THE SUPREM PRAC

1999

Fourth Cumulative Supplement to the 1999 Edition

Up-to-date generally to January 2000

LONDON
SWEET & MAXWELL
2000

Published in 2000 by Sweet & Maxwell Limited of 100 Avenue Road,
London NW3 3PF.
(http://www.smlawpub.co.uk)
Typeset by Mendip Communications Ltd, Frome, Somerset.
Printed in England by Clays Ltd, St Ives plc.

No natural forests were destroyed to make this product; only farmed timber was used and replanted.

SCP Main Work: ISBN 0–421–633–107
Supplement: ISBN 0–421–730–102

CONTENTS

Service information
Table of cases
Table of statutes
Table of statutory instruments
Table of Civil Procedure Rules
Table of Rules of the Supreme Court
Table of Rules of the county court
Table of European and international legislation

VOLUME 1

	Page
ORDER 6	
Writs of Summons: General Provisions	3
ORDER 10	
Service of Originating Process: General Provisions	3
ORDER 11	
Service of Process, etc., out of the Jurisdiction	4
ORDER 13	
Failure to Give Notice of Intention to Defend	5
ORDER 14	
Summary Judgment	6
ORDER 15	
Causes of Action, Counterclaims and Parties	7
ORDER 16	
Third Party and Similar Proceedings	7
ORDER 18	
Pleadings	8
ORDER 20	
Amendment	8
ORDER 22	
Payment into and out of Court	8
ORDER 23	
Security for Costs	9
ORDER 24	
Discovery and Inspection of Documents	10
ORDER 25	
Summons for Directions	11
ORDER 29	
Interlocutory Injunctions, etc.	11
ORDER 30	
Receivers	12
ORDER 32	
Applications and Proceedings in Chambers	12

Place and Mode of Trial 13
ORDER 36
Trials before, and inquiries by Referees and Masters 13
ORDER 38
Evidence 13
ORDER 45
Enforcement of Judgments and Orders: General 14
ORDER 47
Writs of fieri facias 14
ORDER 52
Commital 15
ORDER 54
Applications for Writ of Habeas Corpus 15
ORDER 55
Appeals to High Court from Court, Tribunal or Person: General 16
ORDER 56
Appeals, etc., to High Court by Case Stated, General 16
ORDER 59
Appeals to the Court of Appeal 17
ORDER 62
Costs 26
ORDER 70
Obtaining Evidence for Foreign Courts, etc. 41
ORDER 71
Reciprocal Enforcement of Judgments and Enforcement of European Community Judgments and Recommendations, etc. Under the Merchant Shipping (Liner Conferences) Act 1982 42
ORDER 72
Commercial Actions 42
ORDER 73
Applications Relating to Arbitration 42
ORDER 75
Admiralty Proceedings 42
ORDER 78
County Court Proceedings Transferred or Removed to High Court 44
ORDER 81
Partners 44
ORDER 85
Administration and Similar Actions 44
ORDER 88
Mortgage Actions 45
ORDER 91
Revenue Proceedings 45
ORDER 92
Lodgment, Investment, etc. of Funds in Court: Chancery Division 45

ORDER 93
Applications and Appeals to High Court under Various Acts: Chancery Division 46
ORDER 94
Applications and Appeals to High Court under various Acts: Queen's Bench Division 46
ORDER 104
The Patents Acts 1949 and 1977; The Registered Designs Acts 1949 to 1971; The Defence Contracts Act 1958; The Copyright, Designs and Patents Act 1988 46
ORDER 112
Applications for Use of Blood Tests in Determining Paternity 57
ORDER 113
Summary Proceedings for Possession of Land 59
ORDER 114
References to the European Court 59
COUNTY COURTS OVERVIEW 63
CCR ORDER 5
Causes of Action and Parties 63
CCR ORDER 11
Payment into and out of Court and Between the Parties 63
CCR ORDER 20
Evidence 63
CCR ORDER 25
Enforcement of Judgments and Orders: General 63
CCR ORDER 43
The Landlord and Tenant Acts 1927, 1954, 1985 and 1987 64
CCR ORDER 48D
Enforcement of Fixed Penalties Under the Road Traffic (Vehicle Emissions) (Fixed Penalty) Regulations 1997 64
CCR ORDER 49
Miscellaneous Statutes 66

VOLUME 2

SECTION 1
FORMS

A. PRESCRIBED FORMS 71
B. QUEEN'S BENCH MASTERS' PRACTICE FORMS 72
C. COUNTY COURT FORMS 72

SECTION 2
PRACTICE DIRECTIONS

A. QUEEN'S BENCH MASTERS' PRACTICE DIRECTIONS 73
B. CHANCERY DIVISION PRACTICE DIRECTIONS 75

C. PRACTICE DIRECTIONS, NOTES AND STATEMENTS ISSUED BY THE LORD CHIEF JUSTICE (OR WITH HIS APPROVAL) FOR THE QUEEN'S BENCH DIVISION 75

SECTION 3

TABLES

B. HIGH COURT JUDGMENT TABLE 83
D. TIME TABLE UNDER RSC AND CCR 83

SECTION 4

COURT FEES AND STAMPS

A. SUPREME COURT FEES ORDER 1980 91
B. COUNTY COURT FEES ORDER 1982 91
C. NON-CONTENTIOUS PROBATE FEES ORDER 1981 91

SECTION 5

COURT FUNDS OFFICE RULES AND PRACTICE

B. ADMINISTRATION OF JUSTICE ACT 1982 95
C. COURTS FUNDS RULES 1987 95
D. THE INVESTMENT OF FUNDS IN COURT 100

SECTION 6

ADMIRALTY JURISDICTION AND PROCEEDINGS

A. RSC APPENDIX B 101
B. ADMIRALTY PRACTICE DIRECTIONS 140
D. JURISDICTION 140

SECTION 7

EUROPEAN JURISDICTION

A. GENERAL 142
B. CIVIL JURISDICTION AND JUDGMENTS ACT 1982 143

SECTION 8

HOUSING

B. LAW OF PROPERTY ACT 1925 145
C. ADMINISTRATION OF JUSTICE ACT 1970 145
F. CONSUMER CREDIT ACT 1974 145
G. PROTECTION FROM EVICTION ACT 1977 146
H. RENT ACT 1977 146
K. COUNTY COURTS ACT 1974 147
L. HOUSING ACT 1985 148
M. LANDLORD AND TENANT ACT 1985 150
N. LANDLORD AND TENANT ACT 1987 152
O. HOUSING ACT 1988 153
Q. HOUSING ACT 1996 156

SECTION 9
CONSUMER CREDIT

A. CONSUMER CREDIT ACT 1974 160

SECTION 10
COURT OF PROTECTION

A. GENERAL 163
B. MENTAL HEALTH ACT 1983 163
C. COURT OF PROTECTION RULES 1994 163
G. COURT OF PROTECTION (ENDURING POWERS OF ATTORNEY) RULES 1994 165

SECTION 11
PROBATE JURISDICTION AND PROCEEDINGS

A. SUPREME COURT ACT 1981 166
B. NON-CONTENTIOUS PROBATE RULES 1987 166
D. NON-CONTENTIOUS PROBATE FEES ORDER 1981 169

SECTION 12
TRUSTEES

C. PUBLIC TRUSTEE ACT 1906 170

SECTION 14
LIMITATION

LIMITATION ACT 1980 171

SECTION 15
SOLICITORS

A. SOLICITORS' ACT 1974 175
B. SOLICITORS' ACCOUNTS RULES 1991 176
C. SOLICITORS' ACCOUNTS (LEGAL AID TEMPORARY PROVISION) RULES 1992 176
E. CONDITIONAL FEE AGREEMENTS ORDER 1995 183
F. CONDITIONAL FEE AGREEMENTS REGULATIONS 1995, REGS 1–7 183
G. NOTES ON THE GENERAL LAW RELATING TO SOLICITORS 184

SECTION 16
LEGAL AID

A. LEGAL AID ACT 1988 185
D. CIVIL LEGAL AID (GENERAL) REGULATIONS 1989 185
F. LEGAL AID IN CIVIL PROCEEDINGS (REMUNERATION) REGULATIONS 1994 189

SECTION 17
MISCELLANEOUS PARTIES AND PROCEEDINGS

A. PROCEDURE 191
B. PARTIES GENERALLY 191

SECTION 18

MISCELLANEOUS MATTERS OF PRACTICE

B. CIRCUIT ARRANGEMENTS 193
C. LIST OF DISTRICT REGISTRIES 193
D. COUNTY COURT DIRECTORY 193

SECTION 19

HOUSE OF LORDS APPEALS

A. CIVIL APPEALS 195
B. CRIMINAL APPEALS 198

SECTION 20

JURISDICTIONAL STATUTES AND REGULATIONS

A. MAIN STATUTES 202
B. OTHER STATUTES AND REGULATIONS 210

SECTION 21

MISCELLANEOUS STATUTES

A. ARBITRATION ACT 1950 212
B. ARBITRATION ACT 1975 213
D. ARBITRATION ACT 1986 213
E. ATTACHMENT OF EARNINGS ACT 1971 216
F. CHARGING ORDERS ACT 1979 216
H. CIVIL EVIDENCE ACT 1972 217
J. CIVIL LIABILITY (CONSTRUCTION) ACT 1978 217
K. COMPANIES ACT 1985 217
L. CROWN PROCEEDINGS ACT 1947 217
R. LITIGANTS IN PERSON (COSTS AND EXPENSES) ACT 1975 218
S. OATHS ACT 1978 218
T. HUMAN RIGHTS ACT 1998 218
U. EUROPEAN CONVENTION ON HUMAN RIGHTS 233
Index 235

SERVICE INFORMATION

The Supreme Court Practice is currently published at two yearly intervals. *The Supreme Court Practice 1999* was published in September 1998.

The Supreme Court Practice 1999 consists of two text Volumes, with a separate Index and Tables of Cases, Statutes and Statutory Instruments. It is updated by cumulative supplements and the *Civil Procedure News* (formerly the *Supreme Court Practice News*). *Civil Procedure* was published in March 1999 containing the full text of the Civil Procedure Rules 1998 and all available practice directions, pre-action protocols and forms. *Civil Procedure* (2nd ed.) was published in October 1999 and is up-to-date to October 20, 1999. It contains commentary to the Civil Procedure Rules and Schedules and effectively replaces Volume 1.

Cumulative supplements. These cover all changes and amendments to material in Volumes 1 and 2. Four cumulative supplements are included in the service to the 1999 edition, updating the text every six months. As the supplements are cumulative, they contain all material from previous supplements and old supplements can be discarded if so wished.

A **Stop Press** may be included at the beginning of the supplement, when necessary, to note up any important statutory developments that are issued too late to be included in the main text of the supplement.

Civil Procedure News. A newsletter issued at least 10 times a year (20 issues in total), updating the 1999 edition, *Civil Procedure* (1st and 2nd eds), and the cumulative supplements. It also includes additional background information to Orders and covers topical procedural developments.

Paragraph numbering. Volume 1 is paragraphed using stroke numbers. The number of the Order appears first followed by a rule number. A third number may be given after this which refers to an editorial note. For example:

45/1 refers to O.45, r.1.

45/1/2 refers to the second commentary paragraph to O.45, r.1. Paragraph numbers prefixed with a 'C' relate to the County Court Rules, now situated at the end of Volume 1.

In Volume 2 the Sections are sub-divided, where appropriate, by an alphabetical suffix and then the relevant paragraph number. For example:

15A–4 refers to the fourth paragraph of subsection 'A' of Section 15.

SCP CD ROM Disk. The full text of the **Supreme Court Practice** is now available on CD ROM disk. The disk is updated every six months to include each cumulative supplement as it is published. It also contains *Civil Procedure* (2nd ed.). The disk offers extra search facilities and portability. Please contact the Publishers for further details.

Editorial Queries

All suggestions of an editorial nature should be addressed to the Publishers of The Supreme Court Practice, Sweet & Maxwell Limited, 100 Avenue Road, London NW3 3PF.

Customer Services

Sweet & Maxwell aim to provide all our customers with a fast, efficient and helpful customer care service.

Please call our Customer Services team in Swiss Cottage if you have a query relating to your subscription. You may wish to take out a new subscription, check on the status of a current subscription or check that you have paid a particular subscription.

Our Customer Services department will assist you on all of these matters. The department is divided to take queries from specific geographical regions: please dial the relevant number according to where you are calling from:

London and South East England
Tel: 020-7449-1101
Fax: 020-7449-1144

Central and Southern England and Wales
Tel: 020-7449-1102
Fax: 020-7449-1155

Scotland, Northern England and Ireland
Tel: 020-7449-1102
Fax: 020-7449-1155

Europe and the rest of the world
Tel: +44-1264-342906
Fax: +44-1264-342706

Trade Customers
Tel: 020-7449-1104
Fax: 020-7449-1144

Or you can write to:

Customer Services
Sweet & Maxwell Limited
100 Avenue Road
London
England NW3 3PF
DX: 38861 Swiss Cottage

TABLE OF CASES

References to paragraph numbers in square brackets are to Volume 2
References to paragraph numbers with prefix "C" are to the County Court Rules Supplement

A v. F Co. Ltd; S v. F Co. Ltd (1996) SCTO Digest No. 13 .... 62/A2/28
Abbott v. Bayley, May 1999, *Legal Action* 28, CA .... [80–162]
Aegean Sea Traders Corporation v. Repsol Petroleo SA (The Aegean Sea) [1998] 2 Lloyd's Rep. 39; [1998] C.L.C. 1090, QBD (Adm Ct) 75/37/2
Ager v. Ager [1998] 1 W.L.R. 1074; [1998] 1 All E.R. 703; [1998] 1 F.L.R. 506; [1998] 3 F.C.R. 355; [1998] Fam. Law 253; *The Times*, January 6, 1998; *The Independent*, January 19, 1998 (C.S.), CA .... [16D–246], [20A–172/1], [20A–749/1]
Aiden Shipping Co. Ltd v. Interbulk Ltd; *The Vimeira* [1986] A.C. 965; [1986] 2 W.L.R. 1051; [1986] 2 All E.R. 409; [1986] 2 Lloyd's Rep. 117; 83 L.S.Gaz. 1895; 136 New L.J. 514, HL; reversing [1985] 1 W.L.R. 1222; 129 S.J. 872; [1986] 1 Lloyd's Rep. 107; 82 L.S.Gaz. 3529; 135 New L.J. 1165, CA; reversing (1986) 130 S.J. 429; [1985] 2 Lloyd's Rep. 377 .... 62/2/7
Ali v. Westminster City Council; Nairne v. Camden London Borough Council [1999] 1 W.L.R. 384; [1999] 1 All E.R. 450; (1999) 31 H.L.R. 349; [1998] N.P.C. 135; September 1998, *Legal Action* 26; *The Times*, September 16, 1998; *The Independent*, July 30, 1998, CA .... [8Q–246], [8Q–247/1], [20A–700]
Allen v. Unigate Dairies Ltd. *See* Ridehalgh v. Horsefield.
—— v. Taylor [1992] P.I.Q.R. P255, CA 13/9/18
Allianz Versicherungs-Aktiengesellschaft v. Fortuna Inc. (The Baltic Universal) [1999] 2 All E.R. 625; [1999] 1 Lloyd's Rep. 497, QBD (Comm Ct) .... [21D–38]
Alpine Bulk Transport Co v. Saudi Eagle Shipping Co. (The Saudi Eagle) [1986] 2 Lloyd's Rep. 221 CA 13/9/18
Andrews v. Bradshaw, *The Times*, October 11, 1999, CA .... [21D–59]
Antonelli v. Wade Gery Farr. *See* Ridehalgh v. Horsefield.
Aratra Potato Co. Ltd v. Taylor Joynson Garrett [1995] 4 All E.R. 695; (1995) 145 N.L.J.Rep. 1402, QBD 62/A2/27A
Arbuthnot Latham Bank Ltd v. Trafalgar Holdings Ltd; Chishty Coveney & Co. v. Raja [1998] 1 W.L.R. 1426; [1998] 2 All E.R. 181; [1998] C.L.C. 615; *The Times*, December 29, 1997, CA 25/L/3
Artesian Residential Investments Ltd v. Beck [1999] 3 All E.R. 113; [1999] 22 E.G. 145, CA .... [8O–49]
ASFA Ltd v. RTZ Pension Property Trust Ltd. *See* RTZ Pension Property Trust Ltd v. ARC Property Development Ltd.
Aspen Property Investment plc v. Ratcliffe [1997] 2 Costs L.R. 1, Ch D 62/11/31
Atkinson v. Government of the United States of America *sub nom.* R. v. Brixton Prison Governor, ex p. Atkinson [1971] A.C. 197; [1969] 3 W.L.R. 1074; 113 S.J. 901; [1969] 3 All E.R. 1317, HL; reversing in part, affirming in part 133 J.P. 617; 113 S.J. 690; [1969] 2 All E.R. 1146, DC 56/5/3
Attorney-General for Gibraltar v. May, *The Times*, November 20, 1998 .... 24/14A/3
Avon County Council v. Buscott [1988] Q.B. 656; [1988] 2 W.L.R. 788; [1988] 1 All E.R. 841; (1988) 20 H.L.R. 385; (1988) 86 L.G.R. 569; (1988) 132 S.J. 567; [1988] L.S.Gaz. 13, 1988, 49, CA .... [8Q–31]
Aylesbond Estates Ltd v. Macmillan and Farg March 1999, *Legal Action*, 22, CA ..... [8M–53]

B v. B (Taxation of Costs) [1991] 1 F.L.R. 156; [1991] Fam. Law 102; [1991] F.C.R. 536 .... [16D–221]
BCCI (Overseas) Ltd (In Liquidation) v. Price Waterhouse [1998] Ch. 84; [1997] 3 W.L.R. 849; [1997] 4 All E.R. 781; [1997] 6 Bank L.R. 216; [1998] B.C.C. 511; *The Times*, June 25, 1997, Ch D 24/5/34
Bailey v. IBC Vehicles Ltd [1998] 3 All E.R. 570; (1998) 142 S.J.L.B. 126; *The Times*, April 9, 1998, CA .... 62/20/2, 62/29/6, 62/C/35C, [15F–9]
Banks v. British Steel Corporation. *See* Banks v. Woodhall Duckham Ltd.
—— v. Brown Tawse Ltd. *See* Banks v. Woodhall Duckham Ltd.
—— v. Humphrey & Glasgow. *See* Banks v. Woodhall Duckham Ltd.
—— v. Woodhall Duckham Ltd; Banks v. British Steel Corporation; Banks v. Brown Tawse Ltd; Banks v. Humphrey & Glasgow; *sub nom.* Re Stathams (Wasted Costs Order) [1997] P.I.Q.R. P464, CA 62/11/6
Banque National de Paris Plc v. Montman Ltd, *The Times*, September 7, 1999 .... [21F–7/1]

Barclays Bank Ltd v. Cole [1967] 2 Q.B. 738; [1967] 2 W.L.R. 166; [1966] 3 All E.R. 948; 110 S.J. 844; [1966] C.L.Y. 9961, CA 33/3/1
Barclays Bank plc v. Glasgow City Council. *See* Kleinwort Benson Ltd v. City of Glasgow District Council
—— v. Kent County Council *sub nom.* Kent County Council v. Barclays Bank plc (1998) 76 P. & C.R. 1; [1998] 2 E.G.L.R. 14; [1998] 33 E.G. 76; [1998] R.V.R. 74, CA 62/B/47
Barings plc, *Re. See* Secretary of State for Trade and Industry v. Baker.
Barker, *Re. See* R. v. BHB Community Healthcare NHS Trust.
Barratt Manchester Ltd v. Bolton Metropolitan Borough Council [1998] 1 W.L.R. 1003; [1998] 1 All E.R. 1; [1998] C.L.C. 138; [1997] N.P.C. 142; *The Times*, November 3, 1997, CA 25/L/7
Bassett Road H.A. v. Gough [1998] C.L.Y. 3653, Cty Ct .... [8K–3]
Bates v. Leicester H.A. [1998] Lloyd's Rep.Med. 93, QBD .... [14–17/8]
Beddoe, Re [1893] 1 Ch. 547 .... 62/B/151
Begum v. Tower Hamlets London Borough Council, *The Times*, November 9, 1999, CA; July 1998, *Legal Action* 12, Cty Ct .... [8Q–241], [8Q–246]
Bennett v. Greenland Houchen & Co., [1998] P.N.L.R. 458, CA .... [14–17/3]
Berezovsky v. Forbes Inc., *The Times*, November 27, 1998, CA; reversing *The Times*, January 19, 1998, QBD 11/1/15
Berkeley v. Fulham Football Club. *See* Berkeley v. Secretary of State for the Environment (No. 2).
—— v. Secretary of State for the Environment (No. 2); Berkeley v. Fulham Football Club, *The Times*, April 7, 1998, CA 62/B/55
Berny, The [1979] Q.B. 80; [1978] 2 W.L.R. 387; [1978] 1 All E.R. 1065; [1977] 2 Lloyd's Rep. 533; (1977) 121 S.J. 707 .... [6D–258]
Bevan Ashford v. Geoff Yeandle (Contractors) Ltd (in liquidation) [1998] 3 W.L.R. 172; [1998] 3 All E.R. 238; 59 Con.L.R. 1; [1998] N.P.C. 69; (1998) 148 N.L.J. 587; (1998) 95(16) L.S.G. 27; (1998) 142 S.J.L.B. 151; *The Times*, April 23, 1998, Ch D .... 62/15A/3, 62/A2/27A, [15F–9]
Birmingham Citizens Permanent Building Society v. Caunt [1962] Ch. 883; [1962] 2 2 W.L.R. 323; 106 S.J. 96; [1962] 1 All E.R. 163, Ch D .... [8O–49]
Birmingham Midshires Building Society v. Wretham [1999] 07 E.G. 138, QBD (T & CC) .... [14–18/2]
Bolkiah v. KPMG [1999] 2 W.L.R. 215; [1999] 1 B.C.L.C.; [1999] P.N.L.R. 220; (1999) 149 N.L.J. 16; (1999) 143 S.J.L.B. 35 .... [15G–109]
Borealis AB v. Stargas Ltd; (The Berge Sisar) [1998] 3 W.L.R. 1353; [1998] 4 All E.R. 821; [1998] 2 Lloyd's Rep. 475; [1998] C.L.C. 1589; *The Times*, September 14, 1998, CA; reversing [1997] 1 Lloyd's Rep. 635, QBD (Comm Ct) 15/4/8
Bourns Inc. v. Raychem Corp. (No. 3) [1999] 3 All E.R. 154, CA; (1998) 148 N.L.J. 1809; *The Times*, November 26, 1998, Ch D 62/20/2
Bowmer & Kirkland Ltd v. Wilson Bowden Properties Ltd (1997) 80 B.L.R. 131, QBD (OR) 29/10/6
Braintree District Council v. Clark [1998] C.L.Y. 3724, CA .... [8Q–85]
Brent London Borough Council v. Marks (1999) 31 H.L.R. 343, July 1998, *Legal Action* 11, CA .... [8L–47]
Bridgewater v. Griffiths Review of Taxation, April 29, 1999 (unrep.) .... [16D–91]
Bristol & West plc v. Bhadressa (No. 2), November 13, 1998 (unrep.) 62/2/7
Bristol City Council v. Lovell [1998] 1 W.L.R. 446; [1998] 1 All E.R. 775; (1998) 30 H.L.R. 70; [1998] R.V.R. 133; [1998] E.G.C.S. 29; (1998) 95(9) L.S.G. 30; (1998) 95(14) L.S.G. 23; (1998) 148 N.L.J. 329; (1998) 142 S.J.L.B. 116; [1998] N.P.C. 31; *The Times*, February 27, 1998, HL; reversing (1997) 29 H.L.R. 528; [1996] N.P.C. 130; [1996] E.G.C.S. 140, CA .... [8O–49]
British & Commonwealth Holdings plc (in administration) v. Atlantic Computers Plc. *See* British & Commonwealth Holdings plc (in liquidation) v. Barclays De Zoete Wedd Ltd (No. 2).
—— v. Barclays De Zoete Wedd Ltd (No. 2) (1998) 95(45) L.S.G. 41; *The Times*, November 13, 1998, Ch D 24/13/3
—— v. N. M. Rothschild & Sons Ltd. *See* British & Commonwealth Holdings plc (in administration) v. Barclays De Zoete Wedd Ltd (No. 2).
—— v. Spicer and Oppenheim. *See* British & Commonwealth Holdings plc (in administration) v. Barclays De Zoete Wedd Ltd (No. 2).
British Coal Respiratory Disease Litigation, Re The, January 23, 1998 (unrep.) 62/12/1
British Waterways Board v. Norman (1993) 26 H.L.R. 232; (1995) 159 J.P.N.288; [1993] E.G.C.S. 177; [1994] C.O.D. 262; [1993] N.P.C. 143; *The Times*, November 11, 1993; *The Independent*, November 29, 1993, DC (CS) ... 62/3/1, 62/A2/27A
Brown v. KMR Services. *See* Unilever v. Chefaro Proprietaries.

Burns v. Shuttlehurst Ltd, *The Times*, January 12, 1999 .... 24/7A/3
Burridge v. Stafford; Khan v. Ali [1999] 4 All E.R. 660; *The Times*, September 14, 1999, CA .... [16A–16/2]
Burrows v. Vauxhall Motors Ltd; Mongiardi v. IBC Vehicles [1998] P.I.Q.R. P48; (1997) 94(47) L.S.G. 31; (1997) 141 S.J.L.B. 237; (1997) 147 New L.J. 1273; *The Times*, December 17, 1997, CA 62/10/6
Bushbury Land Rover Ltd v. Bushbury Ltd [1977] F.S.R. 709 .... 29/L/2
Butcher v. Wolfe (1998) 95(43) L.S.G. 33; (1998) 95 (48) L.S.G. 31; [1998] E.G.C.S. 153; *The Times*, November 9, 1998, CA 62/9/9

Cadogan Estates Ltd v. McMahon [1999] E.G.C.S. 80; *The Times*, June 1, 1999, CA .... [8H–179]
Camden London Borough Council v. Gilsenan (1999) 31 H.L.R. 81; June 1998, *Legal Action* 10, CA .... [8L–47]
Capital Prime Plus plc v. Wills, July 1999, *Legal Action* 22, CA .... [8O–72/1]
Carlyle Finance Ltd v. Pallas Industrial Finance Ltd [1999] 1 All E.R. (Comm.) 659, CA .... [9A–62/2]
Cartwright v. Staffordshire & Moorlands District Council [1998] B.P.I.R. 328, CA 62/B/120
Caspian Basin Specialised Salvage Emergency Salvage Administration v. Bouygues Offshore SA (No. 4), *The Times*, August 7, 1998, CA; affirming [1997] 2 Lloyd's Rep. 507; [1997] C.L.C. 1463; (1997) 94 (35) L.S.G. 35; *The Times*, July 3, 1997, QBD (Adm Ct) 75/37/2
Cathiship SA v. Allanasons Ltd; The Catherine Helen [1998] 3 All E.R. 714; [1998] 2 Lloyd's Rep. 511; [1998] C.L.C. 1310; *The Times*, July 25, 1998, QBD (Comm Ct) .... [21D–34]
Charles M. Willie & Co. (Shipping) Ltd v. Ocean Laser Shipping Ltd [1999] 1 Lloyd's Rep. 225, QBD (Comm Ct) .... [21D–38]
Charlesworth v. Relay Roads Ltd (No. 2) [1999] 4 All E.R. 397; [1999] 10 C.L. 65, CA .... [17A–12]
Chief Adjudication Officer v. Foster [1993] A.C. 754; [1993] 2 W.L.R. 292; [1993] 1 All E.R. 705; [1993] C.O.D. 259; (1993) S.J.L.B. 36; *The Guardian*, January 29, 1993; *The Times*, February 1, 1993; *The Independent*, February 2, 1993, HL; affirming [1992] Q.B. 31; [1991] 3 W.L.R. 473; [1991] 3 All E.R. 846, CA .... [8Q–241]
Chiron Corporation v. Organon Teknika. *See* Unilever v. Chefaro Proprietaries.
Chishty Coveney & Co. v. Raja. *See* Arbuthnot Latham Bank Ltd v. Trafalgar Holdings Ltd.
Chohan v. Times Newspapers Ltd, September 7, 1998 (unrep.) 62/A2/15/1
Chohan Clothing Co. (Manchester) Ltd v. Fox Brooks Marshall (a firm), *The Times*, December 9, 1997, CA 10/1/26, 81/3/7
Church Commissioners for England v. Baines. *See* Wellcome Trust v. Hamad.
Circle 33 v. Watt [1999] 4 C.L.D. 355, Edmonton Cty Ct .... [8Q–66]
Circuit Systems Ltd (in liquidation) v. Zuken-Redac (U.K.) Ltd. *See* Norglen Ltd (In Liquidation) v. Reeds Rain Prudential Ltd.
Clark v. Associated Newspapers Ltd [1998] 1 W.L.R. 1558; [1998] 1 All E.R. 959; [1998] R.P.C. 261; [1998] E.C.C. 185; (1998) 21 (3) I.P.D. 21025; (1998) 95 (7) L.S.G. 31; (1998) 148 N.L.J. 157; *The Times*, January 28, 1998; *The Independent*, January 23, 1998, Ch D 62/12/1
Clark Clifford v. First American Corp. *See* First American Corp. v. Al-Nahyan.
Clickex Ltd v. McCann [1999] E.G.C.S. 73; *The Times*, May 26, 1999, CA .... [8O–137]
Clive Brooks and Co. Ltd v. Baynard, *The Times*, April 30, 1998, CA 15/6/17, 23/3/40
Clough v. Tameside and Glossop Health Authority [1998] 1 W.L.R. 1478; [1998] 2 All E.R. 971; [1998] Lloyd's Rep.Med. 69; [1998] 3 F.C.R. 133; [1998] P.I.Q.R. P219; (1998) 42 B.M.L.R. 166, Fam Div 24/5/3, 62/20/2
Cobra Golf Inc. v. Rata [1998] Ch. 109; [1997] 2 W.L.R. 629; [1997] 2 All E.R. 150; [1997] F.S.R. 317; (1997) 20 (2) I.P.D. 20013; *The Times*, October 11, 1996, Ch D 24/5/34
Companhia Europeia de Transportes Aeros SA v. British Aerospace plc, *The Times*, January 12, 1999 .... 15/7/3
Connelly v. R.T.Z. Corporation plc [1998] A.C. 854; [1997] 1 W.L.R. 373; [1997] 4 All E.R. 335; [1997] C.L.C. 1357; [1998] Env.L.R. 318; [1997] I.L.Pr. 805; (1997) 94 (32) L.S.G. 28; (1997) 147 N.L.J. 1346; (1997) 141 S.J.L.B. 199; *The Times*, August 4, 1997, HL; affirming [1997] I.L.Pr. 643; *The Times*, July 12, 1996, CA 16/1/7
Cooper v. P. & O. European Ferries (Dover) Ltd, October 30, 1998 (unrep.) 62/12/1
Copeland v. Smith, *The Times*, October 20, 1999, CA .... [14–17/8]
Coulthard v. Disco Mix Club Ltd [1999] 2 All E.R. 457; *The Times*, March 25, 1999, Ch D .... [14–26/1]

Crescent Oil & Shipping Services Ltd v. Importang U.E.E., December 19, 1996 (unrep.), discussed Issue 6/97 *Supreme Court Practice News* 13/7A/3
Crest Homes plc v. Marks [1987] 1 A.C. 829; [1987] 3 W.L.R. 293; 131 S.J. 1003; [1987] 2 All E.R. 1074; [1988] R.P.C. 21; 137 New L.J. 662; 84 L.S.Gaz. 2362, HL; affirming [1987] 3 W.L.R. 48; [1987] F.S.R. 305; 137 New L.J. 318; 84 L.S.Gaz. 2048, CA 62/20/2
Crook v. Aaron Dale Construction and Roofing Ltd; Crook v. Provincial Insurance plc [1997] P.I.Q.R. P36, CA 15/6/16
—— v. Provincial Insurance plc. *See* Crook v. Aaron Dale Construction and Roofing Ltd.
Croydon (Unique) Ltd v. Wright [1999] 4 All E.R. 257; *The Times*, August 24, 1999, CA .... [20A–814/4]
Curtis v. Chairman of the London Rent Assessment Committee. *See* Spath Holme Ltd v. Chairman of the Greater Manchester and Lancashire Rent Assessment Committee (No. 2).

Danae Air Transport SA v. Air Canada [1999] 2 Lloyd's Rep. 547, CA; [1999] 2 Lloyd's Rep. 105; *The Times*, March 31, 1999, QBD (Comm Ct) .... [21A–206]
Danemark Ltd v. BAA plc [1996] C.L.Y. 692, CA 23/3/21
Darby v. Meehan, *The Times*, November 25, 1998, Ch D .... [17A–32]
Darlington Building Society v. O'Rourke James Scourfield & McCarthy (a Firm), *The Times*, November 20, 1998, CA 20/8/8
Day v. Royal Automobile Motoring Services Ltd, *The Times*, November 24, 1998; *The Independent*, November 2, 1998 (C.S.), CA 13/9/18
Debtor (No. 68/5D/97), Re A [1998] 4 All E.R. 779, Ch D .... [16D–164/1]
—— (No. 510 of 1997), Re A, *The Times*, June 18, 1998, Ch D 62/B/120
—— (No. 620 of 1997), Re A, *The Times*, June 18, 1998, Ch D 62/B/120
de Court, Re, *The Times*, November 27, 1997, Ch D 52/1/23
Delta Crompton Cables Ltd v. Copper Cable Co. Ltd [1997] F.S.R. 850; (1997) 20 (9) I.P.D. 20084, Pat Ct 62/5/7
Demetri v. Westminster C.C., *The Times*, November 11, 1999, CA .... [8Q–246]
Dialworth Ltd v. TG Organisation (Europe) Ltd (1998) 75 P. & C.R. 147, CA 14/4/7
Dimond v. Lovell Transcript [1999] 1 All E.R. 1, CA .... [9A–45/1], [9A–47/1]
Director General of Fair Trading v. First National Bank plc, 1999 HC/01241 .... [9A–159/3]
Domicrest Ltd v. Swiss Bank Corp. [1998] 3 All E.R. 577; [1998] C.L.C. 1451; *The Times*, July 16, 1998; *The Independent*, July 20, 1998 (C.S.), QBD (Comm Ct) .. 11/1/55
Downes v. Cottam. *See* Beddoe, *Re*.
DPP v. Coleman [1998] 1 W.L.R. 1708; [1998] 1 All E.R. 912; [1998] 2 Cr.App.R. 7; (1997) 94 (48) L.S.G. 30; *The Times*, December 13, 1997; *The Independent*, December 2, 1997, QBD 56/1/9
Drew-Morgan v. Hamid-Zadeh [1999] E.G.C.S. 72, CA .... [8N–11]
Drouat Assurances SA v. Consolidated Metallurgical Industries (CMI Industrial Sites) (Case C–351/96) [1998] All E.R. (EC) 483; [1998] C.L.C. 1270; [1998] I.L.Pr. 484; *The Times*, June 10, 1998, ECJ 11/1/70
Dumez France v. Hessiche Landesbank (Case C–220/88) [1990] E.C.R. I–49, ECJ 11/1/55

Eastwood (dec'd), Re, Lloyds Bank Ltd v. Eastwood [1975] Ch. 112; [1974] 3 W.L.R. 454; 118 S.J. 533; [1974] 3 All E.R. 603, CA; reversing [1973] 3 W.L.R. 795; 117 S.J. 487; [1973] 3 All E.R. 1079 .... [21R–6]
Ebert v. Venvil; *sub nom.* Ebert v. Birch [1999] 3 W.L.R. 670; 149 New L.J. 608; *The Times*, April 28, 1999, CA .... [20A–255]
Ebied v. Hopkins. *See* Wellcome Trust v. Hamad.
"Edinburgh Castle", The [1999] 2 Lloyd's Rep. 362 .... [6D–38]
Egmatra A.G. v. Marco Trading Corporation [1999] 1 Lloyd's Rep. 862; [1998] C.L.C. 1552 .... [21D–157]
Elgindata (No. 2), *Re* [1992] 1 W.L.R. 1207; [1993] 1 All E.R. 232; [1993] B.C.L.C. 119; 136 S.J.L.B. 190; [1992] *Gazette*, 15 July, 33; *The Times*, June 18, 1992, CA 62/3/3
Elliott v. Pensions Ombudsman, *The Times*, November 20, 1997; (1998) 142 S.J.L.B. 19; (1997) 94(45) L.S.G. 27, Ch D 62/B/132
Equitas Ltd v. Trygg Hansa Insurance Co. Ltd. *See* Trygg Hansa Insurance Co. Ltd v. Equitas Ltd.
Evans (Application for Judicial Review), Re, October 1, 1998 (unrep.), DC 62/3/6
Ewa, Re [1901] 2 K.B. 642 .... 62/28/4

Falco Finance Ltd v. Gough [1999] C.C.L.R. 16; (1999) 17 Tr.L.R. 526, Macclesfield Cty Ct .... [9A–159/3]
Federal Insurance Co. and Chubb Insurance Co. of Europe S.A. v. Transamerica Occidental Life Insurance Co. [1999] 2 All E.R. 138; [1999] 2 Lloyd's Rep. 286 .... [21D–41/1]

First American Corporation v. Zayed; *sub nom.* First American Corp. v. Al-Nahyan [1998] 4 All E.R. 439; [1998] Lloyd's Rep. Bank. 213[1998] C.L.C. 1225; *The Times,* August 17, 1998; [1998] C.L.Y. 350, CA 70/6/3
Fisher v. Hughes [1998] C.O.D. 281; [1998] E.L.R. 475, QBD 55/7/3
Fitzpatrick v. Sterling Housing Association [1998] Ch. 304; [1998] 2 W.L.R. 225; [1997] 4 All E.R. 991; [1998] 30 H.L.R. 576; [1998] 1 F.L.R. 6; [1998] 1 F.C.R. 417; [1997] Fam. Law 784; (1997) 147 N.L.J. 1275; [1997] E.G.C.S. 122; [1997] N.P.C. 118; *The Times,* July 31, 1997; *The Independent,* July 29, 1997, CA .... [8L–61], [8O–118]
Fletamentos Maritimos S.A. v. Effjohn International B.V. [1997] 2 Lloyd's Rep. 302; [1995] 1 Lloyd's Rep. 311; Lloyd's List, February 8, 1995, QBD 62/11/20
Forbes v. Wandsworth Health Authority [1996] 3 W.L.R. 1108; [1996] 4 All E.R. 881; [1996] 7 Med.L.R. 175; (1996) 93(15) L.S.G. 32; (1996) 146 N.L.J.Rep. 477; (1996) 140 S.J.L.B. 85; *The Times,* March 21, 1996, CA .... [14–17/6], [14–17/8]

Gafford v. Graham [1998] N.P.C. 66; (1998) 95 (21) L.S.G. 36; (1998) 142 S.J.L.B. 155; *The Times,* May 1, 1998, CA 29/L/1
Garston v. Scottish Widows Fund and Life Assurance Society [1998] 1 W.L.R. 1583; [1998] 3 All E.R. 596; [1998] L. & T.R. 230; [1998] 2 E.G.L.R. 73; [1998] 32 E.G. 88; [1998] N.P.C. 109; (1998) 95 (26) L.S.G. 32; (1998) 142 S.J.L.B. 199; [1998] E.G.C.S. 101; *The Times,* July 14, 1998; *The Independent,* July 7, 1998, CA; reversing [1996] 1 W.L.R. 834; [1996] 4 All E.R. 282; [1996] 1 E.G.L.R. 113; [1996] 23 E.G. 131; [1996] N.P.C. 49, Ch D .... [8O–137]
Gaud v. Leeds Health Authority, *The Times,* May 14, 1999, CA .... [14–17/3]
Gbangbola v. Smith & Sherriff Ltd [1998] 3 All E.R. 730, QBD (OR) 62/B/12
General Medical Council v. British Broadcasting Corporation [1998] 1 W.L.R. 1573; [1998] 3 All E.R. 426; (1998) 43 B.M.L.R. 143; [1998] E.M.L.R. 833; (1998) 148 N.L.J. 942; (1998) 95 (25) L.S.G. 32; (1998) 142 S.J.L.B. 182; *The Times,* June 11; *The Independent,* June 17, 1998, 1998, CA 52/1/37
General of Berne Insurance Co., The v. Jardine Reinsurance Management Ltd [1998] 1 W.L.R. 1231; [1998] 2 All E.R. 301; [1998] Lloyd's Rep.I.R. 211; [1998] C.L.C. 768; (1998) 95 (11) L.S.G. 35; (1998) 142 S.J.L.B. 86; *The Times,* February 20, 1998, CA .... 62/A2/27A, [15A–58/28/1]
Globe Equities Ltd v. Globe Legal Services Ltd; Globe Equities Ltd v. Kotrie; Kotrie v. Globe Equities Ltd, *The Times,* April 14, 1999, CA .... [20A–403]
Glouchkov v. Forbes Inc. *See* Berezovsky v. Forbes Inc.
Goldman v. Hesper [1988] 1 W.L.R. 1238; [1988] 3 All E.R. 97; 138 New L.J. 272, CA; affirming 17 Fam. Law 315 .... 62/20/2
Goldtech Investments Ltd v. Mainwaring. *See* Mainwaring v. Goldtech Investments Ltd (No. 3).
Grant v. Travellers Cheque Associates Ltd, *The Times,* April 19, 1995, CA 33/3/1
Gray v. Brown (1993) 25 H.L.R. 144, CA; [1993] 07 E.G. 97; *The Times,* November 3, 1992, CA .... [8O–19]
—— v. Taylor [1998] 1 W.L.R. 1093; [1998] 4 All E.R. 17; [1998] N.P.C. 60; (1998) 95 (20) L.S.G. 34; (1998) 142 S.J.L.B. 141; [1998] E.G.C.S. 62; *The Times,* April 24, 1998, CA .... [8H–4]
Grimaldi Compagnia di Navigazione SpA v. Sekihyo Line Ltd [1999] 1 W.L.R. 708; [1998] 3 All E.R. 943; [1998] 2 Lloyd's Rep. 638; [1998] C.L.C. 1403; *The Times,* July 20, 1998, QBD (Comm Ct) .... [21D–25]

H F Pension Trustees Ltd v. Ellison, *The Times,* March 5, 1999, Ch D .... [14–18/2]
H-S (Minors) (Chambers Proceedings: Right of Audience), Re [1998] 1 F.L.R. 868; [1998] 3 F.C.R. 245; [1998] Fam. Law 328; *The Times,* February 25, 1998, CA .... 32/6/31, 62/A2/38, [15G–107]
Halifax Financial Services Ltd v. Intuitive Systems Ltd [1999] 1 All E.R. (Comm.) 303 .... [20A–185]
Halki Shipping Corp. v. Sopex Oils Ltd [1998] 1 W.L.R. 726; [1998] 2 All E.R. 23; 1 Lloyd's Rep. 465; [1998] C.L.C. 583; [1998] N.P.C. 4; (1998) 142 S.J.L.B. 44; *The Times,* January 19, 1998; *The Independent,* January 12, 1998 (C.S.), CA; affirming [1997] 1 W.L.R. 1268; [1997] 3 All E.R. 833; [1998] 1 Lloyd's Rep. 49; (1997) 94 (28) L.S.G. 26; (1997) 141 S.J.L.B. 172; *The Times,* October 13, 1997, QBD (Adm Ct) .... [21D–25]
Hall v. Yorkshire Bank. *See* Yorkshire Bank v. Hall.
Hammond v. West Lancashire H.A. [1998] Lloyd's Rep. Med. 146; (1998) 95 (14) L.S.G. 23; *The Times,* March 5, 1998, CA .... [14–40/5]
Hanak v. Green [1958] 2 Q.B. 9; [1958] 2 W.L.R. 755; 102 S.J. 329; [1958] 2 All E.R. 141, CA 62/3/3
Harbour and General Works Ltd v. Environment Agency [1999] 2 All E.R. (Comm.) 686; *The Times,* October 22, 1999, CA .... [21D–34]
Hatfield v. Hiscock [1998] C.C.L.R. 68, Cty Ct .... [9A–45/1], [9A–47/1]
Hegab v. Shamash, June 1998, *Legal Action* 13, CA .... [8O–60]

Henderson v. Merrett Syndicates. *See* Unilever v. Chefaro Proprietaries.
—— v. Temple Pier Co. Ltd [1998] 1 W.L.R. 1540; [1998] 3 All E.R. 324; (1998) 95 (20) L.S.G. 35; (1998) 142 S.J.L.B. 156; *The Times*, May 2, 1998; *The Independent*, April 29, 1998, CA .... [14–17/6], [14–17/8]
Herceg Novi (Owners) v. Ming Galaxy (Owners); The Herceg Novi [1998] 4 All E.R. 238; [1998] 2 Lloyd's Rep. 454; [1998] C.L.C. 1487; *The Times*, July 30, 1998, CA; reversing [1998] 1 Lloyd's Rep. 167, QBD (Adm Ct) 75/37/2
Hodgson v. Imperial Tobacco Ltd [1998] 1 W.L.R. 1056; [1998] 2 All E.R. 673; (1998) 41 B.M.L.R. 1; (1998) 95 (15) L.S.G. 31; (1998) 142 S.J.L.B. 93; (1998) 148 New L.J. 241; *The Times*, February 13, 1998; *The Independent*, February 17, 1998, CA 32/13/23, 62/15A/3
Hood Sailmakers Ltd v. Berthon Boat Co. Ltd (1999) 149 New L.J. 529; *The Independent*, May 10, 1999 (C.S.), CA .... [15G–109]
Hough v. P & O Containers Ltd [1998] 3 W.L.R. 851; [1998] 2 All E.R. 978; [1998] 2 Lloyd's Rep. 318; [1998] C.L.C. 947; [1998] I.L.Pr. 713; (1998) 95 (17) L.S.G. 32; (1998) 142 S.J.L.B. 127; *The Times*, April 6, 1998, QBD (Adm Ct) 11/1/61, 11/1/67
Hounslow London Borough Council v. McBride (1999) 31 H.L.R. 143; June 1998, *Legal Action* 11, CA .... [8H–94], [8H–100], [8L–47]
Hughes v. Greenwich London Borough Council [1994] 1 A.C. 170; [1993] 3 W.L.R. 821; [1993] 4 All E.R. 577; 26 H.L.R. 99; [1994] I.C.R. 48; 92 L.G.R. 61; 60 P. & C.R. 487; [1993] E.G.C.S. 166; 90 (46) L.S.Gaz. 38; 137 S.J.L.B. 244; [1993] N.P.C. 137; *The Times*, October 26, 1993, HL; affirming 24 H.L.R. 605; [1992] E.G.C.S. 76; [1992] N.P.C. 73; 157 L.G.Rev. 41; *The Times*, May 22, 1992; *The Independent*, June 4, 1992, CA .... [8L–150]
—— v. Kingston Upon Hull City Council [1999] 2 All E.R. 49; (1998) 95 (44) L.S.G. 36; *The Times*, December 9, 1998; *The Independent*, November 16, 1998 (C.S.) DC .... [15A–58/23/1]
Huyton S.A. v. Jakil S.P.A. [1999] 2 Lloyd's Rep. 83, CA 21A–206
Hyde Park Funding Ltd v. Ioannou [1999] 3 C.L.D. 428, Barnet Cty Ct .... [8C–3]
Hydro Agri Espana SA v. Charles M. Willie & Co. (Shipping) Ltd [1998] C.L.C. 511; *The Times*, March 5, 1998, CA 6/8/6

Iberotravel Ltd v. Pallas Leasing (No. 32) Ltd, Transcript: Chant. 96/0678/B, June 19, 1997; [1997] C.L.Y. 551, CA 62/9/4
INCO Europe v. First Choice Distribution [1999] 1 W.L.R. 270; [1999] 1 All E.R. 820; [1999] C.L.C. 165, CA; (1998) 95(41) L.S.G. 45; (1998) 142 S.J.L.B. 269; *The Times*, October 22, 1998; *The Independent*, October 12, 1998 .... [21D–20]

JFS (U.K.) Ltd v. Dwr Cymru Cyf (1998) 95 (39) L.S.G. 40; (1998) 142 S.J.L.B. 256; *The Times*, October 10, 1998, CA .... [14–42/6]
Jaggard v. Sawyer [1995] 1 W.L.R. 269; [1995] 2 All E.R. 189, CA; [1995] 13 E.G. 132; [1994] E.G.C.S. 139; [1994] N.P.C. 116; *The Independent*, August 22, 1994, (CS) CA; affirming [1998] 1 E.G.L.R. 197 .... 29/L/1
James v. East Dorset Health Authority, *The Times*, December 7, 1999, CA .... [14–17/8]
—— v. Williams [1999] 3 W.L.R. 451; *The Times*, April 13, 1999, CA .... [14–26/1]
John (Julie), Re [1998] C.O.D. 306, QBD 54/1/5
Johnson v. Valks, *The Times*, November 23, 1999, CA 20A–255
Jones and Son v. Whitehouse [1918] 2 K.B. 61, CA .... [15A–58/71]
Joyce v. Dorset County Council [1997] E.L.R. 26, QBD 55/7/3

Karbachian v. Parvazian Transcript: 908/98; May 21, 1998; [1998] C.L.Y. 612, CA 25/L/23
Keary Developments Ltd v. Tarmac Construction Ltd [1995] 3 All E.R. 534; [1995] 2 B.C.L.C. 395; 73 B.L.R. 115, CA 23/3/2
Kent County Council v. Barclays Bank plc. *See* Barclays Bank plc v. Kent County Council.
Khazanchi v. Faircharm Investments Ltd *sub nom.* McLeod v. Butterwick [1998] 1 W.L.R. 1603; [1998] 2 All E.R. 901; [1998] 3 E.G.L.R. 147; (1998) 76 P. & C.R. D8; [1998] E.G.C.S. 46; [1998] N.P.C. 47; (1998) 148 N.L.J. 479; (1998) 95 (17) L.S.G. 31; (1998) 142 S.J.L.B. 142; *The Times*, March 25, 1998, CA; affirming [1996] 1 W.L.R. 995; [1996] 3 All E.R. 236; *The Times*, March 12, 1996, Ch D 45/1/10
Khreino v. Khreino, [2000] 1 F.C.R. 75, CA .... [20A–408]
Kinch v. Bullard [1998] 4 All E.R. 650; [1998] 3 E.G.L.R. 112; [1998] 47 E.G. 140; [1998] Fam. Law 738; [1998] N.P.C. 137; [1998] E.G.C.S. 126; *The Times*, September 16, 1998; *The Independent*, October 12, 1998 (C.S.), Ch D .... [8B–18]
Kingcastle Ltd v. Owen-Owen, The Times, March 18, 1999, CA .... [8L–61], [8O–118]
Kingston upon Thames Royal London Borough Council v. Prince [1998] E.G.C.S. 179; [1998] N.P.C. 158; *The Times*, December 7, 1998; *The Independent*, December 4, 1998 (C.S.); June 1998, *Legal Action* 10, Cty Ct .... [8L–71]

Kinnear v. Falcon Films NV [1996] 1 W.L.R. 920; [1994] 3 All E.R. 42; *The Times*, March 1, 1994, QBD 16/1/7
Kleinwort Benson Ltd v. City of Glasgow District Council (Case C–346/93) [1996] Q.B. 57; [1995] 3 W.L.R. 866; [1995] All E.R. (EC) 514; [1996] 5 Bank L.R. 140; *The Times*, April 17, 1995, ECJ .... [7A–3]
Kuwait Airways Corporation v. Iraqi Airways Co., July 30, 1998 (unrep.) 62/A2/13
Kuwait Airways Corp. v. Iraqi Airways Co. (No. 2) [1994] 1 W.L.R. 985; [1995] 1 All E.R. 790; [1994] 1 Lloyd's Rep. 284; (1994) 138 S.J.L.B. 39; *The Times*, February 19, 1994, CA 62/35/12

L v. L (Legal Aid Taxation) [1996] 1 F.S.R. 873; [1996] 2 F.C.R. 193; [1996] Fam. Law 349; (1996) 140 S.J.L.B. 58; *The Times*, January 26, 1996, CA; reversing [1993] 2 F.L.R. 84; [1994] 2 F.C.R. 185; [1993] Fam. Law 343; *The Times*, February 8, 1993, Fam Div 62/A2/28
Laimond Properties Ltd v. Al-Shakarchi (1998) 30 H.L.R. 1099; [1998] E.G.C.S. 21; (1998) 95 (8) L.S.G. 34; [1998] N.P.C. 19; *The Times*, February 23, 1998, CA .... [8O–175]
Laker Airways Inc. v. F.L.S. Aerospace Ltd, *The Times*, May 21, 1999 .... [21D–59]
Lancashire Fires Ltd v. S.A. Lyons and Co. Ltd (No. 2), *The Times*, July 24, 1999, CA .... [16A–72]
Leachman, Re [1998] C.O.D. 466, QBD 54/1/3
Lewisham London Borough Council v. Adeyemi [1999] E.G.C.S. 74, CA .... [8L–47], [8L–177]
Lismane v. Hammersmith and Fulham London Borough Council (1998) 10 Admin.L.R. 586; (1998) 95 (31) L.S.G. 36; (1998) 142 S.J.L.B. 219; (1998) 162 J.P.N. 926; *The Times*, July 27, 1998, CA .... [8Q–141/1]
Lloyd's Bank Plc v. Wojcik, *The Independent*, January 19, 1998 (C.S.), CA .... [14–42/6]
Locabail (UK) Ltd v. Bayfield properties Ltd (Leave to Appeal); Locabail (UK) Ltd v. Waldorf Investment Corp (Leave to Appeal); Timmins v. Gormley; Williams v. Inspector of Taxes; R. v. Bristol Betting and Gaming Licensing Committee, ex p. O'Callaghan, *The Times*, November 19, 1999, CA .... [20A–169]
Loveday v. Renton (No. 2) [1992] 3 All E.R. 184 .... 62/A2/15/1
Lownes v. Babcock Power Ltd [1998] P.I.Q.R. P253; (1998) 142 S.J.L.B. 84; (1998) 95 (14) L.S.G. 22; *The Times*, February 19; *The Independent*, February 13, 1998, CA 62/28/4
Lowsley v. Forbes [1998] 3 W.L.R. 501; [1998] 3 All E.R. 897; [1998] 2 Lloyd's Rep. 577; (1998) 95 (35) L.S.G. 37; (1998) 142 S.J.L.B. 247; (1998) 148 N.L.J. 1268; *The Times*, August 24, 1998, HL; reversing in part [1996] C.L.C 1370; *The Times*, April 5, 1996, CA .... [14–29/1]
Lubrizol Ltd v. Tyndallwoods, April 8, 1998 (unrep.) 62/11/29

M.B. Building Contractors Ltd v. Ahmed, *The Independent*, November 23, 1998 (C.S.) CA 62/3/3
MSC Mediterranean Shipping Company SA v. Polish Ocean Lines (The Tychy) [1999] 1 All E.R. (Comm) 819; [1999] 2 Lloyd's Rep. 11; *The Times*, April 30, 1999, CA .... [6D–60]
McCauley v. Vine [1999] 1 W.L.R. 1977, CA .... [21G–31/1]
McDonald v. Horn [1995] 1 All E.R. 961; [1995] I.C.R. 685; 144 N.L.J.Rep. 1515; *The Times*, August 10, 1994; *The Independent*, August 8, 1994, CA; affirming *The Times*, October 12, 1993, Ch D 85/2/3
McEvoy v. A.A. Welding and Fabrication Ltd [1998] P.I.Q.R. P266, CA .... [14–40/4]
McLeod v. Butterwick. *See* Khazanchi v. Faircharm Investments Ltd.
Mahon v. Rahn [1998] Q.B. 424; [1997] 3 W.L.R. 1230; [1997] 3 All E.R. 687; [1997] E.M.L.R. 558; *The Times*, June 12, 1997, CA; reversing (unrep., June 19, 1996), QBD 24/14A/2
Mainwaring v. Goldtech Investments Ltd (No. 3) (1998) 95 (45) L.S.G. 38; *The Times*, November 16, 1998; *The Independent*, November 16, 1998 (C.S.), CA; reversing [1997] 4 All E.R. 16, Ch D 62/28/4
Manchester City Council v. Cochrane [1999] 1 W.L.R. 809; *The Times*, January 12, 1999, CA .... [8Q–31], [8Q–47]
—— v. Lawler (1999) 31 H.L.R. 119; June 1998, *Legal Action* 11, CA .... [8Q–66]
—— v. McCann (1998) 95 (48) L.S.G. 31; *The Times*, November 28, 1998; *The Independent*, November 20, 1998, CA 52/1/37
Mannai Investment Co. Ltd v. Eagle Star Life Assurance Co. Ltd [1997] A.C. 749; [1997] 2 W.L.R. 945; [1997] 3 All E.R. 352, HL; reversing [1995] 1 W.L.R. 1508; [1996] 1 All E.R. 55; (1996) 71 P. & C.R. 129; [1996] 1 E.G.L.R. 69; [1996] 06 E.G. 140; [1995] E.G.C.S. 124; [1995] N.P.C. 117; (1995) 139 S.J.L.B. 179; *The Times*, July 19, 1995, CA .... [8O–137]
Manzanilla Ltd v. Corton Property & Investments Ltd [1997] 3 F.C.R. 389; *The Times*, August 4, 1997, CA 62/11/14
Marinari v. Lloyds Bank plc (Case C–364/93) [1995] I.L.Pr. 737; *The Times*, October 19, 1995, ECJ 11/1/55

Maritrop Trading Corp. v. Guangzhou Ocean Shipping Co. [1998] C.L.C. 224, QBD (Comm Ct) 11/1/11
Martin v. Maryland Estates Ltd [1999] E.G.C.S. 63, CA .... [8M–61]
Martin & Biro Swan Ltd v. H. Millwood Ltd (1954) 71 R.P.C. 316 .... 24/2/11
Martin & Miles Martin Pen Co. Ltd v. Scrib (1950) 67 R.P.C. 127, CA 24/2/11
Maryland Estates v. Joseph [1998] 3 All E.R. 193; (1999) 77 P. & C.R. 150; (1999) 31 H.L.R. 269; [1998] 2 E.G.L.R. 47; (1998) 95 (17) L.S.G. 33; (1998) 95 (21) L.S.G. 36; [1998] N.P.C. 70; (1998) 142 S.J.L.B. 157; [1998] 27 E.G. 142; [1998] E.G.C.S. 66; *The Times*, May 6, 1998; *The Independent*, May 1, 1998, CA; affirming [1997] 2 E.G.L.R. 96; [1997] 46 E.G. 155; (1997) 147 N.L.J. 1386, CC (Central London) .... [8K–4]
Mayfair Brassware Ltd v. Aqualine International Ltd (Costs Order) [1998] F.S.R. 135, CA; (1997) 20 (11) I.P.D. 20118, Ch D 62/7/14
Meynell Family Properties Ltd v. Meynell, June 1998, *Legal Action* 12, CA .... [8H–4]
Microsoft Corporation v. Backslash Distribution Ltd, *The Times*, March 15, 1999 .... [16D–192], [16D–241]
Miller v. Eyo [1998] N.P.C. 95; October 1998; *Legal Action* 26, CA .... [8O–19A]
Minmetals Germany GmbH v. Ferco Steel Ltd, *The Times*, March 1, 1999, QBD (Comm Ct) .... [21D–243]
Minster Investments Ltd v. Hyundai Precision and Industry Co. Ltd [1988] 2 Lloyd's Rep. 621; *The Times*, January 26, 1988; *The Independent*, February 23, 1988, QBD (Comm Ct) 11/1/55
Minotaur Data Systems Ltd, Re; *sub nom.* Official Receiver v. Brunt, [1999] 1 W.L.R. 1129, [1999] 3 All E.R. 122, CA; *The Times*, March 18, 1999, CA; reversing [1998] 4 All E.R. 500; [1998] 2 B.C.L.C. 306; [1998] B.P.I.R. 756; *The Times*, June 25, 1998, Ch D .... 62/18/2/1, [21R–4]
Mirpuri v. Jass (1998) 56 Con.L.R. 31, QBD (OR) .... [21A–206]
Mohamed v. Alaga & Co.; *sub nom.* Mohammed v. Alaga & Co. [1999] 3 All E.R. 699; *The Times*, July 29, 1999, CA; [1998] 2 All E.R. 720; (1998) 95 (17) L.S.G. 29; (1998) 142 S.J.L.B. 142; *The Times*, April 2, 1998; *The Independent*, March 27, 1998, Ch D .... [15F–9]
Mongiardi v. IBC Vehicles. *See* Burrows v. Vauxhall Motors Ltd.
Morris v. Wiltshire & Woodspring District Council, January 16, 1998 (unrep.) 62/18/2, 62/A2/37
Mortgage Agency Services v. Bal [1998] 28 L.S.G. 32, CA .... [8C–4]
Mortgage Corporation v. Alexander Johnson, *The Times*, September 22, 1999 .... [14–29/1]
—— v. Lambert & Co. [1999] 42 E.G. 138; *The Times*, October 11, 1999 .... [14–18/2]
Mortgage Funding Corporation Plc v. Kashef-Hamadani, April 26, 1993 (unrep.), CA 62/6/6
Murphy v. Young & Co.'s Brewery plc [1997] 1 W.L.R. 1591; [1997] 1 All E.R. 518; [1997] 1 Lloyd's Rep. 236, CA 62/2/7

Nairne v. Camden London Borough Council. *See* Ali v. Westminster City Council
Nash v. Eli Lilly & Co. [1993] 1 W.L.R. 782; [1993] 4 All E.R. 383, CA; affirming [1992] 3 Med.L.R. 353; *The Times*, October 7, 1992 .... [14–17/6]
National Justice Compania Naviera S.A. v. Prudential Assurance Co. Ltd (The Ikarian Reefer) (No. 2); *sub nom.* Comninos v. Prudential Assurance Co. Ltd [1999] 2 All E.R. (Comm.) 673; 149 New L.J. 1561; *The Times*, October 15, 1999, CA .... [20A–403]
National Westminster Bank v. Story and Pallister [1999] Lloyd's Rep. Bank. 261; *The Times*, May 14, 1999, CA .... [9A–47/1], [9A–57/1]
Nederlandse Reassurantie Groep Holding NV v. Bacon & Woodrow, April 21, 1998 (unrep.) 62/A2/27A
Nelson v. Rye [1996] 1 W.L.R. 1378; [1996] 2 All E.R. 186; [1996] F.S.R. 313; [1996] E.M.L.R. 37; (1997) 61 Conv. 225; *The Times*, December 5, 1995, Ch D .... [14–26/1]
Newham London Borough Council v. Philips (1998) 30 H.L.R. 859; (1998) 96 L.G.R. 788; [1998] 1 F.L.R. 613; (1998) 10 Admin.L.R. 309; [1998] Fam. Law 140; [1997] E.G.C.S. 143; [1997] N.P.C. 149; (1997) 94(45) L.S.G. 27; (1997) 141 S.J.L.B. 251; *The Times*, November 12, 1997, CA .... [8L–61]
News International plc v. Borgognon, Transcript: CHANI 97/1646 CMS 3; March 5, 1998; [1998] C.L.Y. 583, CA; affirming Transcript: CH.1997–N–2577; November 5, 1997, Ch D 11/4/14
Nitikendo v. Leboeuf Lamb Greene Mackay, *The Times*, January 26, 1999, Ch D ... 29/L/1
Nordstern Allgemeine Versicherungs A.G. v. Internav Ltd; Nordstern Allgemeine Versicherungs A.G. v. Katsamas [1999] 2 Lloyd's Rep. 139; *The Times*, June 8, 1999, CA .... [20A–403]
Norglen Ltd (In Liquidation) v. Reeds Rain Prudential Ltd; Circuit Systems Ltd (in liquidation) v. Zuken-Redac (U.K.) Ltd [1997] 3 W.L.R. 177, HL; *The Times*, December 1997; [1996] 1 W.L.R. 864; [1996] 1 All E.R. 945; [1996] 1 B.C.L.C. 690; [1996] B.C.C. 532; *The Times*, December 6, 1995; *The Independent*, January 12, 1996, CA; reversing [1994] E.G.C.S. 21, Ch D 15/6/17, 15/6/18

Northampton Borough Council [1998] E.H.L.R. 59; [1998] 2 F.C.R. 182; (1998) 30 H.L.R. 875; [1998] 1 E.G.L.R. 15; [1997] N.P.C. 159; [1998] 07 E.G. 142; [1997] E.G.C.S. 156; (1998) 95 (10) L.S.G. 28; *The Times*, January 3, 1998; *The Independent*, November 14, 1997, CA .... [8H–180], [8L–175], [8O–253]
Northern Regional Health Authority v. Derek Crouch Construction Co. Ltd [1984] Q.B. 644; [1984] 2 W.L.R. 676; [1984] 2 All E.R. 175; (1984) 128 S.J. 279; (1984) 26 Build.L.R. 1, CA; affirming (1983) 24 Build.L.R. 60, DC .... [21A–41], [21A–85]
Nykredit Mortgage Bank Plc v. Edward Erdman Group Ltd (No. 2) [1997] 1 W.L.R. 1627; [1998] 1 All E.R. 305; [1998] Lloyd's Rep. Bank. 39; [1998] P.N.L.R. 197; [1998] 1 E.G.L.R. 99; [1998] 05 E.G. 150; [1998] C.L.C. 116; (1998) 75 P. & C.R. D28; [1997] N.P.C. 165; (1998) 95 (1) L.S.G. 24; (1998) 142 S.J.L.B. 29; *The Times*, December 3, 1997, HL 62/35/12

O (A Minor) (Costs: Liability of Legal Aid Board), Re; *sub nom.* O (A Minor) (Legal Aid Costs), Re [1997] 1 F.L.R. 465; *The Times*, November 25, 1996, CA .... 62/11/6, 62/11/25, [16A–73]
O'Callaghan v. Coral Racing Ltd, *The Times*, November 26, 1998; *The Independent*, November 26, 1998, CA .... [21A–8]
O'Driscoll v. Dudley H.A. [1998] Lloyd's Rep.Med. 210, CA; reversing [1996] 7 Med.L.R. 408; (1997) 37 B.M.L.R. 146, QBD .... [14–17/8]
Ochwat v. Watson Burton, February 18, 1998 (unrep.) 62/B/83
Official Receiver v. Brunt. *See* Minotaur Data Systems Ltd, *Re.*
Oksuzoglu v. Kay [1998] 2 All E.R. 361; [1998] Lloyd's Rep. Med. 129; (1998) 42 B.M.L.R. 43; *The Times*, February 26, 1998, CA 62/3/3
Oldham v. Sharples [1997] P.I.Q.R. Q82, CA 62/3/3
Oliver v. Calderdale Metropolitan Borough Council, *The Times*, July 7, 1999, CA ..[20A–739/3]
Orange Personal Communications Services Ltd v. Squires, Transcript: FC2 98/5196/1; February 6, 1998; [1998] C.L.Y. 623, CA 14/1/2
Osei Bonsu v. Wandsworth London Borough Council. *See* Wandsworth London Borough Council v. Osei Bonsu.
Owners of the Ship Kumanova v. Owners of the Ship Massira [1998] 2 Lloyd's Rep. 301; *The Times*, February 5, 1998, QBD (Adm Ct) 75/42/8
Oxnard Financing SA v. Rahn [1998] 1 W.L.R. 1465; [1998] 3 All E.R. 19; (1998) 95 (19) L.S.G. 23; (1998) 142 S.J.L.B. 143; *The Times*, April 22, 1998; *The Independent*, April 27, 1998 (C.S.), CA 81/1/21

Paragon Finance plc v. DB Thackerar & Co. [1999] 1 All E.R. 400; (1998) 95 (35) L.S.G. 36; (1998) 142 S.J.L.B. 243; *The Times*, August 7, 1998, CA .... 20/8/8, [14–26/1], [14–42/11]
—— v. Thakerar & Co. *See* Paragon Finance plc v. DB Thackerar & Co.
—— v. Thimbleby & Co. *See* Paragon Finance plc v. Thakerar & Co.
Parkes v. Legal Aid Board [1996] 4 All E.R. 271; [1996] N.P.C. 30, CA; [1994] 2 F.L.R. 850; [1994] 3 F.C.R. 234; [1995] Fam. Law 18; *The Times*, May 24, 1994, Fam Div; [1997] 1 W.L.R. 1547 .... [16D–155]
Parkins v. Westminster City Council (1998) 30 H.L.R. 894; [1998] 1 E.G.L.R. 22; (1998) 75 P. & C.R. D39; [1998] 13 E.G. 145; [1997] E.G.C.S. 163, CA .... [8O–8]
Parsons v. Provincial Insurance plc, February 20, 1998 (unrep.), CA 33/3/1
Patel v. Patel [1999] 3 W.L.R. 322; [1999] B.L.R. 227; *The Times*, April 9, 1999, CA .... [21D–24]
Pavey v. Ministry of Defence, *The Times*, November 25, 1998; *The Independent*, November 25, 1998, CA 14/6/5, 33/2/2, 36/11/2
Pearless de Rougemont & Co. v. Polbrow (No. 2) [1999] 3 All E.R. 355, CA .... [15A–58/54]
Pelling v. Pelling (Costs: Taxation) [1998] 1 F.L.R. 636; [1998] Fam. Law 253, CA 62/28/4
Pharaon v. Bank of Credit and Commerce International SA (in liquidation) [1998] 4 All E.R. 455; (1998) 142 S.J.L.B. 251; *The Times*, August 17, 1998, Ch D 24/5/22
Phelps v. Spon-Smith & Co., *The Times*, November 26, 1999 .... [14–42/5]
Philex plc v. Golban. *See* Ridehalgh v. Horsefield.
Philip Powis Ltd, Re [1998] 1 B.C.L.C. 440; [1998] B.C.C. 756; (1998) 95 (11) L.S.G. 36; *The Times*, March 6, 1998, CA; reversing [1997] 2 B.C.L.C. 481; *The Times*, April 30, 1997; *The Independent*, May 12, 1997 (C.S.), Ch D (Companies Ct) ... [14–40/4]
Picton Jones & Co. v. Arcadia Developments Ltd [1989] 1 E.G.L.R. 42; [1989] 03 E.G. 85, DC .... [15A–58/23/1]
Practice Direction (CPR Pt 4) .... [1A–1A], [8C–4/1], [8K–4/1], [8L–47/1], [8O–49/1]
Practice Direciton (CPR Pt 7) .... [9A–42/4]
Practice Direction (CPR Pt 49) .... [6A–1A], [6D–1], [6D–3]
Practice Direction 49F .... [17B–1]
Practice Direction (Patents Court: Consolidated Practice Direction), May 21, 1998; [1998] 1 W.L.R. 32; [1998] 1 All E.R. 279; [1998] F.S.R. 79; [1998] R.P.C. 18, Ch D **104/0/5**
Practice Direction (Setting Down and Skeleton Arguments), March 6, 1998; [1998] 1 W.L.R. 668; [1998] 2 All E.R. 672 .... 72/2/5, 72/A9, 72/A49, [6B–8]

Practice Direction (No. 1 of 1996) (Queen's Bench Division: Personal Injury Cases), March 1, 1996 .... 62/C/17
Practice Direction (No. 2 of 1998) (Personal Injury Cases), July 31, 1998 .... **62/C/17**
Practice Direction (Allocation of Cases to Levels of Judiciary) .... [20A–735/1
Practice Direction (Civil Appeals)
14.5 .... **[19A–53]**
16.6 .... **[19A–58]**
16.12 .... **[19A–60]**
16.13 .... **[19A–61/1]**
17.1 .... **[19A–63]**
19 .... **[19A–65]–[19A–66]**
25.3 .... [19A–76]
Practice Direction (Costs), February 1, 1999 .... 62/0/3, **[2C–259]**
Practice Direction (County Court Orders Enforcement) [1991] 1 W.L.R. 438 .... 78/2/2
Practice Direction (County Court Orders Enforcement) [1998] 1 W.L.R. 1557; [1998] 4 All E.R. 63 .... 78/2/2
Practice Direction (Court Dress), July 19, 1994; [1994] 1 W.L.R. 1056; [1995] 1 Cr.App.R. 13 .... [2C–207], **[2C–208/1]**
Practice Direction (Court Dress), November 25, 1998 .... **[2C–208/1]**
Practice Direction (Court of Appeal: Leave to Appeal and Skeleton Arguments), November 17, 1998 .... 59/1B/4, 59/9/28, 59/9/28A, 59/9/30, 59/9/32, 59/9/40, 59/9/50, 59/9/71—59/9/75, 59/14/18, 59/14/18A, 59/14/21, 59/14/24, 59/14/25, 59/14/26A, 59/14/26B, 59/14/26C, 59/14/31, 59/14/35A—59/14/36L
Practice Direction (Court of Appeal, Civil Division: Leave to Appeal and Skeleton Arguments) [1999] 1 W.L.R. 2; *The Times*, November 23, 1998 .... 30/1/12
Practice Direction (Court of Appeal: Procedural Changes) [1995] 1 W.L.R. 1191; [1995] 3 All E.R. 850, CA 59/9/30, 59/9/40, 59/9/50
Practice Direction (Criminal Appeals)
3.1 .... [19B–4]
3.2 .... [19B–4]
5.5 .... [19B–16]
9(A) .... [19B–20/1]
12.1 .... **[19B–31]**
12.2 .... [19B–31]
15.1 .... [19B–39]
15.7 .... **[19B–40]**
15.12 .... **[19B–43]**
15.13 .... [19B–44]
16.1 .... **[19B–45]**
19 .... **[19B–49]**, **[19B–50]**
Practice Direction (House of Lords: Civil Procedure Amendments) [1999] 1 W.L.R. 1833, HL ... [19A–7/1], [19A–22/1], [19A–43/1], [19A–53/1], [19A–57/1], [19A–58/1], [19A–60/1], [19A–61/1], [19A–63/1], [19A–66/1], [19A–67/1], [19A–76/1], [19A–99/1], [19A–107/1]
Practice Direction (House of Lords: Criminal Procedure Amendments) [1999] 1 W.L.R. 1830, HL .... [19B–4/1], [19B–16/1], [19B–32/1], [19B–40/1], [19B–43/1], [19B–44/1], [19B–45/1], [19B–50/1], [19B–51/1]
Practice Direction (Judges: Mode of Address) [1982] 1 W.L.R. 101 .... [2C–204/1]
Practice Direction (Judges: Recorder of Cardiff) [1999] 1 W.L.R. 597, Sup Ct .... [2C–204/1]
Practice Direction (Mercantile Court: Bristol) [1993] 1 W.L.R. 1522 para. 11 .... [2C–242]
Practice Direction (Mercantile Court: Bristol (No. 2); *sub nom.* Practice Note (Bristol Mercantile Court: Designation of Judges) [1999] 1 W.L.R. 1278; [1999] 2 All E.R. 1024, QBD .... [2C–242]
Practice Direction (Queen's Bench Masters: 3) (Use of Postal Facilities in the Queen's Bench Division), April 20, 1993 .... [2A–2]
Practice Direction (Queen's Bench Masters: 32) (Enforcement in the High Court of County Court Judgments) June 28, 1991 .... [12A–100]
Practice Direction (Queen's Bench Masters: 32) (Enforcement in the High Court of County Court Judgments) June 28, 1991; August 31, 1998 .... **[2A–100]**
Practice Direction (RSC O.11) .... [7A–3]
Practice Direction (Statements of Case) .... [6D–1]
Practice Direction (Supreme Court: References to the Court of Justice of the European Communites), January 14, 1999 .... 114/0/3, **2C–240A**
Practice Direction (Taxation Procedure Amendment) [1999] 1 W.L.R. 1860, HL .... [19B–20/1]
Practice Directions (Admiralty) .... [6B–1 to 6B–14]

Practice Directions (Chancery Division) .... [2B–1 to 2B–332]
Practice Explanation, November 19, 1997; [1998] 1 W.L.R. 32; [1998] 1 All E.R. 279; [1998] F.S.R. 79; [1998] R.P.C. 18, Ch D 104/0/5
Practice Note (No. 1 of 1998) (Supreme Court Taxing Office: Summonses Under O.62, r.28), January 2, 1998; [1998] 1 All E.R. 383 .... **62/C/35C**
Practice Note (No. 2 of 1998) (Supreme Court Taxing Office: The Indemnity Principle: Recent Cases), August 25, 1998; [1998] 1 W.L.R. 1674 .... **62/C/35C**
President's Direction, December 22, 1969 .... **[11A–20]**
Price Waterhouse v. Bank of Credit and Commerce International SA (in liquidation). *See* Pharaon v. Bank of Credit and Commerce International SA (in liquidation).
Prince v. Robinson (1999) 31 H.L.R. 89; June 1998, *Legal Action* 12, CA .... [8H–10]
Pritchard v. Ford Motor Co. Ltd [1997] 1 Costs L.R. 39, QBD 62/A2/28

Q.'s Estate, Re [1999] 1 Lloyd's Rep. 931; *The Independent*, March 19, 1999 .... [21D–101]
Quantum Claims Compensation Specialists Ltd v. Powell 1998 S.C. 316; 1998 S.L.T. 228; 1998 S.C.C.R. 173; *The Times*, February 26, 1998, OHCS; affirming 1997 S.C.L.R. 242, Sh Ct .... [15F–9]

R, ex p., January 27, 1998 (unrep.), CA 62/11/21
R. v. A Circuit Judge, ex p. Wathen (1976) 33 P. & C.R. 423; *The Times*, January 31, 1976, DC .... [8O–49]
—— v. BHB Community Healthcare NHS Trust; *sub nom.* Barker, Re, *The Times*, October 14, 1998, CA 54.1.5
—— v. Bedwellty Justices, ex p. Williams *sub nom.* Williams v. Bedwellty Justices, [1997] A.C. 225; [1996] 3 W.L.R. 361; [1996] 3 All E.R. 737; [1996] 2 Cr.App.R. 594; (1996) 8 Admin.L.R. 643; (1996) 160 J.P. 549; [1996] Crim.L.R. 906; [1997] C.O.D. 54; (1996) N.L.J.Rep. 1149; (1996) 93(34) L.S.G. 34; (1996) 160 J.P.N. 696; (1996) 140 S.J.L.B. 192; *The Times*, August 6, 1996, HL 56/5/3
—— v. Bournewood Community and Mental Health NHS Trust, ex p. L; *sub nom.* L, Re [1998] 3 W.L.R. 107; [1998] 3 All E.R. 289; [1998] 2 F.L.R. 550; [1998] 2 F.C.R. 501; (1998) 44 B.M.L.R. 1; (1998) 1 C.C.L.Rep. 390; [1998] C.O.D. 312; [1998] Fam. Law 592; (1998) 148 N.L.J. 1014; (1998) 142 S.J.L.B. 195; (1998) 95 (29) L.S.G. 27; *The Times*, June 30, 1998; *The Independent*, June 30, 1998, HL; reversing [1998] 2 W.L.R. 764; [1998] 1 All E.R. 634; [1998] 1 All E.R. 634; (1998) 1 C.C.L.Rep. 201; [1998] C.O.D. 35; (1998) 95 (1) L.S.G. 24; (1998) 142 S.J.L.B. 39; *The Times*, December 8, 1997; *The Independent*, December 5, 1997, CA; reversing *The Independent*, November 3, 1997 (C.S.), QBD 54/1/2
—— v. Brent London Borough Council, ex p. Bariise (1998) 30 H.L.R. 518; June 1998, *Legal Action* 14, CA; reversing December 1997, *Legal Action* 15, QBD .... [8Q–175], [8Q–176]
—— v. Brighton and Hove Council, ex p. Marmont [1998] 2 P.L.R. 48; (1998) 30 H.L.R. 1046; [1998] J.P.L. 670; *The Times*, January 15, 1998, QBD 113/8/14
—— v. Brixton Prison Governor, ex p. Atkinson. *See* Atkinson v. Government of the United States of America.
—— v. Camden London Borough Council, ex p. Cosmo (1998) 30 H.L.R. 817; December 1997; *Legal Action* 15, QBD .... [8Q–172]
—— v. ——, ex p. Pereira (1999) 31 H.L.R. 317; July 1998, *Legal Action* 12, CA; reversing [1998] C.O.D. 318, QBD .... [8Q–159]
—— v. ——, ex p. Mohammed (1998) 30 H.L.R. 315; (1997) 9 Admin.L.R. 639; (1997) 161 J.P.N. 1038; (1997) 94(35) L.S.G. 34; *The Times*, June 20, 1997; *The Independent*, June 12, 1997, QBD .... [8Q–155/1]
—— v. Canons Park Mental Health Review Tribunal, ex p. A. [1995] Q.B. 60; [1994] 2 All E.R. 659; [1994] 3 W.L.R. 630; [1994] C.O.D. 480; 138 S.J.L.B. 75; 91 (22) L.S.Gaz. 33; *The Times*, March 2, 1994, CA; reversing [1994] 1 All E.R. 481; [1994] C.O.D. 125; *The Times*, August 24, 1993; *The Independent*, September 1, 1993, DC .... [80A–191/1]
—— v. Carrick District Council, ex p. Prankerd (The Winnie Rigg) [1998] 2 Lloyd's Rep. 675; (1998) 95 (33) L.S.G. 34; (1998) 142 S.J.L.B. 228; *The Times*, September 1, 1998; *The Independent*, October 5, 1998 (C.S.), QBD 75/12/3
—— v. Central London County Court, ex p. London [1999] 3 W.L.R. 1; [1999] 3 All E.R. 991, *The Times*, March 23, 1999 .... [20A–700]
—— v. Chester and North Wales Legal Aid Area Office (No. 12); Floods of Queensbury Ltd [1998] 1 W.L.R. 1496; [1998] 2 B.C.L.C. 436; [1998] B.C.C. 685; (1998) 95 (4) L.S.G. 34; (1998) 142 S.J.L.B. 43; *The Times*, December 26, 1997, CA; affirming [1998] C.O.D. 222; *The Times*, November 7, 1997; *The Independent*, November 3, 1997 (C.S.), DC .... [16A–21]
—— v. Dean and Chapter of St Paul's Cathedral and the Church in Wales [1998] C.O.D. 130 .... 94/15/4
—— v. DPP, ex p. Bull. *See* R. v. Lord Chancellor, ex p. Child Poverty Action Group.
—— v.——, ex p. Kebilene, *The Times*, March 31, 1999, DC .... [21T–25]

R. v. DPP, ex p. Rechachi. *See* R. v. DPP, ex p. Kebilene.
—— v. Ealing London Borough Council, ex p. Fox (1998) 95 (11) L.S.G. 35; *The Times*, March 9, 1998, QBD .... [8Q–222]
—— v. ——; Surdonja (1998) 95 (43) L.S.G. 32; (1998) 142 S.J.L.B. 284; *The Times*, October 29, 1998, QBD .... [8Q–155/2]
—— v. Gloucester Crown Court, ex p. Chester [1998] C.O.D. 365; *The Independent*, July 6, 1998 (C.S.), QBD 56/1/9
—— v. Haringey London Borough Council, ex p. Erdogan, August 1998; *Legal Action* 23, QBD .... [8Q–155/1]
—— v. Harrow London Borough Council, ex p. Fahia [1998] 1 W.L.R. 1396; [1998] 4 All E.R. 137; (1998) 30 H.L.R. 1124; [1998] 3 F.C.R. 363; (1998) 95 (35) L.S.G. 38; (1998) 148 N.L.J. 1354; (1998) 142 S.J.L.B. 226; [1998] N.P.C. 122; *The Times*, July 24, 1998, HL; affirming (1997) 29 H.L.R. 974, CA; affirming (1997) 29 H.L.R. 94, QBD .... [8Q–178]
—— v. Hillington London Borough Council, ex p. McDonagh (1998) 95 (46) L.S.G. 35; *The Times*, November 9, 1998, QBD 113/8/14
—— v. Inland Revenue Commissioners, ex p. Bishopp; R. v. Inland Revenue Commissioners, ex p. Allan [1999] S.T.C. 531; *The Times*, May 18, 1999 ....[20A–191/1]
—— v. Kensington and Chelsea Royal London Borough; Assiter September 1996; *Legal Action* 13; *The Times*, August 20, 1996, QBD .... [8Q–198/1]
—— v. Knightsbridge Crown Court, ex p. Foot [1998] C.O.D. 165; *The Times*, February 18, 1998, QBD 56/1/2
—— v. Lambeth Borough Council, ex p. Wilson (1998) 30 H.L.R. 64; [1997] 3 F.C.R. 437; (1997) 94(14) L.S.G. 25; (1997) 141 S.J.L.B. 91; *The Times*, March 25, 1997, CA; reversing (1997) 29 H.L.R. 104; (1996) 3 F.C.R. 146; (1996) 8 Admin.L.R. 376; (1996) 160 L.G.Rev. 484; [1996] C.O.D. 281; *The Times*, March 21, 1996, QBD 62/2/9
—— v. Leeds City Council, ex p. Collier, June 1998, *Legal Action* 14, QBD .... [8Q–158]
—— v. Legal Aid Board, ex p. Parsons, *The Times*, April 1, 1999, CA .... [16D–140/1]
—— v. Legal Aid Board No. 15 Area (Merseyside), ex p. Eccleston [1998] 1 W.L.R. 1279; [1998] C.O.D. 482; (1998) 95 (20) L.S.G. 35; (1998) 142 S.J.L.B. 155; *The Times*, May 6, 1998; *The Independent*, May 4, 1998 (C.S.), QBD .... 62/B/155, [16D–115]
—— v. Lincolnshire County Council, ex p. Atkinson *sub nom.* R. v. Wealden District Council, ex p. Wales; R. v. Wealden District Council, ex p. Stratford, (1996) 8 Admin.L.R. 529; [1997] J.P.L. 65; (1996) 160 L.G.Rev. 580; [1995] N.P.C. 145; [1995] E.G.C.S. 145; *The Times*, September 22, 1995; *The Independent*, October 3, 1995, QBD 113/8/14
—— v. London RAP, ex p. Cadogan Estates [1998] Q.B. 398; [1997] 3 W.L.R. 833; (1998) 30 H.L.R. 487; (1998) 76 P. & C.R. 410; [1997] 2 E.G.L.R. 134; [1997] 34 E.G. 88; [1997] C.O.D. 372; [1997] N.P.C. 88; [1997] E.G.C.S. 88; *The Times*, July 10, 1997, QBD .... [8O–99]
—— v. Lord Chancellor, ex p. Child Poverty Action Group; R. v. DPP, ex p. Bull [1998] 2 All E.R. 755; [1998] C.O.D. 267; (1998) 148 N.L.J. 20; *The Times*, February 27, 1998; *The Independent*, February 11, 1998, DC 62/B/151
—— v. Luton Family Proceedings Court Justices, ex p. R., Transcript: FC3 97/6459/D; QBCOF 97/0112/D; January 27, 1998; [1998] C.L.Y. 496, CA 62/11/21
—— v. Marylebone Magistrates' Court, ex p. Westminster City Council, January 13, 1999; May 1999, *Legal Action* 29 .... [8M–77/1]
—— v. Merton London Borough Council, ex p. Sembi, *The Times*, June 9, 1999, QBD .... [8Q–200], [8Q–200/1]
—— v. Newham London Borough Council, ex p. Chowdhury October 1998; *Legal Action* 22, QBD .... [8Q–198/1]
—— v. ——, ex p. Dada [1996] Q.B. 507; [1995] 3 W.L.R. 540; [1995] 2 All E.R. 522; (1995) 27 H.L.R. 502; [1995] 1 F.L.R. 842; [1995] 2 F.C.R. 441; 93 L.G.R. 459; (1996) 29 B.M.L.R. 79; [1995] Fam. Law 410; (1995) 145 N.L.J.Rep. 490; (1996) 160 L.G.Rev. 341; *The Times*, February 3, 1995, CA; reversing [1994] 2 F.L.R. 1027; [1995] 1 F.C.R. 248; [1995] Fam. Law 71; (1995) 159 J.P.N. 28; *The Times*, July 29, 1994; *The Independent*, September 16, 1994, QBD .... [8Q–198/1]
—— v. ——, ex p. Idowu, August 1998; *Legal Action* 21, QBD .... [8Q–155/1]
—— v. ——, ex p. Ojuri (No. 3), August 1998; *Legal Action* 22 .... [8Q–155/2]
—— v. North West Lancashire Health Authority, ex p. A, *The Times*, August 24, 1999, CA .... [21T–2/1]
—— v. Preston Crown Court, ex p. Chief Constable of the Lancashire Constabulary [1998] C.O.D. 272, QBD 56/1/9
—— v. Secretary of State for the Environment and Shropshire County Council, ex p. Parry [1998] C.O.D. 17; [1998] Env.L.R. D5, QBD 94/2/2
—— v. Secretary of State for the Home Department, ex p. Salem [1999] 2 W.L.R. 483, HL 20A–191/1

R. v. Secretary of State for Transport, ex p. Factortame, July 6, 1998 (unrep.), CA ... 62/3/6
—— v. Southwark London Borough Council, ex p. Anderson, July 1999, *Legal Action* 22, QBD ... [8Q–200]
—— v. ——, ex p. Ryder, September 1995; *Legal Action* 15, CA ... [8Q–198/1]
—— v. Tower Hamlets London Borough Council, ex p. Abdul Jolil, October 1998; *Legal Action* 22, QBD ... [8Q–171]
—— v. Wealden District Council, ex p. Stratford. *See* R. v. Lincolnshire County Council, ex p. Atkinson.
—— v. ——, ex p. Wales. *See* R. v. Lincolnshire County Council, ex p. Atkinson.
—— v. Westminster City Council, ex p. Ellioua, ex p. October 1998; *Legal Action* 22, CA ... [8Q–240/1]
RTZ Pension Property Trust Ltd v. ARC Property Development Ltd *sub nom.* ASFA Ltd v. RTZ Pension Property Trust Ltd (1998) 148 N.L.J. 1675; *The Times*, November 26, 1998, CA ... 62/5/4
Rees v. Mabco (102) Ltd, *The Times*, December 16, 1998, CA ... 15/6/8
Regalbourne Ltd v. East Lindsey District Council [1994] R.A. 1; [1993] C.O.D. 297; (1994) 158 L.G.Rev. 81; *The Times*, March 16, 1993, CA; affirming [1992] C.O.D. 493 ... 94/2/2
Reunion Europeen SA v. Spliethoffs Bevrachtingskantoor BV (Case C–51/97), *The Times*, November 16, 1998, ECJ ... 11/1/55
Rezvi v. Brown Cooper [1997] 1 Costs L.R. 109, QBD ... [15A–58/40]
Riccio v. Ford Motor Co. Ltd. *See* Pritchard v. Ford Motor Co. Ltd.
Richard Roberts Holdings Ltd v. Douglas Smith Stimson Partnership [1998] 2 Con.L.R. 60 ... 62/5/4
Ridehalgh v. Horsefield; Allen v. Unigate Dairies Ltd; Antonelli v. Wade Gery Farr; Philex plc v. Golban; Roberts v. Coverite (Asphalters) Ltd; Watson v. Watson (Wasted Costs Orders) [1994] Ch. 205; [1994] 3 W.L.R. 462; [1994] 3 All E.R. 848; [1994] B.C.C. 390; [1994] 2 F.L.R. 194; [1994] Fam. Law 560; [1994] E.G.C.S. 15; (1994) 144 N.L.J.Rep. 231; [1994] N.P.C. 7; *The Times*, January 28, 1994; *The Independent*, February 4, 1994, CA; reversing *The Times*, July 9, 1993; *The Times*, December 29, 1992 ... 62/11/20
Roberts v. Coverite (Asphalters) Ltd. *See* Ridehalgh v. Horsefield.
Ropaigealach v. Barclays Bank plc [1999] 3 W.L.R. 17; (1999) *New Law Journal*, January 29, p. 121; *The Times*, January 6, 1999, CA ... [8C–3]

S v. F Co. Ltd. *See* A v. F Co. Ltd.
—— v. M (Wasted Costs Order) [1998] 3 F.C.R. 665; *The Times*, March 26, 1998, Ch D ... 62/11/14
S-C (Mental Patient: Habeas Corpus), Re, *sub nom.* Simpson-Cleghorn, Re [1996] Q.B. 599; [1996] 2 W.L.R. 146; [1996] 1 All E.R. 532; [1996] 1 F.L.R. 548; [1996] 2 F.C.R. 692; 29 B.M.L.R. 138; [1996] Fam. Law 210; *The Times*, December 4, 1995, CA; [1996] C.O.D. 221, QBD ... 54/1/5
Saab v. Saudi American Bank [1998] 1 W.L.R. 937; [1998] 4 All E.R. 382; [1998] 2 B.C.L.C. 13; [1998] B.C.C. 722; *The Times*, March 11, 1998, QBD ... 10/2/2
Sage v. South Gloucestershire County Council [1998] C.O.D. 384; [1998] E.L.R. 525, QBD ... 55/4/2
Saint v. Barking and Dagenham London Borough Council, November 1998; *Legal Action* 25, CA ... [8C–4], [8L–52], [8O–72]
Sanctuary H.A. v. Baker (1998) 30 H.L.R. 809; [1998] 1 E.G.L.R. 42; [1998] 09 E.G. 150, CA ... [8L–85]
Sasea Finance Ltd (in liquidation), Re [1998] 1 B.C.L.C. 559; *The Times*, December 29, 1997, Ch D ... 62/11/2
Scarth v. Jacobs-Paton, *The Times*, November 2, 1978, CA ... [16D–34]
Seabridge Shipping A.B. v. A.C. Orssleff's Eftf's A/S [1999] 2 Lloyd's Rep. 685 ... [21D–38]
Second WRVS Housing Society Ltd v. Blair (1987) 19 H.L.R. 104, CA ... [8L–47]
Secretary of State for Trade and Industry v. Baker, Barings plc, Re [1998] Ch. 356; [1998] 2 W.L.R. 667; [1998] 1 All E.R. 673; [1998] 1 B.C.L.C. 16; [1998] B.C.C. 888; *The Times*, October 23, 1997; *The Independent*, October 7, 1997, Ch D (Companies Ct) ... 24/5/16
Shapland v. Palmer [1999] 1 W.L.R. 2068; [1999] 3 All E.R. 50; *The Times*, March 31, 1999, CA ... [14–40/4]
Sheldon v. RHM Outhwaite (Underwriting Agencies) Ltd [1996] A.C. 102; [1995] 2 W.L.R. 570; [1995] 2 All E.R. 558; [1995] 2 Lloyd's Rep. 197; 145 N.L.J.Rep. 687; 92(22) L.S.Gaz. 41; 139 S.J.L.B. 119; *The Times*, May 5, 1995; *The Independent*, May 9, 1995; Lloyd's List, May 24, 1995, HL; reversing [1994] 3 W.L.R. 999; [1994] 4 All E.R. 481; *The Times*, July 1, 1994; *The Independent*, July 8, 1994, CA; reversing [1994] 1 W.L.R. 754; [1994] 4 All E.R. 481; *The Times*, December 8, 1993, QBD ... 18/12/18

Shevill v. Presse-Alliance SA (Case C–68/93) [1995] 2 A.C. 18; [1995] 2 W.L.R. 499; [1995] All E.R. (E.C.) 289; [1995] I.L.Pr. 267; [1995] E.M.L.R. 543; *The Times*, April 6, 1995; *Financial Times*, March 21, 1995, ECJ; [1996] A.C. 959; [1996] 3 W.L.R. 420; [1996] 3 All E.R. 929; [1996] E.M.L.R. 533; (1996) 93 (38) L.S.G. 42; (1996) 140 S.J.L.B. 208; *The Times*, July 26, 1996, HL; affirming [1996] A.C. 977; [1992] 2 W.L.R. 1; [1992] 1 All E.R. 409; *The Times*, March 13, 1991; *The Independent*, March 13, 1991; *Financial Times*, March 21, 1991, CA .... 11/1/15, 11/1/55, [7A–1]
Singh v. Bhasin, *The Times*, August 21, 1998, Ch D 62/B/151
Smith v. Leicestershire Health Authority [1998] Lloyd's Rep.Med. 77, CA; (1996) 36 B.M.L.R. 23, QBD .... [14–17/8], [14–40/6]
Smith Kline Beecham Biologicals SA v. Connaught Laboratories Inc. [1999] 4 All E.R. 498, CA; *The Times*, January 14, 1999 .... 24/14A/3
Société d'Informatique Realisation Organisation v. Ameprsand Software B.V. (Case C–432/93) [1995] All E.R. (EC) 783; *The Times*, September 25, 1995; *The Independent*, October 9, 1995 (C.S.), ECJ; (1993) 137 S.J.L.B. 189; (1993) 90 (35) L.S.G. 36; *The Times*, July 29, 1993, CA .... [7A–1]
Soinco SACI v. Novokuznetsk Aluminium [1998] 2 Lloyd's Rep. 337; [1998] C.L.C. 730; *The Times*, December 29, 1997, CA; affirming 1996–Folio No. 1915, QBD (Comm Ct) .... [21A–254], [21D–145]
Soleimany v. Soleimany [1999] Q.B. 785; [1999] 3 W.L.R. 811; [1999] 3 All E.R. 864; [1999] 2 Lloyd's Rep. 65, CA; pet. dis. [1999] 1 W.L.R. 1999, HL; [1998] C.L.C. 779; *The Times*, March 4, 1998, CA .... [21A–248], [21B–23]
Spath Holme Ltd v. Chairman of the Greater Manchester and Lancashire Rent Assessment Committee (No. 2); Curtis v. Chairman of the London Rent Assessment Committee [1998] 3 All E.R. 909; [1997] N.P.C. 173; *The Times*, January 2, 1998, QBD 62/A2/5
Spurr v. Hall (1877) 2 Q.B.D. 615 .... 22/1/20
Stabilad Ltd v. Stephens & Carter Ltd [1998] 4 All E.R. 129, CA 23/3/42
Star News Shops v. Stafford Refrigeration Ltd [1998] 1 W.L.R. 536; [1998] 4 All E.R. 408; (1997) 94 (43) L.S.G. 30; (1997) 141 S.J.L.B. 236; *The Times*, November 18, 1997, CA 24/16/3
Stretch v. West Dorset District Council (No. 2), *The Times*, May 20, 1999, CA .... [16A–75]
Surrey County Council v. Lamond [1999] 12 E.G. 170; [1998] E.G.C.S. 185; *The Independent*, January 25, 1999 (C.S.), CA .... [8L–150]
Swain v. The Law Society [1983] 1 A.C. 598; [1982] 3 W.L.R. 261; [1982] 2 All E.R. 827; (1982) 126 S.J. 464; (1982) 79 L.S.Gaz. 887, HL; reversing [1982] 1 W.L.R. 17; [1981] 3 All E.R. 797; (1981) 125 S.J. 542, CA; [1980] 1 W.L.R. 1335; [1980] 3 All E.R. 615; (1980) 124 S.J. 220 .... [15A–58/23/1]
Swale Storage & Distribution Services Ltd v. Sittingbourne Paper Co. Ltd (1998) 95 (34) L.S.G. 32; (1998) 142 S.J.L.B. 229; *The Times*, July 30, 1998, CA 62/3/3
Symphony Group plc v. Hodgson [1994] Q.B. 179; [1993] 3 W.L.R. 830; [1993] 4 All E.R. 143; 137 S.J.L.B. 134; 143 N.L.J. 725; *The Times*, May 4, 1993; *The Independent*, May 14, 1993, CA 62/2/7

T. E. Beach (Contractors) Ltd v. Thompson, June 2, 1998 (unrep.) 62/5/7
T.G.A. Chapman Ltd v. Christopher [1998] 1 W.L.R. 12; [1998] 2 All E.R. 873; [1998] Lloyd's Rep.I.R. 1; [1997] C.L.C. 1306; *The Times*, July 21, 1997, CA ... 62/2/7
Taber v. MacDonald (1999) 31 H.L.R. 73; June 1998, *Legal Action* 13, DC .... [8M–76/1]
Tadema Holdings Ltd v. Ferguson, *The Times*, November 25, 1999, CA .... [80–93/1]
Tavera v. MacFarlane [1996] P.I.Q.R. P292, CA 13/7/3
Taylor v. Director of the Serious Fraud Office [1998] 3 W.L.R. 1040; [1998] 4 All E.R. 801; *The Times*, November 4, 1998; *The Independent*, November 3, 1998, HL; affirming [1997] 4 All E.R. 887; [1998] E.M.L.R. 463; (1997) 94 (36) L.S.G. 44; (1997) 147 N.L.J. 1309; (1997) 141 S.J.L.B. 216; *The Times*, August 27, 1997; *The Independent*, July 24, 1997, CA 24/14A/2
Thai Trading Co. v. Taylor [1998] Q.B. 781; [1998] 2 W.L.R. 893; [1998] 3 All E.R. 65; [1998] 2 F.L.R. 430; [1998] 3 F.L.R. 606; [1998] P.N.L.R. 698; [1998] Fam. Law 586; (1998) 95 (15) L.S.G. 30; (1998) 123 S.J.L.B. 125; *The Times*, March 6, 1998, CA .... 62/3/1, 62/A2/27A, [15A–58/23/1]
Theakston v. Matthews, *The Times*, April 13, 1998, CA 62/B/128
Thomas Watts & Co. v. Smith, March 16, 1998 (unrep.), CA .... [15A–58/74]
Tobin v. Gwyther, February 8, 1999 (unrep.), CA .... [16A–86]
Tolstoy–Miloslavsky v. Aldington [1996] 1 W.L.R. 736; [1996] 2 All E.R. 556; [1996] P.N.L.R. 335; (1996) 93(1) L.S.G. 22; (1996) 140 S.J.L.B. 26; *The Times*, December 27, 1995, CA; *The Independent*, January 3, 1996 .... 62/11/20
Tower Hamlets London Borough Council v. Long, September 1998; *Legal Action* 25, CA .... [8Q–70]
Transeuropean Carriage Co. v. Abou-Hamdan, July 1998, *Legal Action* 12, Cty Ct .. [8O–147]
Trygg Hansa Insurance Co. Ltd v. Equitas Ltd [1998] 2 Lloyd's Rep. 439; [1998] C.L.C. 979, QBD (Comm Ct) .... [21D–15]

Tsakos Shipping & Trading SA v. Orizon Tanker Co. Ltd (The Centaurus Mar) [1998] C.L.C. 1003, QBD (Comm. Ct) .....[21D–101/1]
Turner & Co. v. O. Palomo S.A.; *sub nom.* Palomo (O.) S.A. v. Turner & Co. [1999] 4 All E.R. 353; *The Times*, August 30, 1999, CA .....[15A–58/71]
Turner Page Music v. Torres Design Associates Ltd, *The Times*, August 3, 1998, CA 62/11/14
Turpitt v. Elizabeth, August 1998; *Legal Action* 21, Edmonton Cty Ct ..... [8O–147]

Ujima H.A. v. Ansah (1998) 30 H.L.R. 831; [1997] N.P.C. 144; *The Times*, November 20, 1997; *The Independent*, October 23, 1997, CA ..... [8O–8]
Ultisol Transport Contractors Ltd v. Bouygues Offshore SA. *See* Caspian Basin Specialised Salvage Emergency Salvage Administration v. Bouygues Offshore SA (No. 4).
UPS Ltd v. Lewis, *The Independent*, February 23, 1998 (CS), CA 14/7/8
Unilever v. Chefaro Proprietaries [1995] 1 W.L.R. 243; [1995] 1 All E.R. 557; [1994] 144 N.L.J.Rep. 160; *The Times*, November 28, 1994; *The Independent*, November 24, 1994; [1994] R.P.C. 567
United Mizrahi Bank Ltd v. Doherty [1998] 1 W.L.R. 435; [1998] 2 All E.R. 230; *The Times*, December 15, 1997, Ch D 29/L/36

Van Uden Maritime BV v. Kommanditgesellschaft in Firma Deco-Line (Case C–391/95), *The Times*, December 1, 1998, ECJ 11/1/70A
Vernon v. Bosley (No. 2) [1999] Q.B. 18; [1997] 3 W.L.R. 683; [1997] 1 All E.R. 614; [1997] P.I.Q.R. P326; (1997) 35 B.M.L.R. 174; [1997] R.T.R. 275; [1997] Fam. Law 476; (1997) 147 N.L.J. Rep. 89; (1997) 94(4) L.S.G. 26; (1997) 141 S.J.L.B. 27; *The Times*, December 19, 1996; *The Independent*, January 21, 1997, CA 24/2/17
Vosnoc Ltd v. Transglobal Projects Ltd [1998] 1 W.L.R. 101; [1998] 2 All E.R. 990; [1998] 1 Lloyd's Rep. 711; [1997] C.L.C. 1345; (1997) 94 (34) L.S.G. 28; (1997) 141 S.J.L.B. 215; *The Times*, August 27, 1997, QBD (Comm Ct) ..... [21D–38]

Wailes v. Stapleton Construction & Commercial Services Ltd; Wailes v. Unum Ltd [1997] 2 Lloyd's Rep. 112, QBD 62/12/1
—— v. Unum Ltd. *See* Wailes v. Stapleton Construction & Commercial Services Ltd.
Walkley v. Precision Forgings Ltd [1979] 1 W.L.R. 606; (1979) 123 S.J. 354; [1979] 2 All E.R. 548, HL; reversing [1978] 1 W.L.R. 1228; (1978) 122 S.J. 645; [1979] 1 All E.R. 102, CA ..... [14–40/4]
Wall v. Lefever [1998] 1 F.C.R. 605; *The Times*, August 1, 1997, CA 62/11/20
Wallace v. Brian Gale & Associates [1998] 1 F.L.R. 1091; [1998] Fam. Law 400; *The Times*, March 5, 1998, CA; affirming 53 Con.L.R. 103; [1997] 2 Costs L.R. 15; *The Times*, March 31, 1997, QBD (OR) 62/B/137
—— v. Manchester City Council [1998] L. & T.R. 279; [1998] E.G.C.S. 114; (1998) 30 H.L.R. 1111; [1998] N.P.C. 115; [1998] 41 E.G. 223; *The Times*, July 23, 1998; *The Independent*, July 17, 1998, CA ..... [8M–13]
Wandsworth London Borough Council v. Osei-Bonsu *sub nom.* Osei Bonsu v. Wandsworth London Borough Council [1998] N.P.C. 141; [1998] E.G.C.S. 148; (1998) 95 (45) L.S.G. 40; (1998) 95 (42) L.S.G. 34; (1998) 148 N.L.J. 1641; *The Times*, November 4, 1998, CA ..... [8O–162], [8O–168]
Warsame v. Hounslow L.B.C., *The Times*, July 21, 1999, CA ..... [8Q–246]
Waterford Wedgwood plc v. David Nagli Ltd [1998] C.L.C. 1011; *The Times*, May 13, 1998, Ch D 16/1/7
—— v. David Nagli Ltd (in liquidation), *The Times*, January 4, 1999, Ch D ..... [16D–244/1]
Watson v. Watson (Wasted Costs Orders). *See* Ridehalgh v. Horsefield.
Wealands v. CLC Contractors Ltd [1999] 2 Lloyd's Rep. 739, CA; [1998] C.L.C. 808, QBD (Comm Ct) ..... [21D–25], [21J–4/1]
Wellcome Trust v. Hamad [1998] Q.B. 638; [1998] 2 W.L.R. 156; [1998] 1 All E.R. 657; (1998) 30 H.L.R. 629; [1998] 1 E.G.L.R. 73; [1998] 02 E.G. 121; *The Times*, October 13, 1997, CA ..... [8H–121]
Welsh Development Agency v. Redpath Dorman Long Ltd [1994] 4 All E.R. 10; [1994] 1 W.L.R. 1409; 38 Con.L.R. 106; 67 B.L.R. 1; 10 Const.L.J. 325; 91(21) L.S.Gaz. 42; 138 S.J.L.B. 87; *The Times*, April 4, 1994; *The Independent*, May 2, 1994 (C.S.), CA ..... [14–29/1]
West Bromwich Building Society v. Mander Hadley & Co. [1998] C.L.C. 814; [1998] N.P.C. 30; *The Times*, March 9, 1998; *The Independent*, March 10, 1998, CA; reversing CH–1995–W–No. 7967, Ch D ..... [14–18/2]
West Kent Housing Association v. Davis [1998] E.G.C.S. 103, CA ..... [8O–49]
Westacre Investments Inc. v. Jugoimport–SPDR Holding Co. Ltd [1999] 1 All E.R. (Comm.) 865; [1999] 2 Lloyd's Rep. 65; *The Times*, May 25, 1999, CA; affirming [1998] 3 W.L.R. 770; [1998] 4 All E.R. 570; [1998] 2 Lloyd's Rep. 111; [1998] C.L.C. 409, QBD (Comm Ct) ..... [21A–248], [21B–23]
Western Bank Ltd v. Schindler [1977] Ch. 1; [1976] 3 W.L.R. 341; [1976] 2 All E.R. 393; (1976) 32 P. & C.R. 352, CA ..... [8C–3]
Weth v. H.M. Att.-Gen., *The Times*, October 12, 1998, CA; reversing November 21, 1997 (unrep.) 62/2/7, 62/B/151

White v. Glass, *The Times*, February 18, 1989, CA .... [14–40/4]
Wilkinson v. Crown Prosecution Service *sub nom.* Wilkinson v. DPP [1998] C.O.D. 387; (1998) 162 J.P. 591; [1998] Crim.L.R. 743; (1998) 162 J.P.N. 625, DC 56/5/3
—— v. DPP. *See* Wilkinson v. Crown Prosecution Service.
Williams v. Bedwellty Justices. *See* R. v. Bedwellty Justices, ex p. Williams.
Wilson v. Webster [1998] 1 F.L.R. 1097; [1998] 2 F.C.R. 575; [1998] Fam. Law 391; (1998) 95 (16) L.S.G. 23; *The Times*, March 5, 1998, CA 52/1/41
Wong v. Vizards [1997] 2 Costs L.R. 46, QBD 62/15/2
Woodchester Lease Management Services Ltd v. Swain [1999] C.C.L.R. 8, CA ...... [9A–99/1]
Woolwich Building Society v. Fineberg [1998] P.N.L.R. 216, CA 62/11/5
Worldham's Park Golf Course Ltd, Re, [1988] 1 B.C.L.C. 554 .... 30/3/2
Wraith v. Wraith [1997] 1 W.L.R. 1540; [1997] 2 All E.R. 526; *The Times*, February 14, 1997 .... [16D–251]

York and Ross v. Casey (1999) 31 H.L.R. 209; [1998] 2 E.G.L.R. 25; [1998] 30 E.G. 110; [1998] E.G.C.S. 26, CA .... [8O–137]
Yorkshire Bank v. Hall, *The Times*, January 14, 1998; *The Independent*, January 11, 1999, CA 88/1/3

Zockoll Group Ltd v. Mercury Communications Ltd [1998] F.S.R. 354, CA 29/L/1

TABLE OF STATUTES

References to paragraph numbers in square brackets are to Volume 2. Paragraph numbers shown in bold indicate where the text of a statute or part thereof is reproduced.

References to paragraph numbers with prefix "C" are to the County Court Rules Supplement

1847 Docks and Piers Clauses Act (10 & 11 Vict., c. 27)
s.44 .... 75/12/3
1906 Public Trustee Act (6 Edw. 7, c. 55) .... [12C–40]
1925 Law of Property Act (15 & 16 Geo. 5, c. 20) .... [8B–18], [16D–155]
1927 Landlord and Tenant Act (17 & 18 Geo. 5, c. 36) C43/18
1939 Limitation Act (2 & 3 Geo. 6, c. 21)
s.19 .... [14–26/1]
1947 Crown Proceedings Act (10 & 11 Geo. 6, c. 44)
s.38(2) .... [21L–94], [21L–94/1]
s.40 .... [21L–97/1]
(2) .... [21L–97]
(3A) .... **[21L–97]**
1949 Patents Act (12, 13 & 14 Geo. 6, c. 87) .... [20A–406]
1950 Arbitration Act (14 Geo. 6, c. 27) .... [21A–8]
s.22 .... [21A–206]
(1) .... [21A–206]
s.27 .... [21D–34]
1954 Landlord and Tenant Act (2 & 3 Eliz. 2, c. 56) C43/18
1957 Public Trustee (Fees) Act (5 & 6 Eliz. 2, c. 12) .... [12C–40]
s.2(2) .... [12C–40]
1960 Caravan Sites and Control of Development Act (8 & 9 Eliz. 2, c. 62) 113/8/14
Administration of Justice Act (8 & 9 Eliz. 2, c. 65) 32/13/23
s.13(2) 52/1/41
1964 Harbours Act (c. 40)
s.26(3) 75/12/3
s.57(1) 75/12/3
1968 Civil Evidence Act (c. 64)
s.14(1) 24/5/34
1970 Administration of Justice Act (c. 31) .... [8C–4]
s.36 .... [8C–3], [8C–4], [8C–4/1]
1971 Attachment of Earnings Act (c. 32)
s.24(2) .... [21E–43]
(b) .... [21E–42]
1973 Administration of Justice Act (c. 15)
s.8 .... [8C–4/1]
1974 Consumer Credit Act (c. 39) .... [8F–6]
s.8(1), (2) .... [9A–47/1]
s.9(1) .... [9A–45/1]
s.10(1)(b) .... [9A–47/1]
s.11 .... [9A–45/1], [9A–46/1], [9A–47/1], [9A–48/1]
1974 Consumer Credit Act—*cont.*
s.12(a) .... [9A–47/1], [9A–48/1]
s.16 .... [9A–54]
(3)(f) .... [9A–53]
(6B)(a) .... [9A–53]
s.88(1)(b) .... [9A–99/1]
s.126 .... [8C–3]
s.129(1)(b) .... [9A–42/3]
s.138 .... [9A–159/3]
s.139(1)(a) .... [9A–42/3]
s.141 .... [9A–42/1]
Solicitors Act (c. 47) .... [15A–58/23/1]
s.23(1),(2) .... [11B–4]
s.31 .... [15F–9]
s.59(2) .... [15–58/23/1]
s.60(3) .... 62/29/6, 62/A2/27A, [15A–58/28/1]
1975 Arbitration Act (c. 3) .... [21B–23]
Litigants in Person (Costs and Expenses) Act (c. 47) .... [21R–4]
s.1(1) 62/18/2/1
Welsh Development Agency Act (c. 70)
s.21A .... [8F–9/4]
Sched. 4 .... [8F–9/1], [8H–58/1], [8O–217/1]
para. 16 .... **[8F–9/1]**
1977 Rent Act (c. 42) .... [8H–4]
s.4(1) .... [8H–15]
(2) .... [8H–15]
s.14(f)(i) .... [8H–53]
s.15(2)(aa) .... [8H–59]
Protection from Eviction Act (c. 43)
s.3A(8)(f),(g) .... [8G–13]
(ga) .... **[8G–13]**
Criminal Law Act (c. 45)
s.6 .... [8C–3]
1978 State Immunity Act (c. 33)
s.12(5) 13/7A/3
(6) 13/7A/3
1979 Charging Orders Act (c. 53)
s.1 .... [21F–7]
s.2 .... [21F–7]
s.3(5) .... [21F–7/1]
1980 Limitation Act (c. 58)
s.11 .... [14–17/3]
s.14 .... [14–17/8]
(1)(c) .... [14–17/8]
(3) .... [14–17/8]
s.14A .... [14–18/2]
(10) .... [14–18/2]
s.21 .... [14–26/1]
(1)(b) .... [14–26/1]

1988 Legal Aid Act—*cont.*
s.2(11) [16A–16/2]
s.17 [16A–16/2], [16D–244/1]
s.18 [16A–16/2]
(4) [16A–75]
s.31(1)(b) [16A–86]
s.32(1) [16A–93]
s.34(3) [16D–192], [16D–241]
Housing Act (c. 50) C49/6, C49/6A, [8O–8]
Pt I [8O–72/1]
s.3 [8O–19A]
s.5(1) [8O–49]
s.6 [8O–49]
s.7(3) [8O–49]
(4) [8O–49]
(6)(b),(7) [8O–49]
s.8 [1C–3], [8O–49]
s.9(6) [8O–49], [8O–72/1]
s.20 [8O–137]
s.21 [8N–11], [8O–147]
(1)(b) [8O–147]
(4) [8O–147]
s.27 [8O–162]
s.35(4)(a),(5) [8O–176]
s.58 [1C–1]
s.152 [1C–1]
s.153(1) [1C–1]
Sched. 1,
para. 11(2) [8O–201]
para. 12 [8O–217/1]
(1)(c) [8O–202]
Sched. 2 [8O–49]
Ground 8 [8O–49], [8O–72/1]
Ground 10 [8O–49]

1989 Children Act (c. 41)
s.12(2) [11B–68]
s.25 59/1B/8
s.31(1)(a) [11B–68]
s.33(3) [11B–68]

1990 Courts and Legal Services Act (c. 41) 62/A2/27A, [2C–208/1], [15E–1]
s.27(2)(e) 32/6/31, [15G–107]
s.54 [15A–24]
s.58 62/A2/27A
(3) [15E–3], [15E–4]
(4) [15E–1]
(5) [15E–1], [15E–4]
(7) [15E–1]
s.74 [20A–738/1]
(1) [20A–655/2]
(2) [20A–655/2]
Sched. 10, para. 58 [15A–24]
Sched. 11 [15A–24]

1991 Civil Jurisdiction and Judgments Act (c. 12) [7A–5]

1993 Judicial Pensions and Retirement Act (c. 8) [19A–1]
Charities Act (c. 10) 62/2/7

1994 Criminal Justice and Public Order Act (c. 33)
s.77 113/8/14

1995 Merchant Shipping Act (c. 21)
s.93 [6D–205]
(1),(2),(3),(4),(5) [6D–204]
s.185(2A) [6D–209]
Environment Act (c. 25)
s.78 [8M–82], [8M–93]

1995 Environment Act—*cont.*
Sched. 10,
para. 25(1) [8M–82]
(2) [8M–93]

1996 Arbitration Act (c. 23) [21D–15], [21D–25]
Pt I [20A–737/2]
s.6(2) [21D–15]
s.9 [21D–25]
s.12 [21D–25], [21D–34]
s.16 [21D–41/1]
(5) [21D–41/1]
s.27(3) [21D–41/1]
s.33 62/B/12
s.42 [21D–93]
s.63(2) 62/B/12
s.91 [21D–213/1]
s.92 [20A–737/2]
s.107 [21D–20]
Sched. 3 [21D–20]
paras 51, 54, 55 [21D–258/1]
Family Law Act (c. 27) [20A–178]
Pt IV 62/A2/19
Trusts of Land and Appointment of Trustees Act (c. 47)
Sched.1 [8L–71]
Housing Act (c. 52) [8O–137], [8Q–66], [8Q–200]
Pt VII [8L–47]
s.1(1) [8Q–3]
(1A) **[8Q–3]**
(1B),(2) [8Q–3]
s.127(2) [8Q–31]
s.128 [8Q–31]
s.155(2)(b) [8Q–85]
(3)–(7) [8Q–85]
s.156 [8Q–88]
s.175(3) [8Q–141/1]
s.176 [8Q–155/2]
s.186(1) [8Q–141/1]
s.188 [8Q–155/2]
s.189(1)(b) [8Q–158]
s.193 [8Q–200], [8Q–200/1], [8Q–246]
s.198(5) [8Q–219/1]
s.199(1)(b) [8Q–222]
s.202 [8Q–246]
(1) [8Q–246]
(f) [8Q–200/1]
s.204 [8Q–200/1], [8Q–240/1], [8Q–246]
(2) [8Q–246]
s.206 [8Q–198/1]
Sched. 15 [8Q–286]

1997 Civil Procedure Act (c. 12)
s.4(2) [20A–8/2]
s.8 [20A–8/2]
Sched. 2,
para. 2(2) [20A–738/1]
(4) [20A–650/1]
(5) [20A–652/1]
(6) [20A–748/1]
(9) [20A–823/1]
Social Security (Recovery of Benefits) Act (c. 27) 22/1/18
s.16 22/5/2
Protection from Harassment Act (c. 40) C45/15A, [1C–10]
s.3 C45/15A
(3) C45/15A

1998 Employment Rights (Dispute Resolution) Act (c. 8)
Sched. 1, para. 6 .... [15A–24]
Bank of England Act (c. 11)
s.23 .... [15A–24]
(2) 92/3A/1
s.43 .... [15A–24]
Sched. 5,
para. 36 .... [9A–54]
para. 41 .... [15A–24]
Sched. 9, Pt I .... [15A–24]
Social Security Act (c.14)
s.86 .... [21D–258/1]
Sched. 8 .... [21D–258/1]
Late Payment of Commercial Debts (Interest) Act (c. 20) C–016, C25/5A/2
s.17 .... 6/L/2
Data Protection Act (c. 29)
Sched. 16, Pt I .... [15A–24]
Government of Wales Act (c. 38)
s.125 .... [10B–34/1]
s.140 ..... [8G–14], [8L–7], [8L–10], [8L–81], [8L–164/1], [8L–173]
s.152 .... [9A–54]
Sched. 12, para. 22 ...... [10B–34/1]
Sched. 13 ..... [8F–9/2], [8H–58/1], [8O–217/1]
Sched. 15,
para. 7 .... [8L–5]
para. 10 .... [8L–107]
para. 12 .... [8M–82]
para. 13 .... [8M–93]
para. 15 .... [8O–177]
Sched. 16,
para. 2 .... [8G–14]
para. 5 .... [8L–10]
para. 6 .... [8L–7]
para. 7 .... [8L–10]
para. 10 .... [8L–81]
para. 11 .... [8L–120]
para. 21 ... [8L–164/1], [8L–173]
para. 82 .... [8Q–4]
para. 83 .... [8Q–4]
Sched. 18,
Pt IV .... [8G–14], [8G–54], [8L–18], [8L–107], [8L–149], [8L–173], [8M–82], [8O–206]
Pt VI .... [8H–60], [8L–81], [8L–120], [8Q–4], [9A–54]
Human Rights Act (c. 42) .. [21T–1]
s.1 .... **[21T–2]**
(2) .... [21U–1]
s.2 .... [21T–3]
(1) .... [21T–2/1]
(b) .... [21T–4]
(c) .... [21T–5]
(d) .... [21T–6]
s.3 .... **[21T–5]**
s.4 .... **[21T–6]**
s.5 .... **[21T–7]**
s.6 .... **[21T–8]**
s.7 .... **[21T–9]**
s.8 .... **[21T–10]**
s.9 .... **[21T–11]**

1998 Human Rights Act—*cont.*
s.10 .... **[21T–12]**
s.11 .... **[21T–13]**
s.12 .... **[21T–14]**
s.13 .... **[21T–15]**
s.14 .... **[21T–16]**
s.15 .... **[21T–17]**
s.16 .... **[21T–18]**
s.17 .... **[21T–19]**
s.18 .... **[21T–20]**
s.19 .... **[21T–21]**
s.20 .... **[21T–22]**
s.21 .... **[21T–23]**
(3) .... [21T–6]
s.22 .... **[21T–24]**
(4) .... [21T–25]
Sched. 1, Pt I (Convention)
Art. 2 .... **[21T–26]**
Art. 3 .... **[21T–27]**
Art. 4 .... **[21T–28]**
Art. 5 .... **[21T–29]**
Art. 6 .... **[21T–30]**
Art. 7 .... **[21T–31]**
Art. 8 .... **[21T–32]**
Art. 9 .... **[21T–33]**
Art. 10 .... **[21T–34]**
Art. 11 .... **[21T–35]**
Art. 12 .... **[21T–36]**
Art. 14 .... **[21T–37]**
Art. 16 .... **[21T–38]**
Art. 17 .... **[21T–39]**
Art. 18 .... **[21T–40]**
Pt II (First Protocol)
Art. 1 .... **[21T–41]**
Art. 2 .... **[21T–42]**
Art. 3 .... **[21T–43]**
Pt III (Sixth Protocol)
Art. 1 .... **[21T–44]**
Art. 2 .... **[21T–45]**
Scotland Act (c. 46)
s.125 .... [7B–38], [21L–94/1], [21L–97/1]
Sched. 8,
para. 7 .... [21L–94/1], [21L–97/1]
para. 18 .... [7B–38]
1999 Tax Credits Act (c. 10) .... [4B–1]
Access to Justice Act (c. 22)
s.24 .... [20A–199], [20A–204], [20A–263/6]
s.59 .... [20A–407]
s.60 .... [20A–422/1]
s.61 .... [20A–202]
s.62 .... [20A–259/2]
s.69(3) .... [20A–143]
s.70 .... [20A–422/2]
s.106 .... [20A–178], [20A–407], [20A–465/15]
Sched. 4,
para. 22 .... [20A–199]
para. 24 .... [20A–263/6]
para. 32 .... [20A–204]
Sched. 15,
Pt II .... [20A–465/15]
Pt III ...... [20A–178], [20A–407], [20A–57/2]

TABLE OF STATUTORY INSTRUMENTS

References to paragraph numbers in square brackets are to Volume 2. Paragraph numbers shown in bold indicate where the text of a statutory instrument or part thereof is reproduced.

1989 Civil Legal Aid (General) Regulations—*cont.*
reg. 107A(4) .... **[16D–208]**
reg. 107B(3)(a) .... [16D–211]
reg. 124 .... [16D–241]
Civil Jurisdiction and Judgments Act 1982 (Amendment) Order (S.I. 1989 No. 1346) .... [7A–4]
art. 9(1) .... [7B–42]
Sched. 1 .... [7B–42]
1990 Civil Jurisdiction and Judgments Act 1982 (Amendment) Order (S.I. 1990 No. 2591) .... [7A–4]
art. 12(1) .... [7B–42]
Sched. 1 .... [7B–42]
1991 High Court and County Court Jurisdiction Order (S.I. 1991 No. 724)
art. 4A .... **[20B–247]**, [20B–261]
art. 5 .... [20B–247], [20B–261]
(1) ....**[20B–247]**
(3) ....[20B–247]
art. 7 ....[20B–249]
art. 8(1)(b) ....[20B–252]
art. 9 ....**[20B–261]**
art. 10 ....[20B–261]
art. 12(b) ....[20B–265]
County Courts (Interest on Judgment Debts) Order (S.I. 1991 No. 1184) C25/0/3, C25/5A/2
Legal Aid in Family Proceedings (Remuneration) Regulations (S.I. 1991 No. 2038) 62/A2/19
1994 Legal Aid in Civil Proceedings (Remuneration) Regulations (S.I. 1994 No. 228) 62/A2/19
reg. 2(2) .... [16F–2]
reg. 4(1) .... [16F–4]
(b) .... [16F–4]
(c) .... [16F–4]
(3) .... [16F–4]
(4) .... [16F–4]
Legal Aid in Family Proceedings (Remuneration) (Amendment) Regulations [S.I. 1994 No. 230) 62/A2/19
Court of Protection Rules (S.I. 1994 No. 3046)
r.9(2)(a) .... [10C–10]
r.21(3) .... [10C–22]
r.79 .... [10C–80]
r.80(1) .... [10C–81]
r.82 .... **[10C–83]**, [10C–101]
r.89 .... [10C–90]
Appendix,
para 1,
column 1 .... [10C–101]
column 2 .... [10C–101]
para 4 .... **[10C–101]**
para 7, column 2 .... [10C–101]
Table 1 .... **[10C–102]**, [10C–104]
Table 2 .... **[10C–103]**, [10C–104]
1994 Court of Protection (Enduring Powers of Attorney) Rules (S.I. 1994 No. 3047)
Sched. 2, column 2 ...... [10G–38]
Unfair Terms in Consumer Contracts Regulations (S.I. 1994 No. 3159) .... [9A–159/3], [21D–213/1]
1995 Conditional Fee Agreements Order (S.I. 1995 No. 1674) .. 62/A2/27A, [15E–1]
Conditional Fee Agreements Regulations (S.I. 1995 No. 1675) 62/A2/27A
1996 Allocation of Housing and Homelessness (Review Procedures and Amendment) Regulations (S.I. 1996 No. 3122) .... [8Q–240]
High Court and County Courts (Allocation of Arbitration Proceedings) Order (S.I. 1996 No. 3215) .... [21D–259]
art. 5(5) ...... **[21D–259]**, [21D–260]
County Court (Amendment No. 3) Rules (S.I. 1996 No. 3218)
r.3 ....C20/14/4
1997 Introductory Tenants (Review) Regulations (S.I. 1997 No. 72) .... [8Q–31]
Allocation of Housing and Homelessness (Amendment) Regulations (S.I. 1997 No. 631) .... [8Q–240]
County Court (Amendment) Rules (S.I. 1997 No. 1837) .... [8M–102/1]
Housing Act 1996 (Commencement No. 11) Order (S.I. 1997 No. 1851) .... [8M–102/1]
Leasehold Valuation Tribunals (Fees) Order (S.I. 1997 No. 1852) .... [8M–102/1]
Leasehold Valuation Tribunals (Service Charges, Insurance or Appointment of Managers Applications) Order (S.I. 1997 No. 1853) .... [8M–102/1]
Rent Assessment Committees (England and Wales) (Leasehold Valuation Tribunals) (Amendment) Regulations (S.I. 1997 No. 1854) .... [8M–102/1]
Social Security (Recovery of Benefits) Regulations (S.I. 1997 No. 2205)
reg. 8 .... 22/5/2
Civil Courts (Amendment No. 3) Order (S.I. 1997 No. 2310) .... [18C–2]

1997 Legal Aid in Family Proceedings (Remuneration) (Amendment) Regulations (S.I. 1997 No. 2394) 62/A2/19
Civil Jurisdiction and Judgments Act 1982 (Gibraltar) Order (S.I. 1997 No. 2602) .... [7A–3]
Civil Courts (Amendment No. 4) Order (S.I. 1997 No. 2762) .... [18C–2], [18D–1]
Road Traffic (Vehicle Emissions) (Fixed Penalty) Regulations (S.I. 1997 No. 3058) C48D
reg. 2(1)(b) C48D/1
(d) C48D/3
(f) C48D/1
reg. 9 .... C48D/1
reg. 10(1) C48D/1
reg. 12 .... C48D/5
1998 Merchant Shipping (Compulsory Insurance: Ships Receiving Transhipped Fish) Regulations (S.I. 1998 No. 209) .... [6D–262]
Scheme for Construction Contracts (England and Wales) Regulations (S.I. 1998 No. 649)
Sched., Pt I, art. 24 .... [21D–93]
Consumer Credit (Increase of Monetary Limits) (Amendment) Order (S.I. 1998 No. 996) ...... [8F–6]
Bank of England Act 1998 (Consequential Amendments of Subordinate Legislation) Order (S.I. 1998 No. 1129) 92/3A/1, 93/23/1
Merchant Shipping (Convention on Limitation of Liability for Maritime Claims) (Amendment) Order (S.I. 1998 No. 1258) .... [6D–209]
European Communities (Enforcement of Community Judgments) (Amendment) Order (S.I. 1998 No. 1259) 71/15/1
Homelessness (Decisions on Referrals) Order (S.I. 1998 No. 1578) .... [8Q–219/1], [8Q–222/1]
Merchant Shipping (Distress Messages) Regulations (S.I. 1998 No. 1691)
reg. 2 .... [6D–205]
Housing Act 1996 (Commencement No. 12 and Transitional Provision) Order (S.I. 1998 No. 1768) .... [8M–102/1]
1998 Merchant Shipping (Liability of Shipowners and Others) Rate of Inter est) Order (S.I. 1998 No. 1795) 75/37/5
Conditional Fee Agreements Order (S.I. 1998 No. 1860)
art. 1 .... **[15E–1]**
art. 2 .... [15E–2]
art. 3 .... **[15E–3]**
(1) .... [15E–3]
art. 4 .... [15E–4]
Rules of the Supreme Court (Amendment) (S.I. 1998 No. 1898) .... 62/13/5, 91/6/1, [1A–21]
r.15 .... 73/31, 73/31/2
r.19 .... 22/0/4
Sched. 1 .... 22/0/4
County Court (Amendment) Rules (S.I. 1998 No. 1899) C11/1, C20/14/4, C43/18, C48D, C49/6, C49/6A, C49/15
County Court (Forms) (Amendment) Rules (S.I. 1998 No. 1900) .... [1C–1]
Assured and Protected Tenancies (Lettings to Students) Regulations (S.I. 1998 No. 1967) ..... [8H–32], [8O–215], [8O–243]
County Court (Interest on Judgment Debts) (Amendment) Order (S.I. 1998 No. 2400) C25/0/3, C25/5A/2
Late Payment of Commercial Debts (Interest) Act 1998 (Commencement No. 1) Order (S.I. 1998 No. 2479) 6/L/2
Sched. 1 .... 6/L/2
Sched. 2 .... 6/L/2
Late Payment of Commercial Debts (Rate of Interest) Order (S.I. 1998 No. 2480) 6/L/2
Late Payment of Commercial Debts (Interest) Act 1998 (Transitional Provisions) Regulations (S.I. 1998 No. 2481) 6/L/2
Late Payment of Commercial Debts (Interest) (Legal Aid Exceptions) Order (S.I. 1998 No. 2482) 6/L/2
Civil Courts (Amendment) (No. 2) Order (S.I. 1998 No. 2910) 18D–1
Civil Procedure (Modification of Enactments) Order (S.I. 1998 No. 2940)
art. 5 .... [20A–216], [20A–220]
(a) .... [20A–8/2]
(b) .... [20A–8/2]

1998 Civil Procedure (Modification of Enactments) Order—*cont.*
art. 6 .. [20A–720/2], [20A–725/1], [20A–726/1], [20A–736/2], [20A–808/2], [20A–809/1]
(b) ....[20A–8/2]
(c) ....[20A–8/2]
Indictments (Procedure) (Modification) Rules (S.I. 1998 No. 3045) 59/1B/1
Rules of the Supreme Court (Amendment No. 2) (S.I. 1998 No. 3049) 30/1/12, 59/1B/3
Reserve Forces Act 1996 (Consequential Provisions, etc.) Regulations (S.I. 1998 No. 3086)
reg. 6 .... [21E–43]
Fair Employment and Treatment (Northern Ireland) Order (S.I. 1998 No. 3162)
art. 105 .... [21D–258/1]
Sched. 5 .... [21D–258/1]
1999 Government of Wales Act 1998 (Housing) (Amendments) Order (S.I. 1999 No. 61) ...... [8O–177], [8O–201/1]
Allocation of Housing and Homelessness (Review Procedures) Regulations (S.I. 1999 No. 71) .... [8Q–219/1], [8Q–240], [8Q–244]
Legal Aid (Prescribed Panels) Regulations (S.I. 1999 No. 166) ...... [16A–93]
Civil Courts (Amendment) Order (S.I. 1999 No. 216) .... [18C–2]
Common Investment (Amendment) Scheme (S.I. 1999 No. 551) ...... [5D–2]
Supreme Court Fees Order (S.I. 1999 No. 687) ...... [4A–1]
Non-Contentious Probate Fees Order (S.I. 1999 No. 688) .... [4C–1], [11D–1]
art. 1 .... **[4C–2]**
art. 2 .... **[4C–3]**
art. 3 .... **[4C–4]**
art. 4 .... **[4C–5]**
art. 5 .... **[4C–6]**
art. 6 .... **[4C–7]**
Sched. 1 .... **[4C–8]**
Sched. 2 .... **[4C–9]**
County Court Fees Order (S.I. 1999 No. 689) ...... [4B–1]
Public Trustee (Fees) Order (S.I. 1999 No. 855) ..... [12C–40], [12C–49]
Civil Procedure Act 1997 (Commencement No. 2) Order (S.I. 1999 No. 1009) .... [20A–2]
1999 High Courts and County Courts (Allocation of Arbitration Proceedings) (Amendment) Order (S.I. 1999 No. 1010) [21D–260]
Civil Courts (Amendment) (No. 2) Order (S.I. 1999 No. 1011) ..... [6D–301], [18C–2]
art. 5 .... [6D–301]
High Court and County Courts Jurisdiction (Amendment) Order (S.I. 1999 No. 1014) .... [20A–749/1]
Non-Contentious Probate (Amendment) Rules (S.I. 1999 No. 1015) .. [11B–8/1]
Court Funds (Amendment) Rules (S.I. 1999 No. 1021) .... [5C–2/1], [5C–6], [5C–19], [5C–27], [5C–37], [5C–42], [5C–46/1], [5C–48/1], [5C–50], [5C–54], [5C–55/1, [5C–59], [5C–60/1], [5C–73], [5C–84/1], [5C–85/1], [5C–92/1]
Civil Legal Aid (General) (Amendment) Regulations (S.I. 1999 No. 1113) .... [16D–21], [16D–45], [16D–129/1], [16D–132/1], [16D–210]
Unfair Terms in Consumer Contracts Regulations (S.I. 1999 No. 2083) .... [9A–159/3]
Unfair Arbitration Agreements (Specified Amount) (S.I. 1999 No. 2167) .... [21D–213/1]
Court of Protection (Amendment) Rules (S.I. 1999 No. 2504) .. [10C–10/1], [10C–80/1], [10C–83/1], [10C–22/1], [10C–81/1], [10C–90/1], [10C–104]
Court of Protection (Enduring Powers of Attorney) (Amendment) Rules (S.I. 1999 No. 2505) .... [10G–39]
Court Court Fees (Amendment) Order (S.I. 1999 No. 2548) .... [4B–1]
Civil Legal Aid (General) (Amendment) (No. 2) Regulations (S.I. 1999 No. 2565) .... [16D–169/1]
Legal Aid in Civil Proceedings (Remuneration) (Amendment) Regulations (S.I. 1999 No. 3098) .... [16F–2/1], [16F–5]
Civil Courts (Amendment) (No. 3) Order (S.I. 1999 No. 3187) .... [18C–2]

TABLE OF CIVIL PROCEDURE RULES

References to paragraph numbers in square brackets are to Volume 2.

1998 Civil Procedure Rules (S.I. 1998 No. 3132) .... [1A–1A], [2A–1], [2C–1], [3D–1], [6D–1], [7A–3], [20A–403], [20A–735/1]
Pt 4 .... [1A–1A], [8C–4/1], [8K–4/1], [8L–47/1], [8O–49/1]
Pt 7 .... [9A–42/4]
Pt 12 .... [3B–1]
Pt 16 .... [6D–1]
Pt 19 .... [17B–1]
Pt 20 .... [6D–1]
Pt 21 .... [17B–1]
Pt 26 .... [20A–737/2]
Pt 27 .... [20A–737/2]
Pt 49 .... [6D–1], [6D–3], [20A–738/2]
r.1.4(2)(e) .... [20A–737/2]

1998 Civil Procedure Rules—*cont.*
r.3.1 .... [17B–1]
r.3.4 .... [20A–735/1]
r.6.16 .... [17B–1]
r.7.9 .... [9A–42/3]
r.12.2(a) .... [9A–42/3]
r.12.10(b)(i) .... [7A–3]
r.18.2 .... [17B–1]
r.19 .... [17B1]
r.19.1 .... [17B–1]
r.19.3 .... [17B–1]
r.26.4 .... [20A–737/2]
r.39.6 .... [17B–1]
r.50.1.2 .... [17B–1]
r.50.1.10 .... [17B–1]
Sched. 1 .... [20A–745/2]
Sched. 2 .. .. [9A–42/2], [9A–42/3], [20A–745/2]

TABLE OF RULES OF THE SUPREME COURT

References to paragraph numbers in square brackets are to Volume 2

1965 Rules of the Supreme Court (Revision) (S.I. 1965 No. 1776) .... [3D–1], [7A–3]
O.2, r.1 .... 81/3/7
(2) 13/7/3, 13/9/9
O.3, r.5 .... 55/4/2, 94/2/2
O.4, r.9 .... 15/5/1
r.10 .... 15/5/1, [17B–1]
O.5, r.6 .... [17B–1]
O.6, r.2(1) .... [17B–1]
r.8(1)(b) 75/4/3
(1A)(b) 75/4/3
O.10, r.2 .... [17B–1]
r.4 .... [17B–1]
O.11 .... [7A–3], [7B–42]
r.1(1) 11/4/14
(2) .... [7A–3]
(a)(ii) 11/1/48
O.12, r.1(2) .... [17B–1]
O.13, r.7(1)(b) 13/7/3
O.14, r.6(2) 33/2/2
O.15 .... [17B–1]
r.4(2) .... [17B–1]
r.6 .... [17B–1]
(2) .... [17B–1]
r.10 .... [17B–1]
r.11 .... [17B–1]
r.12 .... [17B–1]
r.12A 62/B/151
r.14 .... [17B–1]
O.16 .... [6D–1]
r.1(1) 16/1/7
O.17 .... [17B–1]
r.8 .... 62/13/5
O.18 .... 62/12/1
r.8 .... [6D–1]
r.12(1A) 62/3/3
O.20, r.5 .... [14–42/5]
(4) .... [17B–1]
O.23 .... 23/3/42, [17B–1]
r.1 .... [1B–33]
O.24, r.13 .... 24/13/3
O.29, r.1 .... [21D–101/1]
O.32, r.9(1) .... [17B–1]
O.33, r.4 .... [20A–739/3]
r.4A 62/3/3
r.5 .... [20A–739/3]
O.36, r.11(1) 33/2/2
O.55, r.4(4) 55/4/2
r.7(4) 55/7/3
O.59, r.1B 59/1B/2, 59/1B/3, **59/1B**

1965 Rules of the Supreme Court (Revision)—*cont.*
O.59, r.1B(1)(a) 59/1B/6
(b) 59/1B/7
(c) 59/1B/8
(2) 59/1B/4
r.5(1) 59/14/26
O.62 .... 62/28/4
r.2(4) 62/2/7
r.3(3) 62/3/3
r.5 .... 62/5/7
(4) 62/5/7
r.7(4)(b) 62/7/14
r.9(1)(b) 62/9/4
r.10 .... 62/10/6
(1) 62/5/4
r.11(7) 62/11/31
r.13 .... 62/13/5
r.15(2) 62/15/2/1
r.18(2) 62/18/2/1
r.21 .... 62/C/35C
r.22(1) 62/28/4
r.28 .... 62/A2/13, 62/C/35C
(1) 62/10/6
r.29 .... 62/A2/5
(7)(c) 62/29/6
(iii) 62/C/35C
App. 2, para. 2(1)(a) 62/A2/4
O.71, rr.25–39 .... [7A–3], [7B–42]
O.73, r.31(2)(c) 73/31, 73/31/3
O.75 .... [6D–1], [17B–1]
r.4 .... [6D–1]
r.5(7) 75/5/10
r.17 .... [17B–1]
O.77, r.18(1) .... [17B–1]
O.80 .... [17B–1]
r.1 .... [2C–259]
O.81 .... [17B–1]
O.87 .... [17B–1]
O.91, r.6 .... 91/6
(2) 91/6
O.92, r.3A 92/3A
O.93, r.23 .... 93/23
(4) 93/23
O.103 .... [17B–1]
O.104 .... [17B–1]
O.107, r.4 .... [20A–745/2]
O.113 .... 113/8/14
App. B .... [6A–1A]

TABLE OF RULES OF THE COUNTY COURT

References to paragraph numbers in square brackets are to Volume 2. Paragraph numbers shown in bold indicate where the text of a rule or part thereof is reproduced.

1981 County Court Rules (S.I. 1981 No. 1687) .... [3D–1]
O.5, r.1 .... C5/1
O.6 .... [9A–42/2]
O.11, r.1(1A) **C11/1**
O.13, r.10 .... [20A–739/3]
O.19, Pt I .... [20A–737/2]
Pt II .... [20A–738/2]
O.22, r.11 .... [20A–745/2]
(7) .... [20A–745/2]
(8) .... [20A–745/2]
O.24 .... 113/8/14
O.37, r.6(1) .... [8L–47]

1981 County Court Rules —*cont.*
O.43, r.16A .... [8M–102/1]
O.48D C48D
r.1 .... **C48D/1**
r.2 .... **C48D/2**
r.3 .... **C48D/3**
r.4 .... **C48D/4**
r.5 .... **C48D/5**
O.49, r.4 ..... [9A–42/2], [9A–42/3]
r.6(7)(i) C49/6, C49/6A
r.15A **C45/15A**

TABLE OF EUROPEAN AND INTERNATIONAL LEGISLATION

References to paragraph numbers in square brackets are to Volume 2. Figures in bold type indicate where a provision is set out in full.

1950 Rome. Convention for the Protection of Human Rights and Fundamental Freedoms (November 4) .... [21T–1], [21U–1]
- Art. 1 .... [21U–1]
- Art. 13 .... [21U–1], **[21U–2]**, **[21U–3]**
- Art. 25 .... [21T–5]
- Art. 26 .... [21T–5]
- Art. 27(2) .... [21T–5]
- Art. 31 .... [21T–4], [21T–6]
  - (1) .... [21T–4]
- Art. 32 .... [21T–6]
  - (1) .... [21T–6]
- Art. 35 .... [21T–5]
- Art. 46 .... [21T–6]
- Art. 54 .... [21T–6]

1957 Rome. Treaty establishing the European Economic Community (The EEC Treaty) (March 25) .... [7A–1]
- Art. 220 .... [7A–1], [7A–2]

1958 New York Convention on the Recognition and Enforcement of Foreign Arbitral Awards adopted by the United Nations Conference on International Commercial Arbitration (June 10) .... [21B–23], [21D–243]

1968 Brussels Convention on Jurisdiction and the Enforcement of Judgments in Civil and Commercial Matters (E.C. Judgments Convention) (September 27) ..... [7A–1], [7A–3], [7A–4], [7A–5], [7A–6], [7B–42]
- Title I .... [7B–42]
- Title II .... [7B–42]
- Title III .... [7B–42]
- Title VI .... [7A–5]
- Title VII .... [7A–5]
- Art. 2 .... 11/1/55, 11/1/61
- Art. 5(1) 11/1/55
  - (3) 11/1/55
- Art. 6 .... 11/1/55, 11/1/61
  - (2) 11/1/61, 11/1/67
- Art. 16 .... 11/1/48
- Art. 17 .... 11/1/48, 11/1/61, 11/1/67
- Art. 21 .... 11/1/70
- Art. 24 ....11/1/70A

1971 Luxembourg. Protocol on the Interpretation of the 1968 Brussels Judgment Convention by the European Court of Justice (June 3) ...... [7A–1], [7A–3], [7A–4]

1976 London Convention on Limitation of Liability for Maritime Claims (November 19) 75/37/2

1978 Luxembourg. Convention on the Accession of Denmark, Ireland and the United Kingdom to the Convention on Jurisdiction and the Enforcement of Judgments and the Protocol on its Interpretation by the Court of Justice (October 9) .... [7A–2], [7A–3]

1982 Luxembourg. Convention on the Accession of Greece to the Convention on Jurisdiction and the Enforcement of Judgments and the Protocol on its Interpretation by the Court of Justice (October 25) .... [7A–4]

1988 Lugano. Convention on Jurisdiction and the Enforcement of Judgments in Civil Matters (EFTA Judgments Convention) (September 16) .... [7A–5], [7A–6], [7B–67]
- Title VI .... [7A–5]
- Title VII .... [7A–5]
- Art. 5(1) .... [7B–49]
- Art. 17(5) ....**[7B–69/1]**

1989 San Sebastian. Convention on the Accession of Spain and Portugal to the Convention on Jurisdiction and the Enforcement of Judgments and the Protocol on its Interpretation by the Court of Justice (May 26) .... [7A–4], [7A–6]

1992 Maastrict. Treaty on European Unon (February 7) .... [7A–1]

1992 Treaty establishing the European Community (The E.C. Treaty) (The EEC Treaty as amended by the E.U. Treaty) (February 7) .... [7A–1], [7A–5]
1994 Strasbourg. 11th Protocol to the Convention for the Protection of Human Rights and Fundamental Freedoms 1950 (May 11) .... [21T–4], [21T–5]
1996 Protocol amending the 1976 Convention on Liability for Maritime Claims .... [6D–209]
1998 Eleventh Protocol to the 1950 Convention for the Protection of Human Rights and Fundamental Freedoms ..... [21T–6]

VOLUME 1

ORDER 6

WRITS OF SUMMONS: GENERAL PROVISIONS

Summary of principles **6/8/6** [p.54]

After (5)(f), add new sub-paragraph:

(5) (g) The existence of pending proceedings in a foreign jurisdiction between the same parties in respect of the same claim: *Hydro Agri Espana SA v. Charles M. Willie & Co. (Shipping) Ltd, The Times,* March 5, 1998.

Add at end of sub-paragraph (10):

This note was approved in *Hydro Agri Espana SA v. Charles M. Willie & Co. (Shipping) Ltd, The Times,* March 5, 1998.

(a) Interest by contract

Add at end of paragraph: **6/L/2** [p.59]

The Late Payment of Commercial Debts (Interest) Act 1998 provides that an implied term that simple interest will be paid on debts created by contracts to which the Act applies will be incorporated into such contracts. In general terms it applies to debts created by contracts for the supply of goods and services and on such debts interest runs from 30 days after the creation of the debt, however reference should be made to the detailed provisions. The operation of the Act, by Orders made under its provisions, may be restricted to different descriptions of contract: s.17.

Initially (as from November 1, 1998) the operation of the Act has been restricted to debts owed by "large business purchasers" or U.K. Public Authorities to "small business suppliers": The Late Payment of Commercial Debts (Interest) Act 1998 (Commencement No. 1) Order 1988 (S.I. 1998 No. 2479). A large business is defined as one with more than 50 employees and a small business as one with less when calculated in accordance with the provisions of Schedule 2 to these Regulations. These provisions are complex and will have to be considered in detail in the event of dispute. These Regulations by Schedule 1 aso define a "United Kingdom Public Authority".

By The Late Payment of Commercial Debts (Interest) Act 1998 (Transitional Provisions) Regulations 1998 (S.I. 1998 No. 2481) it is to be presumed until the contrary is proved that the business of the purchaser is a large business. On the other hand the onus lies on the supplier to prove that it is a small business. Other regulations provide exemption for certain legal aid fees: S.I. 1998 No. 2482 and for the rate of interest: S.I. 1998 No. 2480. This has been fixed at 8 per cent over base rate.

If interest is claimed under the Act it will have to be pleaded and if the defendant asserts either that the plaintiff is not a small business or that it is not a large business or that the debt does not qualify for some other reason that will have to be pleaded by way of defence.

ORDER 10

SERVICE OF ORIGINATING PROCESS: GENERAL PROVISIONS

Proof of service **10/1/26** [p.83]

Add:

An action should not fail due to a minor defect in service where the plaintiff's messenger handed the writ to one of the defendant's secretaries who then handed it to the defendant as this court in its discretion could rectify the defect: *Chohan Clothing Company (Manchester) Ltd v. Fox Brooks Marshall (a firm), The Times,* December 9, 1997, CA.

Service of writ on agent of overseas principal **10/2/2** [p.84]

Add:

Process could be served on the British branch of an overseas company when the business which was the subject of the dispute between the parties had been carried on both by the British branch and by an overseas eminence of the company: *Saab v. Saudi American Bank* [1998] 1 W.L.R. 937.

ORDER 11

SERVICE OF PROCESS, ETC., OUT OF THE JURISDICTION

2. Standard of Proof

11/1/11 [p.93] *Add before the last sentence of paragraph (2):*

An example of a case where a plaintiff failed to make out a good arguable case is *Maritrop Trading Corp. v. Guangzhou Ocean Shipping Co.* [1998] C.L.C. 224. The plaintiff claimed for damage to cargo against the shipowners and the charterers. It obtained leave to serve out of the jurisdiction against both. The shipowners applied to set aside the leave to serve out on the basis that they were not a party to the bill of lading. The plaintiffs argued that there was a good arguable case that the bill was in fact an owner's bill. This argument was rejected by the court and service was set aside.

11/1/15 **Discretion and forums conveniens**

[p.96] *Add at end:*

An alleged libel published in more than one country could give rise to a cause of action in each country in which the victim was known and in which he claimed to have suffered injury. A multi-jurisdictional libel should not be treated as giving rise to a single cause of action in respect of which the court had to ascertain where the global cause of action arose. The principles applied in the Convention case of *Shevill v. Presse Alliance* (see para. 11/1/55) followed in a non-convention case therefore allowing Russian nationals with a demonstrated connection with this country to sue in England the publisher of an American magazine with a circulation in England: *Berezovsky v. Forbes Inc., The Times,* November 27, 1988, CA.

11/1/48 **Exclusive jurisdiction**

[p.102] *Add at end:*

The second alternative in O.11, r.1(2)(a)(ii) allows service out of the jurisdiction without leave wherever the defendant is domiciled in cases to which either Article 16 or 17 applies.

11/1/55 **Tort or quasi-delict—Art. 5, para. 3**

[p.104] *Add at end:*

In an international carriage operation involving carriage by sea and land the place where the damage to goods arose was the place where the maritime carrier (who was not a party to the bill of lading) was to deliver the goods; it was not the place where the consignee merely discovered the damage. In *Reunion Europeene SA v. Spiethoff's Beverachtingskantoor BV, The Times,* November 16, 1998, the European Court held on an appeal from the Cour de Cassation (France):

(a) That Article 5(1) did not apply as the maritime carrier was not a party to the contract;
(b) That Article 5(3) did apply as against the maritime carrier on the basis of tort and the "harmful event" occurred where the maritime carrier delivered the goods (namely France);
(c) That Article 6 did not apply so as to allow the other defendants who were parties to the contract to be sued in France because none of the defendants was domiciled in France. That this might lead to multiplicity of proceedings was subordinate to the principle that a party who was not domiciled in a contracting state should have his case heard in his court of domicile: Article 2. This undesirable consequence would not arise if the defendants, or any one of them, had been sued in their court of domicile (in this case all were domiciled in Holland).

In the case of a negligent misstatement the "harmful event occurs" where the statement is made not where it is received. In *Domicrest v. Swiss Bank Corp.* [1998] 3 All E.R. 577; *The Times,* July 16, 1998, Rix J. did not follow the domestic decision of Steyn J. in *Minster Investments Ltd v. Hyundai Precision and Industry Co. Ltd* [1988] 2 Lloyd's Rep. 621 that the essence of the cause action was reliance on the statement (*i.e.* acting on it where it was received) not the historical carelessness which led to it being made. Though there was no European Court decision directly on the point, the philosophy behind the decisions in *Dumez France v. Hessiche Landesbank* (Case C–220/88 [1990] E.C.R. 1–49), *Shevill v. Presse Alliance* (above) and *Marinari v. Lloyds Bank* (above) suggested that the place where the statement was made was the correct test for determining jurisdiction.

Third party proceedings—Art. 6, para. 2

11/1/61 *Add at end of paragraph:*

[p.105] Where a defendant properly sued within the jurisdiction wished to claim indemnity or contribution against a third party domiciled in a Convention territory under a contract containing an exclusive jurisdiction clause in favour of another Convention jurisdiction Article 17 operated to prevail over the permissive jurisdiction conferred by Article 6 even though the consequence might be a multiplicity of proceedings: *Hough v. P&O Containers Ltd* [1998] 3 W.L.R. 851; [1998] 2 All E.R. 978; [1998] 2 Lloyd's Rep. 318.

Add:

The words *unless these were instituted solely with the object of removing him* [the third party] *from the jurisdiction of the court which would be competent in his case* refer to the original and not the third party proceedings and provide a narrow test designed to meet a situation where the plaintiff and the defendant are effectively in collusion to bring a claim against the third party in the plaintiff's or defendant's domicile, or otherwise where, even without collusion, the plaintiff had no good reason to sue the defendant, but is hoping that by doing so the defendant will, with the aid of Article 6(2), bring the third party within the plaintiff's domicile.

Where the contract between the defendant and the proposed third party contains an exclusive jurisdiction clause within Article 17 this will override both Article 6 and Article 2 even if the consequence leads to multiplicity of proceedings: *Hough v. P&O Containers* [1998] I.L.Pr. 713 (Rix J.).

Jurisdiction by agreement or "prorogation of jurisdiction" **11/1/67**

Add at end: [p.107]

Article 17 prevails over Article 6(2) to prevent a party to such a contract being added as a third party in proceedings in another convention jurisdiction where a contribution or indemnity is claimed under the terms of the contract even though the result may be a multiplicity of proceedings: *Hough v. P&O Containers Ltd* [1998] 3 W.L.R. 851; [1998] 2 All E.R. 978; [1998] 2 Lloyd's Rep. 318.

Conflict of jurisdictions—lis pendens **11/1/70**

Add: [p.109]

In separate actions in different jurisdictions arising out of the same incident involving insurers as well as the insured, Art. 21 only applied where the interests of the parties were identical. This would be the case where the insured was a party in one jurisdiction and the insurer in the other if in the first jurisdiction the insured had subrogated his rights to the insurer. If there was no subrogation and the insured and the insurer were asserting different interests then Art. 21 did not apply: *Drouot Assurances SA v. Consolidated Metallurgical Industries* [1999] 2 W.L.R. 163; *The Times*, June 10, 1998 (E.C. Case C-351/96).

Insert new note:

Interim measures—Article 24 **11/1/70A**

As noted under para. 11/1/21 dealing with interim injunctions Art. 24 provides that "Application may be made to the courts of a contracting state for such provisional including protective measures as may be available under the laws of that State, even if, under this Convention, the courts of another Contracting State have jurisdiction as to the substance of the matter." [p.109]

The interpretation of this Article was considered by the European Court in *Van Uden Maritime BV v. Kommanditgesellschaft in Firma Deco-Line, The Times*, December 1, 1998 (Case C-391/95) where it was held that an interim payment of a contractual consideration constituted a provisional measure and could be made in the particular circumstances of that case even though the jurisdiction of the court had been excluded by an arbitration clause.

Adding, in the writ of statement of claim, a cause of action other than that for which leave was given to issue and serve **11/4/14**

Add at end of first paragraph: [p.112]

Service of an amendment to a claim made without leave which elaborates an existing cause of action and does not introduce a new one is permissible under the Convention regime whereas it would not be under O.11, r.1(1) where leave to serve an amended writ out of the jurisdiction would be required. The distinction is that under the Convention the right to serve abroad is based on statute whereas in other cases the plaintiff has no right but has to rely on the discretion of the court: *News International v. Bogognon*, CA Trans. CHANI 97/1646 CMS3.

ORDER 13

FAILURE TO GIVE NOTICE OF INTENTION TO DEFEND

(e) Affidavit of service (r.7(1)(b))

Add at end: **13/7/3**

If an affidavit of service cannot be sworn without difficulty the case handler with the plaintiff's solicitor should attend upon the practice master to seek his guidance; this is especially so if it is necessary to seek the discretion of the court to condone an irregularity under O.2, r.1(2). (An [p.151] example of a deficiency not being allowed to vitiate service can be found in *Tavera v. MacFarlane* [1996] P.I.Q.R. P292, CA, where, under the CCR, service of a photocopy of the originating process was, in exceptional circumstances, held to suffice.)

13/7A/3 Grant of leave
[p.153] *Delete the final sentence in the second paragraph and substitute:*

In *Crescent Oil & Shipping Services Ltd v. Importang U.E.E.*, December 19, 1996, unrep. (but discussed in Issue 6/97 of the *Supreme Court Practice News*) the absence of mention of a method for service on a state of a judgment in default of appearance under s.12(5) by s.12(6) was held to be significant and that parties thus cannot agree on an alternative method for such service. Thus such a judgment must be served in the same manner as is required for the writ upon which judgment has been entered.

13/9/9 Application to set aside irregular judgment
[p.158] *Add:*

It is desirable in the supporting affidavit to anticipate any point that may be expected to be taken by the party entering the judgment. If, for example, it is thought it will be contended (although the judgment is technically irregular) that O.2, r.1(2) will be relied upon, this should be anticipated and any facts relevant thereto should be deposed to in the affidavit.

13/9/18 Discretionary powers of the Court
[p.159] *Add at end of first paragraph:*

The previous paragraph was discussed by the Court of Appeal in *Day v. Royal Automobile Motoring Services Ltd, The Times,* November 24, 1998, an appeal from a county court. Although the assessment of the relevant facts in the lower court was held to be wrong and the appeal against the refusal to set aside a default judgment was thus allowed, the approach discussed in the previous paragraph was, seemingly on an *obiter* footing, also considered. Ward L.J., although considering the best guidance could be taken from Sir Roger Ormrod in *Saudi Eagle,* stated he was reluctant to elevate the test to a real likelihood the defendant would succeed. Butler-Sloss L.J. however thought there was no conflict between *Saudi Eagle* and *Allen v. Taylor.* The Editors adhere to the view that, notwithstanding the decision of this two-judge court, the requirement to show "a real prospect of success" survives and that this is not a mere matter of semantics. The introduction of the CPR will result in this higher test being affirmed: see discussion "Summary judgment under the Civil Procedure Rules" in Issue 7/98 of the *Supreme Court Practice News.*

ORDER 14

SUMMARY JUDGMENT

14/1/2 Application of Order 14
[p.163] *Add at end of paragraph 4:*

Fraud can be established on affidavit evidence alone; see *Orange Personal Communication Services v. Squires* (unreported, but noted in [1998] C.L.Y. 623).

14/4/7 Plaintiff's affidavit in reply
[p.173] *Add at end:*

In *Dialworth Ltd v. TG Organisation (Europe) Ltd* (1998) 75 P. & C.R. 147, CA, it was pointed out that it is unnecessary to argue the law in such an affidavit. It is not objectionable however to identify any statutory provision or leading authority relied on. Surprise upon the defendant must be avoided but this can be done as well by letter or serving a written submission.

14/6/5 Trial by Master
[p.191] *Add at end of penultimate paragraph:*

See *Pavey v. Ministry of Defence, The Times,* November 25, 1998, CA.

14/7/8 Costs—High Court or county court scale
[p.193] *Add at end:*

The position suggested in the main work is supported by *UPS Ltd v. Lewis, The Independent,* February 23, 1998, CA. It was there held not to be an abuse of process to apply for summary judgment in the High Court where it was certain, if leave to defend was given, that the action would be transferred to the county court for small claims arbitration.

ORDER 15

CAUSES OF ACTION, COUNTERCLAIMS AND PARTIES

Joinder of parties in the alternative **15/4/8**
Add at end: [p.215]

In *Borealis AB v. Stargas Ltd* [1997] 1 Lloyd's Rep. 635, subject to certain technicalities, subsequent joinder of shippers of propane as an additional defendant was allowed in an action originally brought against its vendors on the basis that it may have deteriorated in transit as the new claim arose out of the same set of facts.

Effect of rule **15/5/1**
In penultimate line of last paragraph delete "O.4, r.10" *and substitute* "O.4, r.9". [p.217]

Intervention by persons not parties **15/6/8**
Add at end: [p.225]

If an application to be added as a defendant is delayed it is essential that merits are shown: *Rees and Another v. Mabco (102) Ltd, The Times,* December 16, 1998, CA.

Mistake as to plaintiff or defendant—misnomer or substitution **15/6/16**
Add after second paragraph: [p.228]

A recent example, under the equivalent CCR, where substitution was permitted (despite failure to rectify the position 20 months after receiving the defence during which the limitation period had expired) is *Crook v. Aaron Dale Construction and Roofing Ltd* [1997] P.I.Q.R. P36.

Application to add, substitute or strike out parties **15/6/17**
Add before final paragraph: [p.229]

The valid assignment of a cause of action by a liquidator of the plaintiff company to its shareholders and former directors to allow the action to proceed with the benefit of the assignees receiving legal aid was not a proper ground to refuse relief (*Norglen Ltd (in liquidation) v. Reeds Rains Prudential Ltd* [1997] 3 W.L.R. 1177, HL(E)). However such an assignment cannot be relied on when the assignor's cause of action has ceased to be valid (*Clive Brooks and Co. Ltd v. Baynard, The Times,* April 30, 1998).

Add at end of final paragraph:

For addition of a further dependant in a fatal accident claim see; "*(41) Statutory particulars,*" paragraph 18/12/44.

Terms as to amendment of parties **15/6/18**
Add at end: [p.229]

It is not possible to impose a term as to the giving of security for costs upon substitution of a party where the new party could not otherwise have been obliged to give such security (*Norglen Ltd (in liquidation) v. Reeds Rains Prudential Ltd* [1997] 3 W.L.R. 1177, HL(E)).

Abatement of action **15/7/3**
Add at end of first paragraph: [p.234]

Where an action stands dismissed for non-compliance with a court order it is not permissible to allow an application to substitute a fresh plaintiff to revive the action even if the applicant is a third party to the action: *Companhia Europeia de Transportes Aeros SA v. British Aerospace plc and Another, The Times,* January 12, 1999.

ORDER 16

THIRD PARTY AND SIMILAR PROCEEDINGS

Service out of the jurisdiction of third party notice **16/1/7**
Add before last paragraph: [p.277]

The view of the Editors expressed in the main work that an autonomous test common to all Convention countries applies to the grant of leave to serve a third party notice out of the jurisdiction has recently been supported. Mr Charles Aldous, Q.C., sitting as a Deputy Judge in the Chancery Division, considered the effect of the Convention in *Waterford Wedgwood plc v. David Nagli Ltd, The Times,* May 13, 1998. He held, after reviewing the cases cited in the main work, that Article 6(2) existed to secure rational and efficient disposal of disputes and in particular to avoid irreconcilable judgments. Differing from the ratio decidendi accepted by the Editors in the main work, he found *Kinnear* only illustrated where it may be expedient for the claim and third party claim to be heard together. He ruled that the decision in *Kinnear* was not intended to derogate from the basic relevant principle of the Convention. This, he determined, was that to override the basic right of the third party to be sued separately in the courts of his domicile it must be shown to be expedient in the interests of justice and good administration that the claims be heard together. He concluded that any domestic third party proceedings which perchance happen to satisfy O.16, r.1(1) are not thus, per se, "any other third party proceedings". Article 6(2) is "intended to have the same meaning and effect in each Contracting State".

The Deputy Judge also ruled that continuing pursuit of the main action, save in exceptional circumstances, was essential. He stated the fact that a defendant, in bringing third party proceedings may enjoy the benefit of legal aid, and might, through lack of means be unable to bring proceedings in another Convention country was an irrelevant consideration. (This may not be the case with other jurisdictions; see *Connelly v. R.T.Z. Corporation plc* [1997] 1 W.L.R. 373 where Lord Goff of Chievely said: "... the availability of financial assistance in this country, coupled with its non-availability in the appropriate forum, may exceptionally be a relevant factor in this context. The question, however, remains whether the plaintiff can establish that substantial justice will not in the particular circumstances be done if the plaintiff has not proceeded in the appropriate forum where no financial assistance is available." Where it is the defendant, rather than the plaintiff, being adversely affected it is expected that discretion will be more readily exercised.)

ORDER 18

PLEADINGS

(15) Fraud

18/12/18 *Add:*

[p.330] See also *Sheldon v. R.H.M. Outhwaite Ltd* [1996] A.C. 102, HL(E).

ORDER 20

AMENDMENT

20/8/8 **Amendments to allow new claims (r.5(5))**

[p.381] *Add:*

An amendment to add a new allegation of intentional wrongdoing by pleading fraud where previously mere negligence had been alleged constituted the introduction of a new cause of action and would not be allowed after the expiry of any relevant limitation period since the new cause of action did not arise out of the same facts or substantially the same facts as a cause of action in respect of which relief had already been claimed in the action. Nor was it possible to circumvent the effect under this sub-rule of the expiry of a period of limitation in respect of a common law claim by seeking to invoke a concurrent equitable jurisdiction where the claims in equity were not different causes of action but merely equitable counterparts of the claims at common law: see *Paragon Finance plc v. Thakerar, The Times*, August 7, 1998, CA.

Where the claim was based on a breach of duty whether arising from contract or in tort, the question whether an amendment pleaded a new cause of action required comparison with the unamended pleading to determine (a) whether a different duty was pleaded; (b) whether the breaches pleaded differed substantially and, where appropriate, (c) the nature and extent of the damage of which complaint was made; see *Darlington Building Society and Another v. O'Rourke, James Scourfield & McCarthy (a Firm), The Times*, November 20, 1998, CA.

ORDER 22

PAYMENT INTO AND OUT OF COURT

22/0/4 **Forms**

[p.407] *Add at end:*

A new Prescribed Form No. 23 has been introduced with effect from September 28, 1998 by RSC(A) O 1998 (S.I. 1998 No. 1898) r.19 and Sched. 1.

Prescribed Form No. 23: such reference is now to the new Prescribed Form No. 23 referred to under 22/0/4 above. **22/1/16** [p.412]

Notice of payment in certifying amount of Social Security Benefits recoverable by State withheld **22/1/18**
Add: [p.412]
The relevant statutory reference with effect from October 6, 1997 is the Social Security (Recovery of Benefits) Act 1997.

See amendment in 22/1/16 above.

Withdrawal of payment in **22/1/20**
Delete reference in second paragraph to Spurr v. Hall. [p.412]

Form **22/2/2**
See amendment in 22/1/16 above. [p.415]

Editorial Note **22/5/2**
Add: [p.420]
With effect from October 6, 1997 the relevant statutory references are the Social Security (Recovery of Benefits) Act 1997, s.16 and reg. 8 of the Society Security (Recovery of Benefits) Regulations 1997 (S.I. 1997 No. 2205).

See amendment in 22/1/16 above.

ORDER 23

SECURITY FOR COSTS

Delete last line of last paragraph and substitute: **23/3/21**
Keary Developments was followed in *Danemark Ltd v. BAA* [1996] 12 C.L., CA where in a late application for additional security the court in allowing the appeal carried out the balancing exercise in favour of the plaintiff where the potenial loss to the plaintiff, if the claim was stifled, was £300,000, whereas the extra exposure of the defendants to costs was only £60,000. Other factors taken into account were that the defendants had not made out a strong prima facie case on the merits and that expert evidence had been introduced into the case at a late stage. [p.436]

Default in giving security **23/3/40**
Add at end of paragraph: [p.441]
An order for security for costs should specify the time limit within which security is to be provided, should stay the proceedings until security is given and provide for automatic dismissal of the action if security is not provided "without further order". These words should be omitted if the court wishes to give further consideration of the matter before the action is dismissed: *Clive Brooks and Co. Ltd v. Baynard, The Times* April 30, 1998. In consequence of this decision a new Queen's Bench Masters' Practice Form has been introduced.

Payment out (rr. 1–3) **23/3/42**
Add at end: [p.441]
Where money is ordered to be paid into court by way of security for costs it is the defendant's costs of trial that are secured. In the event of an appeal by an unsuccessful defendant against the order made at trial, an order requiring the sum lodged by way of security to remain in court pending the outcome of the appeal is within the legitimate scope of the jurisdictional basis on which an order for security is made under O.23 or under s.726: *Stabilad Ltd v. Stephens & Carter Ltd* [1998] 4 All E.R. 129.

ORDER 24

DISCOVERY AND INSPECTION OF DOCUMENTS

24/2/11 **"Relating to any matter in question between them"**
[p.448] *Add as a new second paragraph:*

Discovery is not required of documents which relate to irrelevant allegations in the pleadings which even if substantiated could not affect the result of the action, *Martin & Miles Martin Pen Co. Ltd v. Scrib* (1950) 67 R.P.C. 127 at 131, CA, and *Martin & Biro Swan Ltd v. H. Millwood Ltd* (1954) 71 R.P.C. 316.

24/2/17 **Continuing obligation to give discovery**
[p.450] *The case of Vernon v. Bosley (No. 2) is now also reported at* [1999] Q.B. 18.

Client and non-professional agent or third party

24/5/16 *The case of Secretary of State for Trade and Industry v. Baker is now also reported at* [1998] Ch 356;
[p.458] [1998] 2 W.L.R. 667; [1998] 1 All E.R. 673.

Other advisers

24/5/22 *Add:*
[p.460] The public interest in making confidential documents relating to an alleged fraud of an international bank available to parties to private foreign litigation directed towards exposing such fraud outweighed the public interest in preserving the confidentiality in those documents, *Pharaon and Others v. Bank of Credit and Commerce International SA, Price Waterhouse intervening,* (application for leave to comply with a *subpoena* to produce documents), [1998] 4 All E.R. 455.

Waiver or loss of privilege

24/5/30 *Add at end of seventh paragraph following reference to Balkanbank v. Taher:*
[p.462] Contrast *Clough v. Tameside and Glossop Health Authority* [1998] 1 W.L.R. 1478; [1998] 2 All E.R. 971.

24/5/34 **2. Documents tending to criminate or expose to a penalty**
[p.464] *The case of BCCI (Overseas) Ltd (In Liquidation) v. Price Waterhouse is now also reported at* [1998] Ch. 84.

Add at end of first paragraph:

Proceedings for civil contempt are proceedings for the "recovery of a penalty" within section 14(1) of the Civil Evidence Act 1968 in respect of which there is a privilege against self-incrimination, though for the purposes of civil proceedings pertaining to infringement of intellectual property or passing off such privilege has been withdrawn by section 72 of the Supreme Court Act 1981, see *Cobra Golf Inc. v. Rata,* [1998] Ch. 109; 1997 2 W.L.R. 629; [1997] 2 All E.R. 150

24/7A/3 **"Claim in respect of personal injuries"**
[p.473] *Add:*

A claim for an indemnity under a contract of insurance of which the plaintiff in a personal injury action was the statutory assignee was not "a claim for damages for personal injuries" or "in respect of personal injuries" so as to empower the court to make an order for pre-action discovery against the insurers under s.33(2) of the Supreme Court Act 1981: see *Burns v. Shuttlehurst Ltd, The Times,* January 12, 1999.

24/13/3 **Objection to production**
[p.479] *Add:*

Provided that the test laid down in O.24, r.13 was satisfied the fact that the transcripts of evidence given before two inspectors appointed under s.432 of the Companies Act 1985 was of evidence given under compulsion was no reason for ordering non-disclosure: *British and Commonwealth Holdings plc (in administration) v. Barclays De Zoete Wedd Ltd (No. 2), The Times,* November 13, 1998.

24/14A/2 **Uncertainty as to use of material obtained on discovery**
[p.480] *The case of Mahon v. Rahn is also reported at* [1998] Q.B. 424.

Delete text of seventh and eighth paragraphs and substitute:

In *Taylor v. Director of the Serious Fraud Office* [1998] 3 W.L.R. 1040; [1998] 4 All E.R. 801, HL(E), the House of Lords held that in order to ensure that the privacy and confientiality of those who made, and those who were mentioned in, statements contained in unused material which had come into existence as a result of a criminal investigation were not invaded more than was absolutely necessary for the purposes of justice, compliance by the prosecution with its obligation to disclose all such material to the defence generated an implied undertaking not to use the material for any purpose other than the conduct of the defence; and that, accordingly, documents disclosed to solicitors for one of the accused could not be used for the purposes of the action for defamation by the Plaintiffs; disapproving of *Mahon v. Rahn* [1998] Q.B. 424, CA in such respect. The court further held that the absolute immunity from suit which applied to judges, advocates and witnesses in respect of statements made in court extended also to out of court statements which could fairly be said to be part of the process of investigating a crime or a possible crime with a view to a prosecution; and that, accordingly, the statements made in the letter and the file note were subject to absolute immunity from suit in respect of an action for defamation.

Effect of rule (r.14A) **24/14A/3**
Add at end: [p.481] *

In *Attorney-General for Gibraltar v. May, The Times,* November 20, 1998 it was held that although the Attorney-General was bound by an implied undertaking not to use in criminal proceedings against the defendant taking place in Gibraltar the contents of an affidavit sworn by the defendant under a court order ancillary to an application for a *Mareva* injunction to freeze the defendant's assets, the court would exercise its discretion to release the Attorney-General from the implied undertaking.

Where a judge is invited to familiarise himself out of court with confidential material to which, in open court, only brief reference is made, and the judge subsequently gives a decision based on the material before him, including the confidential documents, such documents may be said to have been "referred to" by the court within the meaning of r.14A (*Smithkline Beecham Biologicals S.A. v. Connaught Laboratories Inc.* [1999] 4 All E.R. 498, CA).

Failure to comply with order for discovery **24/16/3**
The case of Star News Shops v. Stafford Refrigeration Ltd is now reported at [1998] 1 W.L.R. 536; [1998] 4 All E.R. 408, CA. [p.483]

ORDER 25

SUMMONS FOR DIRECTIONS

Contumelious default **25/L/3**
The case of Arbuthnot Latham Bank v. Trafalgar Holdings is now reported at [1998] 1 W.L.R. 1426; [1998] 2 All E.R. 181, CA. [p.500]

(3) Prejudice to the defendant **25/L/7**
The case of Barratt Manchester Ltd v. Bolton Metropolitan B.C. is also reported at [1998] 1 W.L.R. 1003. [p.501]

(15) Originating summons **25/L/22**
Insert new note: [p.505]

Delay caused by Court **25/L/23**
There is no rule of law declaring that delay technically caused by the plaintiff but in reality attributable to the court could not be excusable: *Karbachian v. Parvazian,* May 21, 1998, CA (trans. no. 908/98).

ORDER 29

INTERLOCUTORY INJUNCTIONS, ETC.

(e) Affidavit in support generally
Add at end: **29/10/6**
The affidavit may properly refer to a payment into court; such evidence having been held to be admissible (*Bowmer & Kirkland Ltd v. Wilson Bowden Properties Ltd* (1997) 80 B.L.R. 131). [p.555]

MANDATORY INJUNCTIONS

Add: **29/L/1**
Zockoll Group Ltd v. Mercury Communications Ltd [1998] F.S.R. 354. In *Nitikendo v. Leboeuf Lamb Greene & Mackay, The Times,* January 26, 1999, it was held the overriding consideration to be applied before granting a mandatory order on an interlocutory basis was to decide which course was likely to involve the least risk of injustice if the order was later found to be wrong. [p.563]

Add at end:

That failure to apply promptly for an interlocutory injunction may be treated as acquiescence so leading to a final injunction being refused was reiterated in *Gafford v. Graham, The Times,* May 1, 1998, CA. There (relying on *Jaggard v. Sawyer* [1995] 1 W.L.R. 269, CA) damages were awarded in lieu.

PRINCIPLES AND GUIDELINES TO BE APPLIED IN APPLICATIONS FOR INTERLOCUTORY INJUNCTIONS (AMERICAN CYANAMID CO. CASE)

29/L/2 [p.564] *Add after third paragraph:*

There is a clear distinction between entitlement to interlocutory relief and final judgment; thus where the application falls so far short of satisfying the criteria for granting an interlocutory injunction the applicant can be penalised in costs and in so doing the court may take into account failure to agree to a speedy trial. Discretion so exercised will not readily be interfered with by the Court of Appeal. See *Bushbury Land Rover Ltd v. Bushbury Ltd* [1997] F.S.R. 709, CA.

29/L/36 **Need for injunction restraining dealings with assets**

[p.578] *Add:*

A proviso in a *Mareva* injunction permitting the defendant to use assets otherwise frozen for reasonable legal expenses prevented such use from being a breach of the order and a contempt of court, raising the possibility of solicitors having claim of constructive trust raised against them: *United Mizrahi Bank Ltd v. Doherty* [1998] 1 W.L.R. 435, *The Times,* December 15, 1997.

ORDER 30

RECEIVERS

30/1/12 **Appeal**

[p.606] *Add at end of paragraph:*

and S.I. 1998 No. 3049. See also Practice Direction (Court of Appeal, Civil Division: Leave to Appeal and Skeleton Arguments) ([1999] 1 W.L.R. 2; *The Times,* November 23, 1998).

30/3/2 **Receiver's remuneration**

[p.609] *Add at end of paragraph:*

The plaintiff and the defendant were the only two directors and shareholders in a company from which the defendant stole money. The plaintiff brought proceedings for relief under s.459 of the Companies Act 1985 and for the winding up of the company. Neuberger J. made the winding up order, and ordered under s.461 of the 1985 Act that the remuneration of a receiver who had been appointed should be borne by the defendant's share of the company's assets: *Re Worldhams's Park Golf Course Ltd* [1998] 1 B.C.L.C. 554.

ORDER 32

APPLICATIONS AND PROCEEDINGS IN CHAMBERS

32/6/31 **Rights of audience**

[p.625] *Add:*

Where an individual who met the criteria of s.27(2)(e) of the Courts and Legal Services Act 1990, sought to exercise a right of audience in chambers, the Court had no discretion to bar him doing so: *Re H-S (Minors) (Chambers Proceedings: Right of Audience), The Times,* February 25, 1998.

32/13/23 **Power to direct hearing in Court (rr.11–13)**

[p.633] *Add:*

The right of public to attend hearings in chambers can be summarised as follows:

1. The public had no right to attend hearings in chambers because of the nature of the work transacted in chambers and because of the physical restrictions on the room available but, if requested, permission should be granted to attend when and to the extent that was practical.
2. What happened during the proceedings in chambers was not confidential or secret and

information about what occurred in chambers and the judgment or order pronounced could, and in the case of any judgment or order should be made available to the public when requested.

3. If members of the public who sought to attend could not be accommodated, the judge should consider adjourning the proceedings in whole or in part into open court to the extent that was practical or allowing one or more representatives of the press to attend the hearing in chambers.
4. To disclose what occurred in chambers did not constitute a breach of confidence or amount to contempt as long as any comment which was made did not substantially prejudice the administration of justice.
5. The position summarisd above did not apply to the exceptional situations identified in s.12(1) of the Administation of Justice Act 1960, or where the court with the power to do so, ordered otherwise.

Hodgson v. Imperial Tobacco [1998] 1 W.L.R. 1056; [1998] 2 All E.R. 673, CA.

ORDER 33

PLACE AND MODE OF TRIAL

Effect of rule **33/2/1**
Insert new note:

Trials before Masters **33/2/2**
A Master may try any issue with the consent of the parties (see O.36, r.11(1) and O.14, r.6(2)). **[p.643]**
Where a Master did so, and made a final order, it is appealable only to the Court of Appeal and not to a judge in chambers: *Pavey v. Ministry of Defence, The Times*, November 25, 1998, CA.

Effect of rule **33/3/1**
Add: **[p.643]**
In an action brought against insurers (D) by P for their refusal to meet his claim, defence raised the issue that P's claim was fraudulent. The judge held that this issue did not amount to actionable deceit and refused P's application for jury trial under s.69. On appeal, P accepted this ruling but argued that other aspects of the defence put fraud in issue. The court explained and applied *Grant v. Travellers Cheque Associates Ltd, The Times*, April 19, 1995, CA, and dismissed appeal (*Barclays Bank Ltd v. Cole* [1967] 2 Q.B. 738, CA, referred to): *Parsons v. Provincial Insurance plc*, February 20, 1998, CA, unrep.

Trial with assessors **33/6/2**
In second paragraph delete "11th ed., 1961", *insert* "12th ed., 1997". **[p.651]**

ORDER 36

TRIALS BEFORE, AND INQUIRIES BY, REFEREES AND MASTERS

Trial before Master **36/11/2**
Add at end of note after words "to the Court of Appeal", ": *see Pavey v. Ministry of Defence, The Times*, **[p.684]**
November 25, 1998, CA."

ORDER 38

EVIDENCE

Saving of right to privilege **38/2A/12**
Delete in last line of second paragraph the words "January 27, 1994, unreported", *insert* "*The Times*, **[p.706]**
February 19, 1994."

ORDER 45

ENFORCEMENT OF JUDGMENTS AND ORDERS: GENERAL

45/1/10 Duties of Sheriff
[p.784] *Add:*

A sheriff executing a writ of *fi fa* was not entitld forcibly to re-enter a dwelling house in which the goods were kept, for the purpose of removing them for sale, if the occupant had no knowledge of an intended visit and had locked the premises in the ordinary way and gone about his normal business: *Khazanchi v. Faircharm Investments Ltd; McLeod v. Butterwick*, March 25, 1998, *The Times*, CA.

45/7/7 Indorsement of penal notice or order
[p.803] *Delete note and insert new note:*

45/7/7 Penal Notice

It is a necessary condition for the enforcement of a judgment or order under r.5 by way of sequestration or committal, that the copy of the judgment or order served under this rule should have the requisite warning or "penal notice" displayed on the front of such a copy.

The warning on the front of the copy of the judgment or order should be in the following words or in words to the following effect:

WARNING. To John Doe. Disobedience to this order would be a contempt of court punishable by imprisonment.

In the case of a judgment or order requiring a body corporate to do or abstain from doing an act:

WARNING. To Smith Limited. Disobedience to this order would be a contempt of court punishable by sequestration of the company assets.

If it was sought to provide for possible enforcement proceedings both against the body corporate and against a director or other officer of the company:

WARNING. To Smith Limited and to John Doe. Disobedience to this order would be contempt of court punishable by sequestration of the company's assets and by imprisonment of any individual responsible.

For special forms of warnings required for *Mareva* injunctions and *Anton Piller* orders see the forms of order set out in SCP 1999, Vol. 2, Section 2C, para. 2C–47.

45/7/8 Dispensing with service of documents
[p.804] *Add:*

Paragraph (6) (service of judgment or order not needed if person concerned is shown to have had notice of it) applies only to orders to abstain from doing an act and not to mandatory orders.

Delete the second and third paragraphs of the note.

ORDER 47

WRITS OF FIERI FACIAS

47/1/10 Bankruptcy of debtor
[p.820] *In sub-paragraphs 4 and 5, delete the words* "bankruptcy order" *and substitute the words* "receiving order".

47/1/11 Stays of execution and bankruptcy petitions
[p.821] *Delete sub-paragraph (2) and re-number the sub-paragraphs. In the new sub-paragraph (3), line 1, delete the words* "bankruptcy order" *and substitute the words* "receiving order".

ORDER 52

COMMITTAL

O. Acts calculated to prejudice the due course of justice

Add: **52/1/23** **[p.883]**

A physical assault on a court official, engaged in official business in the administration of justice, is a contempt, *Re de Court, The Times*, November 27, 1997 (Sir Richard Scott V.-C.).

(iii) "contempt . . . in connection with proceedings in an inferior Court"

Add: **52/1/37** **[p.885]**

The power of a county court judge to punish for contempt under s.118 of the County Courts Act 1984 is not limited to dealing with contempts committed in the face of the court but extends to situations where a witness is wilfully insulted on his way to or from court. *Manchester City Council v. McCann and Another, The Times*, November 28, 1998 (Lord Woolf M.R., Henry and Clarke L.JJ.).

Add at end:

The Professional Conduct Committee of the General Medical Council is not part of the judicial system of the state and does not therefore fall within the definition of a "court" for the purposes of contempt proceedings: *General Medical Council v. British Broadcasting Corporation* [1998] 3 All E.R. 426 (Stuart-Smith, Aldous and Robert Walker L.JJ.).

Appeal **52/1/41** **[p.886]**

Add:

There is no jurisdictional bar to prevent an *applicant* in committal proceedings from applying to the Court of Appeal under s.13(2) of the AJA 1960 for a redetermination of the sentence passed on a contemnor by a county court, where it is said that the sentence failed properly to reflect the seriousness of the contempt. However the Court of Appeal will only interfere in exceptional circumstances and where the decision of the court below was plainly wrong: *Wilson v. Webster, The Times*, March 5, 1998 (Sir Stephen Brown P. and Sir Patrick Russell).

ORDER 54

APPLICATIONS FOR WRIT OF HABEAS CORPUS

Habeas corpus **54/1/2** **[p.927]**

Add:

Whether a person is detained is a question of objective fact which does not depend on the presence or absence of consent or knowledge. A person is detained in law if those who have control over the premises in which he is have the intention that he shall not be permitted to leave those premises and have the ability to prevent him from leaving: *R. v. Bournewood Community and Mental Health NHS Trust, ex p.* [1998] 1 All E.R. 635 (Lord Woolf M.R., Phillips and Chadwick L.JJ.).

Application for the writ **54/1/3** **[p.927]**

Add at end:

Where an applicant persists in making hopelessly misconceived applications for habeas corpus, in respect of a particular conviction, constituting a plain abuse of process, the court may direct that no further such applications are to be accepted or processed by the Crown Office in respect of that conviction: *Re Leachman* [1998] C.O.D. 466 (Simon Brown L.J. and Mance J.).

Habeas corpus or judicial review **54/1/5** **[p.929]**

Add at end:

Where an application is made by way of habeas corpus, in circumstances which would have been best dealt with by an application for judicial review, the court will not simply reject it out of hand if the matter can be put into decent procedural shape so as to enable the issue to be resolved: *Re John (Julie)* [1998] C.O.D. 306 (Latham J.).

It was sometimes thought that habeas corpus had advantages over judicial review because of the difference in the burden of proof but in practice that had no practical consequences. Judicial review had advantages over habeas corpus because of the range of remedies available. If a person wrongly detained was released prior to an order for habeas corpus there was no relief which the court could grant, whereas in the case of judicial review it could grant an injunction and, in appropriate cases, damages. In *Re S-C (Mental Patient: Habeas Corpus)* [1996] Q.B. 599, an application for judicial review would have been equally appropriate and would even have had advantages over habeas corpus. Applications for habeas corpus were to be discouraged unless it was clear that no other relief would be required. If both applications were lodged every effort should be made to harmonise the proceedings and the same affidavits should be used. At any interlocutory and final hearing both set of proceedings should be before the court, and in the event of an appeal the same notice of appeal would suffice: *Re Barker; R. v. BHB Community Healthcare NHS Trust and Another, ex p. Barker, The Times,* October 14, 1998 (Lord Woolf M.R., Hobhouse and Thorpe L.JJ.).

ORDER 55

APPEALS TO HIGH COURT FROM COURT, TRIBUNAL OR PERSON: GENERAL

55/4/2 Procedure
[p.937] *Add:*

As to extension under O.3, r.5 of the 28 day period prescribed by r.4(4), where in the case of the Special Educational Needs Tribunal, the tribunal itself had suggested the possibility that it might review its own decision under reg. 31 of its regulations, and the applicant was thus deflected from seeking legal advice, and no prejudice arose, an extension of time would be granted: *Sage v. South Gloucestershire County Council and Another* [1998] C.O.D. 384 (Hidden J.).

55/7/3 Other powers of Court
[p.939] *Add:*

An order for the production of notes or a transcript under r.7(4) will only be made in exceptional and rare circumstances and where it is necessary in order to dispose properly of an issue raised in the appeal: *Joyce v. Dorset County Council* [1997] E.L.R. 26. An order will not be made if its purpose was to conduct a fishing expedition or to add to grounds or to seek to discover grounds on which an appeal could be pursued: *Fisher v. Hughes and Another* [1998] C.O.D. 281 (Keene J.).

ORDER 56

APPEALS, ETC., TO HIGH COURT BY CASE STATED: GENERAL

56/1/2 Appeals from the Crown Court by case stated
[p.942] *Add:*

Where there has been a refusal to state a case it may be conventional and technically correct to apply by way of judicial review for an order of mandamus to compel the Crown Court to state a case, but where the facts are not in dispute it is far better for the true issue to be placed before the Court by way of a straightforward judicial review challenge to the correctness of the Crown Court's adjudication in point of law: *R. v. Knightsbridge Crown Court, ex p. Foot* [1998] C.O.D. 165 (Simon Brown L.J. and Mance J.).

56/1/9 Procedure for obtaining a case stated
[p.944] *Add:*

The power to extend time provided for by r.26(14) of the Crown Court Rules 1982 may be exercised by a judge of the Crown Court alone and there is no requirement that the justices should also participate in that decision. Where an application for an extension of time is made by the prosecution the Crown Court must afford the acquitted defendant an opportunity to be heard in opposition to such an application. Such extensions should not be routinely granted and cogent reasons for doing so will be required from the prosecution. *DPP v. Coleman* [1998] 1 All E.R. 912 (Pill L.J. and Garland J.).

Add:

Where the Crown Court refuses to state a case it should give its reasons for refusal with some particularity: *R. v. Preston Crown Court, ex p. Chief Constable of the Lancashire Constabulary* [1998] C.O.D. 272 (Moses J.). And the same requirement applies where the challenge might be either by way of judicial review or case stated: *R. v. Gloucester Crown Court, ex p. Chester* [1998] C.O.D. 365 (Lord Bingham of Cornhill C.J. and Thomas J.).

56/5/3 Power to state a case
[p.948] *Add:*

In *Wilkinson v. Crown Prosecution Service* [1998] C.O.D. 387 (Lord Bingham of Cornhill C.J. and Cresswell J.) the Divisional Court found it unnecessary to resolve the question whether case stated lies from a decision of examining justices but Cresswell J. observed "In the light of [*Atkinson v.*

Government of the United States of America [1971] A.C. 197] it is doubtful whether the matters sought to be raised in this case were properly ventilated by way of case stated. The appropriate procedure was probably an application for judicial review". Moreover, the court noted that the latter procedure had been followed in *Williams v. Bedwellty Justices* [1996] 3 All E.R. 737, HL.

ORDER 59

APPEALS TO THE COURT OF APPEAL

Leave to Appeal **59/1/91–136** [pp.997–1005]

Delete and substitute:

With effect from January 1, 1999 leave to appeal is required in the case of all appeals to the Court of Appeal, save for three very limited exceptions (see paras 59/1B/1 *et seq.* of this Supplement).

Definition of final and interlocutory orders **59/1A/2** [p.1011]

Add:

The distinction between final and interlocutory orders is no longer relevant for the purposes of deciding whether leave to appeal is required, because leave is now almost universal (see paras 59/1B/1 *et seq.* of this Supplement); but it is still necessary in some cases to know whether or not an order is interlocutory for the purpose of deciding whether a 2–Judge Court has jurisdiction to hear the appeal (see para. 59/1/62 of the Main Work).

Classes of case where leave to appeal is required (O.59, r.1B) **59/1B** [p.1018]

Substitute new rule:

"**1B.**—(1) Every appeal shall be subject to leave except an appeal against—

(a) the making of a committal order;
(b) a refusal to grant habeas corpus; or
(c) an order made under Section 25 of the Children Act 1989 (secure accommodtion orders).

(2) Leave to appeal to the Court of Appeal may be given by the court below or by the Court of Appeal."

History of Rule **59/1B/1** [p.1018]

Delete and substitute:

HISTORY OF RULE

Substituted by S.I. 1998 No. 3045.

Scope of r.1B **59/1B/2** [p.1019]

Delete and substitute:

The new r.1B **59/1B/2**

With effect from January 1, 1999 the new r.1B imposes an almost universal leave requirement (see paras 59/1B/4 to 8 of this Supplement).

Commencement of r.18 **59/1B/3** [p.1019]

Delete and substitute following paragraphs:

Commencement of the new r.1B **59/1B/3**

The new rule applies to all cases where the order sought to be appealed was made after January 1, 1999 and it also applies to orders made before January 1, 1999 unless, prior to that date, (i) an appeal was set down, or (ii) an application for an extension of time for serving notice of appeal or for setting down the appeal was lodged with the Court of Appeal (S.I. 1998 No. 3049, para. 4).

When is leave to appeal required? **59/1B/4**

Leave to appeal is now required in respect of all appeals to the Court of Appeal subject to the three very limited exceptions referred to in paras 59/1B/5 to 59/1B/8. The three exceptional categories where leave to appeal is not required are all cases where the appellant's case is that he has been, or continues to be, wrongly deprived of his liberty.

59/1B/5 **Cases where leave to appeal is not required**

There continues to be an appeal without leave in the following cases only:

Making of a committal order

59/1B/6 There is an appeal as of right against the making of a committal order (r.1B(1)(a)); it is submitted that this exception applies where a suspended committal order has been made as well as to cases where the contemnor has been sentenced to immediate custody. Leave to appeal will, however, now be required in respect of any other order made on a committal application (*e.g.* refusal of the application, imposing a fine or no penalty other than costs, or making an antecedent procedural order, such as adjourning the committal application).

Refusal of habeas corpus

59/1B/7 There is an appeal as of right against a refusal of *habeas corpus* (r.1B(1)(b)), but not any other type of order made on an application for *habeas corpus.*

Making of a secure accommodation order

59/1B/8 Appeal lies without leave against the making in civil proceedings of an order under s.25 of the Children Act 1989 (secure accommodation order) (r.1B(1)(c)); but leave will be required in respect of any other order made on an application under that section.

59/1B/4 **Who may grant leave to appeal?**

[p.1019] *Renumber as 59/1B/9 and at the end of the first sentence substitute:* (r.1B(2)).

Add:

See also paras 8 and 9 of Lord Woolf's Practice Direction of November 17, 1999, set out at para. 59/14/36C of this Supplement.

59/1B/5–19 [pp.1019–1021] *Delete paragraphs* 59/1B/5 to 59/1B/19.

59/9/2 **Time limit for lodging bundles**

[p.1041] *Add new paragraph:*

59/9/2A **Skeleton arguments with bundles**

Four copies of the appellant's advocate's skeleton argument must now be lodged with the appeal bundles (see further para. 59/9/28 of this Supplement).

59/9/13 **Appeal bundles and transcripts for the use of the respondent**

[p.1042] *Add:*

The set of appeal bundles which the appellant's solicitor is required to provide for the respondent's side must now include a copy of the appellant's advocate's skeleton argument.

59/9/24 **In what cases are skeleton arguments required?**

[p.1045] *Add:*

Skeleton arguments now have to be provided for leave to appeal applications which are due to be considered by a single Lord Justice on paper as well as for applications which proceed to an oral hearing (whether before a single Lord Justice or a Full Court). The applicant's skeleton argument has to be lodged with the application bundle (see paras 59/14/10 and 59/14/31 of this Supplement).

59/9/28 **Timetable**

[p.1046] *Delete text and substitute:*

Under Part 2 of Lord Woolf's Practice Direction of November 17, 1998, appellants' skeleton arguments now have to be lodged with the appeal bundles. It is therefore important that the core bundles are finalised early enough to enable the appellant's advocate to have the skeleton argument (with cross references to the paginated core bundles) in time for lodging with those bundles. Four copies of the skeleton argument of the appellant's advocate must be lodged with (but *not* bound in) the appeal core bundles (see paras 31 to 33 of Lord Woolf's Practice Direction which are set out at para. 59/9/75 of this Supplement). A copy of that skeleton argument must be included with the set of bundles which the appellant is required to provide for the use of the respondent (see para. 59/9/13 of this Supplement).

Four copies of the respondent's advocate's skeleton argument must be lodged with the Civil Appeals Documents Room within 21 days after receipt by the respondent's solicitors of the appeal bundle(s) from the appellant's side, or, if earlier, 14 days before the date on which the appeal is listed for hearing (see para. 34 of Lord Woolf's Practice Direction which is set out in para. 59/1/75 of this Supplement).

Add new paragraph:

Supplemental or revised skeleton arguments

No supplemental or revised skeleton arguments can be lodged without the leave of the Court; and leave will only be granted if there are good reasons for doing so (see para. 35 of Lord Woolf's Practice Direction set out at para. 59/9/75 of this Supplement). There would be a good reason for granting such leave if, since the skeleton argument was lodged, there has been a change in the law or admissible fresh evidence has come to light. Leave is not likely to be granted, however, if the need for a supplemental skeleton argument arises out of failure to prepare the case properly when the skeleton was originally lodged; the Court will not countenance "holding" skeleton arguments being lodged with the bundles and then being supplanted by fresh skeleton arguments lodged much closer to the hearing. **59/9/28A**

Fixtures

Delete and substitute new paragraph: **59/9/29** [p.1046]

Skeleton arguments for applications

Skeleton arguments are mandatory for all applications to the Full Court and to a single Lord Justice. **59/9/29**

Short Warned List cases

Delete and substitute new paragraph: **59/9/30** [p.1046]

Full Court applications

Skeleton arguments have to be lodged for all Full Court applications and the timetable is the same as for appeals (see para. 2(5) the Practice Direction of July 26, 1995, set out at para. 59/9/36 of the Main Work, combined with paras 3 and 31 to 35 of Lord Woolf's Practice Direction of November 17, 1998, set out at paras 59/9/71 and 59/9/75 of this Supplement). **59/9/30**

Leave to appeal applications

Delete and substitute new paragraph: **59/9/31** [p.1046]

Applications to a single Lord Justice

Skeleton arguments are required in the case of all applications to a single Lord Justice (see paras 59/14/10 and 59/14/31 of this Supplement). **59/9/31**

Sequential skeleton arguments

Delete text and substitute: **59/9/32** [p.1046]

Subject to any other directions of the court given in any individual case, the effect of the new timetable for skeleton arguments laid down in Lord Woolf's Practice Direction of November 17, 1998 is that all skeleton arguments will now be sequential.

Applications for leave listed for oral hearing

Delete paragraphs 9(2) and (3) of this Practice Direction and insert: **59/9/40** [p.1050]

Those provisions relating to skeleton arguments for leave applications have been superseded by Lord Woolf's Practice Direction of November 17, 1998 (see paras 27 *et seq.* of that Practice Direction set out at paras 59/9/74 and 59/9/75 of this Supplement).

Timetable for skeleton arguments

Delete paragraphs 40 to 46 of this Practice Direction and insert: **59/9/50** [pp.1053 & 1054]

Those provisions relating to the timetable for lodging skeleton arguments for appeals have been superseded by Lord Woolf's Practice Direction of November 17, 1998 (see paras 31 *et seq.* of that Practice Direction set out at para. 59/9/75 of this Supplement).

Case Management

Add new paragraphs: **59/9/70** [p.1060]

PRACTICE DIRECTION (COURT OF APPEAL: LEAVE TO APPEAL AND SKELETON ARGUMENTS)

Introduction

1. This Practice Direction sets out the practice and procedure for dealing with applications for leave to appeal to the Court of Appeal (Civil Division) and for providing skeleton arguments. It has been the subject of consultation with the members of the Court of Appeal, and sets out the collective views of the Court. **59/9/71**

2. The provisions of *Practice Direction (Court of Appeal: Procedural Changes)* dated 26 July 1995 [1995] 1 W.L.R. 1191; [1995] 3 All E.R. 850 (the 1995 Practice Direction) must be read subject to this Practice Direction.

3. Paragraphs 2 and 3 of the 1995 Practice Direction apply (with any necessary modifications) to this Practice Direction.

4. In this Practice Direction:

(a) unless otherwise specified, "the court of first instance" means the court or tribunal which made the decision which is challenged; and

(b) references to the trial judge include, where appropriate, members of tribunals.

* * *

Part 2: Skeleton Arguments

59/9/72 **25.** A skeleton argument is a document prepared by the advocate, which identifies and summarises the points which will be relied on without arguing them fully. For guidance on the form and content of skeleton arguments, see paragraph 37 of the 1995 Practice Direction. Litigants in person may provide a skeleton argument if they wish, but are not required to do so.

Commencement

59/9/73 **26.** Part 2 of this Practice Direction applies to applications lodged and appeals set down in the Court of Appeal before or after 1 January 1999, unless all skeleton arguments have already been lodged prior to that date. In those cases where the bundles were lodged prior to 1 January 1999 and all skeleton arguments have not yet been provided, any skeleton argument not previously lodged must be lodged by 1 February 1999 or, if earlier, not later than 14 days before the hearing.

Skeleton arguments for applications for leave to appeal

59/9/74 **27.** In order to assist the Court of Appeal to deal efficiently with applications for leave to appeal, all represented applicants for leave must provide a skeleton argument.

28. Two copies of the skeleton argument must accompany the bundle of documents which the applicant's solicitors lodge with the Civil Appeals Office for the application. (These copies should be lodged with, but not bound in, the bundle.)

29. If the application is listed for oral hearing at which the Court has directed that both parties are to have the opportunity to attend, the respondent's skeleton argument must be lodged and served within 14 days of receipt of the applicant's bundle (as required by paragraph 9(1) of the 1995 Practice Direction).

30. Where dates are of significance in relation to the proposed appeal, a chronology should be filed and served with the applicant's skeleton argument.

Skeleton arguments for appeals

59/9/75 **31.** The directions relating to the timetable for skeleton arguments in respect of all appeals (whether leave was granted by the court below or the Court of Appeal, or was not required) are now those set out in this Practice Direction. These directions supersede paragraphs 9(2) and (3) and 40 to 46 of the 1995 Practice Direction.

32. Where leave to appeal is granted by the Court of Appeal, the appellant (and any respondent who has lodged a skeleton argument in response to the leave application) may use the same skeleton arguments for the purposes of the appeal (subject to making any minor amendments which they consider necessary, such as changes to page references), or they may prepare fresh skeleton arguments for the purposes of the appeal.

33. The appellant's solicitors must include with the appeal bundle four copies of their skeleton argument. (These copies should be lodged with, but not bound in, the bundle.) The appellant's solicitors must also include a copy of that skeleton argument with the set of bundles served on the respondent. [Appellants are reminded of the obligation to serve a set of bundles on the respondent at the same time as the appeal bundles are lodged with the Civil Appeals Office (see paragraph 21 of the 1995 Practice Direction).]

34. The respondent's solicitors must lodge with the Civil Appeals Office four copies of their skeleton argument within 21 days of the date on which the appellant's bundle was served on them or, if earlier, not later than 14 days before the appeal hearing.

35. No supplemental or revised skeleton arguments may be lodged without the permission of the Court. Permission will only be granted if there are good reasons for doing so.

Application bundle **59/14/10** [p.1083]

Add:

Skeleton arguments are now required in respect of applications to a single Lord Justice (whether they are due to be determined on paper or listed for oral hearing). Two copies of the applicant's advocate's skeleton argument must be lodged with the application bundle(s). If the application is listed for hearing *inter partes,* the respondent's advocate must lodge with the Civil Appeals Office two copies of his skeleton argument within 14 days of the receipt by the respondent's solicitors of the application bundle from the appellant's side.

Circumstances in which leave to appeal will be granted **59/14/18** [p.1084]

Add:

Part 1 of Lord Woolf's Practice Direction of November 17, 1998 (the text of which is set out in paras 59/14/35A and 59/14/35B of this Supplement) lays down guidelines to assist courts in deciding whether leave to appeal should be granted.

Add new paragraph:

Second tier appeals **59/14/18A** [p.1084]

Where the applicant is seeking to be permitted to appeal against a decision of a judge dismissing an appeal to him against a decision given by the court or tribunal below that, a much stricter test is applied in deciding whether leave should be granted (see para. 20 of Lord Woolf's Practice Direction of November 17, 1998, the text of which is set out in paras 59/14/35A and 59/14/35B of this Supplement). In the case of such second tier appeals leave to appeal will not generally be granted unless the case raises an important point of principle or practice, or the case is one which for some other reason should be considered by the Court of Appeal.

1. Mode of applying for leave to appeal **59/14/21** [p.1085]

Delete "£60" *and substitute* "£100". *Add:*

Where leave has been refused by the court below, the judge will normally have endorsed on a form supplied for that purpose his reasons for refusing leave; a copy of that form must be annexed to any application to the Court of Appeal for leave (see para. 21 of Lord Woolf's Practice Direction of November 17, 1998 which is set out at para. 59/14/36K of this Supplement).

4. Application bundle **59/14/24** [p.1085]

Add:

Two copies of the applicant's advocate's skeleton argument must be lodged with the application bundle (see paras 27 and 28 of Lord Woolf's Practice Direction of November 17, 1998, the text of which is set out at para. 59/9/74 of this Supplement).

5. Referral to single Lord Justice **59/14/25**

Delete paragraph and substitute:

Consideration of leave applications paper **59/14/25** [p.1085]

In all represented cases applications to the Court of Appeal for leave to appeal will continue to be referred to a single Lord Justice for consideration on paper, but changes to the system have been made by Part 3 of Lord Woolf's Practice Direction of November 17, 1998 (the text of which is set out in paras 59/14/36L of this Supplement).

If the single Lord Justice (the Assigned Lord Justice) considers that leave to appeal should be granted, he will grant it on paper as under the previous system. If, however, the Assigned Lord Justice is minded to refuse leave, he will not generally make an order on paper refusing leave, but under the new system he will cause a letter to be sent to the applicant's solicitors indicating his preliminary view and giving the applicant the opportunity to consider whether to ask for an oral hearing (see para. 59/14/26A below). In future some applications for leave by litigants in person may be referred to a single Lord Justice for consideration on paper (see para. 40 of Lord Woolf's Practice Direction which is set out at para. 59/14/36L of this Supplement).

59/14/26 **6. Refusal on paper—renewal of application in open court**
Delete paragraph and substitute:

59/14/26 **Grant of leave to appeal by a single Lord Justice**
[p.1085] The system for granting leave to appeal on paper has not changed. The Associate will seal and issue the order granting leave and send copies of it to the applicant's solicitor and to all known respondents. The applicant's solicitor must then serve the notice of appeal and set down the appeal. (The time limit for serving notice of appeal is normally prescribed in the order granting leave and is usually 10 days after the date of the seal on the order. The time limit for setting down is that prescribed by O.59, r.5(1) (see paras 59/5/2 *et seq.* of the Main Work).)

Add new notes:

59/14/26A **Where the single Lord Justice is minded to refuse leave to appeal**
In such cases the Assigned Lord Justice will not normally refuse leave on paper, but will instead direct the office to send a letter to the applicant's solicitor with a schedule annexed setting out the reasons why the Assigned Lord Justice is minded to refuse leave (see para. 38 of Lord Woolf's Practice Direction set out at para. 59/14/36L of this Supplement). If the applicant wishes to pursue the application further, then, within 14 days of receiving that letter, the applicant's solicitor must notify the Civil Appeals Office in writing that the applicant wishes to have the application listed for oral hearing (see paras 38 and 39 of Lord Woolf's Practice Direction set out at para. 59/14/36L of this Supplement). Before deciding to seek an oral hearing of the application, counsel's advice should be sought to check whether there are good reasons for doing so, having regard to the Assigned Lord Justice's preliminary observations. If the application is pursued to an oral hearing, counsel must be prepared to deal with the points raised in those observations. Those who pursue applications to an oral hearing without good grounds may be penalised in costs.

59/14/26B **Where an oral hearing is requested**
If there is an oral hearing of the application, it will be listed before a single Lord Justice or a 2-Judge Court according to the directions given by the Assigned Lord Justice; he will also direct whether it is to be listed *inter partes* or *ex parte* (see para. 38 of the Practice Direction set out at para. 59/14/36L of this Supplement). If a hearing before a 2-Judge Court has been directed, the applicant's solicitor must lodge with the letter requesting an oral hearing a second set of the application bundle(s) and skeleton argument. Wherever possible the Assigned Lord Justice will conduct the oral hearing either sitting alone or with another Lord Justice as the case may be.

59/14/26C **Where there is no request for an oral hearing**
In the absence of a request for an oral hearing having been received within the 14-day time limit, the application will be determined in open court (usually by a single Lord Justice) without further reference to the applicant (see para. 39 of the Practice Direction set out at para. 59/14/36L of this Supplement).

59/14/31 **Skeleton arguments**
[p.1086] *Delete text and substitute:*
Skeleton arguments are now required in respect of applications for leave which are considered on paper as well as for all those which proceed to an oral hearing (whether before a single Lord Justice or a Full Court) (see paras 27 to 29 of Lord Woolf's Practice Direction of November 17, 1998 which is set out at para. 59/9/74 of this Supplement). Two copies of the applicant's advocate's skeleton argument must be lodged with the application bundle(s). If the application is listed for hearing *inter partes*, the respondent's advocate must lodge with the Civil Appeals Office two copies of his skeleton argument within 14 days of the receipt by the respondent's solicitors of the application bundle from the appellant's side (see para. 29 of the Practice Direction set out at para. 59/9/74 of this Supplement).

59/14/35 *Skeleton arguments*
[p.1087] *Add new paragraphs:*

PRACTICE DIRECTION (COURT OF APPEAL: LEAVE TO APPEAL AND SKELETON ARGUMENTS)

Introduction

1. This Practice Direction sets out the practice and procedure for dealing with applications for leave to the Court of Appeal (Civil Division) and for providing skeleton arguments. It has been the subject of consultation with the members of the Court of Appeal, and sets out the collective views of the Court. 59/14/35A

2. The provisions of *Practice Direction (Court of Appeal: Procedural Changes)* dated 26 July 1995 [1995] 1 W.L.R. 1191; [1995] 3 All E.R. 850 (the 1995 Practice Direction) must be read subject to this Practice Direction.

3. Paragraphs 2 and 3 of the 1995 Practice Direction apply (with any necessary modifications) to this Practice Direction.

In this Practice Direction:

(a) unless otherwise specified, "the court of first instance" means the court or tribunal which made the decision which is challenged; and

(b) references to the trial judge include, where appropriate, members of tribunals.

Part 1: Leave to Appeal

5. Part 1 of this Practice Direction comes into force forthwith. 59/14/35B

6. Many appeals require leave; that is, the permission of the court of first instance (the court which made the decision which is challenged) or of the Court of Appeal to bring an appeal.

7. The experience of the Court of Appeal is that many appeals and applications for leave to appeal are made which are quite hopeless. They demonstrate basic misconceptions as to the purpose of the civil appeal system and the different roles played by appellate courts and courts of first instance. Courts of first instance have a crucial role in determining applications for leave to appeal. The guidance in this Practice Direction is designed to ensure that this crucial role is exercised as constructively as possible, and to assist parties, their legal advisers, trial judges and the Court of Appeal to deal justly and effectively with applications for leave to appeal.

From which court should leave to appeal be sought?

8. The court which has just reached a decision is often in the best position to judge whether the case is or is not one where there should be an appeal. It should not leave the decision to the Court of Appeal. Courts of first instance can help to minimise the delay and expense which an appeal involves. Where the parties are present for delivery of the judgment, it should be routine for the judge below to ask whether either party wants leave to appeal and to deal with the matter then and there. However, if the court of first instance is in doubt whether an appeal would have a real prospect of success or involves a point of general principle, the safe course is to refuse leave to appeal. It is always open to the Court of Appeal to grant leave. 59/14/35C

9. The advantages which flow from leave being considered by the court of first instance are lost if the application cannot be listed before the judge who made the decision which is the subject of the application. Where it is not possible for the application for leave to be listed before the same judge, or where undue delay would be caused by so listing it, the Court of Appeal will be sympathetic to applicants who claim that it was impracticable for them to make their applications to the court below and will not require such an application to be made.

The general test for leave

59/14/35D **10.** There is no limit on the number of appeals the Court of Appeal is prepared to hear. It is therefore not relevant to consider whether the Court of Appeal might prefer to select for itself which appeals it would like to hear. The general rule applied by the Court of Appeal, and thus the relevant basis for first instance courts deciding whether to grant leave, is that leave will be given unless an appeal would have no realistic prospect of success. A fanciful prospect is insufficient. Leave may also be given in exceptional circumstances even though the case has no real prospect of success if there is an issue which, in the public interest, should be examined by the Court of Appeal. Examples are where a case raises questions of great public interest or questions of general policy, or where authority binding on the Court of Appeal may call for reconsideration.

11. The approach will differ depending on the category and subject matter of the decision and the reason for seeking leave to appeal, as will be indicated below. However, if the issue to be raised on the appeal is of general importance that will be a factor in favour of granting leave. On the other hand, if the issues are not generally important and the costs of an appeal will far exceed what is at stake, that will be a factor which weighs against the grant of leave to appeal.

A point of law

59/14/35E **12.** Leave should not be granted unless the judge considers that there is a real prospect of the Court of Appeal coming to a different conclusion on a point of law which will *materially* affect the outcome of the case. An appeal on the grounds that there is no evidence to support a finding is an appeal on a point of law, but it is insufficient to show that there was little evidence.

A question of fact

59/13/35F **13.** The Court of Appeal will rarely interfere with a decision based on the judge's evaluation of oral evidence as to the primary facts or if an appeal would involve examining the fine detail of the judge's factual investigation.

14. Leave is more likely to be appropriate where what is being challenged is the inference which the judge has drawn from the primary facts, or where the judge has not received any particular benefit from having actually seen the witnesses, and it is properly arguable that materially different inferences should be drawn from the evidence. In such a case the judge, if he grants leave, should expressly indicate that this is the basis on which leave is given.

15. If a case is one which has involved considering many witnesses and/or documents, it will be especially important that the trial court considers whether to grant leave and, where it refuses leave, gives its reasons for doing so. This is because in a case of this sort the Court of Appeal is less able to assess whether an appeal is appropriate.

Questions of discretion

59/14/35G **16.** The Court of Appeal does not interfere with the exercise of discretion of a judge unless the Court is satisfied the judge was wrong. The burden on an appellant is a heavy one (many family cases do not qualify for leave for this reason). It will be rare, therefore, for a trial judge to give leave on a pure question of discretion. He may do so if the case raises a point of general principle on which the opinion of a higher court is required.

Appeals from interlocutory orders

59/14/35H **17.** An interlocutory order is an order which does not entirely determine the proceedings (see Order 59, rule 1A of the Rules of the Supreme Court 1965). Where the application is for leave to appeal from an interlocutory order, additional considerations arise:

(a) the point may not be of sufficient significance to justify the costs of an appeal;
(b) the procedural consequences of an appeal (*e.g.* loss of the trial date) may outweigh the significance of the interlocutory issue;
(c) it may be more convenient to determine the point at or after the trial.

In all such cases leave to appeal should be refused.

Limited and conditional leave

18. Leave may be limited to one or more points. It may also be conditional, *e.g.* on some special order for costs. If a court grants leave on one or more issues only, it should *expressly* refuse leave on other issues. The reason for this is that the other issues can then only be raised with the leave of the Court of Appeal. **59/14/35I**

19. If an appellant wishes to raise additional issues for which there is no leave to appeal, written notice of this must be given to all other parties and the Court of Appeal within 28 days of leave being granted, or 28 days prior to the hearing, if this is earlier. Unless there are special reasons for making an application earlier, to avoid additional expense the application to raise an additional issue should be dealt with at the outset of the appeal and all parties should normally be prepared to argue the additional issues at that hearing. If, however, a respondent considers the additional points will have a significant effect on the preparation necessary for or the length of the hearing, he may inform the appellant within 14 days of receiving the notice that he requires an application to be made prior to the hearing. An application should then be made in writing within 14 days accompanied, if necessary, by short written submissions, which should be served on the respondent. The respondent may deliver short written submissions within a further 14 days. The court will, where practical, give its decision as to whether the additional point can be argued prior to the hearing of the appeal.

More than one level of appeal

20. Where there has already been one appeal to a court (not a tribunal) against the decision being challenged, for example from a district judge to a Circuit judge or from a Master to a High Court judge, and the application is for leave for a further appeal to the Court of Appeal, a more restrictive approach to the test for leave to appeal should be adopted if there has already been one unsuccessful appeal. Leave should be granted only if the case raises an important point of principle or practice or the case is one which for some other reason should be considered by the Court of Appeal. **59/14/35J**

The Form

21. At Annex A to this Practice Direction [not included in this print] is a generic example of the form which the judge should complete when he grants or refuses leave to appeal, giving his reasons. The reasons for the decision need only be brief, *e.g. difficult point of law* or *pure question of fact.* All parties will, on request, be given a copy of the form. It is the applicant's responsibility to annex the form to his notice of application where he has been refused leave, or to his notice of appeal where he has been granted leave. **59/14/35K**

[For Part 2 see paras 59/9/72 *et seq.* of this Supplement.]

Part 3: Procedure in the Court of Appeal

36. Part 3 of this Practice Direction sets out the procedure which will be followed in the Court of Appeal from 1 January 1999 when dealing with any application for leave to appeal not determined before that date. **59/14/35L**

37. When an application for leave to appeal is referred to the single Lord

Justice on the papers alone and the Lord Justice decides to grant leave, there will be no change from the present practice, but the Lord Justice may give directions for the subsequent progress of the appeal.

38. When the Lord Justice is minded to refuse leave to appeal, his or her reasons for doing so will be sent to the applicant's solicitors (or the applicant, if in person). A letter will accompany the Lord Justice's comments informing the applicant of the right to seek an oral hearing. (An example of the letter that will be sent is at Annex B to this Practice Direction [not included in this print].) The Lord Justice will direct whether the oral hearing should be before one or two Lords Justices.

39. In the absence of a request for an oral hearing being received within 14 days, the application will be determined in open court without further reference to the applicant.

40. At present, only leave applications where the applicant is legally represented are dealt with on paper. In future, some applications from litigants in person may be deemed suitable to be dealt with in the same way.

41. Further information about the procedure on applications for leave to appeal is set out in paragraphs 5 to 10 of the 1995 Practice Direction.

ORDER 62

COSTS

62/0/3 [p.1113] **Related Sources**

To Practice Directions add:

—*Queen's Bench Division and Chancery Division Practice Direction*, February 1, 1999.

62/2/7 [p.1116] **Rule 2(4)—Discretion as to costs**

Add:

T. G. A. Chapman Ltd v. Christopher is now reported at [1998] 1 W.L.R. 12, CA.

In the principles laid down by the Court of Appeal for the guidance of judges at first instance in awarding costs delete guideline (6) and substitute:

(6) The procedure for the determination of costs is a summary procedure, not necessarily subject to all the rules that would apply in an action. Thus, subject to any relevant statutory exceptions, judicial findings are inadmissible as evidence of the facts upon which they were based in proceedings between one of the parties to the original proceedings and a stranger. Yet in the summary procedure for the determination of the liability of a solicitor to pay the costs of an action to which he was not a party, the judge's findings of fact may be admissible. This departure from basic principles can only be justified if the connection of the non-party with the original proceedings was so close that he will not suffer any injustice by allowing this exception to the general rule.

Add after T. G. A. Chapman Ltd v. Christopher:

Guidelines may be deduced from *Symphony Group Plc v. Hodgson*; *Murphy v. Young & Co.'s Brewery Plc* and *T. G. A. Chapman Ltd v. Christopher* (above): two issues need to be considered, first whether there were exceptional circumstances to justify an order against a non party and second to what extent the conduct of that party caused loss to the applicant in the sense of occasioning or increasing the costs: *Bristol & West Plc v. Bhadresa (No. 2)*, November 13, 1998, Lightman J., unreported.

Add:

In relation to the joinder of parties where a plaintiff exercised his rights to a statutory appeal under the Charities Act 1993 and applied for the Charity Commissioners to be joined as defendants to the action it was held that the Court had a discretion to decide whether the Commissioners were proper defendants to the proceedings. On the facts it was neither necessary nor desirable for them to be joined. As to the question of costs the Court found that the plaintiff would be able to recover any costs against the Commissioners even if not party to the action under the principle in *Aiden Shipping Co. Ltd v. Interbulk Ltd (The Vimeira)* [1986] A.C. 965: *Weth v. H.M. Attorney General, The Times,* October 12, 1998, CA.

Supreme Court Act 1981, s.51 **62/2/9** [p.1118]

Add after R. v. Lambeth Borough Council, ex p. Wilson:

The Court of Appeal set aside the costs order against the two housing officers employed by the defendant authority since the order had been made to punish them for the way they had handled (or failed to handle) the case in question: *R. v. Lambeth Borough Council, ex p. Wilson* (1998) 30 H.L.R. 64, CA.

Effect of rule **62/3/1** [p.1121]

Delete reference to British Waterways Board v. Norman

Add at end:

Thai Trading Co. v. Taylor, [1998] 2 W.L.R. 893, [1998] 3 All E.R. 65, CA, and see note at 62/A2/27A.

Insert after Rozhon v. Secretary of State for Wales:

Where a plaintiff in a civil action recovered less than had already been received from the Criminal Injuries Compensation Board, it did not mean that he should not be awarded costs since he had been wholly successful on liability. An award from the CICB did not disentitle the plaintiff from bringing a civil action and it was in the public interest that the CICB should be repaid by the tortfeasor: *Oldham v. Sharples* [1997] P.I.Q.R. Q82, CA.

Rule 3(3) **62/3/3** [p.1122]

Add after Rozhon v. Secretary of State for Wales:

A trial judge may exercise discretion over apportionment of costs in accordance with r.3(3). It is appropriate to apply the rule that costs follow the event with costs being awarded to the successful party on each claim. In a case where two actions involving unrelated issues were consolidated it was appropriate to order apportionment of costs between the parties according to the amount of time each issue had taken at the trial. *Swale Storage & Distribution Services Ltd v. Sittingbourne Paper Co. Ltd, The Times,* July 30, 1998, CA.

After Re Elgindata insert:

The proper approach is to ascertain which side has won overall and then to apply the principle of dealing with the claim and equitable set off as one for the purposes of costs: see *Hanak v. Green* [1958] 2 Q.B. 9. It is then appropriate to consider whether the conduct of the successful party justifies depriving them of any costs, see *Re Elgindata* above; *M.B. Building Contractors Ltd v. Ahmed The Independent,* November 23, 1998 (C.S.), CA.

After Gerdes-Hardy v. Wessex Regional Health Authority, delete note relating to Oksuzoglu v. Kay and insert:

Where on a split trial the judge at first instance found in favour of the plaintiff on the issue of negligence but largely against him on causation, the defendants were ordered to pay the whole of the costs since they could have protected their position before trial of liability by making an offer under RSC, O.33, r.4A to accept a specified proportion of the liability and the inclusion of a claim for psychiatric injury (added with leave at trial) did not constitute the addition of a new cause of action. On appeal Brooke L.J. stated that the Court was entitled to ask itself "who was essentially the winning party?" It will not be distracted from making a just order as to costs by the absence of a payment into Court which the plaintiff obviously would not have accepted or where the defendants did not have a proper opportunity to make a payment into Court, which obviously would not have been accepted. The Court found that the judge at first instance was wrong when applying the third principle in Elgindata (above) not to make a separate order as to the costs of the issues on liability/causation on which the defendants were essentially the winners. The reference to O.33, r.4A was wrong. The defendants had adequately protected themselves by payment in, and if payment in was inapplicable they had protected themselves to a considerable extent by the terms of a Calderbank letter. On the particular facts of the case the defendants were ordered to pay the plaintiff's costs up to the date of trial, save that the plaintiff was ordered to pay the defendants 90 per cent of their costs arising out of the trial of the issues on liability and causation. The defendants were ordered to pay the plaintiff's costs thereafter except for costs of and incidental to an application to re-amend, which the plaintiff had to pay to the defendants. An order for set-off was made in favour of three defendants against any liability they might have to pay damages and costs to the plaintiff. The Court treated the defendants as essentially the winners in relation to the preliminary issues. The Court gave general guidance:

"1. RSC, O.18, r.12(1A) is there to be obeyed, defendants should be able to evaluate a claim and make a payment into Court soon after a statement of claim is served if they wish. The statement of the special damage claim must be fully stated as at the date of the statement of claim. If for any reason a plaintiff's solicitors wish to be relieved of their obligation of commissioning an up to date medical report at the time when proceedings are served they should obtain agreement from the defendant's solicitors about this course or an order from the Court. In any event if the plaintiff's prognosis is still uncertain at the time the statement of claim is served this should be made clear in the statement of claim.

2. If, from a defendant's defence, it is clear that he is suggesting that even if the plaintiff wins on liability he may lose on causation to a very substantial extent, his solicitors must furnish particulars to the defendant's solicitors of their client's claim on the alternative hypothesis (negligence but not much resulting damage) if these are requested. Otherwise if a payment into Court is made they may find themselves in difficulties if they lose on their principal causation allegations on a trial of a preliminary issue.
3. On a trial of a preliminary issue a Court may ask itself "who essentially was the winner?" and make an order as to costs to follow that event in a case in which it may be prudent to take much more care in formulating the preliminary issues to be tried in order to make it easier for a defendant to limit them by admissions.
4. If for any reason a payment into Court is not an available option in a personal injuries action, defendants' solicitors should bear in mind that a notice admitting facts may be a more effective device for limiting their client's liability for costs than a Calderbank letter.
5. O.33, r.4A is available as a device for limiting the incidence of costs where the proportion of a defendant's liability may be in issue. It is not available where there was no suggestion of any contributory negligence."

Per Brooke L.J. in *Oksuzoglu v. Kay* [1988] 2 All E.R. 361, CA.

62/3/6 Judicial Review
[p.1123] *Add:*

Where in judicial review proceedings the respondent attended the *ex parte* hearing, the question of costs arose, on the particular facts of the case the court fond that it was not merely reasonable for the respondent to attend at the *ex parte* stage; reason and justice supported such an attendance. It was accordingly appropriate to exercise the discretion to award costs to the respondents: *Re Evans (Application for Judicial Review)* October 1, 1998, DC (unreported).

Add:

A successful party's costs may be reduced where his unreasonable conduct of the case has increased the costs. Where the Divisional Court has found against an applicant on some issues concerning the seriousness of the applicant's conduct a reduction may be justified: *R. v. Secretary of State for Transport, ex p. Factortame,* July 6, 1998, CA (unreported).

62/5/4 Discontinuance—costs in cause
[p.1127] *Add:*

Where discontinuance is in fact an acknowledgment of defeat the defendant would normally be entitled to costs of the action unless there was good reason for some other order to be made. It might be proper to make no order for costs or to order the defendant to pay the plaintiff's costs in respect of a particular issue or period of time in respect of which costs have been wasted or unnecessarily incurred as a result of the defendant's conduct of the proceedings. In order to justify an order that the defendant pay the plaintiff's costs it would be necessary to show misconduct within the meaning of O.62, r.10(1). No order for costs would be appropriate if that was fair and just in all circumstances. See *Richard Roberts Holdings Ltd v. Douglas Smith Stimson Partnership* [1998] 2 Con. L.R. 60; *RTZ Pension Property Trust Ltd v. ARC Property Developments Ltd, The Times,* November 26, 1998.

62/5/7 Rule 5(4)—Acceptance of payment into Court
[p.1127] *Add after Hudson v. Elmbridge Borough Council:*

See also *Delta Crompton Cables Ltd v. Copper Cable Co. Ltd* [1997] F.S.R. 850, Jacob J.

Add:

The trial judge has no jurisdiction, after acceptance of payment in, to deal with questions of costs otherwise than as provided for by O.62, r.5: *T. E. Beach (Contractors) Ltd v. Thompson,* June 2, 1998 (unreported).

62/6/6 What are costs?
[p.1130] *Add after Gomba Holdings U.K. v. Minories Finance Ltd:*

The Court has no power to require, against the wishes of the plaintiff mortgagees, that the costs be taxed if not agreed or to direct that the plaintiffs recover no other costs by other means. If the mortgagees seek to deduct an excessive sum, the remedy of the defendant mortgagor is to ask for an account and to challenge the figure which the plaintiff mortgagees seek to charge for their costs. At that stage the Court would not be bound by the contractual provisions and would be entitled to say that the costs sought to be charged were excessive and could make the appropriate order at that point. This would however depend on the mortgagees having behaved unreasonably. *Per* Balcombe L.J. in *Mortgage Funding Corporation plc v. Kashef-Hamadani,* April, 26, 1993, CA, unrep.

62/7/14 Rule 7(4)(b)—Gross sum
[p.1134] *Add at end:*

Where the court refused a plaintiff's application for injunctive relief and discharged the defendant from undertakings pending the trial, the judge ordered the plaintiff to pay £3,500 by way of costs to one defendant and £26,000 to another. The Court of Appeal held that it was within the judge's discretion to make such orders for costs as he thought fit and the order which had been made was entirely a matter for his discretion. Since the trial was to take place shortly it was a proper exercise of the discretion to make the order for immediate payment of a lump sum: *Mayfair Brassware Ltd v. Aqualine International Ltd (Costs Order)* [1998] F.S.R. 135, CA.

Rule 9(1)(b)—Payment into Court **62/9/4** [p.1138]

Add:

The rule requires not only that the amount of the payment into Court be considered but that the basis upon which it is made be taken into account: *Iberotravel Ltd v. Pallas Leasing (No. 32) Ltd,* Transcript: Chant. 96/0678/B, June 19, 1997, CA.

Offer **62/9/9** [p.1139]

Add:

Where a plaintiff, in refusing a *Calderbank* bank offer, obtained nothing from the proceedings that could not equally and more cheaply have been obtained by accepting the offer, it was appropriate that the plaintiff should pay the costs. The court commented that a defendant could not ordinarily escape liability for costs merely by offering in place of litigation some form of alternative dispute resolution. In the case in point the dispute between the parties was the basis of valuation of certain property: *Butcher v. Wolfe, The Times,* November 9, 1998, CA.

Proceeding unreasonably **62/10/6** [p.1141]

Add at end:

In a case where a plaintiff has acted unreasonably by commencing proceedings without giving the defendant a sight of the medical report and the matter is subsequently settled on admission and payment into Court, if the payment in is accepted after the time fixed by the rules the Court may make an order under r.10 disallowing the costs. If the payment in is accepted within the time limit no such order may be made, but on taxation of the plaintiff's bill the taxing officer may exercise the powers conferred by r.10 (see O.62, r.28(1)): *Burrows v. Vauxhall Motors Ltd* (1997) 147 New L.J. 1273, CA.

Maintainer or guarantor of action **62/10/7** [p.1142]

Add after Murphy v. Young & Co.'s Brewery plc:

See also note at 62/2/7 on discretion as to costs.

Effect of rule **62/11/2** [p.1142]

Add:

One possible sanction available to the Court, where legal representatives provided the Court with wholly unrealistic time estimates of a case's duration, was to limit the recovery of costs to the estimated duration of the case: *Re Sasea Finance Ltd (in liquidation), The Times,* December 29, 1997, Sir Richard Scott V.-C.

Pursuing a hopeless case **62/11/5** [p.1143]

Add at end:

(Where at a hearing counsel accepted that an application to suspend a warrant of possession was hopeless and counsel, with a senior partner of the solicitors behind him, made no application for an adjournment nor gave an explanation of the conduct of the solicitors, it was held that the solicitors had had a reasonable opportunity to show cause why the order should not be made and, whilst the original application was doomed to failure, that did not of itself justify a wasted costs order but the absence of explanation suggested playing for time and the commonplace nature of the original application rendered it unnecessary for the judge to insist on a full investigation of the solicitors' motivation: *Woolwich Building Society v. Fineberg* [1998] P.N.L.R. 216, CA.)

Legal aid **62/11/6** [p.1143]

Add after Wall v. Lefever:

The Court of Appeal has set out the procedure to be adopted where an assisted party has been unsuccessful, and the unassisted party seeks to recover costs against the Legal Aid Board or under the wasted costs jurisdiction: *Re O (A Minor) (Costs: liability of the Legal Aid Board)* [1997] 1 F.L.R. 465, CA.

Where a party is legally aided the solicitor is under a duty (see Civil Legal Aid (General) Regulations 1989, reg. 82(2)) to serve notice of revocation or discharge of legal aid on all other parties to the proceedings and also on counsel and on the Court hearing the matter. Failure to do so could amount to unreasonable behaviour and costs suffered by other parties as a result of the failure should not be borne by the Legal Aid Board: *Banks v. Woodhall Duckham Ltd; Banks v. British Steel Corporation; Banks v. Brown Tawse Ltd; Banks v. Humphrey & Glasgow, sub nom. Re Stathams (Wasted Costs Order)* [1997] P.I.Q.R. P464, CA.

Procedure **62/11/14** [p.1144]

Add after Manzanilla Ltd v. Corton Property & Investments Ltd:

Fairness requires that any respondent legal representative must be told very clearly what is alleged to have been done wrong and what is claimed. There should be no pleadings and discovery is not appropriate. The applicant will not be permitted to interrogate the respondent lawyer or vice versa. *Per* Pumfrey J. in *S. v. M. (Wasted Costs Order), The Times,* March 26, 1998.

Add:

An application for a wasted costs order was held to be inappropriate where complicated proceedings requiring detailed investigation into the facts would ensue as the procedure was a summary one to be applied in uninvolved and clear cases where unnecessary costs were incurred. *Manzanilla Ltd v. Corton Property* above followed. The summary procedure might also be inappropriate in circumstances where a solicitor was alleged to be in breach of his professional duty to his client: *Turner Page Music v. Torres Design Associates Ltd, The Times,* August 3, 1998, CA.

62/11/20 **General principles**

[p.1145] *Add after Tolstoy-Miloslavsky v. Aldington:*

The Court of Appeal summarised the principles derived from *Ridehalgh v. Horsefield* [1994] Ch. 205; *Tolstoy-Miloslavsky v. Aldington* [1996] 1 W.L.R. 736 and *Wall v. Lefever, The Times,* August 1, 1997. The power to make a wasted costs order is to be found in section 51 of the Supreme Court Act 1981, the principles to be applied include:

(a) Improper conduct is that which would be so regarded "according to the consensus of professional (including judicial) opinion". Unreasonable conduct "aptly describes conduct which is vexatious, designed to harass the other side rather than advance the resolution of the case and it makes no difference that the conduct is the product of excessive zeal and not improper motive . . . the acid test is whether the conduct permits of a reasonable explanation". Negligent conduct was to be understood "in an untechnical way to denote failure to act with the competence reasonably to be expected of ordinary members of the profession". (*Ridehalgh.*)

(b) "Legal representatives will . . . whether barristers or solicitors, advise clients of the perceived weakness of their case and of the risk of failure. But clients are free to reject their advice and insist that cases be litigated. It is rarely if ever safe for a Court to assume that a hopeless case is being litigated on the advice of the lawyers involved . . . it is however one thing for a legal representative to present on instructions a case which he regards as bound to fail, it is quite another to lend his assistance to proceedings which are an abuse of the process of the Court . . . it is not entirely easy to distinguish by definition between the hopeless case and the case which amounts to an abuse of the process, but in practice it is not hard to say which is which and if there is doubt the legal representative is entitled to the benefit of it." (*Ridehalgh.*)

(c) "A solicitor does not abdicate his professional responsibility when he seeks the advice of counsel." (*Ridehalgh.*) Where leading and junior counsel have put their signatures to a statement of claim this "did not exonerate the solicitors from their obligations to exercise their own independent judgment to consider whether the claim could properly be pursued, they were not entitled to follow counsel blindly". (*Tolstoy.*)

(d) "The jurisdiction to make a wasted costs order must be exercised with care and only in clear cases." (*Tolstoy.*) "It should not be used to create satellite litigation which is as expensive and as complicated as the original litigation. It must be used as a remedy in cases where the need for a wasted costs order is reasonably obvious. It is a summary remedy which is to be used in circumstances where there is a clear picture which indicates that a professional adviser has been negligent". (*Wall v. Lefever.*): *Fletamentos Maritimos SA v. Effjohn International BV,* December 10, 1997, CA, unrep.

62/11/21 **The solicitor and counsel relationship**

[p.1145] *Add after Swedac Ltd v. Magnet & Southern plc:*

In circumstances where there was no evidence that a solicitor had expertise in the field of judicial review, the proposition that a solicitor who acted on counsel's advice had to bear responsibility for that advice in all circumstances could not be supported: *ex p. R,* January 27, 1998, CA, unrep.

Add reference:

Ex p. R, R. v. Luton Family Proceedings Court Justice, ex p. R, January 27, 1998, CA (unreported, trans. ref. FC3 97/6459/D; QBCOF 97/0112/D).

62/11/25 **Legal Aid Act 1988**

[p.1147] *Add:*

Re: O (A Minor) (Costs: Liability of Legal Aid Board) is now reported at [1997] 1 F.L.R. 465, CA.

62/11/29 **Judicial review**

[p.1147] *Add after R. v. Camden London Borough Council, ex p. Martin:*

In circumstances where the application for leave included a claim for interim relief by way of interlocutory injunction, the respondent must be said to be a party in so far as costs have been incurred in response to the application for interlocutory relief and the Court accordingly has jurisdiction to make a wasted costs order in relation to those costs: *Lubrizol Ltd v. Tyndallwoods,* April 8, 1998, unrep., Carnwath J.

Other examples **62/11/30**
Insert new note: [p.1148]

Rule 11(7)—Payment of fees **62/11/31**

In a case where the successful litigant changed solicitors and the second solicitors concluded a compromise between the two litigants which included the taxing fees, when the client became insolvent and failed to pay the fees, it was held that the second firm of solicitors were liable to pay them and in the particular circumstances of the case it was not approrpiate to apportion liability between the two firms of solicitors: *Aspen Property Investment plc v. Ratcliffe* [1997] 2 Costs L.R. 1 (James Mumby, Q.C.).

General note **62/12/1**
Add after Glyne Investments Ltd v. Hill Samuel Life Assurance Ltd: [p.1148]

See note at para. 62/3/7. In group litigation where the defendants mounted a full frontal attack on medical evidence underpinning field research programmes which they themselves had helped to set up, the judge found that the defendants' experts, whose evidence was effectively rebutted by two of the plaintiffs' experts, had, by attempting to hold the basis of their written thoughts, lost intellectual and professional credibility. The Court found that the decision to continue the challenge through the defendants' experts after the plaintiffs' experts had completed their evidence amounted to unreasonable conduct of the litigation. Therefore on the generic medical issues it was directed that the defendants should pay the costs on the indemnity basis, whereas in respect of all other issues, in the cases where the plaintiffs succeeded, costs should be on the standard basis: *Re The British Coal Respiratory Disease Litigation* January 23, 1998, Turner J., (unreported). Where cross-examination of a plaintiff took the form of a totally uncalled for personal attack, the Court made an order for costs on the indemnity basis in favour of the plaintiff for that portion of the trial, *Clark v. Associated Newspapers Ltd, The Times,* January 28, 1998, Lightman J.

Add:

Where a party to litigation acted in a way that could be described as disgraceful or deserving of moral condemnation an order for costs on the indemnity basis could be made: *Wailes v. Stapleton Construction & Commercial Services Ltd; Wailes v. Unum Ltd* [1997] 2 Lloyds' Rep. 112, Newman. J.

Add:

Where defendants in a personal injury action alleged fraud on the part of the plaintiff in exaggerating his injuries such allegations had to be supported by evidence. In personal injury cases allegations of fraud must be specifically pleaded in accordance with O.18. It was therefore appropriate to award costs against the defendants on the indemnity basis: *Cooper v. P&O European Ferries (Dover) Ltd,* October 30, 1998, Miss B. Bucknall, Q.C. (Deputy HCJ) (unreported).

Receiver **62/13/4**
Insert new note:

Interpleader proceedings **62/13/5**

In interpleader proceedings where the claimant fails to appear, the court may direct that the sheriff's and execution creditor's costs be assessed by a Master or District Judge. In those circumstances O.62, r.13 applies. See O.17, r.8 as amended by Rules of the Supreme Court (Amendment) 1998 (S.I. 1998 No. 1898) with effect from September 28, 1998.

Effect of rule **62/15/2**
Insert new note:

Rule 15(2) **62/15/2/1**

Where a client had been provided with an estimate of costs on the basis of an hourly rate shortly prior to trial, it was held to be unreasonable that the client should then be charged a higher hourly rate than he was led to believe would be charged. The estimate of costs up to and including trial did not constitute a binding agreement but the correspondence amounted to a clear and considered indication of the clients maximum liability to the solicitors upon which the client was likely to and did rely. The Law Society's *Guide to Professional Conduct of Solicitors* indicates that the final amount payable should not vary substantially from an estimate given unless the client has been informed of the changed circumstances in writing: *Wong v. Vizards* [1997] 2 Costs L.R. 46 (Toulson J.).

Effect of rule **62/15A/2**
Insert new note:

The position of legal representatives acting under conditional fee agreements **62/15A/3**

The existence of a conditional fee agreement does not alter the relationship between the legal adviser and the client. Legal representatives owe the client exactly the same duties and remain under the same duty to the client to disregard their own interests as if there were no conditional fee agreement. The legal representative also owes the same duties to the Court. There is no reason why the circumstances in which a legal representative acting under a conditional fee [p.1153] agreement can be made personally liable for the costs of a party other than his client should differ from those in which a legal representative who is not acting under a conditional fee agreement would be liable. The existence of a conditional fee agreement should make the legal representative's position as a matter of law no worse, so far as being ordered to pay costs is concerned, than it would be if there were no conditional fee agreement. Legal representatives acting under conditional fee agreements are under no more risk of paying costs personally than they would be if they were not so acting. In addition whether or not conditional fee agreements are properly the subject of professional privilege they are not normally required to be disclosed. *Per* Lord Woolf M.R. in *Hodgson v. Imperial Tobacco Ltd* [1998] 1 W.L.R. 1056; [1998] 2 All E.R. 673, CA.

For a note as to the Indemnity Principle and Conditional Fee Agreements in arbitration cases, see para. 62/A2/27A and *Bevan Ashford v. Geoff Yeandle (Contractors) Ltd (in liquidation)* [1998] 3 W.L.R. 172, Sir Richard Scott V.-C.

62/16/4 Next Friend
[p.1154] *In the first line delete:* "damages and".

62/18/2 Effect of rule
Insert new note:

62/18/2A Calculating the costs of a litigant in person
[p.1156] The exercise is as follows. Find out, in respect of the item, what, at the litigant in person charging rate, the total is. Compare that with two thirds of the notional solicitor rate, give the lower of the two items. That does mean that the bill of costs drawn by the litigant in person must be gone through in some detail item by item. *Per* Jacob J. in *Morris v. Wiltshire & Woodspring District Council*, January 16, 1998, (unreported).

Add new note:

62/18/2/1 Official Receiver
* Where an Official Receiver applies under the Company Directors Disqualification Act 1975, s.6 for disqualification of director he is a "litigant in person" within the meaning of the Litigants in Person (Costs and Expenses) Act 1975, s.1(1) and, although salaried, the costs recoverable by him under RSC O.62, r.18(2) are not limited to disbursements (*Re Minotaur Data Systems Ltd* [1999] 1 W.L.R. 1129, CA; [1999] 3 All E.R. 122, CA).

62/20/2 Privilege
[p.1158] *Add after British Coal Corporation v. Denis Rye Ltd:*

By virtue of the circumstances under which a paying party obtaind documents in the course of taxation, a legal obligation was imposed upon him by operation of law not to make collateral use of them. It would not be a breach of the undertaking to use the documents on an appeal from an English judgment: see *Crest Homes Plc v. Marks* [1987] 1 A.C. 829. Privilege in documents may be waived: see *Clough v. Tameside Health Authority* [1982] 2 All E.R. 971. Absent special considerations, and subject to the court's inherent power to override the privilege where the circumstances demand it, the waiver of privilege for documents relied on in a taxation extended
* only as far as the taxation: see *Goldman v. Hesper* above. *Bourns Inc. v. Raychem Corp. (No. 2)*, [1999] 3 All E.R. 154, CA.

Insert new note:

62/20/2A Power to order disclosure
"The Taxing Officer is exercising a judicial function with substantial financial consequences for the parties [...] if [...] some feature of the case alerts him to the need to make further investigation [...] he may seek further information. No doubt he would begin by asking for a letter or some form of written confirmation or reassurance as appropriate. If this were to prove inadequate he might then make orders for discovery or require affidavit evidence [...] it would theoretically be open to him to order interrogatories." *Per* Judge L.J. in *Bailey v. IBC Vehicles Ltd* [1998] 3 All E.R. 570, CA.

62/28/4 Para. (4)
[p.1164] *Insert after Morrow v. Nadeem:*

For the approach of the Court to delay in civil litigation generally see *Arbuthnot Latham Bank Ltd v. Trafalgar Holdings Ltd; Chishty Coveney & Co v. Raja, The Times*, December 29, 1997, CA; and *Lownes v. Babcock Power Ltd, The Times*, February 19, CA.

Add after Morrow v. Nadeem:

In dealing with delay under r.16(4) of the Matrimonial Causes (Costs) Rules 1988 the Court of Appeal (Mummery L.J.) refused leave to appeal on the basis that good practice required a bill to be lodged within the prescribed time and in default for an extension to be sought. In the event that a bill contrary to good practice was lodged late without any application for an extension it was open to the court to proceed with the taxation, the sanction being that if there was no material explanation of the non compliance the Taxing Officer might disallow all or part of the costs: *Pelling v. Pelling (Costs: Taxation)* [1998] 1 F.L.R. 636, CA.

Add:

Taxation under O.62 is based on a single bill of costs and is designed to produce a single certificate under O.62, r.22(1) for the costs allowed by the Taxing Officer. The Taxing Officer had no power to leave a certificate subsisting against one party subject to an order for costs whilst setting it aside for a second party. The common law rule (see *Re Ewa* [1901] 2 K.B. 642) together with the rules confirm that the intention of the rule is that the disallowance of costs against one jointly and severally liable defendant has the effect of disallowing costs against the joint debtor (*Mainwaring v. Goldtech Investments Ltd, The Times,* November 16, 1998, CA.)

Para 7(c) signature of the bill of costs **62/29/6** [p.1167]

Insert new note:

In signing the bill the solicitor certifies that the contents of the bill are correct: "that signature is no empty formality, the bill specifies the hourly rates applied and the care and attention uplift claimed. If an agreement between the receiving solicitor and his client [...] restricted (say) the hourly rate payable by the client, that hourly rate is the most that can be claimed or recovered on taxation [...]. The signature of the bill of costs under the rules is effectively the certificate of an officer of the Court that the receiving party's solicitors are not seeking to recover in relation to any item more than they have agreed to charge their client [...]". *Per* Henry L.J., in *Bailey v. IBC Vehicles Ltd, The Times,* April 9, 1998, CA.

"[...] in view of the increasing interest taken in (the indemnity principle) by unsuccessful parties to litigation coupled with the developing practice in relation to conditional fees, the extension of the client care letter and contentious business agreements under section 60(3) (of the Solicitors Act 1974), in future copies of the relevant documents (where they exist) or a short written explanation [...] should normally be attached to the bill of costs. This will avoid skirmishes which add unnecessarily to the costs of litigation." *Per* Judge L.J., in *Bailey v. IBC Vehicles Ltd* [1998] All E.R. 570, CA.

No inspection by paying party of privileged documents **62/29/8** [p.1167]

Delete note.

Interest on costs **62/35/12** [p.1177]

Delete Kuwait Airways Corporation v. Iraqi Airways Co. (No. 2) and preceding sentence and insert:

Where the House of Lords reduced an award of damages, the plaintiff was ordered to pay the defendant's costs of appeal to the House of Lords and the defendant's costs in the Court of Appeal on the issue of quantum; held: in respect of the Court of Appeal costs, interest ran from the date on which the order for payment was made by the House of Lords and that order could not be backdated to the date of the Court of Appeal's judgment (*Kuwait Airways Corporation v. Iraqi Airways Co. (No. 2)* [1994] 1 W.L.R. 985, CA, overruled). The defendant was entitled to interest on the proportion of damages and costs paid to the plaintiff pursuant to orders made by the Judge and the Court of Appeal and made repayable to the defendant following appeal to the House of Lords: *Nykredit Mortgage Bank plc v. Edward Erdman Group Ltd (No. 2)* [1997] 1 W.L.R. 1627, HL.

Fees to counsel **62/A2/4** [p.1180]

Add new note:

Para. 2(1)(a)—"Before taxation" **62/A2/4A**

"Before taxation" means before the actual taxation by the taxing officer and not the commencement of the taxation proceedings in accordance with rule 29. The amount of the fee is agreed if the solicitor assents to or accepts as payable the amount of the fee in counsel's fee note. The amount of the fee can be agreed by the unilateral act of the solicitor following the receipt of counsel's fee note. If the solicitor does not challenge the amount of counsel's fees, within the three month period allowed by the professional rules of both professions, he may be taken to have assented to and accepted as payable and thereby agreed the amount of counsel's fees. Similarly if the solicitor lodges a signed bill of costs setting out, without qualification, as disbursements counsel's fees he may be taken to be representing to the Court that he assents to and accepts as payable counsel's fees in the amounts set out. *Per* Morland J. in *Spath Holme Ltd v. Chairman of the Greater Manchester and Lancashire Rent Assessment Committee (No. 2)* [1998] 3 All E.R. 909 (Morland J.).

Certificate for three counsel **62/A2/13** [p.1183]

Add:

In deciding whether to grant a certificate for three counsel the court will apply a test of reasonableness, that being the general test in respect of taxation under the current rules. That test would permit some expenditure which could not be described as necessary but which would provide for the convenient conduct of the litigation. The court was better placed than the Taxing

Masters to decide the issue of three counsel: *Kuwait Airways Corporation v. Iraqi Airways Co.*, July 30, 1998 (Mance J.) (unreported).

62/A2/15 Brief Fee—quantum
[p1184] *Insert new note:*

62/A2/15/1 Written submissions

The court made observations on the subject of written closing submissions at the end of a lengthy review of taxation:

"In the hearing of the preliminary issue in this review of taxation the court was occupied for nine hearing days, a daily transcript was obtained and there were in excess of 5,000 documents including original documents before the court. The issues were complex and at the conclusion of the evidence the matter was adjournd so that written submissions could be prepared. These were detailed and of assistance to the court.

As Mr Justice Hobhouse, as he then was, said in *Loveday v. Renton (No. 2)* [1992] 3 All E.R. at 191, final submissions are an ordinary part of the conduct of a trial by a barrister on behalf of his client as part of the work which he accepts an obligation to perform in accepting the brief fee and for which he is remunerated by the brief fee and the agreed refreshers. Thus the preparation of final submissions, whether or not reduced into the form of a written document, is all work that has to be done in any event by counsel.

There may however be circumstances where the case is properly regarded as sufficiently complex or exceptional not to have been covered by the brief fee, and hence for a separate fee to have been specifically agreed for the peparation of written submissions by counsel.

Where such an agreement is made it would in my judgment be perfectly proper for the Taxing Master to consider it allowable in principle subject to taxation of the amount when taxing the bill of costs."

Per Nelson J. in *Chohan v. Times Newspapers Ltd*, Sepember 7, 1998 (unreported).

62/A2/19 Family Division
[p.1185] *After sub-paragraph (2) add:*

Proceedings under Part IV of the Family Law Act 1996 are not included in the category of prescribed family proceedings: see S.I. 1997 No. 2394.

Delete paragraph 2 beginning "the only family proceedings" and substitute:

All other family proceedings are governed by the RSC unless they are legally aided, when the Legal Aid in Civil Proceedings (Remuneration) Regulations 1994 (S.I. 1994 No. 228) which came into force February 25, 1994 apply under the provisions of Regulations 3(2)(C) of the Legal Aid in Family Proceedings (Remuneration) Regulations 1991 as amended by S.I. 1994 No. 230. The provisions of the 1994 Regulations are set out in Vol. 2, p.1445.

62/A2/27A The indemnity principle
[p.1188] *In line 7 delete* "mitigation", *insert* "litigation". *After Gundry v. Sainsbury delete text and reference to British Waterways Board v. Norman.*

After Universal Thermosensors v. Hibben delete remaining text.

Add:

The indemnity principle is to be applied on an item by item basis rather than on a global basis "where applicable the figures in a contentious business agreement provide both a measure and a ceiling for each recoverable item of costs", *per* Sir Brian Neill, *The General of Berne Insurance Co. v. Jardine Reinsurance Management* [1998] 2 All E.R. 301, CA. That judgment related to a contentious business agreement where the hourly rate was agreed. The principle applies even where there is no contentious business agreement: "In my judgment there should be no distinction between those cases where a formal contentious business agreement is in place and which are governed by section 60(3) of the Solicitors Act 1974 and other cases where there is an agreement partly evidenced in writing, an unwritten agreement or no agreement at all, but merely an understanding arising perhaps from a long established relationship . . .": *Nederlandse Reassurantie Groep Holding NV v. Bacon & Woodrow*, April 21, 1998, Tucker, J., unrep.

"In my judgment there is nothing unlawful in a solicitor acting for a party to litigation agreeing to forego all or part of his fee if he loses provided that he does not seek to recover more than his ordinary profit costs and disbursements if he wins." *Per* Millett L.J. in *Thai Trading Co. v. Taylor*, [1998] 2 W.L.R. 893, CA. The Court went on to overrule the decisions in *British Waterways Board v. Norman* (1993) 26 H.L.R. 232, DC, and *Aratra Potato Co. Ltd v. Taylor Joynson Garrett* [1995] 4 All E.R. 695, Garland J.

Conditional fee agreements are permitted by section 58 of the Courts and Legal Services Act 1990 (see Part 15(E) and 15(F) for Conditional Fee Agreements Order and Regulations 1995). A conditional fee agreement relating to a claim to be determined by arbitration was held not to be void for champerty. The Court held that the effect of the Courts and Legal Services Act 1990 and the 1995 Conditional Fee Agreements Order and Regulations which have been substantially complied with was not champertous. *Bevan Ashford v. Geoff Yeandle (Contractors) Ltd (in liquidation),* [1998] 3 W.L.R. 172, Sir Richard Scott V.-C.

The hourly rate **62/A2/28** [p.118]

Add:

L v. L (Legal Aid Taxation) is now reported at [1996] 1 F.S.R. 873, CA.

Add at end:

If a party chooses a particular status or type of solicitor or counsel or one located in a particular area then the costs will have been reasonably incurred if, having regard to the circumstances, a reasonable choice has been made. The question to be asked is whether the solicitor chosen is the sort of solicitor that a person would have instructed with a view to the proper conduct of his case in minimising the costs of litigation. *Per* Hooper J. review of taxation, *A v. F Co. Ltd; S v. F Co. Ltd,* (1996) SCTO Digest No. 13.

Add after Jones v. Secretary of State for Wales & Vale of Glamorgan Borough Council:

Where litigation has been appropriately conducted by a senior partner it is proper to allow an uplift on the hourly rate to take account of the seniority of the solicitor conducting the litigation. The rates to be allowed in any geographical area should be regularly updated and guidance issued by District Judges to local law Societies was to be welcomed. *Pritchard v. Ford Motor Co. Ltd; Riccio v. Ford Motor Co. Ltd* [1997] 1 Costs L.R. 39 (Hooper J.).

Costs of preparing the bill of costs **62/A2/37** [p.1191]

Insert new note:

Amendment of bill of costs **62/A2/37A**

There is no reason in principle why somebody who has put forward a claim (*i.e.* bill of costs) should not amend it whether that course should be permitted is a matter for the discretion of the Court. The normal rule is that amendments will be allowed provided the opposite party is not prejudiced in some way, other than as to costs.

The Courts have never said that one may not amend to increase the amount claimed because there might have been an offer on the basis of the original claim. Even where that has happened it is a matter which the Court can, when it comes to consider the question of costs of the taxation or proceedings before it, take into account.

There is a liability to pay interest on costs, that is a point which can be taken into account in the general exercise of the Court's discretion in relation to the costs of the taxation process. Furthermore it is possible for the paying party to issue an application under O.62, r.28 in relation to the extra costs of other matters that have arisen due to the original bill. They would have to show misconduct and neglect to bring themselves within the rule but it is a matter which the Court can plainly deploy where there has been an amendment. *Per* Jacob J. in *Morris v. Wiltshire & Woodspring District Council, Review of Taxation,* January 16, 1998, unrep.

Rights of audience on taxation **62/A2/38** [p.1191]

Add:

As to rights of audience in Chambers, see *Re H-S (Minors) (Chambers Proceedings: Right of Audience) The Times,* February 25, 1998, CA.

Costs of the Reference **62/B/12**

Add after Everglade Maritime Inc v. Schiffahrtsgesellschaft Detlaf Von Appen mbH The Maria:

Where an arbitrator made a final award in which he ruled in favour of the applicants on some issues and in favour of the respondent on others and ordered the applicants to pay the respondent costs, and in giving reasons for the decision the arbitrator relied on two matters which the parties had not raised, the court found that the arbitrator had not acted in accordance with the general duty, under s.33 of the Act, to act fairly and impartially between the parties. His failure to raise these matters with the parties amounted to a serious irregularity within the meaning of s.63(2) of the Arbitration Act 1996. *Gbangbola v. Smith and Sherriff Ltd* [1998] 3 All E.R. 730 (Judge Lloyd, Q.C., Technology and Construction Court).

Lands Tribunal **62/B/47** [p.1209]

Add:

Where the Lands Tribunal made an award of compensation in 1988 which was subsequently set aside and the matter remitted for redetermination, the Tribunal redetermining the compensation in 1991, interest on costs ran from the date of the 1991 award which was the only effective award on the reference: *Barclays Bank plc v. Kent County Council* [1998] R.V.R. 74, CA.

Town and Country Planning (Assessment of Environment Effects) Regulations 1988 **62/B/55** [p.1211]

Insert new note:

Where the Secretary of State was in breach of an obligation imposed upon him by the statutory provisions it was a matter to be taken into account when awarding costs even though the breach had no effect on the outcome of the proceedings. The Court had its own interest in preserving the high standards of civil administration and it was appropriate to mark its disapproval of the breach by depriving the Secretary of State of a proportion of his costs: *Berkeley v. Secretary of State for the Environment (No. 2), The Times,* April 7, 1998, CA.

62/B/83 **Group Actions**
[p.1216] *Add:*

Where lead actions were fought and lost defendants were not necessarily entitled to all of their costs against the losing plaintiff. Different considerations may arise in group litigation which it may be proper for the Court to reflect in the order for costs. The purpose of a common costs order was to permit a group of plaintiffs whose individual means and probable damages were modest to spread the costs risk amongst all of them in the event of the lead plaintiffs losing, otherwise the burden on the lead plantiffs would be intolerable and no plaintiff would be prepared to lead. If common issues were tried on a preliminary basis a costs sharing scheme might be sensibly limited to those issues but if the litigation proceeded by lead actions it must be contemplated that the group will stand behind the lead plaintiffs for the whole of their costs: *Ochwat v. Watson Burton*, February 18, 1998, Smith J. (unreported).

62/B/120 **Bankrupt**
[p.1221] *Add:*

A creditor who serves a statutory demand, without judgment having already been given in his favour, does so at his own risk on costs. The service of a statutory demand is a step in the bankruptcy proceedings and a cause of action in its own right: *Re A Debtor (No. 620 of 1997), The Times*, June 19, 1998 (Hart J.).

When, following service of the petition, the debt is paid, the appropriate order for costs must reflect the ultimate success of the creditors but must also reflect any avoidable defects in the creditor's proceedings. Where substantial additional costs were incurred, quite unnecessarily by the debtor, because of, *e.g.* adjournments, the proper order should be no order as to costs: *Re A Debtor (No. 510 of 1997), The Times*, June 18, 1998 (Mr Stanley Burnton, Q.C.).

Where a creditor served a statutory demand for payment of taxed costs, the fact that there was a pending review in respect of the taxation was not sufficient ground to set aside the statutory demand: *Cartwright v. Staffordshire & Moorlands District Council* [1998] B.P.I.R. 328, CA.

62/B/128 **Counterclaim**
[p.1223] *Add:*

It is wrong in principle for a judge, having ordered part of a counterclaim to be struck out, to then order that any further proceedings on the counterclaim be stayed until the defendant had complied with an order to pay costs to the plaintiffs. The error was in making an order which at one and the same time allowed part of the counterclaim to proceed and then stayed it until payment of costs which had only been ordered to be paid by the same order. *Theakston v. Matthews, The Times*, April 13, 1998, CA.

62/B/132 **Liquidator**
[p.1223] *Insert new note:*

62/B/132/1 **Ombudsman**

Where two former trustees of a pension fund successfully appealed against a finding of the Pensions Ombudsman and the Ombudsman had participated in the appeal to assist the Court, the guiding principle was to assess the extent to which the appellant's costs had been increased by the Ombudsman's participation. The Court ordered the Ombudsman to pay the increase but otherwise each side was to bear its own costs: *Elliott v. Pensions Ombudsman* (1997) 94(45) L.S.Gaz. 27.

62/B/137 **Post judgment costs**
[p.1224] *Add:*

Where an action was settled by a Tomlin Order which provided for payment of "the costs of the action" it was held that although solicitors' fees reasonably incurred in ensuring that the settlement was carried into effect were recoverable as costs of action, disbursements, such as the hire of a structural expert, could not be regarded as "costs of the action". It should be borne in mind that this decision was based on the interpretation of the wording of the Tomlin Order: *Wallace v. Brian Gale & Associates, The Times*, March 5, 1998, CA.

62/B/150 **Costs, indemnity as to**
[p.1226] *Add after Murphy v. Young & Co.'s Brewery plc:*

See note at para. 62/2/7 discretion as to costs.

62/B/151 **Powers of the court as to costs**
[p.1226] *Add at end of first paragraph:*

A trustee who defends proceedings brought against him in a representative capacity without obtaining a *Beddoe* order will be at risk as to costs. If the court would not have given authority to defend the proceedings in accordance with the principles set out in *Re Beddoe* it would not allow the costs to be paid out of the trust funds either, even if the trustee was advised by counsel that he had a good defence to the claim: *Singh v. Bhasin, The Times*, August 21, 1998 (Mr Alan Boyle, Q.C.).

Add after Re Charge Card Services Ltd:

The discretion to make pre-emptive costs orders, even in cases involving public interest challenges, should be exercised only in the most exceptional circumstances, necessary conditions were that the issues raised were truly ones of general public importance and that the Court had sufficient appreciation of the merits of the claim that it could conclude that it was in the public interest to make the order. The Court also had to have regard to the financial resources of the applicant and the respondent and the amount of costs likely to be in issue: *R. v. Lord Chancellor, ex p. Child Poverty Action Group*; *R. v. DPP, ex p. Bull*, *The Times*, February 27, 1998, DC.

The practice in pre-emptive costs applications is that they should be *inter partes* (see RSC, O.15, r.12A): *Weth v. HM Attorney General*, November 21, 1997, L. Collins, Q.C., Deputy High Court Judge (unreported)

Plaintiff's expenses **62/B/155** [p.1229]

Add:

As to obtaining authority for the expenses of a legally aided plaintiff see *R. v. Legal Aid Board No. 15 Area (Merseyside), ex p. Eccleston*, Sedley J., April 3, 1998, unrep. (See Note at 16D–115.)

PRACTICE DIRECTION NO. 1 OF 1996 **62/C/17** [p.1237]

Delete this Practice Direction and insert Practice Direction No. 2 of 1998:

PRACTICE DIRECTION NO. 2 OF 1998 QUEEN'S BENCH DIVISION—PERSONAL INJURY CASES

Interlocutory Fees: Revised Scales from August 1, 1998—This list of scale fees, which was last increased in March 1996, has been the subject of discussion between the Chief Master and the General Council of the Bar. A list of new fees relating to such cases, which will come into operation in respect of instructions and briefs delivered on or after August 1, 1998, is set out below. **62/C/17**

The fees in the list are the basic amounts proper to be allowed upon taxation in the normal run of personal injury claims where the item has been dealt with fully, on the assumption that the value of the action exceeds £50,000. Save in the case of conference fees, each fee is intended to cover any necessary perusal of papers in connection with the item. A lower fee may be appropriate where the item has not been dealt with comprehensively, was exceptionally simple or if the value of the action when commenced was below £50,000. If a higher fee has been agreed it will need to be justified on taxation.

The fees of Queen's Counsel have been omitted on the basis that they will not ordnarily be instructed in the normal run of personal injury cases.

Item	**Basic fees to be allowed in the normal run of personal injury cases**
Statement of claim	£90.00
Defence without counterclaim	£80.00
Defence (plain submission)	£26.50
Particulars	
request	£42.50
answers	£53.00
Reply with or without defence to counterclaim	£53.00
Third party notice (not to stand as statement of claim	£53.00
Interrogatories and answers	£80.00
Advice on evidence	£106.00
Opinion (including opinion on appeal)	£90.00
Opinion on liability	£95.00
Opinion on quantum	£106.00
Opinion on liability and quantum	£160.00
Opinion on liability, quantum and evidence	£212.00
Notice of appeal to Court of Appeal and counternotice	£80.00

Item	Basic fees to be allowed in the normal run of personal injury cases
Brief on summons before master (short summons)	£132.50
Conference fees (junior counsel)	
first half hour	£64.00
each succeeding half hour	£37.00

Practice Direction dated July 31, 1998

62/C/35B **Practice Direction (Commercial Court: Costs)**

Insert Supreme Court Taxing Office Practice Note No. 1 of 1998 after the above Practice Direction:

SUPREME COURT TAXING OFFICE PRACTICE NOTE NO. 1 OF 1998: SUMMONS UNDER O.62, R.28

62/C/35C Attention is drawn to *Supreme Court Taxing Office Practice Direction (No. 2 of 1992) Direction 3: Wasted Costs Orders and Delay.* The number of such Summonses (especially those seeking a disallowance of costs because of delay on the part of the receiving party) has been steadily increasing. No problems arise where the taxation is to be conducted by a Taxing Master or a Deputy Taxing Master because the Summons can be given the same return day as the taxation to which it relates and will be listed for hearing by the Master or Deputy Master who conducts the taxation. However where the taxation is to be conducted by a Taxing Officer the Summons cannot be heard by him or her and must be heard by a Taxing Master (O.62, r.28(7)). In such cases the Summons Clerk endeavours to give the Summons a return date and time which immediately precedes the time of the taxation so that it may be heard at a time which will be most convenient to the parties. However the following difficulties may occur:

1. Most such r.28 Summonses are taken out in the week preceding the date of the relevant taxation. This places an unduly heavy burden on the Summons Clerk to complete all the arrangements and also causes logistical difficulties in ensuring that the relevant file and bill is given to the Master before the hearing without disrupting the Taxing Officer's preparation for the taxation.
2. R. 28 Summonses in practice delay the taxation hearing before the Taxing Officer. They also delay other hearings in the list of the Master before whom the Summons is heard.
3. In a significant number of cases it is inappropriate to conclude the hearing of the r.28 Summons before the completion of the taxation to which it relates.

In an effort to alleviate these difficulties those wishing to take out such Summonses should:

1. Issue the Summons as soon as possible after it has become clear that the parties are unable to reach agreement, and not leave the issue of the Summons until the week preceding the date of taxation.
2. Give an accurate estimate of the time required for the hearing of the Summons and serve with the Summons any evidence relied on in support of the application, as is required by O.32, r.3(2)(c).

It is intended that the current practice of giving r.28 Summonses a return date and time immediately preceding the time appointed for the taxation will, so far as possible, continue.

If however no Master is available to hear the Summons at that time it will be listed to be heard by the Sitting Master at 10 a.m. on the day appointed for the taxation.

In practice the primary penalties sought and imposed in rule 28 Summonses complaining of delay are: (i) a disallowance equivalent to interest; (ii) disallowance of the costs of the taxation proceedings and the taxing fee. It is also common for additional remedies in respect of a total or partial disallowance of the costs claimed in the bill to be sought. It is possible for the paying party to achieve these objectives in many cases without resorting to r.28. The following suggestions are made:

1. Raising in open correspondence that, if appropriate remedies are not provided by agreement, a penalty as to the costs of taxation (including the taxing fee) will be sought from the Taxing Officer under RSC, O.62, r.27.
2. Further or alternatively indicating that, if additional remedies are appropriate but cannot be agreed a r.28 Summons will be issued after the taxation hearing.
3. The parties should remember that the Taxing Officer has power, under O.62, r.21, to extend the period within which the party is required to begin proceedings for taxation or to do anything in or in connection with those proceedings, on such terms (if any) as he thinks just, even though the application for extension is not made until after the expiration of that period. An appropriate application to the Taxing Officer whether by the Receiving Party or the Paying Party may therefore provide the appropriate remedy.

In some cases a r.28 Summons is issued seeking the total disallowance of the bill. Where the Master is satisfied that such disallowance is sought for tactical purposes only, without any real prospect of obtaining such a disallowance, the Summons may be dismissed with costs on the indemnity basis.

P. T. HURST
Chief Master

PRACTICE NOTE NO. 2 OF 1998, AUGUST 25, 1998
THE INDEMNITY PRINCIPLE: RECENT CASES

Summary of Current Position

1. This note summarises the indemnity principle and some recent cases dealing with it and then sets out certain changes in practice which are necessary in order to take account of those cases. **62/C/35D**

2. The indemnity principle is as follows: an order for costs between parties allows the receiving party to claim from the paying party only an indemnity in respect of the costs covered by the order. Receiving parties cannot therefore recover a sum in excess of their liability to their own solicitors: *Gundry v. Sainsbury* [1910] 1 K.B. 645.

3. On the taxation of a bill, the indemnity principle is to be applied on an item by item basis rather than on a global basis. If the receiving parties and their solicitors have made an agreement limiting the maximum hourly rates payable by the receiving parties or limiting the maximum costs of any other item, that agreement provides both a measue and a ceiling for the hourly rate or the other item in question: *General of Berne Insurance Co. v. Jardine Reinsurance Management* [1998] 2 All E.R. 301, CA.

4. The item by item approach is applicable whether or not the receiving parties and their solicitors have entered into a contentious business agreement: *Nederlandse Reassurantie Groep Holding NV v. Bacon & Woodrow*, April 21, 1998, Review of Taxation, Tucker J. (unreported). Tucker J. stated:

"In my judgment there should be no distinction between those cases where a formal CBA [contentious business agreement] is in place and which are governed by section 60(3) of the 1974 Act and other cases where there is an agreement partly evidenced in writing, an unwritten agreement, or no agreement at all, but merely an understanding arising perhaps from a long-standing relationship ... It is desirable that there should be uniformity in approaches to taxation, and highly undesirable and confusing for different approaches to be adopted according to whether any agreement can be brought within the statutory definition of a CBA. In any event I agree with the editors of the White Book that section 60(3) does no more than express the Common Law doctrine under which costs are given to the successful party by way of indemnity only. I take the view that if in a CBA case an item by item approach should be adopted (which I take to be the effect of the decision of Court of Appeal in *The General of Berne*) then there is no warrant for the adoption of any different approach in other cases."

5. RSC, O.62, r.29(7)(c)(iii) requires the receiving parties' solicitor to sign the bill of costs. In relation to each and every item in that bill that signature is in effect a certificate by the receiving parties' solicitor that the costs claimed for that item do not exceed the costs paid or payable by the receiving parties to their solicitors: *Bailey v. IBC Vehicles Ltd* [1998] 3 All E.R. 570, CA.

6. Where the receiving parties and their solicitors have made an agreement which restricts the hourly rates payable in respect of relevant costs, the hourly rates claimed in the bill of costs should normally coincide with the terms of that agreement: *Bailey v. IBC Vehicles Ltd*, above.

7. In future, information concerning the charging arrangements between the receiving parties and their solicitors should be sent with the bill of costs served on the paying parties: *Bailey v. IBC Vehicles Ltd*, above.

8. The case law summarised above makes clear the obligation placed upon receiving parties and their solicitors to reveal to the paying parties information as to the relevant terms of any agreement or arrangement they have made as to the level or method of charging. The amount and detail of the information to be given must be such as to enable the paying parties to consider the bill of costs served and satisfy themselves that the indemnity principle will not be breached.

9. Further, RSC, O.62, r.29(7)(c)(iii) in effect obliges solicitors for receiving parties to ensure that the bill of costs drawn for taxation is not inconsistent with the terms of any agreement or arrangement fixing or limiting costs and will not lead to a breach of the indemnity principle. In this respect solicitors for receiving parties should take into account the inference that the appropriate rates to claim in the bill should not exceed the rates which the receiving parties have been charged during the course of the proceedings unless for example the solicitors have expressly reserved the right to claim at the conclusion of the proceedings further sums in respect of work already done.

Modification of Taxation Practice

10. These recent decisions require some modifications to be made to taxation practice. In some respects, in some cases, it will not now be possible realistically to comply with the provisions of *SCTO Practice Direction No. 2 of 1992*, in particular paragraphs 1.1, 1.2, 1.5, 1.6, 1.7 and 1.15.

11. It is recognised that agreements and correspondence made or written between solicitors and clients often contain information which is privileged and which may be commercially sensitive. This important point has been taken into account in formulating the changes in taxation practice set out below.

12.(1) In this Note the expression "written agreement or arrangement between solicitor and client" includes any letter or other written information provided by the solicitor to the client explaining how the solicitor's charges are to be calculated.

(2) Receiving parties must give to paying parties a short but adequate written explanation of any agreement or arrangement between solicitor and client which affects the costs claimed againts the paying parties.

The explanation may precede the narrative of the bill or be set out in a separate document attached to the bill served on the paying parties and to the bill filed with the court when proceedings for taxation are commenced.

(3) The receiving parties must attach to the copy of the bill filed with the court a *full copy* of any written agreement or arrangement between solicitor and client which affects the costs claimed in that bill. The Taxing Officer will compare that copy with the written explanation included or served with the bill. If not satisfied that the written explanation given is adequate, the Taxing Officer will give such directions or order as to further disclosure as may be appropriate.

(4) Every bill filed for taxation must contain a certificate substantially in the form set out below which is signed by the solicitor whose bill it is, or, if the costs are due to a firm, by a partner of that firm. The name of the solicitor signing must also be shown in block letters.

> I certify that this bill is both accurate and complete and that, in relation to each and every item it covers, the costs claimed herein do not exceed the costs which the receiving party/parties is/are required to pay me/my firm.

(5) If the costs to be taxed are affected by any written agreement or arrangement between solicitor and client which fixes hourly rates payable by the receiving parties to their solicitors, the bill drawn for taxation may claim costs on the basis of those hourly rates instead of claiming costs on the basis of expense rates and mark-up thereon (the A + B formula).

(6) Paragraphs (2), (3), (4), and (5) above do not apply to employed solicitors in respect of work done on behalf of their employers.

(7) The changes in pactice set out in this Note are to come into operation immediately save to the following extent: in bills filed for taxation before November 1, 1998 the receiving parties are not obliged to supply the new information referred to in paragraph (2) above or the new certificate referred to in paragraph (4) above unless the Taxing Officer so orders. However, in all such cases if the paying parties request the Taxing Officer so to order, the receiving parties will be given reasonable notice to show cause why such an order should not be made. If reasonable notice cannot be given before the date fixed for taxation the Taxing Officer may fix a new date for the hearing and/or fix additional dates for further hearings.

ORDER 70

OBTAINING EVIDENCE FOR FOREIGN COURTS, ETC.

General principles for compliance with foreign request for evidence (rr.1–6) **70/6/3**
Add at end: [p.1321] *

A request could not be denied on the ground of "fishing" if there was sufficient reason to believe that the witness could give relevant evidence to issues in the action and the issue of relevance fell to be determined by the foreign court. It was necessary however to protect witnesses from oppressive requirements such as submitting them to wide ranging examination while at the same time they were under threat of being added as defendants. The test of whether to disallow the request was similar to that applied in setting aside a domestic *subpoena* (*First American Corporation v. Zayed* [1999] 1 W.L.R. 1154, CA, *sub nom. First American Corporation v. Al-Nahyan* [1998] 4 All E.R. 439, CA).

ORDER 71

RECIPROCAL ENFORCEMENT OF JUDGMENTS AND ENFORCEMENT OF EUROPEAN COMMUNITY JUDGMENTS AND RECOMMENDATIONS ETC. UNDER THE MERCHANT SHIPPING (LINER CONFERENCES) ACT 1982

71/15 Interpretation
Add new note:

71/15/1 Amendment
[p.1344] By the European Communities (Enforcement of Community Judgments) (Amendment) Order 1968 (S.I. 1998 No. 1259) the 1972 Order was amended to provide for the registration and enforcement as Community judgments of awards of costs made by the Office of Harmonisation in the Internal Market, the institution which administers the Community trade mark.

ORDER 72

COMMERCIAL ACTIONS

72/2/5 Setting Down and Skeleton Arguments—Practice Direction
[p.1358] *This Practice Direction is now reported at* [1998] 1 W.L.R. 668; [1998] 2 All E.R. 672.

72/A9 V1. Summonses inter partes
[p.1371] *The Practice Direction of March 6, 1998 is now reported at* [1998]; 1 W.L.R. 668; [1998] 2 All E.R. 672.

APPENDIX III SPECIMEN TIME-TABLE FOR HEAVY SUMMONSES

72/A49 *The Practice Direction of March 6, 1998 is now reported at* [1998] 1 W.L.R. 668; [1998] 2 All E.R. 672.
[p.1403]

ORDER 73

APPLICATIONS RELATING TO ARBITRATION

73/31 Enforcement of awards
[p.1425] *In r.31(2)(c) substitute for the words* "may be made" *the words* "shall be made", *RSC(A) 1998 (S.I. 1998 No. 1898), r.15*

73/31/2 Affidavit in support of application
Insert new note:

73/31/2 HISTORY OF RULE—RSC(A) 1998 (S.I. 1998 No. 1898), r.15 amended r.31(2)(c).
[p.1425]

ORDER 75

ADMIRALTY PROCEEDINGS

(2) Wages actions
75/1/23 *Add as a new penultimate paragraph:*
[p.1434] The above-mentioned Orders in Council additionally require a statement to the effect that the consular officer of the state concerned has been notified of the intention to invoke the jurisdiction of the court and has not objected within a period of two weeks from the date of such

notification to be included among the details on which the claim is based at the time when the proceedings are commenced.

Duration of Admiralty Writ in personam for service out of the jurisdiction **75/4/3** [p.1437]

Delete text of note and substitute:

The validity of a writ in personam in admiralty proceedings for service out of the jurisdiction (other than a concurrent writ) is six months in the first instance beginning with the date of issue. Where the original writ was issued not for service out of the jurisdiction, then provided a concurrent writ for service out of the jurisdiction is issued within the period of four months from the date of issue of the original writ, the concurrent writ is valid for service out of the jurisdiction in the just instance for six months beginning with the date of issue of the original writ, see O.6, r.8(1)(b) and (1A)(b). If the aforesaid proviso cannot be complied with, it will be necessary to seek an extension to the validity of the original domestic writ.

Para. (7) "... the United Kingdom has undertaken ..." **75/5/10** [p.1440]

Add:

On April 30, 1998 the U.K. gave a 12 months' notification to the above mentioned states of its intention to terminate the 1968 Treaty and related Protocols. Earlier termination might be achieved by mutual consent of the U.K. and a particular state, as has happened in respect of Armenia with effect from August 11, 1998.

Practice **75/12/3** [p.1446]

Add at end of second paragraph:

Mooring charges do not constitute "ship dues" within the meaning of s.26(3) of the Harbours Act 1964 and as defined by s.57(1) of the 1964 Act. Accordingly there is no power to distain for non-payment of mooring charges under s.44 of the Harbours, Docks and Piers Clauses Act 1847: see *R. v. Carrick District Council, ex p. Prankerd, (The Winnie Rigg)* [1998] 2 Lloyd's Rep. 675.

Note **75/23A/2** [p.1460]

Add at end:

The fees and commission paid by the Marshal to Brokers in addition to their reasonable expenses for carrying out a Judicial sale of a vessel are as follows:

Scale of valuation Fees as from May 25, 1998

Not exceeding £20,000: £200
Exceeding £20,000: £400
Where the condition of the ship and/or the state of the market make it advisable that there should be a dual valuation for both trading and demolition purposes the full fee will apply in respect of the valuation for trading and in addition a fee at half the above rates will apply in respect of the valuation for demolition.

Scale of Commission as from May 25, 1998

6 per cent on the first £5,000
5 per cent on the next £10,000 up to £15,000
3 per cent on the next £15,000 up to £30,000
1 per cent on the balance over £30,000.

Limitation action **75/37/2** [p.1468]

Add at end of first paragraph:

The Court of Appeal has upheld the finding that the decree or declaration can be obtained without liability being first established or admitted: see report of appeal [1998] 2 Lloyd's Rep. 461.

Add at end:

Charterers cannot limit their liability under the 1976 Convention in respect of claims brought by owners against them: see *Aegean Sea Traders Corporation v. Repsol Petroleo SA and Another* [1998] 2 Lloyd's Rep. 39.

In *Herceg Novi (Owners) v. Ming Galaxy (Owners)* [1998] 4 All E.R. 238; [1998] 2 Lloyd's Rep. 454, CA, the Court held that the 1976 Convention was not an internationally sanctioned and objective view of where substantial justice was viewed as lying, but was simply the view of some 30 states. Moreover, the preference for the 1976 convention had no greater justification than for the 1957 regime and, in terms of abstract justice, neither convention was objectively more just than the other. Accordingly, since substantial justice would be done in Singapore, the appeal would be allowed and an unconditional stay of the English action would be granted.

Limitation fund and interest **75/37/5** [p.1469]

Add:

The rate of interest is now:

(a) where the occurrence takes place before September 1, 1998 but the fund is constituted on or after that date—
  (i) 12 per cent from the date of the occurrence until December 31, 1994;
  (ii) 6.75 per cent on and after January 1, 1995 until August 31, 1998; and
  (iii) 8.5 per cent on and after September 1, 1998; or
(b) where the occurrence takes place on or after September 1, 1998, 8.5 per cent.

(Merchant Shipping (Liability of Shipowners and Others) (Rate of Interest) Order 1998 (S.I. 1998 No. 1795)).

75/42/8 **Proved recoverable amount**
[p.1476] *The case of Kumanova v. Massira is now reported at* [1998] 2 Lloyd's Rep. 301.

ORDER 78

COUNTY COURT PROCEEDINGS TRANSFERRED OR REMOVED TO HIGH COURT

78/2/2 **Transfer for enforcement**
[p.1497] *Delete words* "Section 2013" *and substitute words* "Section 20B". *Delete words* "Practice Direction (County Court Orders Enforcement) [1991] 1 W.L.R. 438" *and substitute words* "Practice Direction (County Court Order: Enforcement) [1998] 1 W.L.R. 1557".

ORDER 81

PARTNERS

81/1/21 **Foreign firms**
[p.1529] *Add at end of paragraph:*

The question of whether a Swiss general partnership should be sued in English proceedings in the name of the firm or in the name of the individual partners was considered by the Court of Appeal in *Oxnard Financing SA v. Rahn* [1998] 1 W.L.R. 1465; [1998] 3 All E.R. 19, CA. Under Swiss Law a general partnership was not a corporation but it was an entity distinct from the individual partners in certain respects. It could make contracts in its name, it could sue and be sued in its own name and could own property. The individual partners were liable for the debts of the partnership but could only be sued if a partner became bankrupt or the partnership was dissolved. The plaintiffs had sued the defendants by naming the individual partners in the writ and the defendants sought to set aside the writ on the ground that they could not be sued as individuals under Swiss Law. The Court of Appeal held that as English Law was the *lex fori* and governed the procedure and procedure included how parties sued should be identified and as it allowed partners to be sued as individuals they were properly identified in the writ. Equally because of the substantive provisions of Swiss law they could have been sued in the firm name.

(c) Service upon persons having control or management of partnership business

81/3/7 *Add at end:*
[p.1536] A failure to serve all the partners sought to be made liable did not make the action itself irregular. A minor defect in service, in this case the process server handing the writ in a sealed envelope to the secretary of the partner sought to be served, could be cured under O.2, r.1: *Chohan Clothing Co. (Manchester) Ltd v. Fox Brooks Marshall (a firm), The Times*, December 9, 1997.

ORDER 85

ADMINISTRATION AND SIMILAR ACTIONS

85/2/3 **Pre-emptive cost orders**
[p.1562] *Delete* "MacDonald" *and substitute* "McDonald".

ORDER 88

MORTGAGE ACTIONS

Claims to possession **88/1/3**

Delete the sentence beginning at end of p.1575 "The High Court also has jurisdiction ..." *and substitute:* [p.1575]

Section 21(3) of County Courts Act 1984 overrides the power of the County Court, under s.42(2), to transfer proceedings to the High Court, because s.21(3) is one of the provisions in s.42(7)(b) to which s.42(2) is subject. Therefore possession proceedings within s.21(3) cannot be transferred to the High Court and the High Court has no jurisdiction even if such an order for transfer is made: *Yorkshire Bank v. Hall, The Independent* January 11, 1999, CA.

Evidence in support of applications for payment **88/5/10**

Add at end of paragraph: [p.1580]

Compliance with (c) may exceptionally be waived if it appears right to do so having regard to the cost and difficulty of compliance unless in any case the borrower required such compliance.

ORDER 91

REVENUE PROCEEDINGS

Appeals from value added tax tribunals (O.91, r.6) **91/6**

In O.91, r.6(2), delete words "by single judge of the Queen's Bench Division or, where both parties consent,". [p.1594]

Add at end: **91/6/1**

HISTORY OF RULE [p.1594]

Amended by S.I. 1998 No. 1898.

ORDER 92

LODGMENT, INVESTMENT, ETC., OF FUNDS IN COURT: CHANCERY DIVISION

Payment into court under section 26, Banking Act 1987 (O.92, r.3A) **92/3A**

Delete "Bank of England" *and substitute* "Financial Services Authority". [p.1597]

Add: **92/3A/1**

HISTORY OF RULE [p.1597]

Also amended by S.I. 1998 No. 1129, made by the Treasury pursuant to to s.23(2) of the Bank of England Act 1998.

ORDER 93

APPLICATIONS AND APPEALS TO HIGH COURT UNDER VARIOUS ACTS: CHANCERY DIVISION

93/23 **Proceedings under the Banking Act 1987 (O.93, r.23)**
[p.1612] *In subs. (4) delete the words* "the Bank of England" *and insert the words* "Financial Services Authority".

93/23/1 *Add:*
[p.1612] HISTORY OF RULE
Amended by S.I. 1998 No. 1129.

ORDER 94

APPLICATIONS AND APPEALS TO HIGH COURT UNDER VARIOUS ACTS: QUEEN'S BENCH DIVISION

94/2/2 **Entry and service**
[p.1616] *Add:*
Where, in this context, an application is made to extend time under O.3, r.5 for the service of a notice of motion the reasonable requirements of public administration have a significance which is absent in ordinary *inter partes* litigation, *Regalbourne Ltd v. East Lindsey District Council* [1993] C.O.D. 297 (Sir Thomas Bingham M.R.), and it will only be in rare circumstances, in cases involving public bodies, that the court's discretion is likely to be exercised to extend time: *R. v. Secretary of State for the Environment and Shropshire County Council, ex p. Parry* [1998] C.O.D. 17 (Scott Barker J.).

94/15/4 **Applications for leave to institute or continue proceedings**
[p.1626] *Add:*
The findings of the High Court on which a civil proceedings order has been based are capable of having a bearing on the court's evaluation of the matters which a leave application brings into play: *R. v. Dean and Chapter of St Paul's Cathedral and the Church in Wales* [1998] C.O.D. 130 (Sedley J.).

ORDER 104

THE PATENTS ACTS 1949 AND 1977; THE REGISTERED DESIGNS ACTS 1949 TO 1971; THE DEFENCE CONTRACTS ACT 1958; THE COPYRIGHT, DESIGNS AND PATENTS ACT 1988

104/0/5 **Consolidated Practice Explanation by Laddie J., November 19, 1997**
[p.1704] *Delete this Consolidated Practice Explanation and substitute:*

CONSOLIDATED PRACTICE DIRECTION, MAY 21, 1998 — No. 1998

by Laddie J.

This consolidated and amended Practice Direction supersedes and replaces all previous explanations and directions of the Patents Court. The general guidance applicable to all matters in the Chancery Division, as set forth in the Chancery Guide, also apply to patent actions unless specifically varied below.

Explanatory note

Changes or additions to the Consolidated Practice Explanation dated November 19, 1997 are to be found in the following paragraphs: 2–4, 10, 18–20, 27, 29, 30, 33, 47 and 48. The changes are, in large part, self evident. However special mention should be made of some of the alterations both to the Practice Direction and to the standard form Minute of Order for Directions **104/0/6**

The purpose of paragraphs 18 and 19 of this Practice Direction is to ensure that the court is kept abreast of the latest time estimates for trials and, once those estimates for trials and, once those estimates are in place, to encourage the parties to keep them. Actions which exceed their allotted space in the diary can create difficulties for subsequent fixtures. This is to be avoided if at all possible. It is accepted that sometimes issues may arise which could not have been anticipated and sometimes it is difficult to anticipate the speed and economy with which major witnesses will answer questions under cross examination.

Paragraph 27 of this Practice Direction and paragraph 17 of the standard form Minute of Order for Directions are concerned with the provision of technical primers. The value of these documents has been commented on in a number of recent cases. Practitioners must remember that they start the trial having been exposed over a number of months or longer to the technology in issue. It will be familiar to them. If they are in any doubt on a technical matter they can usually obtain instruction from one or more of the technically qualified experts or support team working on their case. The Patents Court is likely to be faced with the technology for the first time a few days before the commencement of the trial. The same applies to the Court of Appeal in those cases where an appeal is pursued. The provision of primers may significantly assist in the reduction of court time. Nevertheless the production of these documents can be time consuming and expensive and the court's attitude to the need for a primer is likely to be heavily influenced by any agreement between the parties that it is not necessary to have one.

Practitioners should also notice that paragraph 12 of the standard form Minute of Order for Directions has been modified. There is no longer an automatic requirement that advance notice be given of any drawings or photographs on which a party intends to rely. Needless to say, if drawings or photographs form part of or are contained in a report of experiments of which notice must be given, they must be disclosed in advance as well. It should also be remembered that if photographs are to be used as evidence of what they show, expert evidence may be necessary. See *Van der Lely v. Bamfords* [1963] R.P.C. 61.

General

1. All Originating Notices of Motion, Notices of Motion and Summonses concerned with proceedings governed by O.104 are issued in accordance with O.104 r.2(3). Before issuing a Notice of Motion or summons, the applicant should apply to the Clerk in Charge of the Patents Court List for a return date. **104/0/7**

Clerk in charge of the patents court list

2. The clerk to one of the principal assigned patent judges will be in charge of the patents list. Until further notice the clerk in charge of the patents list will be the clerk to Laddie J. He is located in Room TM 7.02 in the Royal Courts of Justice. He can be contacted there or by e-mail (psmith.patent.rcj@gtnet.gov.uk), telephone (0207 936 6518) or fax (0207 936 6439). **104/0/8**

3. The Patents Court diary, together with practice directions and some judgments are now to be found on the Patents Court Website: http://www.open.gov.uk/courts/court/highhome.htm

The Website can also be accessed through the Court Service Website: http://www.courtservice.gov.uk/highhome.htm

4. In the near future it is expected that it will be possible to access decisions of the Court of Appeal in patent matters through the Patents Court Website.

Short applications

104/0/9 **5.** These will normally be listed for hearing at 10 a.m. Parties should liaise with the clerk in charge of the patent list. In addition to these arrangments, the Court will make available a two hour slot from 9.00 a.m. to 11.00 a.m. on Tuesday mornings so as to speed up the hearing and disposition of slightly more lengthy applications. Parties and their representatives will be expected to continue to assist the Court to dispose effeciently of business. In the case of any of the applications referred to in this paragraph, the parties must provide to the Court by not later than 4.00 p.m. on the preceding working day all necessary documents and skeleton arguments. They should also provide drafts of any Order which the Court will be invited to make. It is important for the Court to be provided with accurate estimates of duration so that, where possible, more than one application can be listed for hearing before 10.30 a.m. Parties will be kept to their estimates and, where necessary to achieve this, guillotines are likely to be imposed on oral submissions.

September sittings

104/0/10 **6.** The Patents Court will sit in September. Normally sittings in that month will be reserved for trials and applications with an estimated duration, taking into account any necessary pre-reading by the judge, of five days or less.

Appeals from the Comptroller

104/0/11 **7.** These are governed by O.104, r.19. The Order refers to the "proper officer". He is the Clerk in Charge of the Chancery List (tel: 0207 936 7383). In practice, the file is passed to the Clerk in Charge of the Patents Court List who carries out the duties of the Proper Officer. The appellant has the conduct of the appeal and he or his representative should within two weeks of lodging the appeal contact the Clerk in charge of the Patents Court List with a view to arranging a date for a hearing. Any party appealing from a decision of the Comptroller shall ensure that the appeal is set down as soon as reasonably practical after service of the notice of appeal. Parties are reminded that the provisions relating to the service of skeleton arguments set out in the Chancery Guide apply to appeals from the Comptroller.

Ex Parte Applications

104/0/12 **8.** A party wishing to apply *ex parte* should contact the Clerk in Charge of the Patents Court List. In cases of emergency in vacation or out of normal court hours the application should be made to the duty Chancery Judge.

Documents

104/0/13 **9.** If it is known which judge will be taking the case, papers for the case should be lodged directly with that judge's clerk. Faxed documents of significance (and particularly skeleton arguments) should be followed up by clean direct prints.

10. It is the responsibility of both parties to any application to the Patents Court to ensure that all relevant documents are lodged with the Clerk of the Judge who will be taking the case by noon two working days before the date fixed for hearing unless some longer or shorter period has been ordered by the judge.

11. In substantial matters the judges request that all important documents also be supplied to them on disc in a format convenient for the judge's use. These will include the patent, the witness statements and expert reports.

12. Bundling is of considerable importance and should be approached intelligently. The general guidance given in the Chancery Guide should be followed, though where documents bear their own internal numbering and are within a tabbed file, the whole file need not be paginated.

Simplified Trial

13. Attention is drawn to the ability and willingness of the Patents Court to hear actions on affidavit evidence, if that is the wish of the parties. It is suggested that in appropriate cases solicitors acting for one of the parties should, after close of pleadings, write to the solicitors acting for the other party requesting agreement to a "Simplified Trial". That letter should point out that refusal may be brought to the attention of the judge after judgment and could result in an adverse order on costs. **104/0/14**

14. If the parties agree to a Simplified Trial, one of them should within 14 days after close of pleadings apply for directions which should include:

1. the filing of evidence by affidavit,
2. the trial to be heard on affidavit,
3. limitation of experts,
4. setting down.

15. If agreed directions are sought, no attendance at Court is necessary.

16. A Simplified Trial would not be suitable where cross-examination is likely on any issue of substance nor where any substantial discovery is needed.

Reading guide—time estimates

17. Judges hearing patent actions usually read the basic documents in the action before the action is called on for trial. These will rarely include documents disclosed on discovery. A party setting down a patent action must lodge a certificate stating the estimated length of the trial; and, an estimate of the time needed for the judge to read the documents. **104/0/15**

18. Two weeks before the date set for the commencement of the trial, the parties intending to appear at the trial must send to the clerk in charge of the patent list a certificate, signed by or on behalf of all of them setting out their current estimate of the duration of the trial. If that estimate is significantly longer than the most recent previous estimate, the certificate must be accompanied by a brief written note setting out the reason for the increase.

19. Not less than two working days before commencement of the trial, each party must lodge a certificate stating the estimated length of its oral submissions, its examination in chief (if any) of its own witnesses and its cross examination of witnesses of any other party.

20. The documents in the form to be used at trial must be lodged by the plaintiff's solicitors at least four working days before the date for trial together with a "Reading Guide" for the judge. The "Reading Guide" should be short, non-contentious and if possible agreed. It should not contain argument. It should shortly set out the issues, the parts of the documents that need to be read on each issue and the most convenient order that they should be read. If thought appropriate, the relevant passages in text books and cases should be referred to.

21. Parties are reminded of the court's power to impose guillotines on the duration of submissions and cross examination. This power will be exercised in any case where it is of the view that a case is not being conducted with reasonable expedition.

Narrowing of issues

22. As early as possible the patentee should identify which of the claims of its patent are contended to have independent validity and which of those claims are said to be infringed. This position should be kept under constant review. If there is any reduction of the contentions at any stage the patentee should forthwith notify the other parties. **104/0/16**

Admissions

104/0/17 **23.** With a view to early elimination of non-issues, practitioners are reminded of the desirability of making admissions at an early stage. This may be done even without waiting for a notice to admit facts. It can be done as early as in a defence or reply. For instance in a defence a party may admit the acts complained of or that his article/process has certain of the integers of a claim. In a reply a patentee may be able to admit prior publication of cited documents.

24. The notice to admit facts required by RSC, O.104, r.10 may also include a request to identify points not in dispute. Technically a request seeking admissions in respect of particular integers of a claim may involve a mixed question of fact and law and so not be within the rule. By asking whether or not the defendant disputes that his article/process has certain features of the claim the real dispute can be narrowed. Thus the ambit of discovery and of witness and expert statements will be narrowed.

25. Similarly a patentee ought at an early stage to identify which of his claims he intends to defend independently, see *Unilever v. Chefaro* [1994] R.P.C. 567. A request for admissions directed to him may also include such a request.

26. Requests for admissions should be drawn sensibly. It is not sensible or desirable to frame them *in extenso.*

Technical primers

104/0/18 **27.** In all cases of technical complexity, the court will expect the parties to work from an early stage towards the production of an agreed primer which sets out the basic technology necessary to an understanding of the issues in the case and which can be used to present the Patents Court and any appellate court with a non-contentious background to the case. The issue of whether a technical primer is needed must be addressed by parties before the summons for directions is put before the court. The court will give considerable weight to any agreement between the parties that a primer is not necessary.

Notices to admit facts in an application for a declaration of non-infringement

104/0/19 **28.** Under O.104, r.11(1)(a), a list of documents in an application for a declaration of non-infringement of a patent must be served by each party within 21 days after service of the notice of admissions under r.10(2), or within 21 days after the close of pleadings. However, O.104, r.10 does not expressly cover notices to admit facts and notices of admissions in an application for a declaration of non-infringement of a patent. A rule change will be proposed shortly to broaden the ambit of r.10. In the meantime, the parties to any action for a declaration of non-infringement of a patent are encouraged, where appropriate, to serve notices to admit facts within the period provided in O.104, r.10(1).

Documents referred to in pleadings

104/0/20 **29.** It is desirable that copies of documents referred to in a pleading (*e.g.* documents referred to in the Statement of Claim, advertisements referred to in Particulars of Infringements or documents cited in Particulars of Objections) are served with the pleading. Where any such document requires translation, a translation should be served at the same time.

Skeleton Arguments, pre-trial and post evidence

104/0/21 **30.** In addition to the reading guide parties should lodge skeleton arguments in time for the judge to read them before trial. That should normally be at least two working days before commencement of the trial, but in substantial cases a longer period (to be discussed with the clerk to the Judge concerned) may be needed. It is desirable that each party should summarise what it contends to be the common general knowledge of the man skilled in the art.

31. Following the evidence in a substantial trial a short adjournment may be granted to enable the parties to summarise their arguments in writing before oral argument.

32. In trials where a transcript of evidence is being made and supplied to the judge, the transcript should be accompanied by a version on disc in a format convenient for the judge's use.

Jurisdiction of Masters

33. By virtue of the Practice direction of April 9, 1991 and the operation of **104/0/22**
O.104, r.2 any matter arising under O.104 should be brought directly (by motion or summons) before the Patents Court, save that (i) consent orders (ii) orders on summonses for extension of time (iii) applications for leave to serve out of the jurisdiction and (iv) applications for security for costs may be heard by a Master. Other matters may be dealt with by the Master with the specific authority of a patent judge. However if a matter which a Master may hear is anticipated to be substantial it should normally be taken (by summons or motion) direct to a patent judge.

Agreed Orders

34. The court is normally willing to make consent orders (interlocutory or **104/0/23**
final) without the need for the attendance of any parties. A draft of the agreed order and the written consent of the parties' respective solicitors or counsel should be supplied to the clerk in charge of the Patents List. Where a draft has been substantially amended by hand, it is helpful for a disk of the unamended version to be supplied in accordance with paragraph 7.2 of the Chancery Guide. Unless the judge considers a hearing is needed he will make the order in the agreed terms by initialling it. It will be drawn up accordingly and sent to the parties. This procedure applies both to interlocutory (including procedural directions on an originating motion) and final orders.

Telephone summonses

35. For short (90 minutes or less) matters before the Patents Court, the **104/0/24**
patents judges are willing, unless a matter of general public importance is involved, to hear summonses by telephone conference. The following is the procedure:

36. Unless the matter is very urgent, the parties must agree that a telephone hearing is appropriate.

37. Where it is known that the hearing will be by telephone in advance of issue of the summons it should be marked "by telephone". Where the summons has already been issued then a letter (or fax) from the party issuing it should be sent to the clerk in charge of the patents list indicating that a telephone hearing is desired. Where a notice of motion has already been issued the court may treat the hearing as if by summons.

38. Any bundles to be used should be agreed and sent in advance to the clerk of the judge who will hear the summons. Any last minute documents may be sent by fax. The judge's clerk should be informed by telephone of any such documents and it will be prudent in any event to check with the clerk that the necessary papers are present and correct.

39. The time for hearing should be agreed with the judge's clerk. It should normally be between 9.30 and 10.15 a.m.

40. The party issuing the summons is responsible for setting up the conference call. This may be done by contacting British Telecom on 0800 778877. The call should commence with the judge at precisely the time agreed with the judge's clerk.

41. The costs of the call will be treated as part of the costs of the summons.

42. Loudspeaker telephones may be used unless they interfere with the hearing.

43. To avoid any misunderstandings the parties must agree a minute of order immediately following the hearing of the summons. This may most conveniently be done by one party faxing a signed copy of the minute to the other and that other signing a copy and faxing the completed agreed order to the judge, but other arrangements may be agreed. The judge's clerk will arrange for the order to be drawn up in the same way as an agreed order (see below).

44. The patent judges have arranged for recording of any telephone summons to be made. It will not be transcribed. The tape will be kept by the judge's clerk for a period of six months. Arrangements for transcription, if needed, must be made by the parties.

45. This procedure may be used for most short disputed interlocutory matters. The parties should use it where it will save costs. The procedure is not a substitute for the even cheaper procedure of an agreed interlocutory order.

Pre-trial reviews in patent actions

104/0/25 **46.** Paragraph 3.9 of the Chancery Guide indicates that such a review should be held in a case of over 10 days' estimated duration. However, in a matter before the Patents Court unless any party considers that it would be helpful, there is no need for a pre-trial review.

Rights of audience on hearing of summons

104/0/26 **47.** In patent proceedings most interlocutory matters must come by summons direct before a patent judge. These are heard in chambers. Practitioners are reminded that solicitors have rights of audience on any summons in chambers before the High Court.

48. All Chambers hearing will be open to the public save when they are expressly ordered to be in camera.

Patents judges able and willing to sit out of London

104/0/27 **49.** If the parties so desire, for the purpose of saving time or costs, the Patents Court will sit out of London. This also applies to any other intellectual property case. If such a sitting is desired a request should be made in the first instance to the clerk in charge of the patents list whether the matter is proceeding in a district registry or in London.

Intellectual Property Court Users' Committee

104/0/28 **50.** This considers the problems and concerns of intellectual property litigation generally. Membership of the committee includes the principal patent judges, a representative of each of the Patent Bar Association, the Intellectual Property Lawyers Association, the Chartered Institute of Patent Agents, the Institute of Trade Mark Agents and the Trade Marks Designs and Patents Federation. It will also include one or more other Chancery judges. Anyone having views concerning the improvement of intellectual property litigation is invited to make his or her views known to the committee, preferably through the relevant professional representative on the committee.

Orders following judgment

104/0/29 **51.** Where a judgment is made available in draft before being given in open court and it is desired to ask the court for an order when judgment is given, the parties should, in advance of that occasion, exchange drafts of the desired consequential order. It is highly undesirable that one party should spring a proposal on the other for the first time when judgment is given.

Experiments not part of normal research

52. The position of the admission at trial of evidence of experiments conducted for litigious purposes but not specifically for the case in hand requires clarification. RSC, O.104, r.12 refers to establishing "any fact by experimental proof". This includes experiments done in other jurisdictions or any other experiments not done as part of normal research. **104/0/30**

Experiments done for litigation but not disclosed

53. The Intellectual Property Court Users' Committee has discussed the question of experiments conducted by a party for the purposes of litigation but not disclosed or adduced by it following the judgments in *Honeywell Ltd v. Appliance Components Ltd* (February 22, 1996, unrep.), Jacob J. and *Electrolux Northern Ltd v. Black & Decker* [1996] F.S.R. 595, Laddie J. As a result, in future it shall be a requirement that an expert's report shall include the statement "I know of no experiment which is inconsistent with my evidence". **104/0/31**

Immediate assessment of costs

54. In appropriate cases the Patents Court will adopt a more vigorous approach to costs. In particular, it will be willing to consider application for immediate assessment by the judge who has just tried the case rather than remit the matter for taxation. Such an assessment may be done on the basis of the actual detailed bills sent to clients. Without in any way limiting the court's discretion as to when it will exercise this power, it may in particular be exercised in a case where the delays caused by a taxation of costs may themselves give rise to injustice. **104/0/32**

Applications for interlocutory injunctions: trial dates

55. When an application for an interlocutory injunction is made the plaintiff should, where practicable, make prior inquiries and investigations as to the estimated length of trial and possible trial dates. **104/0/33**

Amendment of patent

56. New rules concerning amendment of a patent in proceedings before the court are to be issued shortly. **104/0/34**

Specimen minute of order for directions

57. The general form minute of order for directions annexed to this practice direction has the approval of the Patents Judges. It is intended only as a guide and may need adaptation for particular circumstances. **104/0/35**

Annex

Standard Form Minute of Order for Directions

(*indicates a provision which may be necessary when a rule, e.g. for automatic discovery, has not been complied with.) **104/0/36**

[UPON THE SUMMONS FOR DIRECTIONS in this Action and Counterclaim]

AND UPON HEARING Counsel for the Plaintiffs and for the Defendants

[AND UPON THE PLAINTIFFS by their Counsel undertaking forthwith to issue a pro forma summons for directions and treating that Summons as before the Court]

AND UPON READING the documents marked in the Court file as having been read

THIS COURT ORDERS THAT

[Transfer

104/0/37 **1.** This Action and Counterclaim be transferred to the Patents County Court.] (If this order is made, no other Order will generally be necessary, though it may be desirable for procedural orders to be made at this time to save the costs of a further application in the County Court).

Proof of Documents

104/0/38 **2.** Legible copies of the specification of the Patent in suit [and any patent specifications or other documents cited in the Particulars of Objections] may be used at the trial without further proof thereof or of their contents.

Amendments to Pleadings

104/0/39 **3.** The Plaintiffs have leave to amend their Writ herein by [ ] and that service of the Writ and the Defendants' acknowledgement of service stand and that the costs of and occasioned by the amendments be the Defendants in any event.

4. The Plaintiffs have leave to amend their Statement of Claim [and Particulars of Infringement] as shown in red on the copy [annexed to the Summons for Directions/as signed by the solicitors for the parties/annexed hereto] and [to re-serve the same on or before [ ] and that re-service be dispensed with] and that the Defendants have leave to serve a consequentially amended Defence within [ ] days [thereafter/hereafter] and that the Plaintiffs have leave to serve a consequentially amended Reply (if so advised) within [ ] days thereafter.

5. (a) The Defendants have leave to amend their Defence [and Counterclaim and Particulars of Objections] as shown in red on the copy [annexed to the Summons for Directions/as signed by the solicitors for the parties/annexed hereto] and [to reserve the same within [ ] days/on or before] [and that re-service be dispensed with] and that the Plaintiffs have leave to serve a consequentially amended Reply (if so advised) with [ ] days thereafter. (b) The Plaintiffs do on or before [ ] elect whether they will discontinue this Action and withdraw their Defence to Counterclaim and consent to an Order for the revocation of Patent No. [ ] ("the patent in suit") AND IF the Plaintiffs shall so elect and give notice thereof in the time aforesaid IT IS ORDERED THAT the patent in suit be revoked and that it be referred to the taxing master to tax the costs of the Defendants and this Action and Counterclaim up to and including [ ] being the date of delivery of the [amended] Particulars of Objections and Counterclaim to the date of this Order [except so far as the same have been increased by the failure of the Defendants originally to deliver the Defence and Counterclaim in its amended form], and to tax the costs of the Plaintiffs in this Action and Counterclaim from [ ] [insofar as they have been increased by the failure of the Defendants aforesaid] AND IT IS ORDERED that the said taxing officer is to set off the costs of the Defendants and of the Plaintiffs when so taxed as aforesaid and to certify to which of them the balance after such set-off is due.

Further and Better Particulars

104/0/40 **6.** (a) The [Plaintiffs/Defendants] do on or before [ ] serve on the [Defendants/Plaintiffs] the Further and Better Particulars of the [ ] as requested by the [Plaintiffs/Defendants] by their Request served on the [Defendants/Plaintiffs] on [ ] [and/or] (b) the [Plaintiffs/Defendants] do on or before [ ] serve on the [Defendants/Plaintiffs] a response to their Request for Further and Better Particulars of the [ ] served on the [Defendants/Plaintiffs] on [ ].

*Admissions**

7. The [Plaintiffs Defendants] do on or before [ ] state in writing whether or not they admit the facts specified in the [Defendants'/Plaintiffs'] Notice to Admit facts dated [ ] and that the said Notice shall stand as a Notice to Admit within the meaning of RSC, O.27, r.2 and RSC, O.62, r.7. **104/0/41**

Security

8. The Plaintiffs do provide security for the Defendants' costs in the sum of £ by [paying the said sum into Court and giving notice of such payment in to the Defendants] [paying the said sum into an account at [ ] Bank of [ ] in the joint names of solicitors for the parties] [giving the Defendants a bond securing the said sum] [in the terms annexed hereto] on or before [ ] and that in the meantime all further proceedings be stayed. **104/0/42**

*Lists of Documents**

9. (a) The Plaintiffs and the Defendants respectively do on or before [ ] make and serve on the other of them a list of the documents which are or have been in their possession custody power or control relating to the matters in question in this Action and Counterclaim and on request file an affidavit verifying such list. (b) In respect of those issues identified in Schedule [ ] hereto discovery shall be limited to those [documents/categories of documents] listed in Schedule [ ]. **104/0/43**

*Inspection**

10. If any party wishes to inspect or have copies of such documents as are in another party's possession power custody or control it shall give notice in writing that it wishes to do so and such inspection shall be allowed at all reasonable times upon reasonable notice and any copies shall be provided within [ ] working days of the request upon the undertaking of the party requesting the copies to pay the reasonable copying charges. **104/0/44**

*Experiments**

11.(a) Where a party desires to establish any fact by experimental proof, including an experiment conducted for the purposes of litigation or otherwise not being an experiment conducted in the normal course of research, that party shall on or before [ ] serve on all the other parties a notice stating the facts which it desires to establish and giving full particulars of the experiments proposed to establish them. **104/0/45**

(b) A party upon whom a notice is served under the preceding subparagraph shall within 21 days serve on the party serving the notice a notice stating in respect of each fact whether or not that party admits it.

(c) Where any fact which a party wishes to establish by experimental proof is not admitted that party may apply to the Court for further directions in respect of such experiments.

[Or where O.104, r.11 has been complied with.]

11.(a) The Plaintiffs/Defendants are to afford to the other parties an opportunity, if so requested, of inspecting a repetition of the experiments identified in paragraphs [ ] of the Notice[s] of Experiments served on [ ]. Any such inspection must be requested within [ ] days of the date of this Order and shall take place within [ ] days of the date of the request.

(b) If any party shall wish to establish any fact in reply to experimental proof that party shall on or before [ ] serve on all the other parties a notice stating the facts which it desires to establish and giving full particulars of the experiments proposed to establish them.

(c) A party upon whom a notice is served under the preceding subparagraph shall within 21 days serve on the party serving the notice a notice stating in respect of each fact whether or not that party admits it.

(d) Where any fact which a party wishes to establish by experimental proof in reply is not admitted the party may apply to the Court for further directions in respect of such experiments.

Notice of models, etc.

104/0/46 **12.** (a) If any party wishes to rely at the trial of this action upon any model, apparatus, cinematograph or video film that party shall on or before [ ] give notice thereof to all the other parties; shall afford the other parties an opportunity within 14 days of the service of such notice of inspecting the same and shall, if so requested, furnish the other party with a sufficient drawing photograph or other illustration of any model or apparatus.

(b) If any party wishes to rely upon any such materials in reply to any matter of which notice was given under sub-paragraph (a) of this paragraph, the party shall within 14 days after the last inspection to be made in pursuance of the said sub-paragraph (a) give to the other parties a like notice, if so requested within 7 days of delivery of such notice shall afford like opportunities of inspection which shall take place within 7 days of such request; and shall in like manner furnish copies of any drawing photograph or illustration of any such model or apparatus.

(c) No further or other model apparatus cinematograph or video film shall be relied upon in evidence by either party save with mutual consent or by leave of the Court.

Written evidence

104/0/47 **13.** (a) Each party may call up to [ ] expert witnesses in this Action and Counterclaim provided that the said party:

(i) supplies the name of such expert to the other parties and to the Court on or before [ ]; and

(ii) no later than [date/[ ] before the date set for the hearing of this Action and Counterclaim] serve upon the other parties a report of each such expert comprising the evidence which that expert intends to give at trial.

(b) Each party shall on or before [ ] serve on the other parties [signed] written statements of the oral evidence which the party intends to lead on any issues of tact to be decided at the trial, such statements to stand as the evidence in chief of the witness unless the Court otherwise directs;

(c) The parties . . . (here insert the particular directions sought, e.g. within 21 days after service of the other party's expert reports and written statements state in writing the facts and matters in those reports and statements which are admitted).

Admissibility of evidence

104/0/48 **14.** A party who objects to any statements of any witness being read by the judge prior to the hearing of the trial, shall serve upon each other party a notice in writing to that effect setting out the grounds of the objection.

Non-compliance

104/0/49 **15.** Where either party fails to comply with the directions relating to experiments and written evidence it shall not be entitled to adduce evidence to which such directions relate without the leave of the Court.

Trial bundles

104/0/50 **16.** Each party shall no later than [28] days before the date fixed for the trial of this Action and Counterclaim serve upon the parties a list of all the documents to be included in the trial bundles. The Plaintiffs shall no later than [21] days before the date fixed for trial serve upon the Defendants an index of the bundles for use at trial.

Technical primer

17.(a) Not later than [6 weeks before the date fixed for the trial of this Action and Counterclaim] the [Plaintiff] shall send to the [defendant] a draft primer setting out the non-contentious technical background necessary to an understanding of the case. **104/0/51**

(b) No later than [three weeks before the date fixed for the trial of this Action and Counterclaim], the [defendant], will return the primer to the [plaintiff] marked with any alterations and additions which it wishes to make or include.

(c) The primer shall be supplied by the [plaintiff] to the clerk to the patent court together with its skeleton argument. If the primer is not agreed in total, it must be marked so as to indicate which parts are agreed and which parts are not agreed. In relation to the latter parts, the alternative wording/illustrations proposed by each party will be included together with legends clearly indicating which party is proposing which form of wording/illustration.

Trial

18. The trial of these proceedings shall be before an Assigned Judge alone in [London], estimated length [ ] days and a pre-reading estimate for the Judge of [ ] days. **104/0/52**

Setting Down

19. Any party may set this action and Counterclaim down for trial [after [date]/forthwith] [to be heard not before [ ] with liberty to apply for an earlier date]. **104/0/53**

Liberty to Apply

120. The parties are to be at liberty on two days' notice to apply for further directions and generally. **104/0/54**

Costs

21. The costs of this Application are to be costs in the Action and Counterclaim. **104/0/55**

ORDER 112

APPLICATIONS FOR USE OF BLOOD TESTS IN DETERMINING PATERNITY

List of testers (rr. 1–6) **112/6/10**

Add to note: [p.1784]

The list of persons appointed by the Lord Chancellor to test blood in cases of disputed paternity was amended with effect from April 27, 1998.

PERSONS APPOINTED BY THE LORD CHANCELLOR TO TEST BLOOD SAMPLES IN CASES OF DISPUTED PATERNITY

Name	Address	Tel No.	Fax No.
Dr D. Lee	National Blood Service, Quernmore Road, Lancaster, LA1 3JP	01524 63456 Ex 65	01524 62602
Dr P. J. Lincoln Dr D. Syndercombe Court	Department of Haematology, The London Hospital Medical College, Turner Street, London, E1 2AD	0207 377 7076	0207 377 7677
Dr S. S. Papiha	Department of Human Genetics, University of Newcastle upon Tyne, 19/20 Claremont Place, Newcastle upon Tyne, NE2 4AA	0191 222 6000 Ex 7574	0191 222 7143
Matthew Greenhalgh Melanie Leyshon Dr Brian McKeown Janine Stickley Dr G. Rysiecki Mrs Amanda Riordan	Cellmark Diagnostics, Blacklands Way, Abingdon Business Park, Abingdon, Oxon, OX14 1DY	01235 528609	01235 528141
Dr P. G. Debenham Mr Jim Thomson Dr J. I. H. Walker	University Diagnostics Ltd., South Bank Technopark, 90, London Road, London, SE1 6LN	0207 401 9898	0207 928 9297
Dr C. N. Maguire Mr M. J. Barber Ms S. M. Hill Ms V. S. Tomlinson Mrs M. G. Younie	The Forensic Science Service, Sandbeck Way, Audby Lane, Wetherby, West Yorkshire, LS22 4DN	0937 581919	0937 587683
Dr S Mastana	Department of Human Services, Loughborough University, Loughborough, Leics. LE11 3TU	01509 223036	01509 223940

THE FOLLOWING FORENSIC SCIENCE SERVICE SCIENTISTS MAY OCCASIONALLY REPORT DISPUTED PATERNITY CASES

Name	Address	Tel No.	Fax No.
Dr W. Basley Dr S. Bolton Dr C. Dark Ms J. Guiness Ms H. Long Ms A. D. Parry Ms C. Thompson	The Forensic Science Service, 6th Floor, Priory House, Gooch Street North, Birmingham, B5 6QQ	0121 607 6828	0121 622 2139

ORDER 113

SUMMARY PROCEEDINGS FOR POSSESSION OF LAND

Making of order for possession **113/8/14** [p.1798]

Add at end:

In an application for judicial review in the context of an application under O.24 CCR (in this context the same as O.113) for summary possession of part of a caravan site designate under The Caravan Sites and Control of Development Act 1960 it was held that a local authority does not have to carry out the investigation set out in the *Gypsy Sites and Unauthorised Camping* (D.o.E. Circular 18/24) before seeking possession: *R. v. Hillingdon LBC, ex p. McDonagh, The Times,* November 9, 1998; *R. v. Brighton and Hove Council, ex p. Marmont, The Times,* January 15, 1998 considered; *R. v. Lincolnshire County Council, ex p. Atkinson, The Times,* September 22, 1995 (a case under s.77 of the Criminal Justice and Public Order Act 1994) not followed.

ORDER 114

REFERENCES TO THE EUROPEAN COURT

Related Sources **114/0/3** [p.1800]

Add:

- Practice Direction—Supreme Court: References to the Court of Justice of the European Communities, January 14, 1999

COUNTY COURT RULES

COUNTY COURTS OVERVIEW

Interest on Judgments C–016 [p.1834]

Add:

See note on interest on "qualifying debts" within the meaning of the Late Payment of Commercial Debts (Interest) Act 1998 at C25/5A/2 in this Supplement.

CCR ORDER 5

Causes of Action and Parties

Joinder of causes of action (O.5, r.1) C5/1 [p.1853]

In the first line of r.1 delete "ons" *and substitute* "one".

CCR ORDER 11

Payment Into and Out of Court and Between the Parties

Payment into court (O.11, r.1) C11/1 [p.1898]

After r.1 of CCR, O.11 insert the following:

(1A) Where a payment under paragraph (1) is made to which the Social Security (Recovery of Benefits) Act 1997 applies, the defendant shall state the gross amount of the compensation, the name and amount of any benefit by which the gross amount is reduced in accordance with section 8 of and Schedule 2 to the 1997 Act, and the net sum paid into court.

Add: C11/1/1 [p.1899]

Amended by the County Court (Amendment) Rules 1998 (S.I. 1998 No. 1899). The new rule requires the extra information referred to when making a payment into court to which the Social Security (Recovery of Benefits) Act 1997 applies.

CCR ORDER 20

Evidence

Note

Add: C20/14/4 [p.1967]

Rule 3 of the County Court (Amendment No. 3) Rules 1996 has been revoked as from September 1, 1998 by the County Court (Amendment) Rules 1998 (S.I. 1998 No. 1899). This amendment has no practical consequences: the revoked r.3 was intended to be transitional and, as already noted in the Main Work, had been held to be *ultra vires*.

CCR ORDER 25

Enforcement of Judgments and Orders: General

Related Sources C25/0/3 [p.1992]

Add at end of sixth bullet point:

The County Courts (Interest on Judgment Debts) Order 1991 has been amended by the County Courts (Interest on Judgment Debts) (Amendment) Order 1998 (S.I. 1998 No. 2400). See C25/5A/2 in this Supplement.

C25/5A/2 **County Court (Interest on Judgment Debts) Order 1991 (S.I. 1991 No. 1184)**
[p.1995] *Add:*

The County Courts (Interest on Judgment Debts) (Amendment) Order 1998 (S.I. 1998 No. 2400) amends the definition of "relevant judgment" in the County Courts (Interest on Judgment Debts) Order 1991. The new rule exends the power to award interest on county court judgments and orders to include not only (as hitherto) judgments for £5,000 or more but also judgments of whatever amount in respect of "qualifying debts" as defined in the Late Payment of Commercial Debts (Interest) Act 1998.

CCR ORDER 43

THE LANDLORD AND TENANT ACTS 1927, 1954, 1985 AND 1987

C43/18 **Application for order under section 24 of the Act of 1987 (O.43, r.18)**
[p.2096] *CCR, O.43, r.18 has been revoked by the County Court (Amendment) Rules 1998 (S.I. 1998 No. 1899) as from September 28, 1998.*

CCR ORDER 48D

ENFORCEMENT OF FIXED PENALTIES UNDER THE ROAD TRAFFIC (VEHICLE EMISSIONS) (FIXED PENALTY) REGULATIONS 1997

C48C/16/4 **"Transfer to and from High Court (Commercial Court)"**
[p.2126] *TheCounty Court (Amendment) Rules 1998 (S.I. 1998 No. 1899) have inserted, immediately after CCR, O.48C, a new CCR, O.48D as follows:*

C48D/1 **Application and interpretation (O.48D, r.1)**
[p.2127] **1.**—(1) This Order applies for the recovery of fixed penalties as defined in regulations 2(1)(b) and 9 of the 1997 Regulations.

(2) In this Order, unless the context otherwise requires—

"authority" means a participating authority as defined in regulation 2(1)(f) of the 1997 Regulations;

"order" means an order made under regulation 10(1) of the 1997 Regulations;

"the Order" means the Enforcement of Road Traffic Debts Order 1993;

"respondent" means the person on whom the fixed penalty notice was served;

"specified debts" means the Part II debts specified in article 2(1)(a) of the Order;

"the 1997 Regulations" means the Road Traffic (Vehicle Emissions) (Fixed Penalty) Regulations 1997.

(3) unless the context otherwise requires, expressions which are used in the 1997 Regulations have the same meaning in this Order as they have in those Regulations.

C48D/2 **The Parking Enforcement Centre (O.48D, r.2)**

2. The parking enforcement established in rule 1A of Order 48B shall have such functions relating to proceedings under this Order and other related matters as the Lord Chancellor may direct.

Requests for Orders and Warrants of Execution (O.48D, r.3) C48D/3

3.—An authority which wishes to take proceedings under this Order shall give notice to the proper officer and, where the proper officer so allows, a combined request for an order and a warrant of execution may be made, and such an order may be enforced and a warrant executed in accordance with the following provisions of this Order.

(2) An authority shall file a combined request for an order and a warrant of execution in the appropriate form or in another manner approved by the proper officer scheduling the fixed penalties in respect of which an order and warrant of execution are sought and Order 50, rule 4A shall not apply to a request under this Order.

(3) The authority shall in the request or in another manner approved by the proper officer—

- (a) certify—
  - (i) that 56 days have elapsed since the issue of the fixed penalty notice,
  - (ii) the amount due under the fixed penalty notice and the date on which it was issued, and
  - (iii) that the amount due remains unpaid;
- (b) give the number of the fixed penalty notice;
- (c) specify (whether by reference to the appropriate code or otherwise) the grounds stated in the fixed penalty notice and in regulation 2(1)(d) of the 1997 Regulations on which the authorised person who issued the fixed penalty notice believed that a fixed penalty was payable with respect to that vehicle;
- (d) state—
  - (i) the name and address of the respondent and where known, his title;
  - (ii) the registration number of the vehicle concerned;
  - (iii) (whether by reference to the appropriate fixed penalty notice number or otherwise) the authority's address for service;
  - (iv) the court fee.

(4) If satisfied that the combined request is in order, the proper officer shall order that the fixed penalty (together with the court fee) may be recovered as if it were payable under a county court order by sealing the request and returning it to the authority.

(5) When the proper officer so orders and on receipt of the sealed request, the authority shall, within 7 days of the sealing of the request, prepare the warrant in the appropriate form.

Documents (O.48D, r.4) C48D/4

4.—(1) Rule 3 of Order 48B shall apply to this Order with the modification referred to in paragraph (2).

(2) The reference to rule 2(2) in rule 3(1) of Order 48B shall be a reference to rule 3(2) of this Order.

Enforcement of Orders (O.48D, r. 5) C48D/5

5.—(1) Rule 5 of Order 48B shall apply to this Order with the modifications referred to in paragraphs (2), (3) and (4)

(2) Paragraphs (3), (4) and (7) of rule 5 shall not apply.

(3) Sub-paragraphs (c) and (d) of rule 5(9) shall not apply.

(4) In paragraph (11) of rule 5, the references to the words "charge certificate" shall be references to the words "fixed penalty notice".

(5) Where a fixed penalty notice is withdrawn under regulation 12 of the 1997 Regulations—

(a) any order made or warrant issued in respect of that fixed penalty notice is deemed to be revoked;
(b) any execution issued on the order shall cease to have effect, and
(c) the authority shall forthwith inform any bailiff instructed to levy execution of the withdrawal of the warrant.

CCR ORDER 49

MISCELLANEOUS STATUTES

C49/6 Housing Act 1988: assured tenancies (O.49, r.6)

[p.2134] *CCR, O.49, r.6(7)(i) has been amended to insert at the beginning the additional words* "the first written tenancy agreement and". *Amended by the County Court (Amendment) Rules 1998 (S.I. 1998 No. 1899)*.

C49/6A Housing Act 1988: assured shorthold tenancies (O.49, r.6A)

[p.2138] *CCR, O.49, r.6A(7)(i) has been substituted as follows:*
"(i) the first written tenancy agreement and the current (or most recent) written tenancy agreement".
Amended by the County Court (Amendment) Rules 1998 (S.I. 1998 No. 1899).

C49/15A Protection from Harassment Act 1997 (O.49, r.15A)

[p.2148] *Insert new rule. The County Court (Amendment) Rules 1998 (S.I. 1998 No. 1899) have inserted immediately after CCR, O.49, r.15, a new CCR, O.49, r.15A as follows:*

15A.—(1) In this rule, "the 1997 Act" means the Protection from Harassment Act 1997.

(2) This rule shall apply to injunctions granted on or after the date of the commencement of this rule and injunctions granted before that date shall be treated as if this rule had not come into force.

(3) Proceedings under section 3 of the 1977 Act to a county court shall be filed—
(a) in the court for the district in which the plaintiff resides or carries on business; or
(b) in the court for the district in which the defendant resides or carries on business.

(4) Where the court grants an injunction under section 3 of the 1997 Act, it shall be issued in the appropriate prescribed form.

(5) An application for the issue of a warrant for the arrest of the defendant under section 3(3) of the 1997 Act shall—
(a) state that it is an application for the issue of a warrant for the arrest of the defendant;
(b) set out the grounds for making the application and be supported by an affidavit or evidence on oath;
(c) state whether the plaintiff has informed the police of the defendant's conduct as described in sub-paragraph (b); and
(d) state whether, to the plaintiff's knowledge, criminal proceedings are being pursued.

(6) Where the court issues a warrant for the arrest of the defendant, the warrant shall be issued in the appropriate prescribed form.

(7) The court before whom a person is brought following his arrest may—
(a) determine whether the facts, and the circumstances which led to the arrest, amounted to disobedience of the injunction, or

(b) adjourn the proceedings and, where such an order is made, the arrested person shall be released and—
   (i) may be dealt with within 14 days of the day on which he was arrested; and
   (ii) be given not less than 2 days' notice of the adjourned hearing.

VOLUME 2

SECTION 1

FORMS

A. PRESCRIBED FORMS

Table of contents **1A–1A**
Add at beginning of table: [p.4]

The forms listed below in A are no longer prescribed. Under the Civil Procedure Rules 1998 the forms to be used in conjunction with the CPR are practice forms and are listed in Table 1 of the Practice Direction supplementing Pt 4. The forms set out below in A, B and C may be used, suitably amended, as precedents where appropriate. The forms in A and B which are required as precedents are in the process of being amended in order to comply with the CPR. It is intended to publish most of these in an Appendix to the Guide to the Queen's Bench Division. A similar exercise is taking place in respect of the forms in C.

No. 23 Notice of Payment into Court **1A–21**
Delete Form No. 23 and substitute the following form: [p.32]

No. 23

Notice of Payment into Court (O.22, rr.1, 2)

[*Heading as in action*]

Take notice that—

The defendant has paid £ into court.

This sum is in satisfaction of (the cause of action) (some of) (all of) (the causes of action) in respect of which the plaintiff claims (namely) and (does) (does not) take into account (the cause of action) (some of) (all of) (the causes of action) in respect of which the defendant counterclaims (namely)

For cases where the Social Security (Recovery of Benefits) Act 1997 applies

The gross amount of the compensation payment is £

The defendant has reduced this sum by £ in accordance with section 8 of and Schedule 2 to the Social Security (Recovery of Benefits) Act 1997, which was calculated as follows:

Name of benefit	Amount

Dated the day of 19

Note—Amended by RSC (Amendment) 1998 (S.I. 1998 No. 1898).

Note—Amended by RSC (Amendment) 1998 (S.I. 1998 No. 1898)

B. QUEEN'S BENCH MASTERS' PRACTICE FORMS

1B–33 [p.81] *Delete Form No. PF44 and substitute:*

No. PF 44

Order for Security for Costs (O.23, r.1)

It is ordered that the plaintiff by p.m. on 199 give security for the defendant's costs in the sum of £ [by payment into court of the same] [by lodging with the defendant's solicitors a (here describe the form of bankers draft etc.)] [in such manner as to the satisfaction of the Master] and that all further proceedings be stayed until security is given. In default of such security being given, the action is struck out with judgment for the defendant and his costs, to be taxed if not agreed.

C. COUNTY COURT FORMS

LIST OF COUNTY COURT FORMS

1C–1 [p.145] *Add:*

County Court (Forms) Rules 1982 have been further amended by the County Court (Forms) (Amendment) Rules 1998 (S.I. 1998 No. 1900). Minor amendments have been made to:

N5A Application for accelerated possession under s.58 of the Housing Act 1988
N5B Application for accelerated possession under s.21 of the Housing Act 1988
N29 Order for possession (mortgaged property)
N31 Order for possession (possession suspended) (mortgaged property)
N64 Suspended Attachment of Earnings Order
N79 Committal Order
N110A Power of arrest attached to an injunction under s.152 or s.153(1) of the Housing Act 1988

1C–3 [p.145] **Attachments to Summons**

Delete "N11A Form of reply to application for possession under s.8 of the Housing Act 1988" *and substitute* "N11A Form of reply to application for possession following issue of a notice under s.8 of the Housing Act 1988".

Delete "N11B Form of reply to application for accelerated possession under s.21 of the Housing Act 1988" *and substitute* "N11B Form of reply to application for accelerated possession following issue of a notice under s.21 of the Housing Act 1988".

1C–6 [p.146] **Forms of Enforcement**

Delete:

N56 Reply to an attachment of earnings application—statement of means

1C–10 [p.147] **Particulars of Claim—Housing**

Add new forms prescribed for use under the Protection from Harassment Act 1997:

N138 Injunction
N140 Warrant of arrest

SECTION 2

PRACTICE DIRECTIONS

A. QUEEN'S BENCH MASTERS' PRACTICE DIRECTIONS

Note **2A–1**
Add new para. at beginning of note: [p.155]
The practice directions set out in A have, in part, been absorbed into the practice directions which now supplement the CPR. Of the remainder, those which still apply will be reproduced, in amended form where necessary, in Guides to the various Divisions, Courts and Offices.

(20) Application by post for private room appointments before the Masters— **2A–27** [p.163]

Delete para. (2)(c) and substitute
(c) The following form properly completed:

APPLICATION FOR APPOINTMENT BEFORE A QUEEN'S BENCH MASTER

ASSIGNED MASTER UNDER O.4, R.1, OR IF NONE WRITE "x" ....

PARTIES IN ACTION ....

TYPE OF SUMMONS (or, if assessment of damages, nature of claim)

....

VALUE OF CLAIM (or, if unliquidated, the approximate sum the Plaintiff reasonably expects to recover) ....

APPLICANT'S AFFIDAVIT EVIDENCE IN SUPPORT:
(tick box if it has been or is ready to be served) ☐
(if none required, write "none") ....

ESTIMATED LENGTH OF HEARING (the Court must be informed forthwith of any material change):
Applicant's Estimate for Entire Hearing ....

Respondent's Estimate for Entire Hearing ....

EARLIEST DATE WHEN ALL PARTIES WILL BE READY FOR HEARING AND OTHER COVENIENT DATES:

For the Applicant ....

For the Respondent ....

DATES TO BE AVOIDED:

For the Applicant ....

For the Respondent ....

NAME OF COUNSEL (if attending and if known):

For the Applicant: ....

For the Respondent: ....

DATE APPLICATION MADE: ....

SOLICITORS MAKING THE APPLICATION:

....

TELEPHONE NUMBER, FAX NUMBER AND REFERENCE:

....

DOCUMENT EXCHANGE: .... ACTION NUMBER: ....

2A–100 **(32) Enforcement in the High Court of County Court Judgments**
[p.176] *Delete text of Practice Direction No. 32 and substitute the following:*

The practice for the enforcement in the High Court of those County Court judgments or orders to which Article 8(1) of the High Court and County Courts Jurisdiction Order 1991 applies shall be as follows:

(1) The applicant shall present to the judgment counter clerk a certificate of judgment of the County Court sealed with the seal of that court, setting out details of the judgment or order to be enforced, together with a copy of the same. There is no fee payable on registration.

(2) The judgment counter clerk will check that the certificate has been signed by an officer of the issuing court (a rubber stamp is not sufficient), dated and that the certificate complies with County Court Rules Order 22, r.8(1A), and in particular with the requirement that on its face it states that it is granted for the purpose of enforcing the judgment (or order) by execution against goods in the High Court.

(3) Provided that paragraphs 1 and 2 have been complied with, the counter clerk will:

(a) Allocate a reference number, letter (according to the plaintiff's name) and year and endorse that on the top right hand corner of certificate and copy.

(b) Date seal the certificate and copy, return the original to the applicant and retain the copy for the court records.

(c) Enter the matter in a special register.

(4) The certificate shall be treated for enforcement purposes as a High Court judgment and interest at the appropriate rate shall run from the date of the certificate.

(5) The title of all subsequent documents shall be as follows:

IN THE HIGH COURT JUSTICE High Court No.
County Court Plaint No.

QUEEN'S BENCH DIVISION
(Sent from the County Court by Certificate dated the day of).

BETWEEN

A.B.
Plaintiff
and
C.D.
Defendant

(6) When a writ of *fieri facias* is issued, the Certificate of Judgment retained by the applicant shall be date sealed by the counter clerk on the bottom left hand corner and indorsed with the designation of the sheriff to whom the process is directed.

Although any application for a stay of execution should be made by summons in the High Court returnable before a Queen's Bench Master, all other applications for enforcement or ancillary relief must be made to the issuing county court.

(7) *District registries*—The above practice shall be followed in the district registries with such variations as circumstances may require.

B. CHANCERY DIVISION PRACTICE DIRECTIONS

Chancery Division Practice Directions

2B–1 to 2B–332 [pp.186–256]

Please delete from para. 2B–1 up to (and including) para. 2B–332. A provisional revised version of the Chancery Guide, first published in 1995, has been published and is authorised by the Vice-Chancellor for use in the Chancery Division from April 26, 1999 until further notice. The Guide includes a substantive revision of the Chancery Division Practice Directions ("CDPDs") which is intended to replace the old Chancery Practice Directions. Because of its importance to practitioners, the Guide is published in full in the second edition of *Civil Procedure.*

Allocation of Actions

2B–123 [p.211]

Insert word "Chief" *before words* "Master Winegarten"; *delete words* "Chief Master Dyson" *and substitute words* "To be announced".

C. PRACTICE DIRECTIONS, NOTES AND STATEMENTS ISSUED BY THE LORD CHIEF JUSTICE (OR WITH HIS APPROVAL) FOR THE QUEEN'S BENCH DIVISION

Introduction to Section 2C

2C–1 [p.258]

Add new para. at beginning of note:

The practice directions set out in C have, in part, been absorbed into the practice directions which now supplement the CPR. Of the remainder, those which still apply will be reproduced, in amended form where necessary, in Guides to the various Divisions, Courts and Offices.

Miscellaneous

2C–11 [p.259]

Add:

47a. References to the Court of Justice of the European Communities

Mercantile and Commercial Lists

2C–12 [p.259]

Insert new paragraph:

Costs

2C–12A [p.273]

52. Queens Bench Division and Chancery Division Practice Direction

2C–66 **Affidavits**
[p.273] *Delete square brackets and reference to* "Room E15" *in the second line of footnote.*

2C–81 **Undertakings given to the Court by the Plaintiff**
[p.276] *Delete square brackets and reference to* "Room E15" *in the second line of footnote.*

2C–96 **Undertakings given to the Court by the Plaintiff**
[p.278] *Delete the words* "Room W.11" *in the first line of footnote. Delete square brackets and reference to* "Room E15" *in second line of footnote.*

2C–107 **Undertakings given to the Court by the Plaintiff**
[p.281] *Delete square brackets and reference to* "Room E15" *in the second line of footnote.*

2C–118 **Undertaking given to the Court by the Plaintiff**
[p.282] *Delete square brackets and reference to* "Room E15" *in the second line of footnote.*

2C–128 **Effect of the Defendant's undertaking**
[p.283] *Delete square brackets and reference to* "Room E15" *in the second line of footnote.*

2C–139 **Effect of the Defendant's undertaking**
[p.284] *Delete square brackets and reference to* "Room E15" *in the second line of footnote.*

2C–148 **Terms of Settlement**
[p.285] *Delete square brackets and reference to* "Room E15" *in the second line of footnote.*

2C–204 **Description**
[p.297] *Add new note:*

*
2C–204/1 **Note**

The *Practice Direction (Judges: Mode of Address)* [1982] 1 W.L.R. 101 has been amended so as to provide that, when sitting in court, the judge who holds the office of recorder of Cardiff shall be addressed as "My Lord" or "My Lady", as the case may be (*Practice Direction (Judges: Recorder of Cardiff)* [1999] 1 W.L.R. 597, Sup.Ct.).

2C–207 **COURT DRESS**
[p.298] *Amend date to July 19, 1994 in heading.*

2C–208 **(B) Practice Direction issued by Lord Chief Justice, April 11, 1995**
[p.298] *Add at end:*

2C–208/1 **(C) Practice Direction issued by Lord Chief Justice, November 25, 1998**

1. On April 23, 1998 the Institute of Legal Executives (ILEX) became an authorised body under the Courts and Legal Services Act 1990 for the purpose of granting rights of audience to its members. Having consulted the Heads of Divisions and ILEX, the Lord Chancellor has decided that it would be appropriate for members of ILEX who are authorised advocates under the Courts and Legal Services Act 1990 to wear court dress when appearing in open court in circumstances in which counsel or solicitors appearing as advocates wear court dress.

2. The Lord Chancellor has also decided to take this opportunity to provide for advocates who may be granted rights of audience by any future bodies authorised for this purpose under the Courts and Legal Services Act 1990. The Lord Chancellor has decided that it would not be appropriate to extend the wearing of wigs.

3. The requirements of Practice Direction (Court Dress) [1994] 1 W.L.R. 1056 of July 19, 1994 are therefore varied as follows: Queen's Counsel wear a short wig and silk (or stuff) gown over a court coat; junior counsel wear a short wig and stuff gown with bands; solicitors and other advocates authorised under the Courts and Legal Services Act 1990 wear a black stuff gown and bands, but no wig.

4. This Direction is made by the Lord Chancellor with the concurrence of the Heads of Divisions and applies throughout the Supreme Court (including the Crown Court) and in county courts.

Rights of Audience of Solicitors in the Supreme Court **2C–240**
Add new paragraph: [p.307]

SUPREME COURT: REFERENCES TO THE COURT OF JUSTICE OF THE EUROPEAN COMMUNITIES NO. 47A

Practice Direction issued by Lord Chief Justice, January 14, 1999

1. Before making a reference to the European Court of Justice under article 177 of the EC Treaty the Court of Appeal and the High Court should pay close attention to (a) the terms of that article, (b) Order 114 of the Rules of the Supreme Court and (c) Prescribed Form 109 (see *The Supreme Court Practice 1999*, volume 2, paragraph 1A–114). **2C–240A**

Close attention should also be paid to the *Guidance of the European Court of Justice on References by National Courts for Preliminary Rulings* incompletely reproduced at [1997] 1 C.M.L.R. 78), and fully set out in Schedule B below.

2. It was the responsibility of the court, not the parties, to settle the terms of the reference. That should identify as clearly, succinctly and simply as the nature of the case permitted the question to which the referring court sought an answer. It was very desirable that language should be used which lent itself readily to translation.

3. The referring court should, in a single document scheduled to the order:

(i) identify the parties and summarise the nature and history of the proceedings;
(ii) summarise the salient facts, indicating whether those were proved or admitted or assumed;
(iii) make reference to the rules of national law (substantive and procedural) relevant to the dispute;
(iv) summarise the contentions of the parties so far as relevant;
(v) explain why a ruling of the European Court was sought, identifying the EC provisions whose effect was in issue;
(vi) formulate, without avoidable complexity, the question(s) to which an answer was requested.

Where the document was in the form of a judgment, as would often be convenient, passages which were not relevant to the reference should be omitted from the text scheduled to the order.

Incorporation of appendices, annexures or enclosures as part of the document should be avoided, unless the relevant passages lent themselves readily to translation and were clearly identified.

4. The referring court should ensure that the order of reference, when finalised, was promptly passed to the Senior Master of the Queen's Bench

Division so that it might be transmitted to Luxembourg without avoidable delay.

The title of the referring court should be stated, as appropriate.

Schedule A listed titles of the divisions and sub-divisions of the Court of Appeal and the High Court.

Schedule B

Guidance of the European Court of Justice on References by National Courts for Preliminary Rulings

The development of the Community legal order was largely the result of co-operation between the Court of Justice of the European Communities and national courts and tribunals through the preliminary procedure under article 177 and the corresponding provisions of the ECSC and Euratom Treaties.

In order to make that co-operation more effective, and so enable the Court of Justice better to meet the requirements of national courts by providing helpful answers to preliminary questions, the Note for Guidance was addressed to all interested parties, in particular to all national courts and tribunals.

It had to be emphasised that the Note was for guidance only and had no binding or interpretative effect in relation to the provisions governing the preliminary ruling procedure.

It merely contained practical information which, in the light of experience in applying preliminary ruling procedure, might help to prevent the kind of difficulties which the court had sometimes encountered.

1. Any court or tribunal of a member state might ask the Court of Justice to interpret a rule of Community law, whether contained in the Treaties or in acts of secondary law, if it considered that that was necessary for it to give judgment in a case pending before it.

Courts or tribunals against whose decisions there was no judicial remedy under national law had to refer questions of interpretation arising before them to the Court of Justice, unless the Court had already ruled on the point or unless the correct application of the rule of Community law was obvious.

2. The Court of Justice had jurisdiction to rule on the validity of acts of the Community institutions. National courts or tribunals might reject a plea challenging the validity of such an act.

But where a national court, even one whose decision was still subject to appeal, intended to question the validity of a Community act, it had to refer that question to the Court of Justice.

Where, however, a national court or tribunal had serious doubts about the validity of a community act on which a national measure was based, it might, in exceptional cases, temporarily suspend application of the latter measure or grant other interim relief with respect to it.

It had then to refer the question of validity to the Court of Justice, stating the reasons for which it considered that the Community act was not valid.

3. Questions referred for a preliminary ruling had to be limited to the interpretation or validity of a provision of Community law, since the Court of Justice did not have jurisdiction to interpret national law or assess its validity.

It was for the referring court or tribunal to apply the relevant rule of Community law in the specific case pending before it.

4. The order of the national court or tribunal referring a question to the Court of Justice for a preliminary ruling might be in any form allowed by national procedural law.

Reference of a question or questions to the Court of Justice generally involved stay of the national proceedings until the Court had given its ruling, but the decision to stay proceedings was one which it was for the national court alone to take in accordance with its own national law.

5. The order of reference containing the question or questions referred to the Court would have to be translated by the Court's translators into the other official languages of the Community.

Questions concerning the interpretation or validity of Community law were frequently of general interest and the Member States and Community institutions were entitled to submit observations. It was therefore desirable that the reference should be drafted as clearly and precisely as possible.

6. The order for reference should contain a statement of reasons which was succinct but sufficiently complete to give the Court, and those to whom it had to be notified, the Member States, the Commission and in certain cases the Council and the European Parliament, a clear understanding of the factual and legal context of the main proceedings.

In particular, it should include

(i) a statement of the facts which were essential to a full understanding of the legal significance of the main proceedings;
(ii) an exposition of the national law which might be applicable;
(iii) a statement of the reasons which had prompted the national court to refer the question or questions to the Court of Justice; and
(iv) where appropriate, a summary of the arguments of the parties.

The aim should be to put the Court of Justice in a position to give the national court an answer which would be of assistance to it.

The order for reference should also be accompanied by copies of any documents needed for a proper understanding of the case, especially the text of the applicable national provisions.

However, as the case-file or documents annexed to the order for reference were not always translated in full into the other official languages of the Community, the national court should ensure that the order for reference itself included all the relevant information.

7. A national court or tribunal might refer a question to the Court of Justice as soon as it found that a ruling on the point or points of interpretation or validity was necessary to enable it to give judgment.

It had to be stressed, however, that it was not for the Court of Justice to decide issues of fact or to resolve disputes as to the interpretation or application of rules of national law.

It was therefore desirable that a decision to refer should not be taken until the national proceedings had reached a stage where the national court was able to define, if only as a working hypothesis, the factual and legal context of the question.

On any view, the administration of justice was likely to be served if the reference was not made until both sides had been heard.

8. The order for reference and the relevant documents should be sent by the national court directly to the Court of Justice, by registered post, addressed to:

The Registry
Court of Justice of the European Communities
L-2925, Luxembourg
(Tel: 00 352 4303 1)

The Court Registry would remain in contact with the national court until judgment was given, and would send copies of the various documents, written observations, report for the hearing, opinion of the advocate-general. The Court would also send its judgment to the national court.

The Court would appreciate being informed about the application of its judgment in the national proceedings and being sent a copy of the national court's final decision.

9. Proceedings for a preliminary ruling before the Court of Justice were free of charge. The Court did not rule on costs.

2C–242 **Mercantile Court (Bristol)**

[p.308] *Delete para. 11 of Practice Direction.*

* *Add new note:*

2C–242/1 **Note**

Paragraph 11 of *Practice Direction (Mercantile Court: Bristol)* [1993] 1 W.L.R. 1522 has been deleted, and the power of presiding judges to designate judges to whom cases may be released by mercantile judge has been removed (*Practice Direction (Mercantile Court Bristol) (No. 2)* [1999] 1 W.L.R. 1278, QBD, *sub. nom. Practice Note (Bristol Mercantile Court: Designation of Judges)* [1999] 2 All E.R. 1024).

Commencement of this Practice Direction

2C–258 *Add new paragraph:*

[p.313]

COSTS

SHORT INTERLOCUTORY HEARINGS

Practice Direction issued by the Lord Chief Justice and the Vice-Chancellor, February 1, 1999

2C–259 1. Judges (at all levels in the judiciary) have a discretionary power to assess summarily the amount of costs to be paid by a party to the litigation to another party (see Order 62 Rule 7(4)(b) of the Rules of the Supreme Court and Order 38 Rule 3(3D) and Rule 19(3) of the County Court Rules 1981). It is desired to encourage a greater use by judges of this power. Accordingly, the following paragraphs apply to every inter partes interlocutory hearing the estimated duration of which does not exceed one day.

2. (i) At the conclusion of the hearing of every inter partes interlocutory application in the High Court and of every inter partes interlocutory application in the County Court to which Order 38 Rule 3(3D) or Rule 19(3) of the County Court Rules 1981 applies, the Court should consider whether or not to assess summarily the amount of the costs of the application to be recoverable by one party from another. Where Order 38 Rule 19(1) of the County Court Rules 1981 applies, the Court is obliged to assess the costs.

(ii) The general rule is that whenever a "costs in any event" order is made the Court should make a summary assessment of costs unless there is good reason not to do so, *e.g.* where the paying party shows substantial grounds for disputing the sum claimed for costs that cannot be dealt with summarily.

(iii) Where costs are assessed summarily, the Court may make an order for payment by some specified date or by instalments. If no such order is made the assessed costs will be payable within 14 days of the date of the order.

(iv) A summary assessment cannot be made where any (paying or receiving) party is either legally aided and/or a person under a disability (Order 80 Rule 1 of the Rules of the Supreme Court).

(v) Order 59 Rule 1B(1)(b) (appeals) applies both to the court's decision to make a summary assessment of costs and to the assessment itself.

3. Unless the Court otherwise directs—

(i) Not later than 24 hours prior to the commencement of the hearing of every interlocutory application each party who intends to seek a "costs in any event" order must supply every other party with a brief summary statement of the amount of the costs of the application that he will seek to recover under that order.

(ii) The statement must state the amount and nature of any disbursements (including counsel's fees) and the amount of the solicitor's profit costs recovery of which will be sought. All amounts must be shown net of VAT. If VAT is to be claimed, the amount of VAT must be separately shown.

(iii) If the solicitor's profit costs have been calculated on the basis of a rate per hour, the statement must specify the number of hours, the rate per hour and the grade of fee earner. If the solicitor's profit costs have been calculated on any other basis, the statement must explain the basis of the calculation thereof.

(iv) The failure by a party without reasonable excuse to comply with sub-paragraph (i) shall be taken into account by the Court in deciding what order in respect of the costs of the application should be made.

(v) The foregoing sub-paragraphs shall not apply where the parties have agreed between them the amount of the costs for which an order for payment should be made.

(vi) A model form for use when complying with sub-paragraph (i) is annexed.

4. This Practice Direction will come into effect on Monday, 1 March 1999. It does not apply to family proceedings in the High Court or in a County Court.

Note

1. This Practice Direction applies only to short interlocutory hearings (including summary judgment applications). This is in order to enable judges who have not previously been accustomed to assessing costs to gain some experience in doing so in short and simple cases. It is intended that when the new Civil Procedure Rules and Practice Directions come into force the restriction of the Practice Direction to interlocutory hearings will be removed. In the meantime, the restriction should not be taken as any discouragement to judges who wish to exercise their power to assess costs in cases not falling within the scope of this Practice Direction from doing so.

2. Order 38 Rule 19(1) of the County Court Rules 1981 requires the Court to assess costs without a taxation (a) where the costs are awarded on the lower scale and (b) where the costs are awarded on Scale 1 and the solicitor for the receiving party so desires. In the cases covered by Order 38 Rule 19(1) an assessment is obligatory not discretionary. In County Courts proceedings, the Court has a discretionary power to assess costs under Order 38 Rule 3(3D) (where costs are awarded on Scale 2), Rule 17B and Rule 19(3) (where costs are awarded on Scale 1 and are not included in the general costs of the action). Thereapart, in County Court proceedings the Court has no power to assess costs. These provisions will no longer apply after 26 April 1999.

3. Paragraph 3 of this Practice Direction applies to all interlocutory hearings the estimated duration of which does not exceed one day. Failure to comply with sub-paragraph (i) may be taken as indicating that the party in default will not be seeking an order for costs.

4. On 26 April 1999 the Costs Practice Direction supplemental to Parts 43 to 48 of the Civil Procedure Rules will come into effect. Paragraphs contained in section 3 of the Costs Practice Direction relating to Part 44 will supersede and replace the provisions of this Practice Direction without materially altering their effect.

Annex

COURT
JUDGE/MASTER CASE REFERENCE
CASE TITLE

[Party]'s Statement of Costs for the hearing on [date]

Description of fee earners*
(1) [name] [grade] [hourly rate claimed]
(2) [name] [grade] [hourly rate claimed]

<u>Attendances on [Party]</u>
[number] hours at £ | £

<u>Attendances on opponents</u>
[number] hours at £ | £

<u>Attendances on others</u>
(1) [number] hours at £ | £
(2) [number] hours at £ | £

<u>Attendances on documents</u>
[number] hours at £ | £

<u>Attendance at hearing</u>
[number] hours at £ | £
[number] hours travel and waiting at £ | £

<u>Counsel's fees [name] [year of call]</u>
Fee for [advice/conference/documents] | £
Fee for hearing | £

<u>Other expenses</u>
[court fees] | £
Others [give brief description] | £ ______

TOTAL | £
Amount of VAT claimed
on solicitors and counsel's fees | £
on other expenses | £
GRAND TOTAL
£ ______

The costs estimated above do not exceed the costs which the [party] is liable to pay in respect of the work this estimate covers.

Dated

Signed
Name of firm of solicitors
[partner] for the [party]

*4 grades of fee earner are suggested: (1) partners and solicitors with over 4 years PQE(2) solicitors with up to 4 years PQE and senior legal executives (3) legal executives and senior para legals (4) trainee solicitors and junior para-legals. In respect of each fee earner routine letters out and routine telephone calls should be claimed at one tenth of the hourly rate.

SECTION 3

TABLES

B. HIGH COURT JUDGMENT TABLE

Note **3B–1 [p.374]**

Add at end:

This table will require substantial amendment given the provisions of Pt 12 of the Civil Procedure Rules. Work is currently underway on suitable High Court Forms and the table will be revised once this work is complete.

D. TIME TABLE UNDER RSC AND CCR

Table showing the times fixed for taking various proceedings **3D–1 [p.390]**

Delete all of Section D and substitute:

D. TIME TABLE UNDER CPR

SHOWING THE TIMES FIXED BY RULE FOR TAKING VARIOUS PROCEEDINGS

[— *As to computation of the times mentioned in this Table, see CPR Pt 2, r.8*] **3D–1**

Tables Showing the Times Fixed for Taking Various Proceedings

Acceptance of Money Paid into Court (Part 36 Payments).	
Money paid into Court in satisfaction can be accepted in satisfaction and the action terminated if notice of such acceptance is given	within 21 days after receipt of notice of payment. Where a payment is made less than 21 days before trial, the offer may only be accepted if the parties agree liability for costs or the court gives permission. (CPR 36.5(6),(7).)
Acknowledgment of Service.	
(a) where the defendant is served with a claim form which states that particulars of claim are to follow the period for acknowledgment of service is	14 days after service of the particulars of claim (CPR 10.2(1)(a)).
(b) in any other case the period for acknowledgment of service is	14 days after service of the claim form (CPR 10.3(1)(b)). (Save where the claim is served overseas—see RSC O.11 r1A and CPR 6.16(4)).
Admission of Documents.	
A party shall be deemed to admit the authenticity of a document disclosed under CPR 31 unless he serves a notice that he wishes the document to be proved at trial. The Notice must be served	by the latest date for serving witness statements or within 7 days of disclosure of the document, whichever is the later (CPR 32.19).

Admissions of Fact.	
A party may serve notice on another party requiring him to admit the facts specified in the notice (CPR 32.18). The notice must be served	no later than 21 days before trial (CPR 32.18(2)).
Admissions of liability to pay. A party may admit the whole or part of a money claim by returning an admission form within	14 days after service of the claim form or where the Claim form specified that Particulars of Claim would follow, 14 days after service of the Particulars of Claim. (CPR 14.2) (But see RSC O. 11 r1A where the Claim is served out of the jurisdiction.)
Appeals. 1. TO HOUSE OF LORDS	See House of Lords Directions and Standing Orders Applicable to Civil Appeals (1996).
2. TO COURT OF APPEAL	See RSC O.59
3. TO DIVISIONAL COURT	See RSC O.53.
4. TO A CIRCUIT JUDGE from a decision of a District Judge	
(a) Where the decision is made in the course of proceedings (whether before or after judgment), by Notice of Appeal served	within 5 days of the order appealed against or such further time as the judge may allow (CCR O.13 r.1(10)–(11)).
(b) Where the judgment or order is final, except where the party has consented to the order, by Notice of Appeal stating the grounds of appeal served	within 14 days of the date on which the judgment or order was given or made (CCR O.37 r.6(2)).
5. APPEALS ON THE SMALL CLAIMS TRACK	
(a) To appeal against an order in proceedings allocated to the Small Claims Track, by application on notice stating the ground relied on, filed	no more than 14 days after the day on which notice of the order was served on him (CPR 27.13(1)).
Applications to set aside and/or direct a re-hearing.	
1. SMALL CLAIMS TRACK	
For a re-hearing, where the award or judgment was given in that party's absence and the party was not represented, made by application on notice filed	no more than 14 days after the day on which notice of the judgment was served on him (CPR 27.11(2)).
2. OTHER CLAIMS	
Where an order striking out a statement of case or party or the whole of proceedings is made in the absence of either party the absent party may apply to set aside the order	under CPR 39.3(3), no time limit specified.
Arrest.	
1. ARREST OF THE PERSON	
Where a person is arrested under a power of arrest attached to an order of the court under Family Law Act 1996 part I, that person must be brought before the court	within 24 hours (Family Law Act 1996 s.47(7)).
Assessment of Costs (Detailed).	
(a) Commencement	
Where the source of the order for detailed assessment is a judgment, direction, order, award or other determination	the assessment proceedings must be commenced within 3 months of the judgment, etc., or 3 months of the lifting of any stay pending appeal. (CPR 47.7).
Where the source of the order for detailed assessment is discontinuance under Part 38	the assessment proceedings must be commenced within 3 months of service of notice of discontinuance or 3 months of dismissal of an application to set aside a notice of discontinuance under CPR 38.4. (CPR 47.7).

Where the source of the order for detailed assessment is acceptance of an offer to settle, or a payment into court under Part 36	the assessment proceedings must be commenced within 3 months after the date when the right to costs arose. (CPR 47.7).
Where the assessment is to be of the costs of an assisted person payable out of the legal fund, the assisted persons solicitor may commence assessment proceedings by filing a request	within 3 months after the date when the right to the detailed assessment arose (CPR 47.17(2)).
(b) Service of points of dispute and reply	
The paying party and any other party to the detailed assessment may dispute any item by serving points of dispute	within 21 days after service of notice of commencement (CPR 47.9).
Where points of dispute are served, the receiving party may serve a reply	within 21 days after service of the points of dispute (CPR 47.13).
(c) Application for a detailed hearing	
Where points of dispute have been served, the receiving party must apply for a detailed assessment hearing	within 3 months of expiry of the period for commencing assessment proceedings (CPR 47.14).
(d) Filing the completed bill of costs	
Where detailed assessment of costs has taken place the time for filing the completed bill is	14 days after the end of the detailed assessment hearing. (CPR 47.16).
(e) Appeals against detailed assessment	
A request for reasons for the decision may be made by the receiving party	when filing the completed bill of costs (CPR 47.23(2)).
A request for reasons for the decision may be made by the paying party	within 7 days of the end of the detailed assessment hearing (CPR 47.23(3))
Where permission is required (under CPR 47.24) to appeal against a detailed assessment decision, a party may seek permission	within 14 days after receiving written reasons under CPR 47.23 or 7 days after the decision if the court directs that written reasons do not need to be obtained (CPR 47.24).
Notice of appeal must be served	within 14 days after service of a court officer's reasons for the decision, or 7 days after the date of the decision if the court has directed that reasons do not need to be obtained. Where permission to appeal is required, within 14 days after the date of the decision to give permission to appeal. (CPR 47.25).

Assessment of Costs (Summary).

Each party who intends to claim costs must prepare a written statement of the costs in any case where a summary assessment will be made (for which see para. 4.4 to the Practice Direction relating to Part 44) and must file and serve it	as soon as possible and in any event not less than 24 hours before the date fixed for the hearing (Practice Direction to CPR 44 para. 4.5(4)).

Attachment of Debts *see* **Garnishee.**
Certiorari, Application for—*See* **Appeals** (3).

Charging Orders.

Service of documents specified in CCR O.31	not less than 7 days before the day fixed for the further consideration of the matter (CCR O.31 r.1(8)).

Claim Form.

Claim form must be served	within 4 months of issue, or 6 months where it is to be served out of the jurisdiction (CPR 7.5).

Claim, Particulars of—*See* **Statements of Case.**

Costs Orders.

Where the court makes an order for costs against a legally represented party and the party is not present when the order is made the party's solicitor must notify his client in writing of the costs order	not later than 7 days after the solicitor receives notice of the order (CPR 44.2).

Default Judgment. *See* **Judgments** (b) and (c).

Defence.—*See* **Statements of Case.**

Discontinuance.

(a) The claimant may discontinue the proceedings wholly or in part by filing notice of discontinuance and serving it on every other party	at any time (CPR 38(1)) save where permission is required by CPR 38(2).
(b) Where a defendant is served with a notice of discontinuance without requiring the court's permission, he may apply to set the notice aside	within 28 days of service of the notice of discontinuance on him (CPR 38.4(2)).
(c) Where costs not paid by discontinuing claimant	
Where all or part of a claim is discontinued the claimant is liable to pay the costs of a defendant against whom the claim was discontinued (CPR 38.6). The remainder of the proceedings may be stayed where the claimant is liable to pay those costs and fails to do so	within 21 days of the date on which the parties agreed the costs payable or 21 days of the date on which the court ordered the costs to be paid (CPR 38.8).

Disclosure and inspection.

(a) On the Fast Track, disclosure will take place	according to the court's directions but typically 4 weeks after notice of track allocation (Practice Direction to Part 28 para. 3.12).
(b) On the Multi-Track disclosure will take place	as directed by the court in exercise of its case management functions (CPR 29.2).
(c) On the Small Claims Track where standard directions apply under CPR 27.4, disclosure will take place by sending to every other party copies of all documents on which the party intends to rely	at least 14 days before the date fixed for the hearing (CPR 27.4(3)).
(d) Where a party has a right to inspect a document the party having the right must give notice of his wish to inspect it and the party who disclosed it must permit inspection	not more than 7 days after the date on which he received the notice, and the party inspecting may request a copy of the document. If the party so requesting undertakes to pay reasonable copying costs the party who disclosed the document must supply a copy within 7 days after the date of the request. (CPR 31.15).

Evidence.

1. BY DEPOSITION

A party intending to put in evidence a deposition at a hearing must serve notice of intention to do so on every party	at least 21 days before the day fixed for the hearing (CPR 34.11(3)).

2. HEARSAY—CIVIL EVIDENCE ACT 1995

(a) Where a party proposes to rely on hearsay evidence does not propose to call the person who made the original statement to give oral evidence, the court may allow another party to call and cross-examine that person, on application	made not later than 14 days after service of the hearsay notice (CPR 33.4(2)).
(b) Where a party tenders as hearsay evidence a statement made by a person but does not call the person who made the statement to give evidence, and another party wishes to call evidence to attack the credibility of the person who made the statement	the party wishing to attach the credibility of the witness must give notice to the party tendering the hearsay evidence not more than 14 days after service of the hearsay notice (CPR 33.5(2)).
(c) Evidence of findings on foreign law. Where a party intends to put in evidence a finding on a question of foreign law by virtue of section 4(2) of the Civil Evidence Act 1972 he must	give any other party notice of his intention, (if there are witness statements) not later than the latest date for serving them or (otherwise) not less than 21 days before the hearing at which he proposes to put the finding in evidence (CPR 33.7).

Execution.

(a) A warrant of execution shall not issue without the leave of the court	after six or more years have elapsed since the date of the judgment or order (CCR O.26 r.5(1)(a)).
(b) A warrant of execution shall in the first instance be valid for	12 months beginning with the date of its issue (CCR O.26 r.6(1)).
(c) A warrant of execution which has not been wholly executed may be renewed from time to time, on application	for a period of 12 months at any one time, beginning with the next day following that on which it would otherwise expire (CCR O.26 r.6(1)).

Garnishee.

(a) Unless otherwise ordered an order to show cause must be served on the Garnishee in the same manner as a fixed date summons	at least 15 days before the return day (CCR O.30 r.3(2)(a)).
(b) Unless otherwise ordered an order to show cause must be served on the judgment debtor in accordance with CPR Part 6	at least 7 days after a copy has been served on the Garnishee and at least 7 days before the return day (CCR O.30 r.3(2)(b)).

Interim payment.

(a) Application for an interim payment under CPR 25.6 may be made	after the end of the period for filing an acknowledgement of service (CPR 25.6(1)).
(b) A copy of an application notice for an order for an interim payment must be served	at least 14 days before the hearing of the application (CPR 25.6(3)).
(c) A respondent to an application for an order for an interim payment who wishes to rely on written evidence must file and serve the witness statement	at least 7 days before the hearing of the application (CPR 25.6(4)).
(d) If the applicant wishes to rely on written evidence in reply he must file and serve the written evidence	at least 3 days before the hearing of the application (CPR 25.6(5)).

Judgments.

1. DEFAULT JUDGMENT

(a) Judgment in default of acknowledgment of service (where permitted by CPR 12.2) may be obtained	where the Defendant has not filed an acknowledgment of service or a defence and the time for doing so has expired (CPR 12.3(1)(b)).
(b) Judgment in default of defence (where permitted by CPR 12.2) may be obtained	where the Defendant has filed an acknowledgment of service but has not filed a defence and the time for doing so has expired (CPR 12.3()(b)).

2. SUMMARY JUDGMENT

(a) Summary Judgment under CPR 24.2 where there is no real prospect of success on the claim or issue, or the defendant has no real prospect of successfully defending the claim or issue. Where a claimant wishes to apply for summary judgment	he may not do so until the defendant has filed an acknowledgment of service or a defence, unless the court gives permission or a practice direction provides otherwise (CPR 24.4(1)).
(b) Where a summary judgment hearing is fixed, the respondent (or the parties, where the hearing is fixed of the court's own initiative) must be given	at least 14 days' notice of the date fixed for the hearing and the issues which it is proposed that the court will decide at the hearing (CPR 24.4(3)).
(c) If the respondent to a summary judgment application wishes to rely on written evidence at the hearing he must file and serve the witness statement	at least 7 days before the summary judgment hearing (CPR 24.5(1)).
(d) If the applicant wishes to rely on a witness statement in reply he must file and serve it	at least 3 days before the summary judgment hearing (CPR 24.5(2)).

(e) Where a summary judgment hearing is fixed of the courts own initiative, any party who wishes to rely on written evidence at the hearing must file and serve it	at least 7 days before the hearing (CPR 24.5(3)(a)) and any party wishing to rely on written evidence in reply must file and serve it at least 3 days before the date of the hearing (CPR 24.5(3)(b)).
3. JUDGMENTS RE-OPENING CREDIT AGREEMENTS (FOR LAND)	
Reopening of agreements under the Consumer Credit Act 1974 relating to land only. Where in any proceedings such as are mentioned in sections 139(1)(b) or (c) of the Consumer Credit Act 1974, the debtor or a surety desires to have a credit agreement reopened he shall give notice to that effect to the court and to every other party	within 14 days after service of the claim form on him (CCR O.49 r.15 as amended by the CPR).

Judicial Review, Application for.—*See* **Appeals**, (3).

Landlord and Tenant Act 1954.

Application for a new tenancy under section 24 of the Act of 1954, period of validity for service limited to	2 months (CCR O.43 r.6(3)).

Litigation Friends.

(a) A person who wishes to act as litigation friend for a defendant or a claimant must file the authorisation (under the Mental Health Act 1983 Part VII) or the certificate of suitability stating that he satisfies the conditions of CPR 21.4(3)	in the case of a person wishing to act as litigation friend for a claimant, at the time when the claim is made, and in the case of a person wishing to act as litigation friend for a defendant, at the time when he first takes a step in the proceedings on behalf of the defendant (CPR 21.5(4) and (5)).
(b) When a party ceases to be a child at age 18 the litigation friend's appointment ceases. Where a party ceases to be a patient, the litigation friend's appointment continues until ended by court order. The child or patient must then serve notice complying with CPR 21.9(4) and if he does not do so	within 28 days after the date on which the litigation friend's appointment ceases, the court may on application, strike out any claim or defence brought by him (CPR 21.9(5)).

Mandamus, Application for.—*See* **Appeals** (3).

New Trial. *See* **Applications to set aside and/or direct a re-hearing** *and* **Appeals** *and* RSC O.59 rr.2 and 11.

Notice to admit facts.—*See* **Admissions of Fact.**

Notice to admit documents.—*See* **Admission of Documents.**

Orders—Administration.

(a) Where a debtor is ordered to furnish a list of creditors under the Attachment of Earnings Act 1971 section 4(1)(b), the list shall be filed	within 14 days after the making of the order unless otherwise directed (CCR O.39 r.2(3)).
(b) Where an administration order is revoked under CCR O.39 r.13A(2) or r.13A(3)(a), any party affected may apply on notice for the District Judge to consider the matter afresh	by application made within 14 days of service of the order on him (CCR O.39 r.13A(4)).

Part 20 Claims.

(a) Counterclaims against parties may be made without permission if the Part 20 claim is served	with the defence or at any other time with the court's permission (CPR 20.4(2))
(b) Counterclaims against non-parties may be made	only with the court's permission (CPR 20.5(1)).

(c) Claims for a contribution or an indemnity from a co-defendant may be made — without notice at any time after the defendant seeking the indemnity or contribution has filed an acknowledgment of service or a defence (CPR 20.6).

Particulars of Claim—*See* Statements of Case.

Possession Proceedings.—*See* Recovery of Land.

Recovery of Land, Summary Proceedings for.

(a) The day fixed for the hearing of an originating application for the summary possession of land shall, except in the case of urgency and by leave of the court, be — in the case of residential premises, not less than 5 days after the day of service and in the case of other land not less than 2 days after the day of service (CCR O.24 r.5(1)).

(b) No warrant of possession shall be issued after the expiry of — 3 months from the date of the order without leave of the court (CCR O.24 r.6(2)).

(c) Interim possession orders.

(i) A claim for an interim possession order must be made — within 28 days of the date on which the applicant first knew, or ought reasonably to have known, that the respondent or any of the respondents was in occupation (CCR O.24 r.9(d)).

(ii) The applicant for an interim possession order shall serve on the respondent the documents prescribed by CCR O.24 r.11 — within 24 hours of the issue of the application (CCR O.24 r.11(1)).

(iii) An interim possession order must be served — within 48 hours of the judge or district judge's approving the draft order (CCR O.24 r.13(1)).

Reply—*See* Statements of Case.

Service—*See* Statements of Case.

Setting Aside.—*See* Applications to set aside and/or direct a re-hearing.

Small Claims proceedings under CPR Part 27.

(i) if the district judge decides to hold a prelminary hearing under CPR 27.6 the court will and give the parties — not less than 14 days' notice of the date fixed for the hearing (CPR 27.6(3)).

(ii) if no preliminary hearing is directed to be held, or once the preliminary hearing has taken place, the court shall give the parties — not less than 21 days' notice of the date fixed for the before hearing (CPR 27.6(5)).

(iii) each party shall send to every other party copies of all documents on which he intends to rely, including any experts reports — not less than 14 days before the date fixed for the hearing (CPR 27.4(3)).

Statements of Case.

I—Service

(a) Particulars of Claim — must be contained in or served with the claim form or served within 14 days after service of the claim form, or within the time allowed for service of the claim form, if less (CPR 7.4).

(b) Acknowledgment of service—*See* **Acknowledgment of Service.**

(c) Defence (and Counterclaim) (Subject to circumstances appearing in CPR 15.4(2)) — serve within 14 days after service of Particulars of Claim or 28 days after service of Particulars of Claim where the Defendant has served an acknowledgment of service under CPR Part 10 (CPR 15.4(1)). (See also CPR 20.7 and **Part 20 Claims**).

(d) Reply — file and serve when the Claimant files the allocation questionnaire (CPR 15.8).

II—Statements of Case—Amendment.

Any party may amend any statement of case of his	(i) at any time before it has been served (even if filed) (CPR 17.1(1)); or (ii) if it has been served, with the consent of the parties or the permission of the court (CPR 17.1(2)).

Striking Out.

Application to set aside an order striking out all or part of a statement of case of the court's own initiative. A party served with the order may apply to set it aside	within such period as the court specifies or (if no period is specified) not more than 7 days after the date on which the order was served on the party making the application (CPR 3.3(6)).

Subpoena—*See* **Summons—Witness.**

Summons—Witness.

(a) A witness summons may not be issued without leave if the party issuing it wishes (i) the witness to attend a hearing apart from the trial or any date which is not the date fixed for trial, or (ii) to have the summons issued less than	7 days before the date of the trial (CPR 34.3(2)).
(b) The witness summons will be binding if it is served	at least 7 days before the date on which the witness is required to attend, unless the court directs a shorter period (CPR 34.5(1) and (2)).

Third Party Notice—*See* **Part 20 Claims.**

Trial, Arrangements for.

(a) Unless the court orders otherwise, the claimant must file a trial bundle containing documents required by a relevant practice direction and any court order	and not more than 7 days and not less than 3 days before the start of the trial (CPR 39.5(2)).
(And see the Practice Direction to CPR Part 39).	

Warrant of Execution.—*See* **Execution.**

Warrant of Possession.—*See* **Recovery of Land, Summary Proceedings For, (b).**

Witness Statements.—*See* **Evidence (4).**

Witness Summons.—*See* **Summons—Witness.**

SECTION 4

COURT FEES AND STAMPS

A. SUPREME COURT FEES ORDER 1980

Note 4A–1 [p.413]

Delete paras 4A–1 to 4A–12. Replace with new note:

Note 4A–1

The Supreme Court Fees Order 1980 has been replaced by The Supreme Court Fees Order 1999 (S.I. 1999 No. 687). This can be found in the second edition of *Civil Procedure.*

B. COUNTY COURT FEES ORDER 1982

Note 4B–1 [p.422]

Delete paras 4B–1 to 4B–4. Replace with new note:

Note 4B–1 *

The County Court Fees Order 1982 has been replaced by The County Court Fees Order (S.I. 1999 No. 689). This can be found in the second edtion of *Civil Procedure.* The County Court Fees Order 1999 was amended by the County Court Fees (Amendment) Order 1999 (S.I. 1999 No. 2548) so as to replace references to family credit and disability working allowance with references to working families' tax credit and disabled person's tax credit, following the changes made by the Tax Credits Act 1999.

C. NON-CONTENTIOUS PROBATE FEES ORDER 1981

Note 4C–1 to 4C–8 [p.428]

Delete paras 4C–1 to 4C–8 and insert:

C. THE NON-CONTENTIOUS PROBATE FEES ORDER 1999 (S.I. 1999 NO. 688)

Note 4C–1

This Order replaces the Non-Contentious Probate Order 1981.

4C-2 **Citation and commencement**

1. This Order may be cited as the Non-Contentious Probate Fees Order 1999 and shall come into force on 26th April.

4C-3 **Interpretation**

2. In this Order, unless the context otherwise requires—

(a) a fee referred to by number means the fee so numbered in Schedule 1 to this Order;

(b) "assessed value" means the value of the net real and personal estate (excluding settled land if any) passing under the grant as shown—

(i) in the Inland Revenue affidavit (for a death occurring before 13th March 1975), or

(ii) in the Inland Revenue account (for a death occurring on or after 13th March 1975), or

(iii) in a case in which, in accordance with arrangements made between the President of the Family Division and the Commission of Inland Revenue, or regulations made under section 256(1)(a) of the Inheritance Tax Act 1984 and from time to time in force, no such affidavit or account is required to be delivered, in the oath which is sworn to lead to the grant,

and in the case of an application to reseal a grant means the value, as so shown, passing under the grant upon its being resealed;

(c) "authorised place of deposit" means any place in which, by virtue of a direction given under section 124 of the Supreme Court Act 1981 original wills and other documents under the control of the High court (either in the principal registry or in any district registry) are deposited and preserved;

(d) "grant" means a grant of probate or letters of administration;

(e) "district registry" includes the probate registry of Wales, any district probate registry and any sub-registry attached to it;

(f) "the principal registry" means the Principal Registry of the Family Division and any sub-registry attached to it.

4C-4 **Fees to be taken**

3. The fees set out in column 2 of Schedule 1 to this Order shall be taken in the principal registry and in each district registry of the items described in column 1 in accordance with and subject to any directions specified in column 1.

4C-5 **Exclusion of certain death gratuities**

4. In determining the value of any personal estate for the purposes of this Order there shall be excluded the value of a death payable under section 17(2) of the Judicial Pensions Act 1981 or section 4(3) of the Judicial Pensions and Retirement Act 1993, or payable to the personal representative of a deceased civil servant by virtue of a scheme made under section 1 of the Superannuation Act 1972.

4C-6 **Exemptions, reductions and remissions**

5.—(1) Where it appears to the Lord Chancellor that the payment of any fee prescribed by this Order would, owing to the exceptional circumstances of the particular case, involve undue hardship, he may reduce or remit the fee in that case.

(2) Where by any convention entered into by Her Majesty with any foreign

power it is provided that no fee shall be required to be paid in respect of any proceedings, the fees specified in this Order shall not be taken in respect of those proceedings.

(3) Where any application for a grant is withdrawn before the issue of a grant, a registrar may reduce or remit a fee.

(4) Fee 7 shall not be taken where a search is made for research or similar purposes by permission of the President of the Family Division for a document over 100 years old filed in the principal registry or a district registry or another authorised place of deposit.

Revocations 4C–7

6. The Orders specified in Schedule 2 shall be revoked, except as to any fee or other sum due or payable under those Orders before the commencement of this Order.

SCHEDULE 1

FEES TO BE TAKEN 4C–8

Column 1 Number and description of fee	*Column 2* Amount of fee
1. Application for a grant On an application for a grant (or for resealing a grant) other than on an application to which fee 3 applies, where the value of the estate exceeds £5,000	£50
2. Personal application fee Where the application under fee 1 is made by a personal applicant (not being an application to which fee 3 applies) fee 2 is payable in addition to fee 1, where the value of the estate exceeds £5,000	£80
3. Special applications For a duplicate or second or subsequent grant (including one following a revoked grant) in respect of the same deceased person, other than a grant preceded only by a grant limited to settled land, to trust property, or to part of the estate	£15
4. Caveats For the entry or the extension of a caveat	£15
5. Search On an application for a standing search to be carried out in an estate, for each period of six months including the issue of a copy grant and will, if any (irrespective of the number of pages)	£5
6. Deposit of wills On depositing a will for safe custody in the principal registry or a district registry	£15
7. Inspection On inspection of any will or other document retained by the registry (in the presence of an officer of the registry)	£15
8. Copy documents On a request for a copy of any document whether or not provided as a certified copy:	
(a) for the first copy	£5
(b) for every subsequent copy of the same document if supplied at the same time	£1
(c) where copies of any document are made available on a computer disk or in other electronic form, for each such copy	£3

Column 1 Number and description of fee	*Column 2* Amount of fee
(d) where a search of the index is required, in addition to fee 8(a), (b) or (c) as appropriate, for each period of 4 years searched after the first 4 years	£3
9. Oaths Except on a personal application for a grant for administering an oath,	
9.1 for each deponent to each affidavit	£5
9.2 for marking each exhibit	£2
10. Determination of costs For determining costs	The same fees as are payable from time to time for determining costs under the Supreme Court Fees Order 1999 (the relevant fees are set out in fee 10 in Schedule 1 to that Order)
11. Settling documents For perusing and settling citations, advertisements, oaths, affidavits, or other documents, for each document settled	£10

SCHEDULE 2

ORDERS REVOKED

4C–9

Title	*S.I. number*
The Non-Contentious Probate Fees Order 1981	S.I. 1981/861
The Non-Contentious Probate Fees (Amendment) Order 1981	S.I. 1981/1103
The Non-Contentious Probate Fees (Amendment) Order 1986	S.I. 1986/705
The Non-Contentious Probate Fees (Amendment) (No. 2) Order 1986	S.I. 1986/2185
The Non-Contentious Probate Fees (Amendment) Order 1987	S.I. 1987/1176
The Non-Contentious Probate Fees (Amendment) Order 1989	S.I. 1989/1140

SECTION 5

COURT FUNDS OFFICE RULES AND PRACTICE

B. ADMINISTRATION OF JUSTICE ACT 1982

Management and investment of funds in court 5B–1

In s.38(2) delete "of" *and substitute* "or". [p.446]

C. COURTS FUNDS RULES 1987

Table of contents 5C–2

After Table of Contents add new note: [p.452]

Note 5C–2/1

These Rules have been amended by the Court Funds (Amendment) Rules 1999 (S.I. 1999 No. 1021). For "plaintiff" wherever it appears, substitute "claimant"; and for "proper officer" substitute "court officer".

Interpretation 5C–5

Delete r.2(1) and substitute: [p.454]

(1) Unless the context otherwise requires, expressions used in these Rules shall have the same meaning as in the Civil Procedure Rules 1998, and those Rules are referred to in these Rules as the "CPR".

After para. (1) insert:

(1A) A reference in these Rules to "R.S.C." or "C.C.R." followed by an Order by number is a reference to the Order with that number in the relevant Schedule to the CPR.

In para. (2), in the definition of person under disability, for "minor" *substitute* "child". *Delete the definition of Proper Officer. After the definition of person under disability insert:*

"Royal Courts of Justice" means the Supreme Court at the Royal Courts of Justice and does not include any District Registry.

In the definition of Suitors' money, before "county court" *insert* "District Registry or". *Delete the definition of Taxing Officer.*

Note 5C–6

Add at beginning: [p.455]

Amended by the Court Funds (Amendment) Rules 1999 (S.I. 1999 No. 1021).

Certificate of a Master or Taxing Master 5C–18

For "taxed" *wherever it appears, substitute* "assessed". *For* "Taxing Officer" *wherever it appears, substitute* "Costs Officer". *For* "taxation" *substitute* "detailed assessment". [p.457]

5C–19 Note
[p.458] *Add new para. at beginning of note:*
Amended by the Court Funds (Amendment) Rules 1999 (S.I. 1999 No. 1021).

5C–26 Lodgment on receipt of a Lodgment Schedule
[p.459] *In sub-para. (1)(ii)(b), for* "an" *substitute* "a witness statement or".

5C–27 Note
[p.459] *Add new para. at beginning of note:*
Amended by Court Funds (Amendment) Rules 1999 (S.I. 1999 No. 1021).

5C–33 Lodgment on receipt of a Lodgment Schedule
[p.460] *In sub-para. (2), before* "affidavit" *insert* "witness statement or".

5C–34 Lodgment on receipt of a written request
[p.460] *In sub-para. (i), delete:*
"the lodgment is made under R.S.C. Order 75, rule 24, and".

Delete sub-para. (iii) and substitute:
(iii) in any division of the High Court where the lodgment is made under:
(a) CPR Part 36 in satisfaction of a claim and the request is accompanied by a copy of the claim form and the notice of payment into court; or
(b) CPR rule 37.3 (where the defendant wishes to rely on a defence of tender before claim) and the request is accompanied by a copy of the claim form and a copy of the defence;

5C–37 Note
[p.461] *Add new para. to beginning of note:*
Amended by the Court Funds (Amendment) Rules 1999 (S.I. 1999 No. 1021).

5C–41 Lodgment of money into court
[p.461] *Delete para. (1) and substitute:*
(1) Money to be lodged in the Royal Courts of Justice in accordance with rules 14 or 15, except money representing the proceeds of sale or redemption of National Savings Stock, shall be paid directly into the Court Funds Office.

Delete para. (2). In para. (3), for "paragraphs (1) or (2)" *substitute* "paragraph (1)". *In para. (5), before* "shall", *insert* "or into a District Registry or county court under rule 19". *Delete para. (6) and substitute:*
(6) The effective date of lodgment of money lodged in the Royal Courts of Justice shall be:
(i) in the case of cash or a banker's draft, the date of its receipt in the Court Funds Office;
(ii) in the case of a cheque or instrument other than a banker's draft the date of its receipt in the Court Funds Office or such later date as the Accountant General may determine;
(iii) in the case of a lodgment to which paragraph (5) applies, the date certified by the Bank as that on which the money was placed to an account for the credit of the Accountant General.

In para. (7), before "county court" *insert* "District Registry or". *For* "County Court Rules" *substitute* "Civil Procedure Rules". *After para. (7) insert:*
(8) The effective date of lodgment of money paid in under paragraph (7) shall be the date of its receipt in the court office.

Note 5C–42

Add new para. at beginning of note: [p.461]

Amended by the Court Funds (Amendment) Rules 1999 (S.I. 1999 No. 1021).

Securities transferable by delivery and deposit of effects 5C–46

In para. (4), delete "County Court Rules" *and substitute* "Civil Procedure Rules". *Insert new note:* [p.462]

Note 5C–46/1

Amended by the Court Funds (Amendment) Rules 1999 (S.I. 1999 No. 1021).

Payment of suitors' money into a county court 5C–48

Delete r.19 and substitute: [p.463]

19. Where suitor's money is to be paid into a District Registry or a county court—

(a) it may be paid by post or otherwise into the court office;

(b) payment may be made during office hours on any day on which the office is open;

(c) the court officer shall give a receipt for it.

Insert new rule:

19A. The effective date of lodgment of money paid in under rule 19 shall be the date of its receipt in the court office.

In r.22 before "county court" *insert* "District Registry or". *In r.23 delete* "pursuant to County Court Rules". *Delete r.24 and substitute:*

24. Where—

(a) money has been paid into court in a claim proceeding in the Royal Courts of Justice; and

(b) the claim is transferred to a District Registry or county court, the court officer of the court to which the claim is transferred shall notify the Accountant General and, on receipt of such a notice, the Accountant General shall deal with it as if it had been transferred to him under Rule 31.

Note 5C–48/1

Insert new note:

Amended by the Court Funds (Amendment) Rules 1999 (S.I. 1999 No. 1021).

Appropriation 5C–49

Delete r.25 and substitute: [p.463]

25.—Where a defendant has paid money into court in accordance with a court order and wishes to treat the whole or any part of the money paid into court as a CPR Part 36 payment (in these Rules referred to as "appropriation") he shall file a notice of appropriation with the Accountant General.

(2) The effective date of appropriation shall be the date of the receipt of the notice of appropriation by the Accountant General.

(3) Where a defendant wishes to appropriate money which has been paid into a District Registry or county court and placed to a basic account under rule 31(4) he shall also file a copy of the notice of appropriation at that court.

(4) On receipt of a notice of appropriation the Accountant General shall note the relevant account accordingly and shall withdraw the sum mentioned in the notice from the basic account.

(5) The Accountant General shall place money in the basic account 21 days

after he has received the notice of appropriation, unless before that date he receives—

(a) a request for payment from the claimant; or

(b) if the money was paid into a District Registry or county court, notification from that court that a request for payment from the claimant has been received.

(6) Where, before appropriation, interest has accrued on the money in question the interest may be included in the appropriation, and this rule shall apply to the interest in the same way as it applies to the money lodged.

5C–50 Note
[p.464] *Add at beginning of note:*

Amended by the Court Funds (Amendment) Rules 1999 (S.I. 1999 No. 1021).

5C–53 Interest on money placed to an interest bearing account
[p.464] *In para. (3), for* "Accrued", *substitute* "Unless the Accountant General directs otherwise, accrued".

5C–54 Note
[p.465] *Add at beginning of note:*

Amended by the Court Funds (Amendment) Rules 1999 (S.I. 1999 No. 1021).

5C–55 Time for placing money to an interest bearing account
[p.465] *After para. (3) insert:*

(4) This rule does not apply to money—

(a) paid into court; or

(b) appropriated

to which Rule 31 applies.

5C–55/1 Note
Add new note:

Amended by the Court Funds (Amendment) Rules 1999 (S.I. 1999 No. 1021).

5C–58 Money paid in satisfaction, etc.
[p.465] *Delete para. (1) and substitute:*

(1) Where, in the Royal Courts of Justice, money has been

(a) paid into court in accordance with CPR Part 36; or

(b) appropriated in accordance with CPR rule 37.2

in satisfaction of a claim, it shall only be placed to a basic account 21 days after the effective date of lodgment or appropriation and not before.

Delete para. (2) and substitute:

(2) Where money has been paid into a District Registry or county Court in satisfaction of a claim, the court officer shall remit the amount of the payment to the Court Funds Office 22 days after the effective date of payment into that court.

Insert after para. (2):

(2A) Paragraphs (1) and (2) shall not apply where a request for payment from the claimant is received before the expiration of the time limits specified in those paragraphs.

In para. (3) before "county court" *insert* "District Registry or".

5C–59 Note
[p.466] *Add at beginning of note:*

Amended by the Court Funds (Amendment) Rules 1999 (S.I. 1999 No. 1021).

Interest on money paid in satisfaction **5C–60**

In paras (1) and (2), before "county court" *wherever it appears, insert* "District Registry or" *and delete* "paragraphs (4) and (5)" *wherever it appears and substitute* "paragraph (4)". *In para. (2) before* "county court" *insert* "District Registry or". *Delete para. (4) and substitute:* [p.466]

(4) Where money has been:

(a) (i) placed to a basic account under rule 31(1) or 31(4); or

(ii) paid into a District Registry or county court and subsequently appropriated in satisfaction of a claim; and

(b) accepted by the claimant within the time limit specified in CPR rule 36.11,

no interest shall be payable after the effective date of lodgment or appropriation, or where there has been more than one lodgment or appropriation, after the latest effective date of lodgment or appropriation.

Note **5C–60/1**

Delete paras (5) and (6). Insert new note:

Amended by the Court Funds (Amendment) Rules 1999 (S.I. 1999 No. 1021).

Time for investment **5C–66**

In first line, delete word "this" *preceding words* "Part IV". [p.467]

Dealing with foreign currencies **5C–71**

In para. (1)(i) delete "under R.S.C. Order 22, rule 1" *and substitute* "in the Supreme Court in accordance with CPR Part 36". [p.468]

Note **5C–73**

Add at beginning of note: [p.468]

Amended by the Court Funds (Amendment) Rules 1999 (S.I. 1999 No. 1021).

Payment out without order of money lodged in satisfaction **5C–82**

Delete para. (3). In para. (4)(i), for the words "R.S.C. Order 22" *to* "as the case may be," *substitute* "CPR rule 36.17(2)". *Delete para. (4)(v) and substitute:* [p.471]

(v) (a) payment into court has been made less than 21 days before the start of the trial; or

(b) the claimant has not accepted a payment into court within the time limit in CPR rule 36.11.(1);

except in the circumstances provided by CPR rule 36.11(2)(i).

Note **5C–84/1**

Add at end: [p.472]

Amended by the Court Funds (Amendment) Rules 1999 (S.I. 1999 No. 1021).

Payment out to defendant without order **5C–85**

Delete r.45 and substitute: [p.472]

Payment out of interest

45. Where money lodged or appropriated by the defendant in satisfaction of the whole of the claim has been accepted and paid to the claimant, the Accountant General shall pay any accrued interest remaining in court in respect of that claim to the defendant but no interest shall be payable after the date on which the claimant serves notice of acceptance.

Note **5C–85/1**

Add new note:

Amended by the Court Funds (Amendment) Rules 1999 (S.I. 1999 No. 1021).

5C–92 [p.473] **Payment of suitors' money out of a county court**

Delete r.50 and substitute:

Payment of suitors' money out of a District Registry or county court

50.—(1) Subject to the provisions of this rule, the court officer of each District Registry or county court shall appoint a day in the week on which all payments out of court shall be made, and may appoint a different day from time to time.

(2) In each week on the appointed day the court officer shall, without demand, pay to each entitled person all money to which that person has become entitled since the appointed day in the previous week.

(3) Money paid out of court under paragraph (2) shall be paid by crossed payable order to the person entitled to it or to his solicitor and the court officer shall, at the same time, furnish him with a statement of the money so paid.

(4) Notwithstanding anything in this rule, the court officer may, on request, pay money out of court to the person who he is satisfied is entitled to it on a day other than the appointed day.

5C–92/1 **Note**

Add new note:

Amended by the Court Funds (Amendment) Rules 1999 (S.I. 1999 No. 1021).

D. THE INVESTMENT OF FUNDS IN COURT

5D–2 [p.512] **Common Investment Funds**

In (3) delete from "Also invested" *to* "resident outside the United Kingdom.)" *and substitute* "Withdrawn on April 5, 1999 by the Administration of Justice CIF (Amendment) Scheme 1999 (S.I. 1999 No. 551)".

In the last line of para. 5D–2, delete "February 1 and August 1" *and substitute* "withdrawn on April 5, 1999 by the Administration of Justice CIF (Amendment) Scheme 1999 (S.I. 1999 No. 551).

SECTION 6

ADMIRALTY JURISDICTION AND PROCEEDINGS

A. RSC APPENDIX B

SPECIAL ADMIRALTY FORMS

Special Admiralty Forms **6A–1A** [p.519]

Delete the text of this Section and substitute:

A. CPR—SPECIALIST PRACTICE DIRECTION—ADMIRALTY

SPECIAL ADMIRALTY FORMS TABLE OF CONTENTS

Description of Form

6A–1A [p.519]

Form No.		*Para.*
ADM 1	Claim form (Admiralty claim in rem)	6A–1
ADM 1A	Claim form (Admiralty claim in personam)—NOTE	6A–2
ADM 1B	Notes for claimant on completing an in rem claim form	6A–3
ADM 1C	Notes for defendant on replying to an in rem claim form	6A–3/1
ADM 2	Acknowledgment of service/response pack (Admiralty claim in rem)	6A–4
ADM 3	Preliminary act	6A–5
ADM 4	Application and undertaking for arrest and custody	6A–6
ADM 5	Outline form of declaration (affidavit) in support of application for warrant of arrest	6A–7
ADM 6	Notice to consular officer of intention to apply for warrant of arrest	6A–8
ADM 7	Request for caveat against arrest	6A–9
ADM 8	Request for caveat against arrest after constitution of a limitation fund	6A–10
ADM 9	Warrant of arrest	6A–11
ADM 10	Standard directions to the admiralty marshal	6A–12
ADM 11	Request for caveat against release	6A–13
ADM 12	Application and undertaking for release	6A–14
ADM 13	Application for judgment in default of filing an acknowledgment of service and/or defence or preliminary act	6A–15
ADM 14	Order for sale of a ship	6A–16
ADM 15	Claim form (Admiralty limitation claim)	6A–17
ADM 15A	Notes for claimant on completing a claim form in an Admiralty limitation claim	6A–18
ADM 15B	Notes for defendant (Admiralty limitation claim)	6A–19
ADM 16	Notice of admission of right of claimant to limit liability	6A–20
ADM 16A	Defence to admiralty limitation claim	6A–21
ADM 16B	Acknowledgment of service/response pack (Admiralty limitation claim)	6A–22
ADM 17	Application for restricted decree of limitation	6A–23
ADM 18	Restricted decree of limitation	6A–24
ADM 19	Decree of limitation	6A–25
ADM 20	Defendant's claim in a limitation claim	6A–26
ADM 21	Outline form of declaration (affidavit) as to inability of a defendant to file and serve statement of case under a decree of limitation	6A–27
ADM 22	Notice of appeal against Registrar's decision on a reference	6A–28

6A–1

Claim Form (Admiralty claim in rem)

In the	High Court of Justice Queen's Bench Division Admiralty Court
Claim No.	
Issue date	

Admiralty claim in rem against

of the Port of

Claimant

Defendant(s)

Brief details of claim

The Admiralty Registry within the Royal Courts of Justice, Strand, London WC2A 2LC is open between 10am and 4.30pm Monday to Friday. District Registries with Admiralty jurisdiction are open between 10am and 4pm.
Please address all correspondence to the admiralty registry and quote the claim number.

Claim No.	

Particulars of Claim (attached) (to follow)

Statement of Truth
*(I believe) (The Claimant believes) that the facts stated in these particulars of claim are true.
*I am duly authorised by the claimant to sign this statement

Full name ______________________________

Name of claimant's solicitor's firm ______________________________

signed ______________________ position or office held ______________________
*(Claimant) (Litigation friend) (Claimant's solicitor) (if signing on behalf of firm or company)

*delete as appropriate

Claimant's or claimant's solicitor's address to which documents or payments should be sent if different from overleaf including (if appropriate) details of DX, fax or e-mail.

ADM 1A

Admiralty claim form—(Admiralty claim in personam)

6A–2 An Admiralty Claim in personam shall be commenced on a Part 7 claim form as adapted for a Commercial Court claim, save for taking into consideration any logical or textual modifications made to the "Notes for Claimant on completing a claim form" in the Commercial Court, in order to accord with the practice of the Admiralty Court.

The formats for Part 7 and Part 8 claim forms for Commercial Court claims, the notes and response packs thereto together with certain other forms as adapted shall apply to an Admiralty action in personam (or in rem, if applicable) with the appropriate alterations.

MODIFICATIONS TO THE NOTES FOR CLAIMANT (Commercial Court)

Part 7 and Part 8 Claim forms.

HEADING:—

An Admiralty Claim form must be issued in the Royal Courts of Justice or a District Registry. Use whichever of the following is appropriate:—

"In the High Court of Justice Queen's Bench Division
Admiralty court"
and "......... District Registry"
(inserting the name of the District Registry)

or

"In the High Court of Justice Queen's Bench Division,
Admiralty Court
Royal Courts of Justice".

PARTICULARS OF CLAIM:—

Part 7 Claim form
Substitute "within 75 days after service of the claim form"
for the words "within 28 days after acknowledgment of service"

Notes for Claimant on completing an IN REM claim form

6A–3

Further information may be obtained from the Admiralty & Commercial Registry, room E200 Royal Courts of Justice, London, WC2A 2LL. Tel. 0171 936 6112 Fax. 0171 936 6245.

Please read all these guidance notes before you begin completing the claim form. The notes follow the order in which information is required on the form.

You may only issue an IN REM claim form in the Admiralty Court of the High Court (The High Court means either a District Registry attached to a County Court or the Royal Courts of Justice in London).

Staff can help you fill in the claim form and give information about the procedure once it has been issued. But they cannot give legal advice. If you need legal advice, for example, about the likely success of your claim or the evidence you need to prove it, you should contact a solicitor or a Citizens Advice Bureau.

If you are filling in the claim form by hand, please use black ink and write in block capitals.

Copy the completed claim form and the defendant's notes for guidance so that you have one copy for yourself, one copy for the court and one copy for each Defendant. **You will need an additional copy of the claim form if you are seeking to arrest a vessel.** Send or take the forms to the court office with the appropriate fee. The court will tell you how much this is.

N.B. The time for filing an Acknowledgment of Service in an IN REM claim is within 14 days of service of the CLAIM FORM irrespective of whether or not the PARTICULARS OF CLAIM are served with it. The CLAIM FORM must therefore be served with the forms on which the defendant may reply to your claim.

Notes on completing the claim form

Heading

You should add to the heading the name of the court in which you are issuing:

either 'Royal Courts of Justice' or

'............................ District Registry'

(inserting name of the District Registry)

Ship and port details

You should supply the name of the vessel or vessels you are proceeding against and the **Port of Registry** (**not** the Port where the vessel may be berthed). If you do not know the Port of Registry you should insert 'port of registry unknown'. If you are proceeding in addition or separately against other property, e.g. cargo, you should describe it.

Claimant details

As the person issuing the claim, you are called the 'claimant'. The person you are suing is called the 'defendant'. Claimants who are under 18 years old (unless otherwise permitted by the court), or patients within the meaning of the Mental Health Act 1983, must have a litigation friend to issue and conduct court proceedings on their behalf. Court staff will tell you more about what you need to do if this applies to you.

The Claimant in an in rem claim, whether or not an individual, may be named or described. If not named, you must provide a name upon the request of any other party. If described rather than named you must still give an address. See below as to the appropriate address.

Descriptions that may be used are 'The owners of the ship 'X' or 'The owners of cargo lately laden on board the vessel 'Y'. Court staff can advise you of other acceptable descriptions.

You must provide the following information about yourself according to the capacity in which you are suing. When suing as:—

an individual by name:
All known forenames and surname, (where Mr, Mrs, Miss, Ms or Other e.g. Dr) and residential address (including postcode and telephone number) in England and Wales.

an individual by name who is under 18 write '(a child by Mr John Smith his litigation friend)' after the child's name

a patient within the meaning of the Mental Health Act 1983
write "(by Mr John Smith his litigation friend)" after the patient's name

as an individual trading under another name
you must add the words "trading as" and the trading name e.g. "Mr John Smith trading as Smith's Groceries"

in a representative capacity
you must say what that capacity is e.g. "Mr John Smith as the representative of Mrs Mary Smith (deceased).

in the name of a club or other unincorporated association
add the words "suing on behalf of" followed by the name of the club or other unincorporated association.

a firm
Enter the name of the firm followed by the words "a firm" e.g. "Bandbox—a firm" and an address for service which is either a partner's residential address or the principal or last known place of business.

a corporation (other than a company)
Enter the full name of the corporation and the address which is either its principal office or any other place where the corporation carries on activities and which has a real connection with the claim

a company registered in England and Wales:
Enter the name of the company and an address which is either the company's registered office or any place of business that has a real, or the most, connection with the claim.

an overseas company (defined by s.744 of the Companies Act 1985):
Enter the name of the company and either the address registered under s.691 of the Act or the address of the place of business having a real or the most, connection with the claim.

Defendant details

The defendant **must** be described and not named.

'The owners and/or demise charterers of the ship "Z"', unless it is known that the ship either is, or is not, under demise charter when the claim can be issued simply against 'the owners of the ship "Z"' or 'the demise charterers of the ship "Z"'.

In ownership and/or possession actions, the defendant may be described as 'all other persons claiming ownership and/or possession of the ship "A"'.

When action is taken against cargo and/or freight the defendant may be described as 'owners of cargo now or lately laden on board the ship "X"' together with the freight earned thereon.

The defendant in an action against the proceeds of a Judicial sale by the Admiralty Marshal should be described as 'the owners of the proceeds of sale of the vessel "Y"'.

Permutations of the above can be used as appropriate. The Court staff will advise you as necessary.

Brief details of claim

Note: the facts and full details about your claim should be set out in the 'particulars of claim' (see note under 'Particulars of Claim').

You must set out under **this** heading:

- a concise statement of the nature of your claim in rem
- the remedy you are seeking
- if your claim is for money, the amount you are claiming
- the amount of any interest you are claiming

If your claim is in foreign currency you should endorse the claim form with a certificate as to the sterling equivalent. Court staff will inform you of the appropriate certificate.

Particulars of claim

You may include your particulars of claim on the claim form in the space provided or in a separate document which you should head 'Particulars of Claim'. It should include the names and/or descriptions of the parties, the court, the claim number and your address for service and also contain a statement of truth. You should keep a copy for yourself, provide one for the court and one for each defendant.

Separate particulars of claim can either be served

- with the claim form **or**
- within 75 days after the date on which the claim form was served, provided that the service of the particulars of claim is not later than 12 months from the date of issue of the claim form.

Note: If the particulars of claim are not contained or served with the claim form you must include the following statement "Particulars of claim will follow if an acknowledgment of service is filed indicating an intention to defend the claim."

Your particulars of claim must include

- a concise statement of the facts on which you rely
- a statement (if applicable) to the effect that you are seeking aggravated damages or exemplary damages
- details of any interest which you are claiming
- any other matters required for your type of claim as set out in the relevant practice directions

Note: You are not required to complete and serve particulars of claim if your claim is in respect of a collision between ships.

Address for documents

Insert in this box the address at which you wish to receive documents and/or payments, if different from the address you have aleady given under the heading 'Claimant'. The address must be in England or Wales. If you are willing to accept service by DX, fax or e-mail, add details.

Statement of truth

This must be signed by you, by your solicitor or your litigation friend, as appropriate.

Where the claimant is a registered company or a corporation the claim must be signed by either the director, treasurer, secretary, chief executive, manager or other officer of the company or (in the case of a corporation) the mayor, chairman, president or town clerk.

Notes for defendant on replying to an in REM claim form

6A–3/1

Please read these notes carefully—they may help you decide what to do about this claim. Further information can be obtained from the Admiralty & Commercial Registry, Royal Courts of Justice, Strand, London, WC2A 2LL.

You must file an acknowledgment of service within 14 days of the date of service of the Claim Form on your property (or a Solicitor acting on your behalf) irrespective of whether or not particulars of claim are served with it.

If you do not file an acknowledgment of service, judgment may be given against you and if the property described on the claim form is under arrest of this court, it may be sold by order of the court.

You may either:

- pay the amount claimed
- provide security for the claim in a form acceptable to the Claimant
- admit that you owe all or part of the claim and ask for time to pay or
- dispute the claim.

The notes below tell you what to do.

The response pack, which should accompany the claim form, will tell you which forms to use for your reply.

Court staff can help you complete the forms of reply and tell you about court procedures. But they cannot give legal advice. If you need legal advice, for example about the likely success of disputing the claim, you should contact a solicitor or a Citizens Advice Bureau immediately.

Costs and Interest: Additional costs and interest may be added to the amount claimed on the front of the claim form if judgment is given against you.

Once your completed acknowledgment of service is received by the court, the claimant will send you the particulars of claim, unless previously sent to you.

Your response and what happens next

How to pay

Do not bring any payments to the court—they will not be accepted.

When making payments to the claimant, quote the claimant's reference (if any) and the claim number.

Make sure that you keep records and can account for any payments made. Proof may be required if there is any disagreement. It is not safe to send cash unless you use registered post.

Admitting the Claim

Claim for specified amount

If you admit all the claim, take or send the money, including any interest and costs, to the claimant at the address given for payment on the claim form within 14 days of receipt of the particulars of claim.

If you admit all the claim and you are asking for time to pay, complete Form N9A and send it to the claimant at the address given for payment on the claim form, within 14 days of receipt of the particulars of claim. The claimant will decide whether to accept your proposal for payment. If it is accepted, the claimant may request a judge to give judgment against you and you will be sent an order to pay. If your offer is not accepted, the judge will decide how you should pay or, if your vessel is under arrest, may order that your vessel be sold in order to satisfy the judgment.

If you admit only part of the claim, complete Form N9A and Form N9B (see "Disputing the Claim" overleaf) send them to the court within 14 days of receipt of the particulars of claim. At the same time send copies of the completed Forms N9A and N9B to the claimant who will decide whether to accept your part admission. If it is accepted, the claimant may request a judge to give judgment against you and the court will send you an order to pay or, if your vessel is under arrest, order that your vessel be sold in order to satisfy the judgment. If your part admission is not accepted, the case will proceed as a defended claim.

Claim for unspecified amount

If you admit liability for the whole claim but do not make an offer to satisfy the claim, complete Form N9C and send it to the court within 14 days of receipt of the particulars of claim. At the same time send a copy of the completed Form N9C to the claimant within the same period. The claimant may request a Judge to give judgment against you for an amount to be decided by the court, and costs. If your vessel is under arrest, the Judge may at the same time order that your vessel be sold.

If you admit liability for the claim and offer an amount of money to satisfy the claim, complete Form N9C and send it to the court within 14 days of receipt of the particulars of claim. At the same time send a copy of the completed Form N9C to the claimant. The claimant must indicate within 14 days if the

ADM1C Defendants notes (4.99)

Printed on behalf of The Court Service

offer is acceptable and send you a copy. If a reply is not received, the claim will be stayed. If the amount you have offered is accepted, the claimant may request a Judge to give judgment against you for that amount.

If you have requested time to pay which is not accepted by the claimant, the rate of payment will be decided by the court, or, if your vessel is under arrest the court may order the vessel to be sold by the court.

If your offer in satisfaction is not accepted.

The claimant may apply to the court for judgment against you for an amount to be decided by the court, and costs.

If your vessel is under arrest, order that your vessel be sold. You and the claimant will be sent a copy of the court's order.

Disputing the Claim

If you are being sued as an individual for a specified amount of money and you dispute the claim, the claim may be transferred to your home court i.e. the one nearest your home or your solicitor's business address if different from the court where the claim was issued.

If you need longer than 14 days to prepare your defence or to contest the court's jurisdiction to try the claim, completion of the acknowledgment of service form will allow you 28 days from the date of service of the particulars of claim to serve your defence or make an application to contest the court's jurisdiction. The court will tell the claimant that your acknowledgment of service has been received.

If the case proceeds as a defended claim, the action will be allocated to the multi-track and the claimant will apply for a date to be fixed for a Case Management Conference before a Judge. You and the claimant will be required to file a completed case management information sheet at least 7 days before the Conference.

Further details are available from the Admiralty & Commercial Registry.

If your vessel is under the arrest of the court and you are disputing the claim you may nevertheless obtain the release of the vessel if you are able to offer security for the claim in a form acceptable by the claimant.

Claim for specified amount

If you wish to dispute the full amount claimed or wish to claim against the claimant (a counterclaim), complete Form N9B and send it to the court within 14 days of receipt of the particulars of claim. Send a copy of the completed Form N9B to the claimant within the same period.

If you admit part of the claim, complete the defence Form N9B and the Admission Form N9A and send them to the court within 14 days of receipt of the particulars of claim. At the same time send copies of the completed Forms N9B and N9A to the Claimants within the same period.

If you dispute the claim because you have already paid it, complete Form N9B and send it to the court within 14 days of receipt of the particulars of claim. At the same time send a copy of the completed Form N9B to the Claimant within the same period. The Claimant will decide whether to proceed with the claim or withdraw it and notify the court and you within 28 days. If the claimant wishes to proceed, the case will proceed as a defended claim.

Claim for unspecified amount/non-money claims

If you dispute the claim or wish to claim against the Claimant (counterclaim), complete Form N9D and send it to the court within 14 days of receipt of particulars of claim. At the same time send a copy of the completed Form N9D to the claimant.

Personal injuries claims:

If the claim is for personal injuries and the claimant has attached a medical report to the particulars of claim, in your defence you should state whether you:

agree with the report **or**

dispute all or part of the report **and** give

your reasons for doing so **or**

neither agree nor dispute the report **or**

have no knowledge of the report

Where you have obtained your own medical report, you should attach it to your defence.

If the claim is for personal injuries and the claimant has attached a schedule of past and future expenses and losses, in your defence you must state which of the items you:

agree **or**

dispute **and** supply alternative figures where appropriate **or**

neither agree nor dispute or have no knowledge of

Statement of Truth

This must be signed by you, by your solicitor or your litigation friend, as appropriate.

Where the defendant is **a registered company or a corporation** the response must be signed by either the director, treasurer, secretary, chief executive, manager or other officer of the company **or** (in the case of a corporation) the mayor, chairman, president or town clerk.

6A–4

Response Pack
Admiralty claim in rem

You should read the 'notes for defendant' attached to the claim form which will tell you when and where to send the forms

Included in this pack are:

- either **Admission Form N9A** (if the claim is for a specified amount) or **Admission Form N9C** (if the claim is for an unspecified amount or is not a claim for money)
- either **Defence and Counterclaim Form N9B** (if the claim is for a specified amount) or **Defence and Counterclaim Form N9D** (if the claim is for an unspecified amount or is not a claim for money)
- **Acknowledgment of service** (see below)

You are required to complete an Acknowledgment of Service form within 14 days from service of the Claim Form on you whether or not Particulars of claim are served with the Claim Form.

	Complete
If you admit the claim or the amount claimed and/or you want time to pay	the admission form
If you admit part of the claim	the admission form and the defence form
If you dispute the whole claim or wish to make a claim (a counterclaim) against the claimant	the defence form
If you need longer than 14 days to prepare your defence or to contest the court's jurisdiction to try the claim, completion of the acknowledgment of service form will allow you 28 days from service of particulars of claim to do so	the acknowledgment of service
If you do nothing, the claimant may ask a judge to give judgment against you and, if your vessel is under arrest, also request that your vessel be sold	

Acknowledgment of Service
Admiralty claim in rem

In the High Court of Justice Queen's Bench Division Admiralty Court	
Claim No.	
Claimant(s) (including ref.)	
Defendant(s)	

Description of defendant(s):—

Full name of person described above:—

....

....

Nature of ownership of property

The court office at

is open between 10am and 4.30pm Monday to Friday. Please address forms or letters to the Court Manager and quote the claim number.

Address to which documents about this claim should be sent (including reference if appropriate)

		if applicable
	fax no.	
	DX no.	
Tel. no. Postcode	e-mail	

If you do not file an acknowledgment of service within 14 days of the claim form on you, whether or not particulars of claim are served with it, judgment may be given against you.

Tick the appropriate box

1. I intend to defend all of this claim ☐
2. I intend to defend part of this claim ☐
3. I intend to contest jurisdiction ☐

If you file an acknowledgment of service but do not file a defence within 28 days of the date of service of the particulars of claim, judgment may be given against you.

If you do not file an application within 28 days of the date of service of the particulars of claim it will be assumed that you accept the court's jurisdiction and judgment may be given against you.

Signed (Defendant) (Defendant's Solicitor) (Litigation friend)

Position or office held (if signing on behalf of firm or company)

Date

ADM 3

Preliminary Act

In The High Court of Justice
Queen's Bench Division
Admiralty Court 6A–5

Claim No.

Claimant(s)

Defendant(s)

PRELIMINARY ACT ON BEHALF OF ....

PART 1

1

The names of the ships which came into collision and their ports of registry

2

The length breadth gross tonnage horsepower and draught at the material time of the ship and the nature and tonnage of any cargo carried by the ship

3

The date and time (including the time zone) of the collision

4

The place of the collision

5

The direction and force of the wind

6

The state of the weather

7

The state, direction and force of the tidal or other current

8

The position, the course steered

and speed through the water of the ship when the other ship was first seen or immediately before any measures were taken with reference to her presence, whichever was the earlier

9

The lights or shapes (if any) carried by the ship

10

(a) The distance and bearing of the other ship if and when her echo was first observed by radar

(b) The distance, bearing and approximate heading of the other ship when first seen

11

What light or shape or combination of lights or shapes (if any) of the other ship was first seen

12

What other lights or shapes or combinations of lights or shapes (if any) of the other ship were subsequently seen before the collision, and when

13

What alterations (if any) were made to the course and speed of the ship and the earlier of the two times referred to in article **8** up to the time of collision, and when, and what measures (if any) other than alterations of course of speed, were taken to avoid the collision, and when

14

The heading of the ship, the parts of each ship which first came into contact and the approximate angle between the two ships at the moment of contact

15

What sound signals (if any) were given, and when

16

What sound signals (if any)

were heard from the other ship,
and when

PART 2

State:

(1) that the information in Part 1 is incorporated in Part 2;
(2) any other facts and matters upon which the party filing this Preliminary Act relies;
(3) all allegations of negligence or other fault on which the party filing this Preliminary Act relies:
(4) the relief or remedy which the party filing this Preliminary Act claims

Statement of Truth

*(I believe) (The Claimant believes) (The defendant believes) that the facts stated in this Preliminary Act are true
*I am duly authorised by the (claimant) (defendant) to sign this statement

Full name ....

Name of claimant's/defendant's solicitor's firm ....

signed .... position or office held ....

*(Claimant) (Defendant) ('s litigation friend) (if signing on behalf of firm or company)

*delete as appropriate

ADM 4

Application and undertaking for arrest & custody

6A–6

IN THE HIGH COURT OF JUSTICE
QUEEN'S BENCH DIVISION
ADMIRALTY COURT
Admiralty claim in rem against:

Claim No.

The Admiralty Marshal is requested to execute the

Warrant in the above action lodged herewith by the arrest

of ....
....

lying/expected to arrive at ....

....

A personal undertaking is hereby given to pay on demand the fees of the Marshal and all expenses incurred, or to be incurred, by him or on his behalf in respect of the arrest, or endeavours to arrest, the property and the care and custody of it while under arrest and of its release, or endeavours to release it.
Dated day of
To be signed by the Solicitor
or by his Clerk for him ....

....

Office use only:

I confirm that at: on:
no Caveats have been filed or entered against the arrest of the above property.

Signed ....

ADM 5

Outline form of Declaration (Affidavit) in support of application for Warrant of Arrest

Apart from the usual requirements for an affidavit as defined by the Practice Direction supplementing CPR part 32, continue as follows:— 6A–7

"The Claimant's claim is [state nature of claim] I am informed by [name and occupation of informant] and verily believe that the Claimant's claim has not been satisfied.

The property to be arrested is the ship [name] of the port of [port of registry].

The amount of security for the claim sought by the Claimant is [state amount if known]

The relevant notice [if required] [exhibit No.] has been sent to the consular office of [name of country or State]."

If the claim falls under section 21(4) of the Supreme Court Act 1981 and it does **not** carry a maritime lien or other charge the affidavit should further include:—

"The ship [name of ship to be arrested] is the ship [or is one of the ships] against which the action is brought and is [or is not] the ship in connection with which the claim in the action arose.

In my belief the person who would be liable on the claim in an action in personam ["the relevant person"] is [name].
The grounds of my belief are [state them].

In my belief [name of relevant person] was when the cause of action arose the owner [or the charterer or in possession or control [as the case may be] of the ship [name of the ship in connection with which the claim arose]. The grounds of my said belief are [state them].

In my belief [name of relevant person] was on the [date Claim Form was issued] the beneficial owner of all the shares in the ship [name of ship in connection with which the claim arose and is the ship to be arrested] or was the charterer of it under a charter by demise. The grounds of my said belief are [state them]

(**OR**, if the ship to be arrested is not the one in connection with which the claim arose)

In my belief [name of relevant person] was on the [date Claim Form was issued] the beneficial owner as respects all the shares in the ship [name of ship to be arrested]. The grounds of my said belief are [state them]"

ADM 6

Notice to Consular Officer of intention to apply for Warrant of Arrest

6A–8 **To the Consular Officer of (name of State)**

The ship (name) of the Port of

TAKE NOTICE THAT as solicitors for [name or description of party seeking arrest] we did on the day of 19 [or we intend to] institute proceedings in the Queen's Bench Division, Admiralty Court, of the High Court of Justice against the above-mentioned ship in respect of a claim [or Counterclaim] by [name or description of party seeking arrest] for [state nature of claim or counterclaim] and that we intend to apply to the Admiralty Court to arrest the said ship.

Dated this day of 19

[Signed]

Solicitors for

ADM 7

Request for Caveat against Arrest

[Description of property giving name, if a ship] 6A–9

We of

[solicitors for of]

request a caveat against the arrest of

[description of property giving name, if a ship] and hereby

undertake to acknowledge issue or service of the claim form in

any action that may be begun in the High Court of Justice against the said and, within 3 days after receiving

notice that such an action has been begun, to give security in the action in the sum not exceeding or to pay that

sum into court. We consent that the claim form and any other

documents in the action may be left for us at

Dated the day of [Signed]

ADM 8

Request for Caveat against Arrest after constitution of a Limitation Fund

6A–10 [Description of property giving name, if a ship]

We of

[solicitors for of]

request a caveat against the arrest of

[description of property giving name, if a ship], having

constituted a limitation fund in Claim No.

in respect of damage arising from the relevant incident, namely

[describe briefly the incident]; and undertake hereby to

acknowledge issue or service of the Claim Form in any action that may be begun against the property described in this request.

We consent that the Claim Form and any other document may be left for us at

Dated the day of [Signed]

ADM 9

Warrant of Arrest

6A–11

In The High Court of Justice
Queen's Bench Division
Admiralty Court

Claim No.

Admiralty claim in rem against:

Claimant(s)

Defendant(s)

ELIZABETH THE SECOND, by the Grace of God, of the United Kingdom of Great Britain and Northern Ireland and of Our other realms and territories Queen, Head of the Commonwealth, Defender of the Faith:

To the Admiralty Marshal of Our High Court of Justice, and to all singular his substitutes, Greeting. We hereby command you to arrest the ship of the port of and to keep same under arrest until you should receive further orders from Us.

WITNESS , Lord High Chancellor of Great Britain, the day of

The Claimant's claim is for [copy from Claim Form]

Taken out by

Solicitors for the

Certificate as to Service

On the day of

the within-named ship

lying

was arrested by virtue of

for a short time on*

of the said ship, and on taking off the process, by leaving

a copy thereof fixed in its place.

*State on which part
of the outside of the
ship's superstructure

Signed

Date

ADM 10

Standard Directions to the Admiralty Marshal

6A–12

In The High Court of Justice
Queen's Bench Division
Admiralty Court

Claim No.

Admiralty claim in rem against:

Claimant(s)

Defendant(s)

IT IS ORDERED THAT the Admiralty Marshal be at liberty at any time:—

(a) To take measures to preserve the ship " "
its machinery and equipment;

(b) to move the said ship up to 5 miles within the limits of the port where it is lying under arrest, either for
its safety or to comply with the requirements of the
Port Authority;

(c) to supply the minimum victuals, domestic fuel and water
necessary to avoid hardship to the crew.

Dated the day of

The Admiralty Registrar.

ADM 11

Request for Caveat against Release

[Description of property giving name, if a ship] 6A–13

We of
[solicitors for of]

request the entry of a caveat against the release of the above-named property or the proceeds of sale thereof paid into Court by the Admiralty Marshal.

The intending caveator claims to have a right of action in rem

against the above-mentioned property or proceeds of sale for

[state nature of claim in rem and the approximate amount

claimed, if known]

Dated the day of [Signed]

ADM 12

Application and undertaking for release

6A–14

IN THE HIGH COURT OF JUSTICE
QUEEN'S BENCH DIVISION
ADMIRALTY COURT

Claim No.

Admiralty action in rem against:

The Admiralty Marshal is requested to release in the above action the ....

lying ....

A personal undertaking is hereby given to pay the fees of the Marshal and all expenses incurred, or to be incurred, by him or on his behalf in respect of the arrest, or endeavours to arrest, the property and the care and custody of it while under arrest and of its release, or endeavours to release it.

Dated day of

To be signed by the Solicitor
or by his Clerk for him ....

....

Office use only:

I confirm that at: on :
no Caveats have been filed or entered against release of the above property.

Signed ....

ADM 13

Application for Judgment in default of filing an Acknowledgment of Service and/or Defence or Preliminary Act

6A–15

In The High Court of Justice
Queen's Bench Division
Admiralty Court

Claim No.

Admiralty claim in rem against:

Claimant(s)

Defendant(s)

TAKE NOTICE that the Claimant(s) will make an application on day the day of at am/pm,

by Counsel for an Order that:

(1) Judgment in default of filing an Acknowledgment of Service [and or Defence] [or Preliminary Act] be given for the Claimant(s) in the sum of with interest thereon [or in an amount to be assessed] and for their costs of this Claim including the costs of this application to be assessed if not agreed.

[2] [if applicable] The vessel " " be Appraised and Sold by the Admiralty Marshal. [see Form for the terms of the order for sale]

Dated the day of

To the Defendant(s) and/or Caveators or as the case may be.

ADM 14

Order for sale of a ship

6A–16

In The High Court of Justice
Queen's Bench Division
Admiralty Court

Claim No.

Admiralty claim in rem against:

Claimant(s)

Defendant(s)

BEFORE:

UPON HEARING

and upon reading the affidavits of

[no Acknowledgment of Service and or Defence or Preliminary Act having been filed on behalf of the Defendant(s)]

IT IS ORDERED THAT:

(1) the ship " " be appraised and sold by the Admiralty Marshal [before judgment (if applicable)]

(2) the Admiralty Marshal do choose one or more experienced persons to appraise the vessel and certify its true value in writing.

(3) the Admiralty Marshal do sell the vessel on his Conditions of Sale for the highest price that can be obtained for it, but not for less than the certified value without an order of Court

(4) the Admiralty Marshal do pay the proceeds of sale of the vessel into Court.

(5) on completion of the sale the Admiralty Marshal do countersign and file the Certificate of Value together with an account of his fees and expenses.

(6) the Solicitors on behalf of the Claimant [or as may be] do within .... give to the Admiralty Marshal a personal undertaking to pay on demand the fees and expenses of the Marshal incurred by him or on his behalf in respect of the appraisement and sale of the property, or of endeavours to appraise or to sell the property.

[OR BE SOLD IN SUCH OTHER WAY AS THE COURT MAY ORDER]

Dated the day of

6A–17

Claim Form (Admiralty limitation claim)

In the	High Court of Justice Queen's Bench Division Admiralty Court
Claim No.	
Issue date	

Claimant(s)

Defendant(s)

Details of limitation claim (*see also overleaf*)

Named defendant's name and address

The Admiralty Registry within the Royal Courts of Justice, Strand, London WC2A 2LC is open between 10am and 4.30pm Monday to Friday. District Registries with Admiralty jurisdiction are open between 10am and 4pm.
Please address all correspondence to the admiralty registry and quote the claim number.

Claim No.	

Details of limitation claim *(continued)*

Full name ____________________

Name of claimant's solicitor's firm ____________________

signed ____________________ position or office held ____________________
*(Claimant) (Litigation friend) (Claimant's solicitor) (if signing on behalf of firm or company)

*delete as appropriate

Claimant's or claimant's solicitor's address to which documents or payments should be sent if different from overleaf including (if appropriate) details of DX, fax or e-mail.

Notes for Claimant on completing a claim form in an admiralty limitation claim 6A–18

Further information may be obtained from the Admiralty & Commercial Registry, Room E200 Royal Courts of Justice, London, WC2A 2LL. Tel. 0171 936 6112 Fax. 0171 936 6245.

Please read all these guidance notes before you begin completing the claim form. The notes generally follow the order in which information is required on the form.

You may only issue an Admiralty Limitation Claim Form in the Admiralty Court of the High Court (The High Court means either a District Registry (attached to a County Court) or the Royal Courts of Justice in London).

Staff can help you fill in the claim form and give information about the procedure once it has been issued. But they cannot give legal advice. If you need legal advice, for example, about the likely success of your claim or the evidence you need to prove it, you should contact a solicitor or a Citizens Advice Bureau.

If you are filling in the claim form by hand, please use black ink and write in block capitals.

You should file a sworn declaration at the court with your completed claim form:

- proving the facts you rely on in your claim; and
- stating the names and addresses (if known) of all persons who to your knowledge have claims against you in respect of the occurrence to which the claim relates (other than named defendants)

Copy the completed claim form, the defendant's notes for guidance and your sworn declaration so that you have one copy for yourself, one for the court and one for each 'named' defendant (see defendant details below). Send or take the forms to the court office with the appropriate fee. The court will tell you how much this is.

Each named defendant must be served with copies of the claim form, notes for guidance, your declaration and a response pack (ADM Form Nos 15, 15A, 15B, 16 and 16A).

Notes on completing the claim form

Heading

You should add to the heading the name of the court in which you are issuing:

either 'Royal Courts of Justice' or

'................................ District Registry'

(inserting name of the District Registry)

Defendant details

At least one of the defendants in a limitation claim **must** be named.

All other defendants may be described e.g. "and all other persons claiming or being entitled to claim damages by reason of, or rising out of the collision between the ship "Alpha" and the ship "Omega" which occurred in the English Channel on or about the 6th October, 1999".

Claimant and named defendant details

The Claimant must be named not described.

As the person issuing the claim, you are called the "claimant"; the person you are suing is called the "defendant". Claimants who are under 18 years old (unless otherwise permitted by the court), and patients within the meaning of the Mental Health Act 1983 must have a litigation friend to issue and conduct court proceedings on their behalf. Court staff will tell you more about what you need to do if this applies to you.

You must provide the following information about yourself **and** the named defendants according to the capacity in which you are suing and in which the defendant is being sued.

When suing or being sued as:—

an individual: All known forenames and surname, (whether Mr, Mrs, Miss, Ms or Other e.g. Dr) and residential address (**including** postcode and telephone and any fax or e-mail number) in England and Wales. Where the defendant is a proprietor of a business, a partner in a firm or an individual sued in the name of a club or other unincorporated association, the address for service should be the usual or last known place of residence **or** principal place of business of the company, firm or club or other unincorporated association.

Where an individual is: under 18 write "(a child by Mr. John Smith his litigation friend)" after the child's name.

If the child is conducting proceedings on their own behalf write "(a child)" after the child's name.

a patient within the meaning of the Mental Health Act 1983 write "(by Mr. John Smith his litigation friend)" after the patient's name.

trading under another name you must add the words "trading as" and the trading name e.g. Mr. John Smith trading as Smith's Groceries".

suing or being sued in a representative capacity you must say what that capacity is e.g. "Mr John Smith as the representative of Mrs Mary Smith (deceased).

suing or being sued in the name of a club or other unincorporated association add the words "suing/sued on behalf of" followed by the name of the club or other unincorporated association.

a firm enter the name of the firm followed by the words "a firm" e.g. "Bandbox—a firm" and an address for service which is either a partner's residential address or the principal or last known place of business.

a corporation (other than a company) enter the full name of the corporation and the address which is either its principal office **or** any other place where the corporation carries on activities and which has a real connection with the claim

a company registered in England and Wales enter the name of the company and an address which is either the company's registered office **or** any place of business that has a real, or the most, connection with the claim.

an overseas company (defined by s.744 of the Companies Act 1985) enter the name of the company and either the address registered under s.691 of the Act **or** the address of the place of business having a real, or the most, connection with the claim.

Details of claim

Under this heading you must set out:

- a brief description of the incident for which you are claiming to have your liability limited, including the date and place of the incident
- that your claim is limited to the provisions of the Merchant Shipping Act 1995
- that you are seeking all necessary and proper directions for the purposes of ascertaining and distributing the amount of your liability between the parties who are entitled to receive it.

Named defendant's name and address

Enter in this box the full name and address of the named defendant(s) to be served with the claim form (i.e. one claim form for each defendant)

An Admiralty Limitation Claim form may NOT be served outside of England & Wales unless:

(a) the case falls within section 22(2)(a) to (c) of the Supreme Court Act 1981; or

(b) the defendant has submitted to or agreed to submit to the jurisdiction of the Admiralty Court; or

(c) the Admiralty Court has jurisdiction over such claim under any applicable Convention

Address for documents

Insert in this box the address at which you wish to receive documents, if different from the address you have aleady given under the heading "Claimant". The address you give must be either that of your solicitors or your residential or business address and must be in England or Wales. If you live or carry on business outside of England and Wales, you can give some other address within England and Wales. If you are willing to accept service by DX, fax or e-mail, add details.

Notes for defendant (admiralty limitation claim)

6A–19

Please read these notes carefully – they will help you decide what to do about this claim.

Further information may be obtained from the Admiralty & Commercial Registry, Room E200, Royal Courts of Justice, Strand, London, WC2A 2LL. Tel. 0171 936 6112 Fax. 0171 936 6245.

You have only a limited time to reply to this claim – the notes below tell you what to do.

You may either:

dispute the court's jurisdiction or contend that the court should not exercise it

admit the claimant's right to limit liability

dispute the claim

The response pack, which should accompany the claim form, will tell you which forms to use for your reply

If you **do not** respond in any way the court may grant the claimant a Limitation Decree in your absence

Court staff can tell you about procedures but they cannot give legal advice. If you need legal advice, you should contact a solicitor or Citizens Advice Bureau immediately.

Responding to this claim

Time for responding

You have from the date the claim form was served on you: 14 days to file an acknowledgment of service disputing the court's jurisdiction

or

28 days to file a completed defence or admission of the claimant's right to limit liability

(or, if the claim form was served outside of England and Wales, within the time specified by RSC Order 11 r.1A.)

If the claim form was:

- sent by post, the date of service is taken as the second day after posting (see date of postmark on the envelope)
- delivered or left at your address, the date of service will be the day after it was delivered.
- handed to you personally, the date of service will be the day it was given to you.

Completing the acknowledgment of service

You should tick either

- Box A – if you dispute the court's jurisdiction **or**
- Box B – if you contend that the court should not exercise its jurisdiction

and complete all the other details on the form.

You should send the completed form to the court and at the same time send a copy to the claimant.

You should file also an application at the court within 14 days of filing of your acknowledgment of service. The court will arrange a hearing date for the application.

If you do not file the application you will be treated as having accepted that the court has jurisdiction to hear the claim.

Completing the admission

You should complete admission form ADM16 and send it to the court and at the same time send a copy to the claimant. The claimant may file an application for the court to issue a restricted limitation decree limiting liability against any of the named defendants in the claim form who have filed an admission.

Completing the defence

You should file defence form ADM16A at the court and at the same time send a copy to the claimant. Within 7 days of filing of your defence (or filing of defence of other named defendants or expiry of the time for doing so) the claimant must apply for an appointment before the Admiralty Registrar for a case management conference. The court will give directions at this appointment for the future conduct of the case.

Statement of truth

This must be signed by you, by your solicitor or your litigation friend, as appropriate.

If you do nothing

The claimant may apply for a limitation decree against you.

6A-20 Notice of admission of right of claimant to limit liability

In the High Court of Justice Queen's Bench Division Admiralty Court	
Claim No.	

Claimant(s)

Defendant(s)

TAKE NOTICE THAT pursuant to Part Y, rule 8.1(7) Admiralty Proceedings, the following defendant(s) *(name them)*

admit the right of the claimant in this action to limit their liability in accordance with the provisions of *(give details of the relevant Act)*

Signed

Date

Defence to admiralty limitation claim

In the High Court of Justice
Queen's Bench Division
Admiralty Court

6A–21

Claim No.	

Claimant(s)

Defendant(s)

You have a limited number of days to file and serve this form. See notes for guidance attached to the claim form.

Signed (To be signed by you or by your solicitor or litigation friend)	*(I believe) (The defendant believes) that the facts stated in this form are true. *I am duly authorised by the defendant to sign this statement **delete as appropriate*	**Position or office held** (if signing on behalf of firm or company)	
Date			

Give an address to which notices about this case can be sent to you	Postcode	if applicable	
		fax no.	
		DX no.	
	Tel. no.	e-mail	

6A–22

Response Pack
(Admiralty Limitation claim)

You should read the 'notes for defendant' attached to the claim form which will tell you when and where to send the forms

Included in this pack are:

Admission Form ADM 16	Defence Form ADM 16A	Acknowledgment of service *(see below)*

	Complete
If you wish to dispute the court's jurisdiction or argue that the court should not exercise its jurisdiction	the acknowledgment of service
If you admit the right of the claimant to limit liability	the admission form
If you dispute the claim	the defence form
If you do nothing, the claimant may apply for a restricted limitation decree against you	

Acknowledgment of Service
(Admiralty limitation claim)

Defendant's full name if different from the name given on the claim form

....

....

In the High Court of Justice Queen's Bench Division Admiralty Court	
Claim No.	
Claimant (including ref.)	
Defendant	

Address to which documents about this claim should be sent (including reference if appropriate)

		if applicable	
		fax no.	
		DX no.	
Tel. no.	Postcode	e-mail	

Tick the appropriate box

A I intend to dispute jurisdiction ☐

B I intend to argue that the court should not exercise its jurisdiction ☐

You should file an application at the court within 14 days of service of this acknowledgment of service or you will be treated as having accepted the court's jurisdiction.

Signed		**Position or office held** (if signing on behalf of firm or company)		**Date**
	(Defendant) (Defendant's Solicitor) (Litigation friend)			

The Admiralty Registry within the Royal Courts of Justice, Strand, London WC2A 2LC is open between 10am and 4.30pm Monday to Friday. District Registries with Admiralty jurisdiction are open between 10am and 4pm.
Please address all correspondence to the admiralty registry and quote the claim number.

ADM 17

Application for restricted Decree of Limitation

IN THE HIGH COURT OF JUSTICE 6A–23
QUEEN'S BENCH DIVISION
ADMIRALTY COURT

Claim No.

Claimant(s)

Defendant(s)

TAKE NOTICE THAT the Claimant(s) will apply to The Admiralty Registrar on day the day of

(1) for leave [if necessary] to amend the Claim Form in this action so that the Defendants are only those named Defendants as have admitted the Claimant's right to limit liability pursuant to the Merchant Shipping Act 19 . . .

(2) for a Decree of Limitation pursuant to the Merchant Shipping Act 19 . . . restricted to their liabilities against the above-mentioned Defendants described in paragraph (1) above.

(3) for an Order that the fund in Court be paid out and distributed as follows;

(4) the costs of this application be

Dated the day of

To; The Defendants as above.

ADM 18

Restricted Decree of Limitation

6A–24 IN THE HIGH COURT OF JUSTICE
QUEEN'S BENCH DIVISION
ADMIRALTY COURT

Claim No.

Claimant(s)

Defendant(s) [restricted to those Defendants who have admitted the Claimant's right to limit liability]

BEFORE:

UPON CONSENT OF the Claimants and the above-named Defendants

AND UPON reading the affidavit [or declaration] of

IT IS ORDERED BY DECREE

(1) That by reason of the Merchant Shipping Act 19

the Claimants are not answerable in damages in respect of claims by the above-named Defendants or persons claiming through or under them, beyond the amount of Special Drawing Rights, in respect of the loss, damage and delay caused to any property or to the infringement of any rights through the Claimants' act or omission or through the act or omission of any person on board the vessel " " in the navigation or management of the " " when the " " collided with the " " in the on the day of .

(2) the limitation tonnage of the " " ascertained in accordance with the provisions of the Merchant Shipping Act 19 is tonnes, that the amount of the Limitation fund calculated in accordance with the Act is Special Drawing Rights and that the liability of the Claimants to the above named Defendants is £ together with simple interest thereon from the day of [day of the collision] to this day and no more [or as may be agreed between the parties to the action]

(3) the Claimants having constituted a limitation fund by payment into Court of the said amount on [date of payment into Court], all further proceedings against them by the above-named Defendants arising out of this occurrence be stayed.

(4) the fund in Court including all accrued interest to the date of payment out be paid out and distributed as follows:

(5) the costs of this application be

ADM 19

Decree of Limitation

IN THE HIGH COURT OF JUSTICE 6A–25
QUEEN'S BENCH DIVISION
ADMIRALTY COURT

Claim No.

Claimant(s)

Defendant(s)

BEFORE:

UPON HEARING Solicitors (Counsel) for the Claimants and Defendants

AND UPON reading the affidavit [or declaration] of

IT IS ORDERED BY DECREE

(1) That by reason of the Merchant Shipping Act 19 the Claimants are not answerable in damages beyond the amount of Special Drawing Rights, in respect of the loss, damage and delay caused to any property or to the infringement of any rights through their act or omission or through the act or omission of any person on board the " " in the navigation or management of the " " when the " " collided with the " " on the day of

(2) That the limitation tonnage of the " " ascertained in accordance with the provisions of the Merchant Shipping Act 19 is tonnes, that the amount of the Limitation Fund calculated in accordance with the Act is Special Drawing Rights and that the liability of the Claimants is £ together with simple interest thereon from the day of [day of the collision] to this day and no more.

(3) That the Plaintiffs having constituted a Limitation Fund by payment into Court of the said amount on the day of , all further proceedings in any action against them arising out of this occurrence be stayed.

(4) That after deduction of the above sum together with the simple interest thereon, the remainder of such sum

paid into Court by the Claimants on the day of , and any interest accrued thereon be paid out to the Claimants.

(5) That the Claimants place a single advertisement in each of three Newspapers, namely identifying the action and specifying the decree made in this action and further specifying a period of for the filing of claims and the issue of applications to set the decree aside.

(6) That the sum of £ together with the simple interest thereon be rateably distributed among the several person who make out their claims against the fund and that within 7 days of the time for filing claims or declarations, the Admiralty Registrar will fix a date for a case management conference at which directions will be given for the further conduct of the proceedings.

(7) That [order as to costs]

Dated the day of ,

ADM 20

Defendant's Claim in a Limitation Claim

IN THE HIGH COURT OF JUSTICE 6A–26
QUEEN'S BENCH DIVISION
ADMIRALTY COURT

Claim No.

Claimant(s)

Defendant(s)

The Defendants' claim is for damages arising out of the above-mentioned collision. On day of , the Claimants were granted a decree limiting their liability for the collision to Special Drawing Rights. Due to the collision the Defendants suffered damage and loss as follows;

With interest pursuant to section 35A of the Supreme Court Act 1981 and cost.

To the Claimants and their Solicitors.

To all other Defendants and their Solicitors.

Statement of Truth

*(I believe)(The Claimant believes)(The defendant believes) that the facts stated in this Preliminary Act are true
*I am duly authorised by the (claimant) (defendant) to sign this statement

Full name ....

Name of claimant's/defendant's solicitor's firm ....

signed ....   position or office held ....

*(Claimant) (Defendant) ('s litigation friend)   (if signing on behalf of firm or company)

*delete as appropriate

ADM 21

Outline form of Declaration (Affidavit) as to inability of a Defendant to file and serve Statement of Case under a Decree of Limitation

6A–27 Apart from the usual requirements for an affidavit as defined by the Practice Direction supplementing CPR part 32, continue as follows:—

"The [intended] Defendant [name] is unable to file and serve a Statement of Case within the time fixed under the Decree of Limitation made in this action on the [date] as he requires further information to enable him to decide whether or not to dispute the Claimant's right to Limit Liability in the following respects [state them]

OR

"The [intended] Defendant [name] requires a further [state period] in which to file and serve an application to set aside the said Decree of Limitation [state reasons for request]

OR

"The [intended] Defendant [name] requires a further [state period] in which to file and serve his Statement of Case under the said Decree of Limitation [state reason for request].

ADM 22

Notice of Appeal against Registrar's Decision on a Reference

In The High Court of Justice 6A–28
Queen's Bench Division
Admiralty Court

Claim No.

[Admiralty claim in rem against:]

Claimant(s)

Defendant(s)

TAKE NOTICE that the Claimants [or Defendants] will make an

application on day the day of

at am/pm, [by Counsel] that;

(1) the decision of the Admiralty Registrar herein dated the day of , upon the Claimant(s)

[or Defendant(s)] claim in the Reference be [set aside or varied by (specify the variation sought) or as the case may be].

(2) the costs of this application be

Dated the day of

B. ADMIRALTY PRACTICE DIRECTIONS

6B–1 to 6B–14 [p.529–532] *Delete all text in these paragraphs, keeping only first and second sentences of para. 6B–3 (substituting "claim form" for "writ"). See generally Practice Direction—Admiralty in second edition of Civil Procedure.*

D. JURISDICTION

6D–1 [p.534] **Introductory note**

Add new paragraph at end:

The following changes in terminology to achieve compliance with the Civil Procedure Rules and the ethos thereof should be made to the text in this Section:

- For "writ" substitute "claim form"
- For "plaintiff" substitute "claimant"
- For "action" substitute "claim"
- For "suit" substitute "claim"
- For "indorsement" substitute "statement of claim or of case"
- For "motion" substitute "application".

References in the notes to the former rules should be read where possible as references to the corresponding provision of the CPR and in particular the Practice Direction—Admiralty under CPR Pt 49. Precise correlation is not possible but the following table can be referred to:

Former rule	New provision
RSC, O.75	Practice Direction—Admiralty under CPR Pt 49
RSC, O.75, r.4	Above mentioned Practice Direction, paras 3.1(2), 4.4 and 9.1(6)
RSC, O.16	CPR Pt 20
RSC, O.18, r.8	CPR Pt 16 and Practice Direction—Statements of Case
SCP 1999, Vol. 1, paras 75/1/18, 75/1/22 to 75/1/28	See notes under CPR Pt 49—Practice Direction—Admiralty, para. 1

6D–3 [p.535] **Admiralty jurisdiction generally**

Delete penultimate paragraph and substitute:

It is now possible for a judgment creditor in a claim *in rem* to arrest both in respect of a national judgment *in rem* as well as a foreign judgment *in rem.* See Practice Direction supplementing CPR Pt 49—Admiralty, para. 6.1.

6D–11 [p.535] **Release on bail in possession action**

Add at end:

The provision of bail is now exceedingly rare.

6D–38 [p.538] **Note**

Add at end:

* See also *The "Edinburgh Castle"* [1999] 2 Lloyd's Rep. 362.

6D–60 [p.541] **subs. (4)(b)(i) "... charterer ..."**

Add new paragraph at end:

A slot charterer of spaces on a container ship for the carriage of goods is capable of coming within the definition of a charterer in s.21(4)(b) of the Supreme Court Act 1981 despite the fact that a slot charter gave control of only part of the vessel to the charterer, *MSC Mediterranean Shipping Company SA v. Polish Ocean Lines (The Tychy),* [1999] 2 Lloyd's Rep. 11, CA.

Ship 6D–73 [p.544]

Delete "para. 6D–8" *and substitute* "para. 6D–9".

Duty to assist ships, etc., in distress 6D–204 [p.549]

In s.93(1), after the words "a signal of distress" *insert* "from an aircraft"; *and for the words* "a ship or" *substitute the word* "an". *Delete subs. (2). In subs. (3), for* "subsections (1) and (2)" *substitute* "subsection (1)". *Delete subs. (4). In subs. (5), delete the words* ", and, if his ship has been requisitioned, from the duty imposed by subsection (2) above,". *In the sidenote, for* "ships, etc." *substitute* "aircraft".

Note 6D–205 [p.550]

Add at end:

Section 93 is amended by The Merchant Shipping (Distress Messages) Regulations 1998 (S.I. 1998) No. 1691), reg. 2.

Note 6D–209

Delete text from "at time of publication" *to end. Substitute:*

as at June 1999 see only under s.185(2A), the Merchant Shipping (Convention on Limitation of Liability for Maritime Claims) (Amendment) Order 1998 (S.I. 1998 No. 1258)—not in force until the 1996 Protocol amending the 1976 Convention on Liability for Maritime Claims comes into force internationally.

"Owners" 6D–235 [p.556]

Delete "para. 6D–225" *and substitute* "para. 6D–226".

"Owners" 6D–252 [p.557]

Delete "para. 6D–225" *and substitute* "para. 6D–226".

"Reasonable opportunity" 6D–258 [p.558]

Delete "The Berry" *and substitute* "The Berny".

Note 6D–262 [p.560]

Delete text from "at the time of writing" *to end. Substitute:*

as at June 1999 see hereunder the Merchant Shipping (Ship Receiving Transhipped Fish) Regulations 1998 (S.I. 1998 No. 209), effective April 1998.

County Court Admiralty Jurisdiction 6D–301 [p.562]

Delete text and substitute:

As from April 26, 1999 there is no Admiralty jurisdiction in the county court, see The Civil Courts (Amendment) (No. 2) Order 1999 (S.I. 1999 No. 1011). However, the county court retains Admiralty jurisdiction in respect of Admiralty proceedings commenced in or transferred to it before April 26, 1999 see art. 5 of the said 1999 Order.

SECTION 7

EUROPEAN JURISDICTION

A. GENERAL

7A–1 **The Brussels Convention**

[p.565] *Please delete existing section A and replace with following:*

7A–1 **The Brussels Convention**

When the EEC Treaty (now called the E.C. Treaty (as a result of the Treaty of Maastricht on European Union) and also referred to as the Treaty of Rome) was signed in 1957, the six original Member States agreed by Art. 220 that they would enter into negotiations with each other "with a view to securing for the benefit of their nationals ... the simplification of formalities governing the reciprocal recognition and enforcement of judgments of courts or tribunals and of arbitration awards". Subsequently, the Convention on Jurisdiction and Enforcement of Judgments in Civil and Commercial Matters was signed at Brussels on September 23, 1968 on behalf of these States (the Brussels Convention).

This Convention went beyond Art. 220 in that it was not confined to the recognition and enforcement of judgments, but also contained rules of jurisdiction applicable in all States. No provision was, however, made for the recognition of arbitration awards. In 1971 the Member States concluded a Protocol on the Interpretation of the 1968 Convention by the European Court of Justice (the 1971 Protocol). This provides for references for preliminary rulings on questions of interpretation of the Convention to be made to the Court by appellate courts of the Contracting States (see text of 1971 Protocol at para. 7B–132 below).

The object of the Conventions is not to unify the rules of substantive law and of procedure of the different contracting states, but to determine which courts have jurisdiction in disputes relating to civil and commercial matters in relations between the contracting states and to facilitate enforcement of judgments (Case C–68/93 *Shevill v. Presse Alliance* [1995] I.L.Pr. 267). However, the Conventions establish an enforcement procedure which constitutes an autonomous and complete system independent of the legal systems of the contracting states (*Société d'Informatique Realisation Organisation v. Ampersand Software B.V.* [1995] All E.R. (E.C.) 783).

7A–2 **Accession of United Kingdom**

When the United Kingdom, together with Denmark and Ireland, joined the European Community, it undertook to accede to any Conventions provided for by Art. 220 of the Treaty of Rome and "to enter into negotiations with the original Member States in order to make the necessary adjustments thereto". The result was a Convention signed on October 9, 1978 amending the Brussels Convention and the 1971 Protocol and providing for the accession to them of the United Kingdom, Denmark and Ireland. In this instance, the amendments went well beyond mere "necessary adjustments".

7A–3 **Civil Jurisdiction and Judgments Act 1982**

This Act has as its main purpose the implementation of the Brussels Convention as amended by the 1978 Accession Convention and the 1971 Protocol. The Act gives the Conventions the force of law in the United Kingdom and requires judicial notice to be taken of them. They are set out, as s.2 states, for "convenience of reference" in the Act. Thus, the English text of the Brussels Convention (as it was at that time) is found in Sched. 1, the 1971 Protocol in Sched. 2 and the relevant provisions of the Accession Convention are in Sched. 3. It is open to the U.K. islands and territories to ask that the Brussels Convention should be extended to them (see in this respect the Civil Jurisdiction and Judgments Act 1982 (Gibraltar) Order 1997) at para. 7D–1 below).

The Civil Jurisdiction and Judgments Act 1982 also contains rules of jurisdiction and rules for the enforcement of judgments as between the constituent parts of the United Kingdom, England and Wales, Scotland, and Northern Ireland. To this end, the Act sets out in Sched. 4 a modified version of the jurisdictional rules found in the Brussels Convention and in addition contains a number of special provisions dealing with recognition and enforcement of judgments. It should be noted that the provisions of the 1982 Act, including the Brussels Convention and the 1971 Protocol (amended as explained below), contained in this Section of *The Supreme Court Practice*, are confined to those dealing with the allocation of jurisdiction among the courts of the E.C. Member States. Schedule 4 of the 1982 Act contains provisions modelled on the Convention for the allocation business between the three separate jurisdictions within the U.K. Its interpretation is a matter solely within the jurisdiction of the United Kingdom national courts (Case C–346/93 *Kleinwort Benson Ltd v. City of Glasgow District Council, The Times*, April 17, 1995).

The Civil Procedure Rules, the Rules of the Supreme Court which survive, and the relevant

Practice Directions give procedural effect to the provisions of the Act and the Conventions. The principal rules are paras 1.4 and 1.5 of the Practice Direction to RSC O.11 (form of certificate on claim form when service abroad is to be effected without permission), RSC O.11, r.1(2) (cases where service permissible under the Conventions); CPR r.12.10(b)(i) (application to enter default judgment in Convention cases); RSC O.71, rr.25–39 (reciprocal enforcement of judgments under the Conventions) and reference should be made to those rules and directions and the notes thereto. For applications under RSC O.71, rr.25–39 it is advisable to use the appropriate Practice Form (see PF 159QB to 164QB, Section 1B, paras 1B–123 to 1B–126).

Accession of other States 7A–4

Section 14(1) of the 1982 Act provides that the Act (including the texts of the Conventions in the Schedules) may be amended by Order in Council. The Civil Jurisdiction and Judgments Act 1982 (Amendment) Order 1989 (S.I. 1989 No. 1346) modified the Act in consequence of a revision of the Brussels Convention and the 1971 Protocol occasioned by the accession to them of Greece by a Convention signed in Luxembourg on October 25, 1982. The Civil Jurisdiction and Judgments Act 1982 (Amendment) Order 1990 (S.I. 1990 No. 2591) brought into effect in the U.K. revisions occasioned by the accession of Spain and Portugal as a result of the San Sebastian Convention signed on May 28, 1989 (as to ratification elsewhere, see para. 7A–6 below). The revisions made to the Brussels Convention on these occasions have not always been confined to what could be called "necessary adjustments" to cope with the accessions of new jurisdictions but in addition have included some changes thought necessary in the light of problems encountered in operating the provisions of the Convention over the years within the Member States.

E.C. and EFTA—The Lugano Convention 7A–5

The Lugano Convention on Jurisdiction and the Enforcement of Judgments in Civil Matters was made between the Member States of the E.C. and those of the European Free Trade Association (EFTA). This Convention is very closely modelled on the Brussels Convention although there is no provision for references on interpretation to be made to the European Court. The Civil Jurisdiction and Judgments Act 1991 (brought into effect on May 1, 1992) gives the Lugano Convention the force of law in the U.K. and amends the 1982 Act so as to incorporate references in it to this Convention (as to ratification elsewhere, see para. 7A–6 below). By this statute the English text of the Convention is inserted in the 1982 Act as Sched. 3C. This text of the Lugano Convention is not incorporated in this Section of *The Supreme Court Practice* but differences between the two Conventions are noted, except in relation to Titles VI and VII where the differences are more substantial.

Ratification 7A–6

The San Sebastian Convention (see para. 7A–4 above) has been ratified by all Member States. (The U.K. ratified the San Sebastian Convention on September 13, 1991, with entry into force on December 1, 1991.) The Lugano Convention has been ratified by all E.C. and EFTA Member States. (The U.K. ratified the Lugano Convention on February 5, 1992, with entry into force on May 1, 1992.)

Up-to-date information as to the progress of ratification by EFTA Member States acceding to the Brussels Convention may be obtained from the Lord Chancellor's Department, International Division, 28 Old Queen Street, London SW1H 9HP, or from the International Litigation Procedure Reports. The information contained therein is updated monthly.

B. CIVIL JURISDICTION AND JUDGMENTS ACT 1982

Domicile and seat of the Crown 7B–37 [p.577]

In s.46(3), after para. (a) insert:

(aa) the Crown in right of the Scottish Administration has its seat in, and in every place in, Scotland,

In subs. (7), after "Kingdom" *insert* ", the Scottish Administration".

Note 7B–38 [p.577]

Add at end:

Subss. (3) and (7) are amended by the Scotland Act 1998 (c.46), s.125, Sched. 8, para. 18.

Note 7B–42 [p.578]

Delete and insert new paragraph:

The text set out below is the version of the 1968 Convention as inserted in Sched. 1 to the 1982 Act by the Civil Jurisdiction and Judgments Act 1982 (Amendment) Order 1990 (S.I. 1990 No. 2591), art. 12(1), Sched. 1, following upon the accession to the European Community of Spain and Portugal. For the earlier version of the Convention inserted following the accession of Greece, see the Civil Jurisdiction and Judgments Act 1982 (Amendment) Order 1989 (S.I. 1989 No. 1346), art. 9(1), Sched. 1. Section 3(3) of the 1982 Act, as amended, states that:

"the reports by Mr. P. Jenard on the 1968 Convention and the 1971 Protocol; and the reports by Professor Peter Schlosser, Professor Demetrios I. Evrigenis, Professor K.D. Kerameus, Mr. Martinho de Almedia Cruz, Mr. Manuel Desantes Real and Mr. P. Jenard on the various Accession Conventions between 1978 and 1989,"

may be considered in ascertaining the meaning or effect of any provision in the Convention and "shall be given such weight as is appropriate in the circumstances". These reports were published in the Official Journal of the European Communities. For a basic commentary on the text of Titles I and II see notes to RSC O.11 in Vol. 1 and particularly notes at Vol. 1, paras 11/1/48 to 11/1/74. For a basic commentary on the text of Title III see notes to RSC O.71 rr.25–39 in Vol. 1. For more detailed analysis of the Conventions see the leading textbooks, *e.g.* Dicey & Morris, *Conflict of Laws*, 12th ed., and Briggs & Rees, *Civil Jurisdiction and Judgments*, 2nd ed.

7B–49 **"In matters relating to individual contracts of employment"**
[p.579] *Add at end:*

The corresponding Point in Art. 5 of the Lugano Convention reads:

"A person domiciled in a Contracting State may, in another Contracting State, be sued:

1. In matters relating to a contract, in the courts for the place of performance of the obligation in question; in matters relating to individual contracts of employment, this place is that where the employee habitually carries out his work, or if the employee does not habitually carry out his work in any one country, this place shall be the place of business through which he was engaged;"

7B–67 **"Tenancies of immovable property"**
[p.582] *Add at end:*

The corresponding point in the Lugano Convention reads:

"however, in proceedings which have as their object tenancies of immovable property concluded for temporary private use for a maximum period of six consecutive months, the courts of the Contracting State in which the defendant is domiciled shall also have jurisdiction, provided that the tenant is a natural person and neither party is domiciled in the Contracting State in which the property is situated;"

7B–69 **Note**
[p.582] *Add new note:*

7B–69/1 **"Individual contracts of employment"**

In the Lugano Convention the points within Art. 17 are numbered and the final point, numbered 5, reads as follows: "In matters relating to individual contracts of employment an agreement conferring jurisidiction shall have legal force only if it is entered into after the dispute has arisen."

7B–139 **Article 5**
[p.594] *Insert comma after word* "question" *in (1).*

SECTION 8

HOUSING

B. LAW OF PROPERTY ACT 1925

Regulations respecting notices **8B–18** [p.610]

Add at end:

See also *Kinch v. Bullard* [1998] 4 All E.R. 650, Ch D.

C. ADMINISTRATION OF JUSTICE ACT 1970

Add new paragraph after (b): **8C–3** [p.615]

Administration of Justice Act 1970, s.36 has not abrogated the mortgagee's common law right to take possession of property (see *Western Bank Ltd v. Schindler* [1977] Ch. 1, CA, and *Ropaigealach v. Barclays Bank plc* [1999] 3 W.L.R. 17, (1999) *New Law Journal*, January 29, p.121, CA). Parliament did not intend s.36 to give mortgagors protection from mortgagees who took possession without the assistance of the Court (*cf.* Criminal Law Act 1977, s.6 and Consumer Credit Act 1974, s.126 where specific protection has been given to mortgagors from forcible re-entry).

Add at end:

Note also *Hyde Park Funding Ltd v. Joannou* [1999] 3 C.L.D. 428 (Barnet County Court) where mortgagees brought possession proceedings and a possession order was granted. Later they obtained a warrant. On the morning of the proposed eviction the borrower applied to a district judge to suspend the warrant. That application was dismissed and the borrower was evicted. The borrower appealed to a circuit judge. The lender contended that as the warrant had been executed, the court no longer had jurisdiction to suspend under Administration of Justice Act 1970, s.36. HHJ Connor allowed the appeal. On appeal from a district judge, a circuit judge can exercise all of the jurisdiction that the district judge had and can make any order that the district judge could have made. In view of new evidence adduced on the appeal, the correct order was to suspend on terms. The district judge's order was set aside and possession restored.

Forms of order **8C–4/1**

Add new note:

County Court Forms N29 (Order for possession (mortgaged property) and N31 (Order for possession of mortgaged land suspended under the Administration of Justice Act 1970, s.36 and the Administration of Justice Act 1973, s.8) have been retained by the Practice Direction to CPR Pt 4, Table 3.

"a reasonable period" **8C–4** [p.615]

Add at end:

See also *Mortgage Agency Services v. Bal* [1998] 28 L.S.G. 32, CA (s.36 ceases to apply after execution of warrant); *cf. Saint v. Barking and Dagenham LBC*, November 1998, *Legal Action* 25, CA (oppression where warrant executed without prior notification to tenant who was in prison and without inviting him to renew his application for housing benefit).

F. CONSUMER CREDIT ACT 1974

Time orders **8F–6** [p.624]

Add:

The Consumer Credit (Increase of Monetary Limits) Order 1998 (S.I. No. 996) increased the limit of loans which come within the Act from £15,000 to £25,000. The change applies to loans granted after May 1, 1998.

8F–9 **Note**
[p.630] *Add new notes:*

8F–9/1 **Welsh Development Agency Act 1975—Schedule 4**
Displacement of legislation preventing possession

16. If the Secretary of State certifies that possession of a house which—

(a) has been acquired by the Agency under s.21A above; and

(b) is for the time being held by the Agency for the purposes for which it was acquired,

is immediately required for those purposes, nothing in the Rent (Agriculture) Act 1976, the Rent Act 1977 or the Housing Act 1988 shall prevent the Agency from obtaining possession of the house.

8F–9/2 **Note**
Amended by Government of Wales Act 1998, Sched. 13.

8F–9/3 **The Agency**
i.e. The Welsh Development Agency.

8F–9/4 **Section 21A**
This gives the Welsh Development Agency power to acquire land by agreement or compulsorily if authorised to do so by the Secretary of State.

G. PROTECTION FROM EVICTION ACT 1977

8G–13 **Excluded tenancies and licences**
[p.632] *Delete s.3A(8)(f). In s.3A(8)(g), delete* "or Housing for Wales" *and add:*

3A(8)(ga) the Secretary of State under section 89 of the Housing Associations Act 1985.

8G–14 **Note**
Add at end:
and Government of Wales Act 1998, s.140 and Sched. 16, para. 2 and Sched. 18, Pt IV.

H. RENT ACT 1977

8H–4 **Protected tenants and tenancies**
[p.640] *Add:*
See too *Gray v. Taylor, The Times,* April 24, 1998; [1998] 4 All E.R. 17; [1998] E.G.C.S. 62, CA; and *Meynell Family Properties Ltd v. Meynell,* June 1998, *Legal Action* 12, CA.

8H–10 **Statutory tenants and tenancies**
[p.641] *Add:*
See too *Prince v. Robinson,* June 1998, *Legal Action* 12, CA.

Add reference (1999) 31 H.L.R. 89, CA to *Prince v. Robinson.*

8H–15 **Dwelling-houses above certain rateable values**
[p.641] *Section 4(1) should read:*
A tenancy which is entered into before April 1, 1990 or (where the dwelling-house had a rateable value on March 31, 1990) is entered into on or after April 1, 1990 in pursuance of a contract made before that date is not a protected tenancy if the dwelling-house falls within one of the Classes set out in subsection (2) below.

8H–32 **"specified educational institution**
[p.645] *Add at end:*
The earlier regulations have now been consolidated by the Assured and Protected Tenancies (Lettings to Students) Regulations 1998 (S.I. 1998 No. 1967).

Landlord's interest belonging to local authority, etc. 8H–53 [p.647]

Delete s.14(f). In s.14(i) delete "Residency" *and insert* "Residuary".

Note 8H–54 [p.648]

At end add:

and The Government of Wales Act 1998, Sched. 18, Part IV.

"landlord" 8H–58 [p.648]

Add new note:

Welsh Development Agency 8H–58/1

Note that some tenants of the Welsh Development Agency do not enjoy security of tenure. See para. 8FA–1, The Welsh Development Agency Act 1975, Sched. 4 as inserted by Government of Wales Act 1998, Sched. 13.

Landlord's interest belonging to housing association, etc. 8H–59 [p.648]

Delete s.15(2)(aa).

Note 8H–60 [p.648]

Add at end:

and Government of Wales Act 1998, Sched. 18, Pt VI.

Grounds for possession of certain dwelling-houses 8H–94 [p.653]

Add new reference (1999) 31 H.L.R. 143, CA to *Hounslow LBC v. McBride.*

Reasonable 8H–100 [p.654]

Add new reference (1999) 31 H.L.R. 143, CA to *Hounslow LBC v. McBride.*

Effect on sub-tenancy of determination of superior tenancy 8H–121 [p.657]

Wellcome Trust v. Hamad—add reference [1998] Q.B. 638.

Breach of any other tenancy obligation 8H–179 [p.671]

Add at end:

A proviso in a contractual tenancy giving the landlord a right of re-entry if the tenant becomes bankrupt is an obligation under the subsequent statutory tenancy within the meaning of Case 1 (*Cadogan Estates Ltd v. McMahon* (1999) *The Times*, June 1; [1999] E.G.C.S. 80, CA).

Nuisance or annoyance 8H–180 [p.671]

Northampton Borough Council v. Lovatt—add reference (1998) 30 H.L.R. 875.

K. COUNTY COURTS ACT 1984

"lease", "lessee", "lessor", "under-lease", "under-lessee" 8K–3 [p.678]

Add at end:

It has been held in a county court that the divorced wife of a lessee, although not herself a lessee within the meaning of s.138, was a beneficial co-owner and so entitled to apply for an extension of time under s.138(4) and to pay the arrears on behalf of the lessee (*Bassett Road HA v. Gough* [1998] S C.L.Y. 3653, Central London County Court).

Provisions as to the forfeiture for non-payment of rent 8K–4 [p.678]

Add:

In *Maryland Estates v. Joseph, The Times,* May 6, 1998; [1998] 3 All E.R. 193; [1998] 27 E.G. 142; [1998] E.G.C.S. 66; (1998) L.S.Gaz. 95/17, p.32, CA, the Court of Appeal, allowing an appeal by landlords, held that the words used in County Courts Act 1984, s.138(3) ("the lessee pays into court . . . all the rent in arrear") are not to be construed to mean that the court can order payment only of the rent in arrear at the date of the summons. It is to be assumed that leases continue after service of summonses and that tenants remain under an obligation to pay sums reserved in leases as rent and that "all the rent in arrear" means the rent payable up to the date stated in the order.

Add references (1999) 77 P. & C.R. 150; (1999) 31 H.L.R. 269, CA to *Maryland Estates Ltd v. Joseph.*

Forms of order 8K–4/1

Add new note:

Forms N27 (Judgment for claimant in Action of Forfeiture for non-payment of rent), N27(1) (Judgment for claimant—for Non Payment of Rent where order refused under Rent Acts) and N27(2) (Judgment for claimant—for Non Payment of rent where order suspended under Rent Acts) have been retained by the Practice Direction to CPR Pt 4, Table 3.

L. HOUSING ACT

8L–4 Other descriptions of authority
[p.682] *In s.4(a) for* ", a new town corporation or the Development Board for Rural Wales" *substitute* "or a new town corporation".

8L–5 Note
[p.682] *Add at end:*
and the Government of Wales Act 1998, Sched. 15, para. 7.

8L–6 Housing associations
[p.682] *In s.5(4)(b), delete* "Housing for Wales" *and replace with* "The Secretary of State".

8L–7 Note
[p.683] *Add to end:*
Amended by the Government of Wales Act 1998, s.140 and Sched. 16, para. 6.

8L–9 The Corporation
[p.683] *In s.6A(1) delete* "Housing for Wales" *and replace with* "The Secretary of State".
In s.6A(1) delete "the Corporation" *and replace with* "the Relevant Authority".
In s.6A(2) delete "Housing for Wales" *and replace with* "The Secretary of State".
In s.6A(3) delete "the Corporation" *and replace with* "the Relevant Authority".

8L–10 Note
[p.684] *Add:*
Amended by Government of Wales Act 1998, s.140 and Sched. 16, paras 5 and 7.

8L–17 The landlord condition
[p.684] *Delete* "the Development Board for Rural Wales" *in s.80(1).*

8L–18 Note
[p.685] *Add:*
Amended by Government of Wales Act 1998, Sched. 18, Pt IV.

8L–47 "reasonable"
[p.690] *Add:*
As to reasonableness, see too *Camden LBC v. Gilsenan*, June 1998 *Legal Action* 10, CA: decision by circuit judge that it was reasonable to make a possession order upheld. The trial judge had differentiated between acts done by the defendant and acts done by her visitors. See also *Brent LBC v. Marks*, July 1998 *Legal Action* 11, CA: appeal by tenant against suspended possession on terms that the tenant pay current rent and £2.50 allowed. Following *Second WRVS Housing Society Ltd v. Blair*, the judge ought to have had more regard to the fact that current rent was being paid by deductions made by the DSS quarterly in arrears and that the benefit system was both causing and then dealing with the arrears. Looking at the overall position this was a responsible tenant whose position had stabilised. On a new exercise of the court's discretion, a possession order might not be made. And see *Hounslow LBC v. McBride*, June 1998 *Legal Action* 11, CA: after agreement between the parties in possession proceedings based upon Housing Act 1985 Grounds 1 and 2 a District Judge made a suspended possession order by consent without hearing evidence. Later the council alleged that Ms McBride had broken the conditions of the suspended order and applied for a warrant of possession. The Court of Appeal confirmed that both the possession order and the warrant should be set aside. A distinction has to be drawn between a form of order which contains an admission as to those matters on which the jurisdiction to make the order rests (e.g. reasonableness) and an order such as this one which did not. The bar against appealing against an order made by consent contained in CCR, O.37, r.6(1) did not apply.

Add new reference (1999) 31 H.L.R. 343, CA to *Brent LBC v. Marks*. *Add new reference* (1999) 31 H.L.R. 143, CA to *Hounslow LBC v. McBride*. *Add new reference* (1999) 31 H.L.R. 81, CA to *Camden LBC v. Gilsenan*.

Add at end:

See too *Lewisham LBC v. Adeyemi* [1999] E.G.C.S. 74, CA where the court dismissed a tenant's appeal against a possession order, where the tenant claimed that the judge, when considering reasonableness had failed to take into account whether the local authority would have a duty to rehouse under the Housing Act 1996, Pt VII. It is not for the court to make a pre-emptive decision on the possible outcome of an application that might or might not be made to the local authority. Entitlement to Pt VII accommodation is confined to the judgement of the local authority. It is not for the court to anticipate the outcome of that decision. The judge was well aware of the self-evident consequence of a possession order. The legal and practical consequences of homelessness however were not before the court, nor need they have been as they were for the local authority to determine.

Forms of order 8L–47/1

Add new note:

Forms N26A (Order that claimant have Possession (Assured tenancies)) and N28 (Order for Possession (possession suspended) (rented property)) have been retained by the Practice Direction to CPR Pt 4, Table 3.

Extended discretion of court in certain proceedings for possession 8L–52

Add at end: [p.692]

; and *Saint v. Barking and Dagenham LBC*, November 1998 *Legal Action* 25, CA (oppression where warrant executed without prior notification to tenant who was in prison and without inviting him to renew his application for housing benefit).

Persons qualified to succeed tenant 8L–61

Newham LBC v. Philips—add reference (1998) 30 H.L.R. 859. [p.694]

Add reference (1998) 96 L.G.R. 788, CA *to Newham LBC v. Philips. Add new reference* [1998] Ch. 304, CA *to Fitzpatrick v. Sterling HA.*

After above reference add:

and *Kingcastle Ltd v. Owen-Owen* (1999) *The Times*, March 18, CA (adjournment of possession proceedings pending the outcome of the appeal to the House of Lords in *Fitzpatrick v. Sterling HA* appropriate provided that court correctly exercises its discretion and takes into account prejudice to both parties).

"qualified to succeed" 8L–71

Add: [p.696]

It has been held in a county court decision that if a minor would be entitled to succeed, by operation of the Trusts of Land and Appointment of Trustees Act 1996, Sched. 1, the tenancy should be held on trust for him or her: *Kingston upon Thames RLBC v. Prince*, June 1998 *Legal Action* 10, Staines County Court

Assignments by way of exchange 8L–80

In s.92(2A)(a) delete "Housing for Wales" *and replace with* "The Secretary of State". [p.697]

Note 8L–81

Add: [p.698]

and by the Government of Wales Act 1998, s.140 and Sched. 16, para. 10 and Sched. 18, Pt VI.

Assignments by way of exchange 8L–85

Sanctuary H.A. v. Baker—add reference (1998) 30 H.L.R. 809, CA. [p.698]

Meaning of "landlord authority" 8L–106

In s.114(1) and (2) delete "the Development Board for Rural Wales". *In s.114(1) and (2), after* "trust" *insert* "or". [p.701]

Note 8L–107

Add at end: [p.701]

and the Government of Wales Act 1998, Sched. 15, para. 10 and Sched. 18, Pt IV.

Index of defined expressions: Part IV 8L–119

In s.117 omit "the Corporation: section 6A". *After* "registered social landlord: section 5(4) and (5)" *add* "the Relevant Authority: section 6A". [p.703]

Note 8L–120

Add at end: [p.703]

and the Government of Wales Act 1998, Sched. 16, para. 11 and Sched. 18, Pt VI.

8L–138 **Premises occupied in connection with employment**
[p.705] *In para. 2(1) delete* "the Development Board for Rural Wales".

8L–149 **Note**
[p.707] *Add* "and the Government of Wales Act 1998, Sched. 18, Pt IV."

8L–150 **Sched. 1, para. 2—employees**
[p.707] *At the end of the second para. add:*

The correct approach to be taken by a court in the light of *Hughes v. Greenwich LBC* is to find out what duties the employee was required to perform. Having regard to the nature of these duties, the court should then ask itself the question whether or not it was practicable for those duties to be carried out if the employee did not live on the premises in question. Where there was a requirement to attend at the premises where the occupant was employed both in and out of hours and where it would not be practicable to carry out those duties without living at the provided premises, such occupation was "for the better performance of his duties". (See *Surrey County Council v. Lamond* [1999] 12 E.G. 170, CA where it was held that there was a clear distinction between the position of a caretaker and that of a headmaster as in *Hughes v. Greenwich LBC.*)

8L–160 **Ground 7**
[p.709] *Delete* "the Development Board for Rural Wales".

8L–164 **Ground 10A**
[p.710] *Delete* "Corporating" *and insert* "Corporation or Scottish Homes".

8L–164/1 **Note**
Add new note:

Amended by the Government of Wales Act 1998, s.140 and Sched. 16, para. 21.

8L–166 **Ground 12**
[p.710] *Delete* "the Development Board for Rural Wales".

8L–172 **Part V—approval of redevelopment schemes for purposes of Ground 10A**
[p.711] *Delete* "registered social landlord, the corporation, and not the Secretary of State" *in para. 6. Substitute:*

social landlord registered in the register maintained by the Housing Corporation under section 1 of the Housing Act 1996 or a housing association registered in the register maintained by Scottish Homes under section 3 of the Housing Associations Act 1985, the Housing Corporation, or Scottish Homes (and not the Secretary of State).

8L–173 **Note**
[p.712] *Add:*

and by Government of Wales Act 1998, s.140 and Sched. 16, para. 21 and Sched. 18, Pt IV.

8L–175 **Sched. 2, Ground 2—nuisance or annoyance**
[p.712] *Northampton B.C. v. Lovatt—add reference* (1998) 30 H.L.R. 875.

8L–177 **Sched. 2, Ground 5—tenancy obtained by false statement**
[p.713] *Add at end:*

and *Lewisham LBC v. Adeyemi* [1999] E.G.C.S. 74, CA.

M. LANDLORD AND TENANT ACT 1985

8M–13 **Damages**
[p.718] *Add at end:*

In *Wallace v. Manchester City Council, The Times,* July 23, 1988; [1998] 41 E.G. 223, CA, Morritt L.J. said:

> "First, the question in all cases of damages for breach of obligation to repair is what sum will, so far as money can, place the tenant in the position he would have been in if the obligation to repair had been duly performed by the landlord. Second, the answer to that question inevitably involves a comparison of the property as it was for the period when the landlord was in breach of his obligation with what it would have been if the obligation had been performed. Third, for the periods when the tenant remained in occupation of the property, notwithstanding the breach of the obligation to repair the loss to him requiring compensation is the loss of comfort and convenience which results from living in a property which was not in the state of repair it ought to have been if the landlord performed his obligation ... Fourth, if the tenant does not remain in occupation but, being entitled to do so, is forced by the landlord's failure to repair to sell or sublet the property he may

diminution of the price or recoverable rent occasioned by the landlord's failure to perform his covenant to repair."

He continued:

"... the sum required to compensate the tenant for the distress and inconvenience ... may be ascertained in a number of different ways, including but not limited to a notional reduction in the rent. Some judges may prefer to use that method alone ... some may prefer a global award for discomfort and inconvenience ... and others may prefer a mixture of the two ... But, in my judgment, they are not bound to assess damages separately under heads of both diminution in value and discomfort because in cases within the third proposition those heads are alternative ways of expressing the same concept. Morritt L.J. said that the source of the money with which to pay the rent (*e.g.* housing benefit) is irrelevant to the extent of the discomfort and inconvenience suffered by the tenant and what would be proper monetary compensation for it."

Limitation of service charges: reasonableness **8M–53** [p.723]

At end of first para. delete "s.31A—see below" *and substitute* "s.31C—see para. 8M–101".

Add after first para:

In *Aylesbond Estates Ltd v. Macmillan and Garg* (March, 1999) Legal Action 22, CA landlords sought forfeiture of a long lease for arrears of ground rent and service charges. The lessees defended on the basis that the service charges were excessive and unreasonable and counterclaimed for breach of covenant for quiet enjoyment and/or nuisance, including the cost of the installation of sound insulation. During an interlocutory appeal, the Court of Appeal considered whether the case should be transferred to the Leasehold Valuation Tribunal under s.19(2A). The Court of Appeal, in refusing to transfer, noted that not all the disputes between the parties were capable of being referred to the LVT which only had jurisdiction to determine the reasonableness of service charges. The LVT could not consider relief from forfeiture, disputes about ground rent, or the counterclaim. Although "the question of costs is of course uppermost", in view of s.20C (power of ocurt to order that costs in proceedings should not be added to service charges), there were no good costs reasons why the case should be sent to the LVT. Although the LVT is "an expert tribunal" and "following an inspection ... could reach a decision on the service charge dispute more quickly and easily, and therefore perhaps less expensively, than a judge who does not have that experience" the Court noted that there were not currently any proceedings before the LVT. Proceedings before the LVT could be a "somewhat lengthy and a somewhat costly exercise" whereas the court case was ready for trial.

Limitation of service charges **8M–61** [p.726]

Add at end:

cf. though *Martin v. Maryland Estates Ltd* [1999] E.G.C.S. 63, CA where at first instance a judge refused to grant landlords a dispensation under s.20(9), holding that they had not acted reasonably in failing to inform the tenants of the need for additional works. The landlords' appeal was dismissed. The cost of all the works, including the additional items, was almost double the amount estimated in the s.20 notice. Although it had not been practical for the landlords to comply with all the requirements, that did not justify a total dismissal of the requirements resulting in the tenants not being informed of the additional works. The judge had been entitled to conclude that the landlords had not acted reasonably. The Court of Appeal also held that the judge had been correct to dismiss the landlords' claim under s.20(1) for £1,000 towards the cost of the additional works. A common sense approach is required when deciding how one batch of "qualifying works" is to be divided from another for the purposes of s.20(1).

Insert new note: **8M–76/1**

See *Taber v. MacDonald*, February 18, 1998, noted in *New Law Property*, June 1998; *Legal Action* 13, DC: held that a landlord had a reasonable excuse for not producing documentation regarding the composite charge for several properties because the lease provided that the lessee could refer the matter to arbitration. As he had not availed himself of that opportunity the landlords had a reasonable excuse for not producing the documents.

Add new reference (1999) 31 H.L.R. 73, QBD *to Taber v. MacDonald.*

Note **8M–77** [p.729]

Add new note:

Trivial offences **8M–77/1**

In *R. v. Marylebone Magistrates' Court, ex p. Westminster City Council*, January 13, 1999 (May 1999) Legal Action 29, QBD, a landlady of six flats, was summonsed for failing without reasonable cause to perform a duty imposed by Landlord and Tenant Act 1985, s.21. A stipendiary magistrate stayed the summons because he was satisfied that the offence allegedly committed was "so trivial that it did not justify the bringing of proceedings". Westminster, who had prosecuted the case, applied for judicial review. Although leave was refused because the case was "extremely old" and "stale", Collins J. said "it would be wrong for a court to decide that it was an abuse of the process of the court to prosecute if the summary did not contain all that was required by Parliament. Of course, the court might take the view that no penalty should follow. It might even take the view in an appropriate case that that be coupled with some sort of costs sanction." Section 21 is not limited to cases where there is a "wilful and inexcusable" failure to produce documents. Collins J. also said that it is better for such challenges to be brought by way of case stated rather than by judicial review since it would mean that the court was provided with the magistrates' reasons in every case.

8M–81 Exception: tenants of certain public authorities

[p.730] *In s.26(1) delete* "the Development Board for Rural Wales". *After* "a local authority," *add* "a National Park authority, or".

8M–82 Note

[p.730] *Add at end:*

Environment Act 1995, s.78, Sched. 10, para. 25(1) and the Government of Wales Act, Sched. 15, para. 12 and Sched. 18, Pt IV.

8M–92 Meaning of "qualified accountant"

[p.731] *In s.28(6), after* "a local authority," *add* "National Park authority", *and for* ", a new town corporation or the Development Board for Rural Wales" *substitute* "or a new town corporation".

8M–93 Note

[p.731] *Add at end:*

Environment Act 1995, s.78, Sched. 10, para. 25(2) and the Government of Wales Act, Sched. 15, para. 13.

Note

8M–102 *Add new note:*

[p.733]

8M–102/1 Implementation

Housing Act 1996 (Commencement No. 11) Order 1997 (S.I. 1997 No. 1851) brought this provision into force on September 1, 1997, but only in relation to county court proceedings commenced on or after that date. However Housing Act 1996 (Commencement No. 12 and Transitional Provision) Order 1998 (S.I. 1998 No. 1768) which came into force on August 11, 1998 enables county courts to transfer to LVTs actions begun before September 1, 1997 which concern the reasonableness of service charges.

The fees and procedure which apply in LVTs are set out in the Leasehold Valuation Tribunals (Fees) Order 1997 (S.I. 1997 No. 1852), the Leasehold Valuation Tribunals (Service Charges, Insurance or Appointment of Managers Applications) Order 1997 (S.I. 1997 No. 1853) and the Rent Assessment Committees (England and Wales) (Leasehold Valuation Tribunals) (Amendment) Regulations 1997 (S.I. 1997 No. 1854). The County Court (Amendment) Rules 1997 provide a new CCR O.43, r.16A stating that where a county court transfers to a LVT any proceedings relating to the reasonableness of service charges, the court shall send notice of the transfer to all parties and certified copies of all entries in the court records to the LVT.

N. LANDLORD AND TENANT ACT 1987

8N–11 Notification by landlord of address for service of notices

[p.737] *Add at end:*

A notice requiring possession against an assured shorthold tenant served under the Housing Act 1988, s.21, whether or not it is valid in its own right as a s.21 notice, may constitute notice within the meaning of s.48(1) if it informs the tenant of the name and address of the landlord's agent without limitation or qualification. The fact that it is not served for the purposes of s.48(1) and that it does not state that the address is one at which "notices (including notices in proceedings) may be served" on the landlord may be irrelevant. There may be cases where a suitably worded possession summons served with another document might constitute notice within s.48—see *Drew-Morgan v. Hamid-Zadeh* [1999] E.G.C.S. 72, CA.

O. HOUSING ACT 1988

"fully mutual housing association" **8O–8**

Ujima H.A. v. Ansah—add reference (1998) 30 H.L.R. 831. *Parkins v. Westminister City Council—add reference* (1998) 30 H.L.R. 894. [p.740]

"let" **8O–19**

Add new note: [p.742]

Sharing accommodation **8O–19A**

Note *Miller v. Eyo,* October 1998, *Legal Action* 26, CA where the terms of the plaintiff's tenancy were that she had exclusive use of her bedroom with shared use of a living room, kitchen and bathroom/WC. Initially the only other bedroom in the flat was occupied by another tenant, but when she moved out the landlord and her family moved into the other bedroom and started to share the other parts of the flat with the plaintiff. Following *Gray v. Brown* (1993) 25 H.L.R. 144, CA the Court of Appeal held that in the absence of an express term in the tenancy that the landlord had the right to re-enter and occupy, the tenancy came with s.3 and was assured. For a landlord to avoid this situation, a landlord's right to re-enter must be "clear and specific".

Orders for possession **8O–49**

Add at end: [p.747]

As to reasonableness (s.7(4)) see *West Kent Housing Association v. Davis* [1998] E.G.C.S. 103, CA.

Delete the final paragraph and insert:

Where a landlord is seeking possession under one of the mandatory grounds for possession (*e.g.* Ground 8) during the fixed term of a tenancy, the court has no power to grant relief from forfeiture under the County Courts Act 1984, s.138. In *Artesian Residential Investments Ltd v. Beck* [1999] 3 All E.R. 113, CA; [1999] 22 E.G. 145, CA a fixed term assured tenancy agreement * included a proviso for re-entry and determination if the rent was at any stage fourteen days in arrears. The defendant fell into rent arrears before the expiry of the term and, the landlord brought possession proceedings relying on the Housing Act 1988, Sched. 2, Grounds 8 and 10. A possession order was made, but the defendant later paid all the arrears and applied for suspension of the possession order, relying upon the relief from forfeiture provisions of the County Courts Act 1984, s.138. HHJ Mitchell granted relief but the Court of Appeal held that the Housing Act 1988, s.5(1) sets out the only routes for bringing an assured tenancy to an end. There is no need for a parallel claim for forfeiture to prevent the contractual tenancy continuing after the granting of an order for possession under the Act. By its express words, s.5(1) makes it abundantly clear that an order for possession brings a tenancy to an end. This construction is also borne out by s.7(7) which provides that, when the court makes an order for possession on grounds relating to a fixed term tenancy which has come to an end, any ensuing statutory periodic tenancy which arises on the ending of the fixed term tenancy ends (without any notice or regardless of the period) on the day on which the order takes effect.

Furthermore, s.7(3) is explicit, obliging the court mandatorily to make an order for possession if satisfied that any of the grounds in Sched. 2 is established subject, *inter alia,* to s.6. Section 7(6)(b) does no more than require provision for, *e.g.*, forfeiture to be included in the terms of the tenancy, and does not set up forfeiture as an independent ground for terminating the tenancy. As a matter of principle there is no room for applying s.138. As there is no exercise of a right of re-entry or forfeiture for non-payment of rent, its requirements are not met.

Note that in practice, where a tenant faces a claim for possession under mandatory Ground 8 (eight weeks arrears at the date of service of a s.8 notice and at the hearing), the only way to obtain time to pay rent arrears (or to sort out housing benefit) is to apply for an adjournment *before* evidence has been heard. It is arguable that at that stage the court has an inherent jurisdiction to adjourn. (See *e.g. R. v. A Circuit Judge, ex p. Wathen* (1976) 33 P.&C.R. 423, QBD; *Birmingham Citizens Permanent BS v. Caunt* [1962] Ch. 883, Ch D; and *Bristol CC v. Lovell* [1998] 1 W.L.R. 446, HL.) Once evidence has been given and the court is satisfied that Ground 8 is made out, there is no power to adjourn and the court must make an outright possession order—see the Housing Act 1988, ss.7(3) and 9(6).

Forms of order **8O–49/1**

Forms N26A (Order that Claimant have possession (Assured tenancies)) and N28 (Order for Possession (possession suspended) (rented property)) have been retained by the Practice Direction to CPR Pt 4, Table 3.

8O–60 "the court considers it just and equitable to dispense with the requirement of such a notice"

[p.749] *Add:*

See too *Hegab v. Shamash*, June 1998 *Legal Action* 13, CA: appeal by tenant against decision to dispense with requirement for notice allowed because the judge had failed to take into account two matters, namely the fact that the tenant had paid a deposit of £4,000 in relation to a proposed purchase of the premises which had not been refunded and that the landlord had not paid the costs of the earlier proceedings concerning an illegal eviction.

8O–72 Extended discretion of court in possession claims

[p.751] *Add at end:*

See also *Saint v. Barking and Dagenham LBC*, November 1988, *Legal Action* 25, CA (oppression where warrant executed without prior notification to tenant who was in prison and without inviting him to renew his application for housing benefit).

8O–72/1 On any of the grounds in Part I

The extended discretion to stay or suspend does not apply where the landlord has satisfied one of the mandatory grounds for possession—s.9(6). See however *Capital Prime Plus plc v. Wills* (July 1999) Legal Action 22, CA where the landlord had consented to the suspension of the original possession order even though there were over two months' arrears. The Court of Appeal held that the order had not been made under Ground 8 and so, on subsequent default, the court did have power to suspend a warrant.

8O–93 Increase of rent under assured periodic tenancies

[p.753] *Add new note:*

*

8O–93/1 **"landlord may serve on the tenant"**—Service of notice on landlord's agent's address is valid service under this section (*Tadema Holdings Ltd v. Ferguson, The Times*, November 25, 1999, CA).

8O–99 Determination of rent by rent assessment committee

[p.755] *Add reference* (1998) 76 P.&C.R. 410, QBD *to R. v. London RAP, ex p. Cadogan.*

8O–118 Succession to assured periodic tenancy by spouse

[p.758] *Add new reference* [1998] Ch. 304, CA *to Fitzpatrick v. Sterling HA*. After that reference add: and *Kingcastle Ltd v. Owen-Owen* (1999) *The Times*, March 18, CA (adjournment of possession proceedings pending the outcome of the appeal to the House of Lords in *Fitzpatrick v. Sterling HA* appropriate provided that court correctly exercises its discretion and takes into account prejudice to both parties).

8O–137 Assured shorthold tenancies: pre-Housing Act 1996

[p.761] *Add:*

Compare *York and Ross v. Casey* [1998] 30 E.G. 110; [1998] E.G.C.S. 26, CA where, following *Mannai Investment Co. Ltd v. Eagle Star Life Assurance Co. Ltd* [1997] 3 All E.R. 352, HL, the Court of Appeal held that a notice is valid even if it contains a minor misdescription if, in its contextual setting, it informs a reasonably minded recipient how the notice is to operate. There is no material difference between contractual and statutory notices and accordingly the *Mannai* test is equally applicable to statutory notices. In this case where the section 20 notice gave a commencement date of September 28, 1996 but a date for termination of the tenancy of September 6, 1996, there was no doubt that the termination date was wrong. The real question was whether the correct termination date was sufficiently clear. In looking at a letter which accompanied the notice, there was no doubt that the termination date was understood to be March 27, 1997. See too *Garston v. Scottish Widows* [1998] 1 W.L.R. 1583, CA

Add new reference (1999) 31 H.L.R. 209, CA *to York and Ross v. Casey.*

At the end of sub-para. (c) add:

See too *Clickex Ltd v. McCann* [1999] E.G.C.S. 73; (1999) *The Times*, May 26, CA where a landlord served a s.20 notice on December 20, 1995 indicating that the term of the proposed assured shorthold tenancy would be from December 21, 1995 to June 23, 1996. However, the tenancy agreement was changed to provide for a term of six months from January 8, 1996 because, said the landlord, a previous tenant was late moving out. The Court of Appeal held that the notice was not valid. The fact the dates were in complete conflict with each other meant that it was not obvious or evident to the reasonable recipient as to when the term ended. There was no existing authority to justify the judge looking into circumstances beyond the documents themselves. The tenant was an assured tenant, not an assured shorthold tenant.

8O–147 Recovery of possession on expiry or termination of assured shorthold tenancy

[p.764] *Add:*

As to section 21(4), see too *Transeuropean Carriage Co. v. Abou-Hamdan*, July 1998 *Legal Action* 12, West London County Court.

Add at end of second paragraph, between "(see above)" and "Uncertainty":

It has been held in the county court that a s.21 notice served before the commencement of the tenancy is not valid because at that stage there was no relationship of landlord and tenant, as required by s.21(1)(b)—see *Turpitt v. Elizabeth*, August 1998, *Legal Action* 21, Edmonton County Court.

Damages for unlawful eviction **8O–162** [p.768]

Add at end of penultimate paragraph:

See too *Wandsworth LBC v. Osei-Bonsu, The Times*, November 4, 1998, CA.

Add after paragraph ending "s.27(6)(b)":

A landlord's contention that s.27 only applies where "the seriousness of the landlord's conduct is established to a high degree and where he makes the tenant's position so intolerable that he is driven out of the property" was rejected by the Court of Appeal in *Abbott v. Bayley* (May 1999) Legal Action 28, CA.

The measure of damages **8O–168** [p.769]

Add at end:

See too *Wandsworth LBC v. Osei-Bonsu, The Times*, November 4, 1998; *New Law Journal*, November 6, 1998, at 1641, CA.

New protected tenancies and agricultural occupancies restricted to special cases **8O–175** [p.772]

Add new reference (1998) 30 H.L.R. 1099, CA *to Laimond Properties Ltd v. Al-Shakarchi.*

Removal of special regimes for tenancies of housing associations, etc. **8O–176** [p.772]

In s.35(4)(a) *for* "a housing action trust established under Part III of this Act or the Development Board for Rural Wales" *substitute* "or a housing action trust established under Part III of this Act".

In s.35(5) delete "Housing for Wales" *and replace with* ", where that interest becomes held by him as a result of the exercise by him of the functions under Part III of the Housing Associations Act 1985, the Secretary of State,".

Note **8O–177** [p.774]

Add:

, Government of Wales Act 1998, Sched. 15, para. 15 and the Government of Wales Act 1998 (Housing) (Amendments) Order 1999 (S.I. 1999 No. 61).

Crown tenancies **8O–201** [p.778]

At end of para. 11(2), after "Crown Estate Commissioners" *add:*

or it is held by him as a result of the exercise by him of the functions under Part III 1985 of the Housing Associations Act 1985 .

Note **8O–201/1**

Add new note:

Amended by the Government of Wales Act 1998 (Housing) (Amendments) Order 1999 (S.I. 1999 No. 61).

Local authority tenancies, etc. **8O–202** [p.778]

Delete para. 12(1)(c).

Note **8O–206** [p.780]

Add at end:

and the Government of Wales Act 1998, Sched. 18, Pt IV.

Para. 8 **8O–215** [p.781]

Add at end:

The earlier regulations have now been consolidated by the Assured and Protected Tenancies (Lettings to Students) Regulations 1998 (S.I. 1998 No. 1967).

Para. 12—Welsh Development Agency **8O–217/1**

Add new note:

Note that some tenants of the Welsh Development Agency do not enjoy security of tenure. See para. 8FA–1, The Welsh Development Agency Act 1975, Sched. 4 as inserted by the Government of Wales Act 1998, Sched. 13.

"specified educational institution" **8O–243** [p.786]

Add at end of first paragraph:

The earlier regulations have now been consolidated by the Assured and Protected Tenancies (Lettings to Students) Regulations 1998 (S.I. 1998 No. 1967).

8O–253 **Ground 14**
[p.788] *Northampton Borough Council v. Lovatt—add references* (1998) 30 H.L.R. 875; 91 L.G.R. 548.

Q. HOUSING ACT 1996

8Q–3 **The register of social landlords**
[p.797] *In s.1(1) delete* "Corporation" *and replace with* "Relevant Authority". *Also delete* "at the head office of the Corporation". *After subs. (1) add:*

(1A) In this Part "the Relevant Authority" means the Housing Corporation or the Secretary of State, as provided by section 56.

(1B) The register maintained by the Housing Corporation shall be maintained at its head office.

Delete subs. (2).

8Q–4 **"corporation"**
[p.797] *Delete existing paragraph and replace with new note:*

8Q–4 **Note**

As amended by the Government of Wales Act 1998, Sched. 16, paras 82 and 83 and Sched. 18, Pt VI.

8Q–31 **Introductory tenancies**
[p.803] *After the end of the seventh para. add:*

See too *Manchester City Council v. Cochrane* (1999) *The Times*, January 12; [1999] 1 W.L.R. 809, CA where the Court of Appeal held that the word "shall" in s.127(2) means that once the requirements of s.128 have been complied with, the county court has no discretion but to make an order for possession.

Delete the eighth para. beginning "The Act is silent" *and replace with:*

The Act is silent as to the methods by which tenants may challenge review decisions. This is not dealt with in the Introductory Tenancies (Review) Regulations either and so tenants' only redress if they are dissatisfied with a review decision is to apply for judicial review. In view of the decisions in *Manchester C.C. v. Cochrane* [1999] 1 W.L.R. 809; (1999) *The Times*, January 12, CA, and *Avon C.C. v. Buscott* [1988] Q.B. 656; [1988] 1 All E.R. 841, CA, county courts hearing subsequent possession proceedings cannot hear public law defences based upon tenants' complaints about the review procedure or decisions. The private law rights of tenants under introductory tenancies are no more than a right to remain in possession until an order for possession is made. In such cases, tenants have to apply for the possession proceedings to be adjourned pending determination of their applications for judicial review.

8Q–47 **Proceedings for possession**
[p.806] *Add at end:*

and *Manchester City Council v. Cochrane* [1999] 1 W.L.R. 809; (1999) *The Times*, January 12, CA

8Q–66 **"local authority"**
[p.809] *Add:*

As to the words "in the locality", see *Manchester CC v. Lawler*, June 1998 *Legal Action* 11, CA.

Add new references (1999) 31 H.L.R. 119, CA *to Manchester CC v. Lawler and Circle 33 v. Watt* [1999] 4 C.L.D. 355, Edmonton County Court.

8Q–70 **Power to grant injunctions against anti-social behaviour**
[p.809] *Add at end:*

In *Tower Hamlets LBC v. Long*, September 1998, *Legal Action* 25, the Court of Appeal held that an immediate sentence of imprisonment was appropriate where a tenant had waged a personal vendetta against another tenant in breach of an injunction. However a prison sentence of three months was reduced to three weeks.

8Q–85 **Arrest and remand**
[p.813] *Add at end:*

Note that s.155(2)(b) and s.155(3)–(7) are still not in force. The DETR have no immediate plans for implementation. See too *Braintree District Council v. Clark* [1998] C.L.Y. 3724, CA.

Remand for medical examination and report **8Q–88** [p.813]
Add at end:
Note that s.156 is still not in force. The DETR have no immediate plans for implementation.

Asylum-seekers and their dependents **8Q–141** [p.822]
Insert new note:

"accommodation ... available for his occupation" **8Q–141/1**
Accommodation only counts for s.186(1) purposes if it is reasonable to continue to occupy it—see s.175(3) and *Lismane v. Hammersmith and Fulham LBC, The Times,* July 27, 1998, CA (not reasonable for family to remain in single bed-sit in HMO which was a fire hazard).

"available for his occupation" **8Q–155** [p.823]
Insert new notes:

Interim duty to accommodate **8Q–155/1**
See *R. v. Camden LBC, ex p. Mohammed, The Times,* June 20, 1997, QBD (summarised at 8Q–240); *R. v. Newham LBC, ex p. Idowu,* August 1998, *Legal Action* 21, QBD: and *R. v. Haringey LBC, ex p. Erdogan,* August 1998, *Legal Action* 23, QBD.

Suitability of interim accommodation **8Q–155/2**
Accommodation provided under the interim duty to accommodate must be suitable. Lack of resources does not relieve councils from this mandatory duty. Section 188, when read with s.176, does not permit councils to split families in accommodation in separate dwellings (*R. v. Ealing LBC, ex p. Surdonja, The Times,* October 29, 1998, QBD). When discharging their interim duties under s.188 local authorities should give individual consideration to the circumstances of particular applicants. The duty cannot be met by booking all applicants into bed and breakfast accommodation—*R. v. Newham LBC, ex p. Ojuri (No. 3),* August 1998, *Legal Action* 22 (Collins J.).

dependent children **8Q–158** [p.824]
Add:
It has been held that the test to be applied under Housing Act 1985, s.59(1)(b) (now Housing Act 1996, s.189(1)(b)) was whether dependent children resided with the applicant, not whether there was any "greater residency" with another adult (*R. v. Leeds CC, ex p. Collier,* June 1998, *Legal Action* 14, QBD).

Vulnerable **8Q–159** [p.824]
Add:
In *R. v. Camden LBC, ex p. Pereira,* July 1998, *Legal Action* 12, CA, after reviewing recent authorities, the Court of Appeal stated that vulnerability involves not just the issue of whether applicants can find and keep accommodation, but also whether they are less able to fend for themselves in coping with the state of homelessness. The assessment required is a composite one and an individual is not homeless under the "coping with homelessness" approach unless s/he would suffer injury of detriment which an ordinary homeless person would not.

Add new reference (1999) 31 H.L.R. 317, CA *to R. v. Camden LBC, ex p. Pereira.*

"deliberately does or fails to do ..." **8Q–171** [p.825]
Add at end of first paragraph:
See too *R. v. Tower Hamlets LBC, ex p. Abdul Jolil,* October 1998, *Legal Action* 22, QBD.

Eviction following arrears **8Q–172** [p.826]
R. v. Camden, ex p. Cosmo—add reference (1998) 30 H.L.R. 817.

"reasonable for him to continue to occupy" **8Q–175** [p.827]
Add new reference (1999) 31 H.L.R. 50, CA *to R. v. Brent, ex p. Bariise.*

Departure after violence **8Q–176** [p.828]
Add:
The decision in *R. v. Brent LBC, ex p. Bariise* has been reversed on appeal—see June 1998, *Legal Action* 14, CA.

Settled accommodation **8Q–178** [p.828]
Delete in penultimate line (1997) 29 H.L.R. 974, CA *and substitute* [1998] 1 W.L.R. 1396, [1998] 4 All E.R. 137, HL.

Add new reference (1998) 30 H.L.R. 1124, HL *to R. v. Harrow LBC, ex p. Fahia*

8Q–198 **"homeless intentionality"**
[p.831] *Add new note:*

8Q–198/1 **"accommodation is available for occupation"**
See too s.206; *R. v. Newham LBC, ex p. Dada* [1996] Q.B. 507; *R. v. Southwark LBC, ex p. Ryder*, September 1995, *Legal Action* 15, CA (CAT95/556); *R. v. Kensington and Chelsea RLB, ex p. Assiter*, September 1996, *Legal Action* 13, QBD and *R. v. Newham LBC, ex p. Chowdhury*, October 1998, *Legal Action* 22, QBD.

8Q–200 **Duty to persons with priority need who are not homeless intentionally**
[p.831] *After fourth para., add:*
The 1996 Act does not give any time limit by which a housing authority has to comply with its duty under s.193 (*R. v. Merton LBC, ex p. Sembi* (1999) *The Times*, June 9, QBD and *R. v. Southwark LBC, ex p. Anderson*, July 1999 Legal Action 22, QBD).

8Q–200/1 **Reviews**
Add new note:
A decision as to suitability of s.193 accommodation is amenable to review under s.202(1)(f)) and subsequent appeal to the county court under s.204. That is the appropriate route for any challenge. Would-be applicants should bear in mind that remedy and should not apply for judicial review (*R. v. Merton LBC, ex p. Sembi* (1999) *The Times* June 9, QBD).

* *Add new notes:*

[p.835]
8Q–219/1 **Note**
The Allocation of Housing and Homelessness (Review Procedures) Regulations 1999 (S.I. 1999 No. 71) include a specific provision for reviews of decisions made under s.198(5). See too the Homelessness (Decisions on Referrals) Order 1998 (S.I. 1998 No. 1578).

8Q–222 **Referral of case to another local housing authority**
[p.836] *Add:*
See too *R. v. Ealing LBC, ex p. Fox, The Times*, March 9, 1998, QBD: voluntary work may be employment for the purposes of s.199(1)(b).

Add new note:

8Q–222/1 Homelessness (Decisions on Referrals) Order 1998 (S.I. 1998 No. 1578) provides a mechanism for resolving disputes between housing authorities about whether or not the conditions of referral from one authority to another exist. Such questions are to be decided by a person to be appointed from a panel established by the Local Government Association.

8Q–240 **Reviews**
In third para. delete:
The Allocation of Housing and Homelessness (Review Procedures and Amendment) Regulations 1996 (S.I. 1996 No. 3122) as amended by the Allocation of Housing and Homelessness (Amendment) Regulations 1997 (S.I. 1997 No. 631) provide that:

Substitute:
The Allocation of Housing and Homelessness (Review Procedures) Regulations 1999 (S.I. 1999 No. 71) provide that:

[p.838] *Add new note:*

8Q–240/1 **Reconsideration of review**
Councils are not precluded from reconsidering review decisions, but there is no requirement that they should do so. If a council fails to reconsider a review, the remedy for the applicant is to appeal the original review decision in the county court in accordance with s.204. The High Court should not entertain an application for judicial review in such circumstances because another remedy (*i.e.* appeal in the county court) is available—*R. v. Westminster C.C., ex p. Ellioua*, October 1998, *Legal Action* 22, CA.

8Q–241 **Appeals**
[p.839] *Add:*
It is generally accepted that county courts hearing section 204 appeals should act on the same principles as in applications for judicial review. See *Chief Adjudication Officer v. Foster* [1993] A.C. 705, HL and *Begum v. Tower Hamlets LBC*, July 1998, *Legal Action* 12, Bow County Court.

8Q–244 **"regulations"**
[p.840] *Delete existing text. Replace with:*
See the Allocation of Housing and Homelessness (Review Procedures) Regulations 1999 (S.I. 1999 No. 71).

Right of appeal to county court on point of law 8Q–246

Delete existing text and substitute: [p.840] *

An appeal on "any point of law" includes, not only matters of legal interpretation, but also the full range of issues which would otherwise be the subject of an application to the High Court for judicial review (*e.g.* procedural error and questions of power, irrationality, and adequacy or inadequacy of reasons) (*Begum (Nipa) v. Tower Hamlets L.B.C., The Times,* November 9, 1999, CA). Under this section, a county court has jurisdiction to hear an appeal against a local housing authority's decision that it had discharged its duty to a homeless person under s.193 of the Act (*Warsame v. Hounslow L.B.C., The Times,* July 21, 1999, CA).

An appeal must be brought within 21 days of the applicant's being notified of the decision on his request made under s.202(1) (s.204(2)). An applicant has no right to request a further review of a decision made on such request. Where, in the exercise of discretion, the decision-making body reconsiders its decision, any appeal to a county court must be made within 21 days as aforesaid, that is to say, within 21 days of the applicant's being notified of the decision made on his original request (*Demetri v. Westminster C.C., The Times,* November 11, 1999, CA).

A county court has no jurisdiction under the County Courts Act 1984, s.38 to grant an interlocutory injunction requiring a local authority to provide accommodation for a person proceeding with an appeal under s.204 (*Ali v. Westminster C.C.* [1999] 1 W.L.R. 384, CA).

See further the commentary to s.202.

"review" 8Q–247

Add new note: [p.840]

Accommodation pending appeal 8Q–247/1

County courts have no power to grant mandatory injunctions requiring local authorities to provide accommodation pending the hearing of s.204 appeals. Authorities have a discretion as to whether or not they provide accommodation in such circumstances. Challenges to the exercise of that discretion can only be made by judicial review—*Ali v. Westminster City Council; Nairne v. Camden LBC,* September 1998, *Legal Action* 26, CA.

Add new references [1999] 1 W.L.R. 384; [1999] 1 All E.R. 450; (1999) 31 H.L.R. 349; CA *to Ali v. Westminster CC; Nairne v. Camden LBC.*

Schedule 15 8Q–286

Add at end: [p.848]

Note that Sched. 15 is still not in force. The DETR have no immediate plans for implementation.

SECTION 9

CONSUMER CREDIT

A. CONSUMER CREDIT ACT 1974

9A–42 *Add new notes:*
[p.851]
9A–42/1 Introductory note re procedure

The county court has exclusive jurisdiction to hear a claim to enforce a regulated agreement against a debtor or hirer, s.141.

9A–42/2 Land

CPR Sched. 2, CCR, O.49, r.4 governs the procedure for consumer credit claims relating to the recovery of land. For related rules about the matters to be included in the particulars of claim, see CPR Sched. 2, CCR, O.6.

9A–42/3 Goods

Claims to enforce regulated consumer hire agreements and regulated consumer credit agreements relating to goods shall be made in accordance with the "Consumer Credit Act procedure" set out in the Consumer Credit Practice direction (which supplements CPR r.7.9). A judgment in default of service or in default of defence is not obtainable on a claim for delivery of goods that are subject to a regulated agreement, CPR r.12.2(a). Except where the claim relates to the recovery of land, the Consumer Credit Practice direction also deals with originating applications by the debtor or hirer for a time order (under s.129(1)(b)) or to re-open an agreement as being an extortionate credit bargain (under s.139(1)(a)). Where the claim relates to the recovery of land, such applications are dealt with by CPR Sched. 2, CCR, O.49, r.4.

9A–42/4 Money claims

A claim by a creditor to enforce a regulated agreement which relates only to money (*i.e.* not goods or land) is to be started by a claim form issued in accordance with CPR Pt 7—see the Consumer Credit practice direction, para. 3.3.

9A–45/1 Subs. (1)
[p.856] *Add at end of paragraph:*

The term "credit hire agreement" is sometimes used to describe a hire agreement under which payment for the hire of goods is deferred for a period after the hire had come to an end. It involves the provision of credit because the duty to pay is contractually deferred for a significant period after payment has been earned, *Hatfield v. Hiscock* [1998] C.C.L.R. 68 and *Dimond v. Lovell*, [1999] 3 All E.R. 1, CA. (See further the notes to s.11.)

9A–46/1 Running-account and fixed-sum credit
[p.857] *Add after first sentence:*

A "credit hire" agreement has been held to be an example of fixed-sum credit—see notes to s.11.

9A–47/1 Restricted-use credit and unrestricted-use credit
[p.858] *Add after first paragraph:*

Hatfield v. Hiscock [1998] C.C.L.R. 68, involved a "credit hire" agreement for the hire of a motor vehicle for a period not exceeding 3 months and under which the payment for the hire was deferred for a period after the hire had come to an end. This agreement was held to involve fixed-sum credit, albeit the amount of the credit was incapable of being quantified until some weeks or months after the agreement was made. In *Dimond v. Lovell* [1999] 1 All E.R. 1, the Court of Appeal held a similar "credit hire" agreement to be: a personal credit agreement within s.8(1); a consumer credit agreement within s.8(2); an agreement for fixed-sum credit within s.10(1)(b), and; a debtor-creditor-supplier agreement within s.12(a).

Add at end:

An agreement can only be "to finance . . ." or "to refinance . . ." within s.11 where it contains an express or implied term that the credit shall be used for that purpose. It is not enough that the parties had a common purpose or intention that the credit be used for that purpose, *National Westminster Bank v. Story and Pallister*, [1999] Lloyd's Rep. Bank 261, CA.

Debtor-creditor-supplier agreements

9A–48/1 [p.859]

Add after last line of second paragraph:

A "credit hire" agreement has been held to be a debtor-creditor-supplier agreement within s.12(a)—see notes to s.11.

Exempt agreements

9A–53 [p.862]

In s.16(3)(f) delete "Bank of England" *and substitute* "Financial Services Authority". *In s.16(6B)(a), the words* ", Housing for Wales" *are repealed.*

Note

9A–54 [p.863]

Add at end:

; the Bank of England Act 1998, Sched. 5, para. 36. Section 16 is amended by the Government of Wales Act 1998 (c.38), s.152, Sched. 18, Pt VI.

Exempt agreements

9A–54/1 [p.863]

In sixth bullet point add after "A debtor-creditor agreement": "(made on or before July 31, 1999)".

Add after sixth bullet point:

- A debtor-creditor agreement which is of a type offered only to a certain class or classes or persons and not offered to the public generally and where the cost of the credit is low, *i.e.* where there is no charge other than interest for the credit and where the annual rate of that interest (the A.P.R.) cannot at any time exceed a rate 1 per cent higher than the highest of the base rates operated by the main English and Scottish banks 28 days earlier.
- A debtor-creditor agreement which is of a type offered only to a certain class or classes or persons and not offered to the public generally, where there can be no increase in the charge for credit and where the cost of the credit is low, *i.e.* where the annual rate of the charge for credit (the A.P.R.) does not exceed a rate 1 per cent higher than the highest of the base rates operated by the main English and Scottish banks at the close of business 28 days before the date on which the agreement is made.
- A debtor-creditor agreement (made on or after August 1, 1999) where the creditor is a credit union and rate of the total charge for credit (the A.P.R.) does not exceed 12.7 per cent.

Multiple agreements

9A–57/1 [p.864]

Add at end:

The opposing view to Professor Goode's is put by the draftsman of the Act, Francis Bennion, in *Multiple Agreements under the Consumer Credit Act 1974* [1999] C.I.C.C. 1. It is that an agreement, whether "unitary" or not, which falls into more than one category of agreement under the Act, is a multiple agreement and that those aspects of the agreement falling into any one such category are to be treated as a separate agreement—*i.e.* that part is to be treated as being, even though it is not in fact, a separate agreement. The difference between the two views can be vital because the effect of treating a part of an agreement as a separate agreement can be to cause that part to fall within the financial limits of the Act when otherwise it would not be a regulated agreement. When the matter surfaced in *National Westminster Bank v. Story and Pallister* [1999] Lloyd's Rep. Bank. 261, CA, Bennion's article was not referred to and the Court of Appeal avoided the issue by deciding that the two different parts, or aspects, of the agreement in that case were both within the same category of agreement within the Act, both involving unrestricted-use credit.

Deemed agency

9A–62/2 [p.869]

Add at end:

For a situation where at common law the dealer was held (contrary to the usual position) to have been expressly authorised by the finance company to accept the debtor's offer to enter a conditional sale agreement, thereby making the agreement by releasing the vehicle to the debtor upon the latter signing the finance company's proposal form, see *Carlyle Finance Ltd v. Pallas Industrial Finance Ltd* [1999] 1 All E.R. (Comm.) 659, CA.

Contents and effects of default notice

9A–99/1 [p.890]

Add after second line:

The usual default is a failure to pay instalments. In that case, the action required to remedy the default, and which s.88(1)(b) requires the default notice to specify, is payment of the arrears together with any default interest owing on those arrears. If the default notice specifies a figure more than the giver of the notice is entitled to demand, then the default notice is invalid: *Woodchester Lease Management Services Ltd v. Swain*, [1999] C.C.L.R. 8, CA although the court might overlook an error which was no more than *de minimis*.

9A–159/3 [p.916] **Interest rates**

Add at end:

Where it is impossible to establish that an agreement is extortionate, it may nevertheless be possible to challenge one or more of its terms under the Unfair Terms in Consumer Contracts Regulations 1994. In *Falco Finance Ltd v. Gough* [1999] C.C.L.R. 16 (Macclesfield County Court), a mortgage loan agreement provided for repayment in 300 monthly payments. It provided for a dual rate of interest. The higher rate involved monthly payments of £449. The lower (concessionary) rate involved monthly payments of £324 and would be payable only so long as all payments were made on time. The agreement also provided for a rebate on early settlement, which rebate was to be calculated according to the "rule of 78" with the settlement date for calculation deferred for six months. It was held that the provisions relating to the dual rate of interest were both extortionate within s.138 and also unfair under the 1994 Regulations. Those provisions: (i) were not based on any attempt to assess the loss caused to the creditor by a late payment; (ii) were harsh because they made it virtually impossible for the debtor to maintain the concessionary rate, (iii) were harsh because loss of the concession was irrevocable. The provision for calculation of the redemption rebate was held to be unfair within the 1994 Regulations. The Regulations came into force on July 1, 1995 and presumably therefore do not apply to any contract made before that date. The 1994 Regulations were repealed and replaced with effect from October 1, 1999 by the Unfair Terms in Consumer Contracts Regulations 1999. These are a slightly modified version of the 1994 Regulations. For an analysis of the application of the 1994 Regulations to a clause in a loan agreement imposing default interest at the contractual rate on outstanding arrears, including after judgment, see *Director General of Fair Trading v. First National Bank plc*, 1999 HC/01241, where Evans-Lombe J. held such a clause not to be an unfair term.

9A–161/1 [p.917] **Restrictions on court's ability to re-open agreement**

Add at end:

See also *Extortionate Credit Bargain Claims and the Limitation Rules* (1998) 142 S.J. 274.

SECTION 10

COURT OF PROTECTION

A. GENERAL

Fixed costs 10A–176 [p.994]

Delete "£520", *substitute* "£560". *Delete* "£130", *substitute* "£135".*Delete* "£146", *substitute* "£150". *Delete* "£400", *substitute* "£430".*Delete* "£455", *substitute* "£485". *Delete* "£273", *substitute* "£280". *In Category V (a) delete* "£100" *and substitute* "£105". *In Category V (b) delete* "£282" *and substitute* "£295". *In penultimate paragraph substitute* "1999" *for* "1998" *throughout.*

B. MENTAL HEALTH ACT 1983

Correspondence of patients 10B–34 [p.1012]

In s.134(3)(c), after "Parliamentary Commissioner for Administration," *insert* "the Welsh Administration Ombudsman,".

Note 10B–34/1 [p.1013]

Add at end:

Subs. (3) (c) amended by the Government of Wales Act 1998 (c.38), s.125, Sched. 12, para. 22.

C. COURT OF PROTECTION RULES 1994

Procedure for short order or direction without appointment of receiver 10C–10 [p.1022] *

In rule 9(2)(a) delete "£5,000" *and substitute* "£10,000".

Note 10C–10/1 *

Add new note:

Amended by The Court of Protection (Amendment) Rules 1999.

Notice of hearing 10C–22 [p.1024] *

In rule 21(3) for the words "according to the practice of the Chancery Division, would have been required to be served with the summons if the application had been made in the High Court", *substitute* "would have been required to be served with the application notice if the application notice had been made in the High Court".

Note 10C–22/1 *

Add new note:

Amended by The Court of Protection (Amendment) Rules 1999.

Commencement fee 10C–80 [p.1037] *

In rule 79 delete the words "or other originating process".

Note 10C–80/1 *

Add new note:

Amended by The Court of Protection (Amendment) Rules 1999.

10C–81 **Administration fee**
[p.1037] *In rule 80(1) delete the words* "issue of the first application for" *and* "or other
* originating process".

10C–81/1 **Note**
* *Add new note:*
Amended by The Court of Protection (Amendment) Rules 1999.

10C–83 **Fee on taxation**
[p.1038] *Delete rule 82 and substitute:*
*

Fee on detailed assessment of costs

82. A fee is payable in respect of the detailed assessment of costs and on an appeal against a decision made in a detailed assessment of costs.

10C–83/1 **Note**
* *Add new note:*
Amended by The Court of Protection (Amendment) Rules 1999.

10C–90 **Supreme Court costs rules to apply**
[p.1040] *Delete rule 89 and substitute:*
*

Civil Procedure rules to apply

89.—(1) Subject to the provisions of these Rules, Parts 43, 44, 47 and 48 of the Civil Procedure Rules 1998 ("the 1998 Rules") shall apply, with the modifications in paragraph (2) and such other modifications as may be necessary, to costs incurred in relation to proceedings under these Rules as they apply to costs incurred in relation to proceedings in the High Court.

(2) The modifications referred to in paragraph (1) are:

(a) in rule 43.2(1)(c) of the 1998 Rules, costs officer shall include
  (i) a judge;
  (ii) the Master.
(b) in rule 43.2(1)(d) of the 1998 Rules, authorised court officer shall include an officer of the court;
(c) rule 44.3(2) of the 1998 Rules (costs follow the event) does not apply;
(d) rules 44.9 to 44.12 of the 1998 Rules (costs on small claims and fast tracks and on track allocation or reallocation) do not apply;
(e) rules 48.1 to 48.3 (costs payable by or to particular persons) and 48.7 to 48.10 (costs relating to solicitors and other legal representatives) of the 1998 Rules do not apply.

(3) Where the court orders costs to be assessed by way of detailed assessment, the detailed assessment proceedings will take place in the High Court.

10C–90/1 **Note**
* *Add new note:*
Amended by The Court of Protection (Amendment) Rules 1999.

10C–101 **Appendix**
[p.1046] *In para. 1, column 1, delete the words* "or other originating process". *In column 2 delete* "£100" *and*
* *insert* "£200". *Delete para. 4 and substitute:*

Detailed assessment of costs (rule 82) 4.—(1) On the filing of a request for a detailed assessment of costs	£160
(2) On an appeal against a decision made in a detailed assessment of costs or on an application to set aside a default costs certificate	£50

In para. 7, column 2, delete "£250" *and substitute* "£300", *and delete* "£100" *and substitute* "£125".

Table 1 10C–102 [p.1046] *

Delete Table 1 and substitute

TABLE 1 (Fee No. 2)

Income Band	Clear Annual Income		Fee
	Exceeding	Not Exceeding	
(i)		£2,000	£100
(ii)	£2,000	£5,000	£180
(iii)	£5,000	£10,000	£450
(iv)	£10,000	£15,000	£800
(v)	£15,000	£25,000	£1,200
(vi)	£25,000		£1,750

Table 2 10C–103 [p.1047] *

Delete Table 2 and substitute:

TABLE 2 (Fee No. 6)

Income Band	Clear Annual Income		Fee
	Exceeding	Not Exceeding	
(i)		£2,000	£200
(ii)	£2,000	£5,000	£600
(iii)	£5,000	£10,000	£1,500
(iv)	£10,000	£15,000	£3,000
(v)	£15,000	£25,000	£3,800
(vi)	£25,000		£4,600

Delete text of "NOTE" *and substitute:* *

NOTE

In relation to fees 2 and 6, and their respective Tables, where income exceeds the lower limit of a band by less than the difference between the fee for that band and the fee for the next lower band, the fee charged shall be the fee for the lower band.

Note 10C–104 *

Add new note:

Tables 1 and 2 are amended by The Court of Protection (Amendment) Rules 1999.

G. COURT OF PROTECTION (ENDURING POWERS OF ATTORNEY) RULES 1994

Schedule 2 10G–38 [p.1085] *

In column 2, delete "£50" *and insert* "£75". *Delete* "£10" *and substitute* "£25". *Add new note:*

Note 10G–39 *

Amended by The Court of Protection (Enduring Powers of Attorney) (Amendment) Rules 1999.

SECTION 11

PROBATE JURISDICTION AND PROCEEDINGS

A. SUPREME COURT ACT 1981

11A–20 **Note**
[p.1098] *Add to note:*

PRESIDENTS DIRECTION DATED NOVEMBER 3, 1998

As from November 9, 1998, records of all grants of representation made in the Principal Registry and in district probate registries, kept pursuant to s.111 of the Supreme Court Act 1981, shall be maintained in the form of a computer record. Annual calendar books will continue to be prepared and will incorporate the information held on computer.

The information held on computer and in the annual calendar books will comprise:

(a) the full name of the deceased and any alias names;
(b) the last address of the deceased;
(c) the date of death and domicil of the deceased;
(d) the name(s) and address(es) of the executor(s) or administrator(s);
(e) the type of grant;
(f) the gross and net values of the estate or in the case of an excepted estate the limits within which the estate falls;
(g) the name and address of the extracting solicitor (if any) or the fact that the grant was obtained by way of personal application;
(h) the date of the grant and the issuing registry.

The President's Direction, as published in the Registrar's circular dated December 22, 1969, is revoked.

B. NON-CONTENTIOUS PROBATE RULES 1987

11B–1 **Arrangement of rules**
[p.1105] *Add the words* "or probate practitioners" *to the end of the title of rule 4.*

[p.1106] *After rule 62 add the words* "62A. Exercise of a registrar's jurisdiction by another registrar" to the Arrangement of Rules list.

11B–4 **Interpretation**
[p.1106] *Insert in the definition of* "personal applicant" *the words* "or probate practitioner" *after the word* "solicitor".

Add following the definition of "personal applicant":
"probate practitioner" means a person to whom s.23(1) of the Solicitors Act 1974 does not apply by virtue of s.23(2) of that Act.

Application of other rules **11B–8**
Delete rule 3 and substitute: [p.1107]

3. (1) Subject to the provisions of these rules and to any enactment, the Rules of the Supreme Court 1965 as they were in force immediately before 26th April 1999 shall apply, with any necessary modifications to non-contentious probate matters, and any reference in these rules to those rules shall be construed accordingly.

(2) Nothing in Order 3 of the Rules of the Supreme Court shall prevent time from running in the Long Vacation.

Note **11B–8/1**
Add new note:
Amended by the Non-Contentious Probate (Amendment) Rules 1999 (S.I. 1999 No. 1015).

Application for grants through solicitors **11B–9**
Add to the end of title the words "or probate practitioner". *Insert in paragraphs (1)* [p.1107] *and (2) after both occurrences of the word* "solicitor" *the words* "or probate practitioner".

Personal applications **11B–12**
Insert at the end of paragraph (3)(a) the words "unless a judge, district judge or [p.1107] registrar permits". *Insert after the words* "solicitor" *in r.5(3)(b) the words* "or probate practitioner".

Grants where two or more persons entitled in same degree **11B–54**
Omit in paragraph (1A) of r.27 the words: "appointed by reference to their being" [p.1116] *and* "and not by their names". *Delete paragraph (7) of r.27 and substitute:*

"(7) The issue of a Summons under this rule in a registry shall be noted forthwith in the index of the pending grant applications."

Grants on behalf of minors **11B–68**
Add after paragraph (1)(a) of r.32: [p.1120]

"(aa) a person who has or is deemed to have parental responsibility for the minor by virtue of section 12(2) of the Children Act 1989 where the court has made a residence order under Section 8 of that Act in respect to the minor in favour of that person; or".

Insert at the end of paragraph (1)(b) of r.32 the word "or".

Add after paragraph (1)(b) of r.32:

"(c) a local authority which has, or is deemed to have, parental responsibility for the minor by virtue of section 33(3) of the Children Act 1989 where the court has made a care order under section 31(1)(a) of that Act in respect of the minor and the local authority is designated in that order".

Grants in case of mental incapacity **11B–74**
Substitute in paragraph 4 of r.35 for the words: "two or more other persons" *the* [p.1122] *words* "other person".

Insert at the beginning of paragraph (5) of r.35 the words: "Unless the applicant is the person authorised in paragraph (2)(a) above,".

11B–79 Renunciation of probate and administration

[p.1123] *Insert after paragraph 2 of r.37:*

"(2A) Renunciation of a probate 11B–90 and administration by members of a partnership—

(a) may be affected, or

(b) subject to paragraph (3) below, may be retracted by any two of them with the authority of the others and any such renunciation or retraction shall recite such authority."

11B–89 Standing searches

[p.1125] *Insert after the word* "solicitor" *in r.43(3)(a) the words* "or probate practitioner".

11B–90 Caveats

[p.1125] *Insert after the word* "solicitor" *in r.44(2) and 44(3)(a) the words* "or probate practitioner".

Delete paragraph (4) of r.44 and insert:

"(4) An index of caveats entered in any registry or sub-registry shall be maintained and upon receipt of an application for a grant, the registry or sub-registry at which the application is made shall cause a search of the index to be made and the appropriate district judge or registrar shall be notified of the entry of a caveat against the sealing of a grant for which the application has been made."

Delete in paragraphs (5), (9), (10) and (12) of r.44 the words "nominated registry" *and insert the words* "registry in which the caveat index is maintained".

Add after paragraph (14) of r.44:

"(15) In this rule 'nominated registry' means the registry nominated for the purpose of this rule by the senior district judge or in the absence of any such nomination the Leeds District Probate Registry".

11B–95 Citations

[p.1127] *Insert the word* "solicitor" *in r.46(2) the words* "or probate practitioner".

11B–109 Applications for rectification of a will

[p.1131] *Insert in paragraph 3 of r.55 after the word* "prejudiced" *the words* "or such other person who might be prejudiced".

11B–113 Index of grant applications

[p.1132] *Delete r.57 and insert:*

"**Index of grant applications**

57.—(1) The senior district judge shall maintain an index of every pending application for a grant made in any registry or sub-registry.

(2) Every registry or sub-registry in which application is made shall cause the index to be searched and shall record the result of the search."

"Exercise of a registrar's jurisdiction" **11B–119A** [p.1133]

Add after r.62:

"Exercise of a registrar's jurisdiction

62A. A registrar may hear and dispose of an application under these Rules on behalf of any other registrar by whom the application would otherwise have been heard, if that other registrar so requests or an application in that behalf is made by a party making an application under these Rules; and where the circumstances require it, the registrar shall, without the need for any request or application, hear and dispose of the application."

Service of summons **11B–123**

Substitute in paragraph (1) of r.66 for the second occurrence of the words "judge or district judge" *the words* "judge, district judge or registrar". [p.1134]

Caveat **11B–129**

In Form 3 insert the words "or probate practitioner" *after the first occurrence of the word* "solicitor" *and the words* "probate practitioner" *after the second occurrence of the word* "solicitor". [p.1135]

Warning to Caveator **11B–130**

In Form 4 insert the words "or probate practitioner" after both occurrences of the word "solicitor". Substitute the words "[The nominated registry as defined by rule 44(5)]" *for the words* "[The Registry in which the caveat index is maintained]" *and the words* "[name and address of the nominated registry]" *for the words* "[name and address of the registry in which the caveat index is maintained]". [p.1135]

Appearance to Warning or Citation **11B–131**

In Form 5 insert the words "probate practitioner" *after the words* "solicitor". [p.1136]

D. NON-CONTENTIOUS PROBATE FEES ORDER 1981

Delete existing text and insert:

[This Order has been revoked and replaced by the Non-Contentious Probate Fees Order 1999. See Section 4, paras 4C–1 *et seq.*] **11D–1** [p.1139]

SECTION 12

TRUSTEES

C. PUBLIC TRUSTEE ACT 1906

12C–40 **"Fees"**
[p.1158] *Delete para. and substitute:*

See the Public Trustee (Fees) Act 1957, and Public Trustee (Fees) Order 1999 (S.I. 1999 No. 855). By s.2(2) of the Public Trustee (Fees) Act 1957, the Public Trustee has power in certain cases to direct that the fees in force immediately before April 1, 1957 shall continue to apply.

12C–49 **Audit Fee**
[p.1161] *Delete para. and substitute:*

Under the Public Trustee (Fees) Order 1999 (S.I. 1999 No. 855) a fee of £750 is payable to the Public Trustee in addition to the remuneration of the auditor. An additional fee may be charged for conducting a hearing in accordance with r.37 of the Public Trustee Rules 1912 and for duties of an unusual, complex or exacting nature.

SECTION 14

LIMITATION

Time limits for actions for personal injuries 14–17/3
In seventh paragraph, after the reference to Ackbar v. C.F. Green & Co. Ltd, add: [p.1211]
Where an employee brings an action against his employers for failing to advise him as to the benefits he was entitled to on suffering personal injury in the course of his employment, the claim is not a claim in respect of personal injury subject to the three year time limit in s.11 but a claim for negligent advice (*Gaud v. Leeds Health Authority, The Times*, May 14, 1999, CA). *

After the reference to Hopkins v. Mackenzie add:
But a claim against solicitors for alleged mishandling of a case, causing clinical depression, is a claim which includes damages for personal injuries: *Bennett v. Greenland Houchen & Co.* [1998] P.N.L.R. 458, CA.

Time limit for actions from date of knowledge 14–17/6
After the third paragraph, add: [p.1212]
In *Smith v. Leicestershire H.A.* (1996) 36 B.M.L.R. 23, May J. (as he then was) held that the Court was bound by the majority decision in *Forbes* to adopt an objective test when applying Section 14(3). The case contains a useful review of the leading decisions on the question of knowledge.

Add at end of paragraph above:
The Court of Appeal has held in *Smith* at [1998] Lloyd's Rep. Med. 77, that the Court was free to decide which of the two conflicting decisions in *Nash* and *Forbes* it should follow. It expressly approved the observations of Evans L.J. in *Forbes* that the test of objectivity and reasonableness should be applied. It posed the question "what would the reasonable person have done placed in the situation of the plaintiff?" The Judge's decision on knowledge was overruled on the facts.

After the reference to Halford v. Brookes, add:
Only in exceptional circumstances would the name of a party liable for a wrongdoing be a fact ascertainable "only with the help of expert advice": *Henderson v. Temple Pier Co. Ltd* [1998] 1 W.L.R. 1540, CA.

Time limit for actions from date of knowledge 14–17/7
In eighth paragraph, after the reference to Hepworth v. Ker, add: [p.1213]
However, circumstances may arise in which a claimant may be fixed with constructive knowledge of facts his advisers, as reasonably competent legal representatives, ought to have acquired (see *Henderson v. Temple Pier Co. Ltd*, explained in para. 14–17/8 below). *

Time limit for actions from date of knowledge 14–17/8
At the end of the fourth paragraph of the note add: [p.1214]
A patient whose condition deteriorates following an operation, and who inferred that the operation had not been a success but who had nothing to alert him to the fact that he had been injured during the operation, cannot be said to be fixed with knowledge by s.14 (*James v. East Dorset Health Authority, The Times*, December 7, 1999, CA). *

At the end of the fifth paragraph of the note add: *
Section 14(3) does not give an extended period of limitation to a claimant whose legal representatives acted dilatorily in acquiring information as to the identity of the defendant (see s.14(1)(c)), being information which was obtainable without the application of particular expertise; in such circumstances, the claimant may be fixed with constructive knowledge of facts his advisers, as reasonably competent legal representatives, ought to have acquired (*Henderson v. Temple Pier Co. Ltd* [1998] 1 W.L.R. 1540, [1998] 3 All E.R. 324, CA; note also *Copeland v. Smith, The Times*, October 20, 1999, CA).

At the end of the sixth paragraph of the note add:
The relevance of a parent's knowledge was treated in *Bates v. Leicester H.A.* [1998] Lloyd's Rep. Med. 93 as related to the information which the plaintiff would have acquired from his parents on the assumption that he ought reasonably to have pressed them for more information. The judge's decision in *O'Driscoll* on constructive knowledge was reversed by the Court of Appeal on the facts: see [1998] Lloyd's Rep. Med. 210, CA.

14–18/2 **Knowledge of plaintiff in negligence actions**

[p.1215] *At the end of the second paragraph of the note add:*

In *West Bromwich Building Society v. Mander Hadley & Co., The Times,* March 6, 1998, CA (a case where the plaintiff wished to guard against future unascertained claims against it outside the limitation period by issuing protective writs claiming contribution) Millett L.J. observed that it was not clear why Parliament had confined the operation of section 14A so that it was not available for claims in negligence framed in contract; nor why Parliament had not provided that a contingent cause of action should not be treated for limitation purposes as accruing before the contingency occurred. But it was not for the courts to extend the limitation period in hard cases by permitting writs to be issued at a time when the plaintiff was unaware of any valid basis for the claim.

[p.1216] *At the end of the third paragraph add:*

But knowledge of facts relating to a cause of action not relied on by the plaintiff in his claim, being a cause of action truly separate from that on which he does rely, will not enable the defence of limitation to succeed: *Birmingham Midshires Building Society v. Wretham* [1999] 07 E.G. 138, a case where the differing nature of the various duties of a solicitor acting for a purchaser or mortgagee is discussed.

At the end of the eighth paragraph add:

Thus it was held in *HF Pension Trustees Ltd v. Ellison, The Times,* March 5, 1999, that the plaintiffs had knowledge for the purposes of s.14A at the time when they made payments under a transfer even though they did not know, and could not have known, at the time that the transfer would subsequently be held unlawful. Mere ignorance that the known facts might give rise to a claim in law could not postpone the running of time.

After the eighth paragraph of the note insert:

It has been held at first instance that estimates as to the value of a lender's security submitted to the collections department of a commercial lender by debt collection agents are insufficient evidence of possible inaccuracies in the initial valuation of the lender's security to put the lender on notice for the purposes of s.14A(10) (*Mortgage Corporation v. Lambert & Co., The Times,* October 11, 1999).

14–26 **Time limit for actions in respect of trust property**

[p.1221] *Add new note after para. 14–26:*

14–26/1 **Section 21—actions for breach of trust and breach of fiduciary duty**

For a consideration of the legislative history of s.21 see *Paragon Finance plc v. DB Thackerar & Co.* [1999] 1 All E.R. 400, CA. That case elucidates the true nature of the distinction between two different classes of persons described as constructive trustees, namely (1) those holding on trust by virtue of taking possession of property on trust for or on behalf of others before the occurrence of the transaction impeached, and (2) those to whom the description applies only by reason of that transaction. It was held that, arguably, s.21 of the 1980 Act, and its predecessor s.19 of the Limitation Act 1939, have not abrogated that distinction and that s.21 is intended to apply only to trustees of the first description. The limitation period applicable to those of the second description, whether the case against them be put in damages for fraud at common law or by a corresponding claim in equity "for an account as constructive trustee", is six years, though the start of the period may be deferred in such latter cases. Likewise, a claim against an agent for an account in equity, absent any trust, was subject to the statutes of limitation. His liability to account for more than six years before the issue of the writ depended on whether he was, not merely a fiduciary (for every agent owes fiduciary duties to his principal), but a trustee, *i.e.* on whether he owed fiduciary duties *in relation to the money* (*Nelson v. Rye* [1996] 2 All E.R. 186 disapproved). See
* also *Coulthard v. Disco Mix Club Ltd* [1999] 2 All E.R. 457, following *Paragon.* On the question of the extent to which an executor *de son* is in the same position as a trustee for the purposes of s.21(1)(b), see *James v. Williams* [1999] 3 W.L.R. 451, CA, and the authorities referred to therein.

14–29 **Time Limit for actions to enforce judgments**

[p.1221] *Insert note to section 24 as follows:*

14–29/1 The House of Lords has held that proceedings to execute a judgment debt (in that case by charging and garnishee orders) were not an action upon a judgment within the meaning of s.24(1). Action meant a fresh action. But recovery of interest was barred by the lapse of 6 years under subs. (2), and s.32 of the Act did not apply to extend that period: *Lowsley v. Forbes* [1998] 3
* W.L.R. 501, HL. The normal rule is that, where there is a dispute as to whether a claimant's claim was time-barred, the claimant has to commence a fresh action in which the viability of the limitation defence can be determined (*Welsh Development Agency v. Redpath Dorman Long Ltd* [1994] 1 W.L.R. 1409, CA, see para. 14–42/5 below). It has been held at first instance that this rule does not apply where there is an issue under s.32(2) as to whether any fact relevant to the

claimant's right of action had been deliberately concealed and the deliberateness of the breach is an essential element of the new cause of action (*Mortgage Corporation v. Alexander Johnson, The Times*, September 22, 1999).

At end of this note add: 14–38/1 [p.1226] *

The normal rule is that, where there is a dispute as to whether a claimant's claim was time-barred, the claimant has to commence a fresh action in which the viability of the limitation defence can be determined (*Welsh Development Agency v. Redpath Dorman Long Ltd* [1994] 1 W.L.R. 1409, CA, see para. 14–42/5 below). It has been held at first instance that this rule does not apply where there is an issue under s.32(3) as to whether any fact relevant to the claimant's right of action had been deliberately concealed and the deliberateness of the breach is an essential element of the new cause of action (*Mortgage Corporation v. Alexander Johnson, The Times*, September 22, 1999).

Action begun after expiry of primary limitation period— 14–40/4 [p.1231]

Add at the end of numbered paragraph 3:

Where a writ against the original defendant was struck out in the reasonable belief that it was a nullity the case was to be regarded as an exception to the rule in *Walkley*, so that discretion could be exercised to permit fresh proceedings to be brought against a second defendant added after the expiry of the limitation period. The Court of Appeal also considered, without deciding, whether *White v. Glass* had added to the rule in *Walkley* a requirement that the first action must have been properly constituted against the same defendants: *McEvoy v. A.A. Welding and Fabrication Ltd* [1998] P.I.Q.R. P266, CA. See also *Shapland v. Palmer* [1999] 1 W.L.R. 2068, CA; * [1999] 3 All E.R. 50, CA in which it was held that where an action against a driver for negligence followed an earlier dismissed action against the driver's employers, there was an exception to the principle in *Walkley*. The two actions were not indistinguishable.

In *Re Philip Powis Ltd, The Times*, March 9, 1998, CA the applicant, who had a pending action for personal injuries on the date of the defendant company's dissolution sought a declaration under section 651(1) of the Companies Act 1985 that the dissolution was void in order to commence a second action outside the primary limitation period. The Judge described the decision in *Walkley* as a formidable obstacle for the applicant. But the Court of Appeal, holding that the termination of the first action was not brought about by any act of the applicant and that an application under section 33 would have reasonable prospects of success, held that the decision in *Walkley* should not necessarily be regarded as an obstacle and that the Judge had failed to give proper weight to the conduct of the company under section 33(3)(c), namely the liquidation and dissolution of the company without making any provision for its liability, if any, to the applicant. The appeal against dismissal of the application under section 651 was allowed.

Discretion to disapply relevant limitation period 14–40/5 [p.1232]

At the end of this paragraph add, as a new para of the note:

Section 33(3)(c) relates to the conduct of the defendant after the cause of action arose. A health authority with a policy of destroying patients' X-rays after three years, even those of patients known to be contemplating actions in negligence and whose solicitors had requested notes, would have any prejudice pleaded in a limitation defence significantly discounted: *Hammond v. West Lancashire H.A., The Times*, March 5, 1988, CA.

At the end of the note, add as a separate paragraph: 14–40/6 [p.1233]

Section 33 cannot be construed by reference to the procedural stage at which it comes into play. Thus in a case where negligence and causation were actually established by the decision of the Court on the merits, the Court had nonetheless to apply the provisions of section 33(3)(b). The plaintiff succeeded on causation on the evidence in 1996 but might not have done so if the trial had taken place even 20 years earlier. The claim failed because it was statute-barred: *Smith v. Leicestershire H.A.* (1996) 36 B.M.L.R. 23.

Add at the end of above paragraph:

The Court of Appeal has disagreed in *Smith* with the judge's reasoning on the s.33 point and has overruled the decision on this and other grounds—"Causation does not change with the passage of time": See [1998] Lloyd's Rep. Med. 77, CA, at 92.

Discretion to disapply relevant limitation period 14–40/7 [p.1233] *

After reference to Halford v. Brooks, add:

Where the reasons for the delay on the part of the plaintiff are due mainly to misleading advice given to him by his legal representatives, s.11 should be disapplied under s.33 as, having regard to the requirements of s.33(3)(a), the delay resulting from their defaults should not be laid at his door (*Das v. Ganju, The Times*, May 4, 1999, CA (delay exceeding five years from expiration of primary limitation period for personal injury action)).

Relationship of s.35 with Rules of the Supreme Court 14–42/5 [p.1237] *

After reference to Goose v. Wilson Sandford & Co. add:

A writ may be amended out of time under RSC O.20, r.5 to include new cause of action which had been pleaded within time limits in the statement of claim but was inadvertently omitted from the writ (*Phelps v. Spon-Smith & Co., The Times*, November 26, 1999).

14–42/6 **Subsection (3)**

[p.1237] *In the second paragraph of the note, after the sentence ending* "until after the limitation period has expired", *add:*

See *Lloyd's Bank Plc v. Wojcik, The Independent,* January 19, 1998, CA.

[p.1238] *At end of the second paragraph add:*

The word "claim" in s.35(3) should be construed as a claim for relief. Accordingly, where a defendant had previously pleaded a defence stating that the plaintiff had extended time for payment of a debt, that was not a claim in the legal sense. There was power under s.35(3) to grant leave to amend to plead a counterclaim even though it was founded on a cause of action which was statute-barred: *JFS (U.K.) Ltd v. Dwr Cymru Cyf, The Times,* October 10, 1998, CA.

14–42/11 **Adding or substituting a new cause of action or a new party**

[p.1240] *After the sixth paragraph of the note, add as a new paragraph:*

An amendment to allege intentional wrongdoing by pleading fraud where previously only negligence had been alleged amounts to the introduction of a new cause of action: *Paragon Finance plc v. Thakerar & Co., The Times,* August 7, 1998, CA.

SECTION 15

SOLICITORS

A. SOLICITORS' ACT 1974

Note 15A–24 [p.1257]

Add:

Courts and Legal Services Act 1990: s.54 is amended and repealed in part by the Bank of England Act, s.23, Sched. 5, para. 41 and s.43, Sched. 9, Pt I respectively. Schedule 10, para. 58 is repealed by the Data Protection Act 1998, Sched. 16, Pt I, and Sched. 11 is amended by Employment Rights (Dispute Resolution) Act 1998, Sched. 1, para. 6.

Subsection (2) 15A–58/23/1 [p.1269]

Insert new note:

This section merely provides that nothing in the Act shall give validity to arrangements of the kind specified. The Act does not legitimise any arrangements which would otherwise be lawful but neither does it make them unlawful if they are otherwise lawful. The Court of Appeal found nothing in the 1974 Act which prohibits the charging of contingent fees. The fact that the Solicitors Practice Rules 1990 make it professional misconduct for a solicitor to enter into any agreement, even for his normal fee, where this is dependent on achieving a successful result in litigation, did not of itself make the practice contrary to law (following *Picton Jones & Co. v. Arcadia Developments Ltd* [1989] 1 E.G.L.R. 42). The Court found that the rules were based on a perception of public policy derived from judicial decisions which were flawed, *Thai Trading Co. v. Taylor*, [1998] 2 W.L.R. 893, CA.

Add at end of above paragraph:

In *Hughes v. Kingston Upon Hull City Council* [1999] 2 All E.R. 49, DC, the Divisional Court decided that *Thai Trading* (above) had been decided *per incuriam* because *Swain v. The Law Society* [1983] 1 A.C. 598, HL decided that the Solicitors Practice Rules (1990, rule 8) had the force of statute. Since that decision the Law Society's Practice Rules have been altered to enable contingent fee agreements, as envisaged in *Thai Trading*, to be entered into by solicitors.

Subsection (3) 15A–58/28/1 [p.1269]

Insert new note:

The words "any costs" in the phrase "an order for the payment of any costs" in section 60(3) relate not to costs at large or to the costs payable by the receiving party to his own solicitor but to the costs and items of costs to be identified on the party and party taxation as the proper and recoverable costs. The words "those costs" clearly refer to the same costs.

The operation of the cap than becomes readily intelligible. Where applicable the figures in the contentious business agreement provide both a measure and a ceiling for each recoverable item of costs. *Per* Sir Brian Neill in *The General of Berne Insurance Co. v. Jardine Reinsurance Management Ltd, The Times*, February 20, 1998, CA.

Add: 15A–58/40

Where a bill has been delivered to a client, that bill may be withdrawn later and substituted by a [p.1272]
second bill if the client consents or with the leave of the court. The first bill is not conclusive evidence of the reasonableness of the amounts charged in it although it may be relevant evidence. Taxation of the second bill would be valid and not without jurisdiction. *Rezvi v. Brown Cooper*, (1997) 1 Costs L.R. 109 (Newman J.).

"To recover any costs" 15A–58/54 [p.1275]

Add at end:

It is non performance of a contract to provide legal services by a solicitor, where a firm of solicitors is asked to provide a solicitor and, without telling the client that the adviser is not a solicitor, provides such an adviser. Accordingly, the firm of solicitors was not entitled to recover anything by way of costs. (*Pearless de Rougemont & Co. v. Pilbrow (No. 2)* [1999] 3 All E.R. 355, CA.)

If 12 months have expired from the delivery of the bill 15A–58/71 [p.1280] ★

Add at end:

A solicitor's client who no longer has a right to claim taxation of the bill of costs under s.70, after expiry of the statutory time limit, is nevertheless entitled to challenge the reasonableness of the sum claimed by the solicitor as due (*Turner & Co. v. O. Palomo S.A.* [1999] 4 All E.R. 353, CA, *sub nom. O. Palomo S.A. v. Turner & Co., The Times*, August 30, 1999, CA; see also *Jones and Son v. Whitehouse* [1918] 2 K.B. 61, CA).

15A–58/74 **Inherent jurisdiction to order taxation**

[p.1280] *Add:*

Where solicitors sued for their costs and the defendant counterclaimed for negligence, all of which allegations failed, the court (the time for applying for taxation having expired) nonetheless made an order that the solicitors' bill should be examined. "Where a quantum meruit is claimed for work done, the benefit of which has been obtained under a contract, but where the contract sum has not been agreed, there may be an order for judgment for the plaintiff with the quantum to be assessed. The judicial assessment should be carried out by a Taxing Master. It is the Taxing Masters that have the requisite expertise for that purpose", *per* Sir Richard Scott, Vice-Chancellor, *Thomas Watts & Co. v. Smith*, March 16, 1998, CA (unreported).

B. SOLICITORS' ACCOUNTS RULES 1991
C. SOLICITORS' ACCOUNTS (LEGAL AID TEMPORARY PROVISION) RULES 1992

15C–5 **Note**

[p.1294] *Add new note and add Solicitors' Account Rules 1998 below:*

The Solicitors' Accounts Rules 1998 which came into force on July 22, 1998 consolidate the Solicitors Accounts Rules 1991, the Solicitors Accounts (Legal Aid Temporary Provision) Rule 1992, the Accountants Report Rules 1991, the contents of the Accounts Rules chapter (chap. 28) of the 1996 Guide to the Professional Conduct of Solicitors; and the guidance contained in Annex 28E of the Guide (Deposit Interest). Firms may choose to implement the new rules immediately, if this is done the rules must be adopted in their entirety and not selectively. All firms must implement the rules by May 1, 2000.

SOLICITORS' ACCOUNTS RULES 1998

15C–6 **Receipt and transfer of costs**

[p.1294] **19.**—(1) A *solicitor* who receives money paid in full or part settlement of the *solicitor's* bill (or other notification of *costs*) must follow one of the following four options:

(a) determine the composition of the payment *without delay*, and deal with the money accordingly:

(i) if the sum comprises *office money* only, it must be placed in an *office account*;

(ii) if the sum comprises only *client money* (for example an unpaid *professional disbursement*—see rule 2(2)(s), and note (v) to rule 2), the entire sum must be placed in a *client account*;

(iii) if the sum includes both *office money* and *client money* (such as unpaid *professional disbursements*; purchase money; or payments in advance for court fees, stamp duty, Land Registry registration fees or telegraphic transfer fees), the *solicitor* must follow rule 20 (receipt of mixed payments); or

(b) ascertain that the payment comprises only *office money*, and/or *client money* in the form of *professional disbursements* incurred but not yet paid, and deal with the payment as follows:

(i) place the entire sum in an *office account* at a *bank* or *building society* branch (or head office) in England and Wales; and

(ii) by the end of the second working day following receipt, either pay any unpaid *professional disbursement*, or transfer a sum for its settlement to a *client account*; or

(c) pay the entire sum into a *client account* (regardless of its composition), and transfer any *office money* out of the *client account* within 14 days of receipt; or

(d) on receipt of *costs* from the Legal Aid Board, follow the option in rule 21(1)(b).

(2) A *solicitor* who properly requires payment of his or her *fees* from money held for the *client* or *controlled trust* in a *client account* must first give or send a bill of *costs*, or other written notification of the *costs* incurred, to the *client* or the paying party.

(3) Once the *solicitor* has compiled with paragraph (2) above, the money earmarked for *costs* becomes *office money* and must be transferred out of the *client account* within 14 days.

(4) (4) A payment on account of *costs* generally is *client money*, and must be held in a *client account* until the *solicitor* has complied with paragraph (2) above. (For an exception in the case of legal aid payments, see rule 21(1)(a).)

(5) (5) A payment for an *agreed fee* must be paid into an *office account*. An "agreed fee" is one that is fixed—not a *fee* that can be varied upwards, nor a *fee* that is dependent on the transaction being completed. An *agreed fee* must be evidenced in writing.

Treatment of payments to legal aid practitioners

21.—(1) *Payments from the Legal Aid Board*: Two special dispensations apply **15C–7**
to payments from the Legal Aid Board:

(a) An advance payment in anticipation of work to be carried out, although *client money*, may be placed in an *office account*, provided the Board instructs in writing that this may be done.

(b) A payment for *costs* (interim and/or final) may be paid into an *office account* at a *bank* or *building society* branch (or head office) in England and Wales, regardless of whether it consists wholly of *office money*, or is mixed with *client money* in the form of:
  (i) advance payments for *fees* or *disbursements*; or
  (ii) money for unpaid *professional disbursements*;

provided all money for payment of *disbursements* is transferred to a *client account* (or the *disbursements* paid) within 14 days of receipt.

(2) *Payments from a third party*: If the Legal Aid Board has paid any *costs* to a *solicitor* or a previously nominated *solicitor* in a matter ("green form" *costs*, advance payments or interim *costs*), or has paid *professional disbursements* direct, and *costs* are subsequently settled by a third party:

(a) The entire third party payment must be paid into a *client account*.

(b) A sum representing the payments made by the Board must be retained in the *client account*.

(c) Any balance belonging to the *solicitor* sending a report to the Board containing details of the third party payment.

(d) The sum retained in the *client account* as representing payments made by the Board must be:
  (i) either recorded in the individual *client's* ledger account, and identified as the Board's money;
  (ii) or recorded in a ledger account in the Board's name, and identified by reference to the *client* or matter;

and kept in the *client account* until notification from the Board that it has recouped an equivalent sum from subsequent legal aid payments due to the *solicitor.* The retained sum must be transferred to an *office account* within 14 days of notification.

Withdrawals from a client account

15C–8 22.—(1) *Client money* may only be withdrawn from a *client account* when it is:

(a) properly required for a payment to or on behalf of the *client* (or other person on whose behalf the money is being held);
(b) properly required for payment of a *disbursement* on behalf of the *client*;
(c) properly required in full or partial reimbursement of money spent by the *solicitor* on behalf of the *client*;
(d) transferred to another *client account*;
(e) withdrawn on the *client's* instructions, provided the instructions are for the *client's* convenience and are given in writing, or are given by other means and confirmed by the *solicitor* to the *client* in writing;
(f) a refund to the *solicitor* of an advance no longer required to fund a payment on behalf of a *client* (see rule 15(2)(b));
(g) money which has been paid into the account in breach of the rules (for example, money paid into the wrong *separate designated client account*)—see paragraph (4) below; or
(h) money not covered by (a) to (g) above, withdrawn from the account on the written authorisation of the *Society*. The *Society* may impose a condition that the *solicitor* pay the money to a charity which gives an indemnity against any legitimate claim subsequently made for the sum received.

(2) *Controlled trust money* may only be withdrawn from a *client account* when it is:

(a) properly required for a payment in the execution of the particular *trust*, including the purchase of an investment (other than money) in accordance with the *trustee's* powers;
(b) properly required for payment of a *disbursement* for the particular *trust*;
(c) properly required in full or partial reimbursement of money spent by the *solicitor* on behalf of the particular *trust*;
(d) transferred to another *client account*;
(e) transferred to an account other than a *client account* (such as a *building society* share account or an account outside England and Wales), but only if the *trustee's* powers permit, or to be properly retained in cash in the performance of the *trustee's* duties;
(f) a refund to the *solicitor* of an advance no longer required to fund a payment on behalf of a *controlled trust* (see rule 15(2)(b));
(g) money which has been paid into the account in breach of the rules (for example, money paid into the wrong *separate designated client account*)—see paragraph (4) below; or
(h) money not covered by (a) to (g) above, withdrawn from the account on the written authorisation of the *Society*. The *Society* may impose a condition that the *solicitor* pay the money to a charity which gives an indemnity against any legitimate claim subsequently made for the sum received.

(3) *Office money* may only be withdrawn from a *client account* when it is:

(a) money properly paid into the account to open or maintain it under rule 15(2)(a);
(b) properly required for payment of the *solicitor's costs* under rule 19(2) and (3);
(c) the whole or part of a payment into a *client account* under rule 19(1)(c);
(d) part of a *mixed payment* placed in a *client account* under rule 20(2)(b); or
(e) money which has been paid into a *client account* in breach of the rules (for example, interest wrongly credited to a *general client account*)—see paragraph (4) below.

(4) Money which has been paid into a *client account* in breach of the rules must be withdrawn from the *client account* promptly upon discovery.

(5) Money withdrawn in relation to a particular *client* or *controlled trust* from a *general client account* must not exceed the money held on behalf of that *client* or *controlled trust* in all the *solicitor's general client accounts* (except as provided in paragraph (6) below).

(6) A *solicitor* may make a payment in respect of a particular *client* or *controlled trust* out of a *general client account*, even if no money (or insufficient money) is held for that *client* or *controlled trust* in the *solicitor's general client account(s)*, provided:
(a) sufficient money is held for that *client* or *controlled trust* in a *separate designated client account*; and
(b) the appropriate transfer from the *separate designated client account* to a *general client account* is made immediately.

(7) Money held for a *client* or *controlled trust* in a *separate designated client account* must not be used for payments for another *client* or *controlled trust.*

(8) A *client account* must not be overdrawn, except in the following circumstances:
(a) A *separate designated client account* for a *controlled trust* can be overdrawn if the *controlled trustee* makes payments on behalf of the *trust* (for example, inheritance tax) before realising sufficient assets to cover the payments.
(b) If a sole practitioner dies and his or her *client accounts* are frozen, the *solicitor*-manager can operate *client accounts* which are overdrawn to the extent of the money held in the frozen accounts.

Method of and authority for withdrawals from client account

23.—(1) A withdrawal from a *client account* may be made only after a specific authority in respect of that withdrawal has been signed by at least one of the following: **15C–9**
(a) a *solicitor* who holds a current practising certificate;
(b) a Fellow of the Institute of Legal Executives of at least three years standing who is employed by such a *solicitor*;
(c) in the case of an office dealing solely with conveyancing, a licensed conveyancer who is employed by such a *solicitor*; or
(d) a *registered foreign lawyer* who is a partner in the practice or, in the case of a *recognised body*, a director.

(2) There is no need to comply with paragraph (1) above when transferring money from one *general client account* to another *general client account* at the same *bank* or *building society*.

(3) A withdrawal from a *client account* in favour of the *solicitor* or the practice must be either by way of a cheque to the *solicitor* or practice, or by way of a transfer to the *office account* or to the *solicitor's* personal account. The withdrawal must not be made in cash.

Part C. INTEREST

When interest must be paid

15C–10 **24.**—(1) When a *solicitor* holds money in a *separate designated client account* for a *client*, or for a person funding all or part of the *solicitor's fees*, the *solicitor* must account to the *client* or that person for all interest earned on the account.

(2) When a *solicitor* holds money in a *general client account* for a *client*, or for a person funding all or part of the *solicitor's fees* (or if money should have been held for a *client* or such other person in a *client account* but was not), the *solicitor* must account to the *client* or that person for a sum in lieu of interest calculated in accordance with rule 25.

(3) A *solicitor* is not required to pay a sum in lieu of interest under paragraph (2) above:

(a) if the amount calculated is £20 or less;

(b) (i) if the solicitor holds a sum of money not exceeding the amount shown in the left hand column below for a time not exceeding the period indicated in the right hand column:

Amount	*Time*
£1,000	8 weeks
£2,000	4 weeks
£10,000	2 weeks
£20,000	1 week

(ii) if the solicitor holds a sum of money exceeding £20,000 for one week or less, unless it is fair and reasonable to account for a sum in lieu of interest having regard to all the circumstances;

(c) on money held for the payment of counsel's fees, once counsel has requested a delay in settlement;

(d) on money held for the Legal Aid Board;

(e) on an advance from the *solicitor* under rule 15(2)(b) to fund a payment on behalf of the *client* in excess of funds held for that *client*; or

(f) if there is an agreement to contract out of the provisions of this rule under rule 27.

(4) If sums of money are held intermittently during the course of acting, and the sum in lieu of interest calculated under rule 25 for any period is £20 or less, a sum in lieu of interest should still be paid if it is fair and reasonable in the circumstances to aggregate the sums in respect of the individual periods.

(5) If money is held for a continuous period, and for part of that period it is held in a *separate designated client account*, the sum in lieu of interest for the rest of the period when the money was held in a *general client account* may as a result be £20 or less. A sum in lieu of interest should, however, be paid if it is fair and reasonable in the circumstances to do so.

(6)(a) If a *solicitor* holds money for a *client* (or person funding all or part of the *solicitor's fees*) in an account opened on the instructions of the *client* (or that person) under rule 16(1)(a), the *solicitor* must account to the *client* (or that person) for all interest earned on the account.

(b) If a *solicitor* has failed to comply with instructions to open an account under rule 16(1)(a), the *solicitor* must account to the *client* (or the person funding all or part of the *solicitor's fees*) for a sum in lieu of any net loss of interest suffered by the *client* (or that person) as a result.

(7) This rule does not apply to *controlled trust money*.

Amount of interest

25.—(1) *Solicitors* must aim to obtain a reasonable rate of interest on money held in a *separate designated client account*, and must account for a fair sum in lieu of interest on money held in a *general client account* (or on money which should have been held in a *client account* but was not). The sum in lieu of interest need not necessarily reflect the highest rate of interest obtainable but it is not acceptable to look only at the lowest rate of interest obtainable. **15C–11**

(2) The sum in lieu of interest for money held in a *general client account* (or on money which should have been held in a *client account* but was not) must be calculated

- on the balance or balances held over the whole period for which cleared funds are held
- at a rate not less than (whichever is the higher of) the following
  - (i) the rate of interest payable on a *separate designated client account* for the amount or amounts held, or
  - (ii) the rate of interest payable on the relevant amount or amounts if placed on deposit on similar terms by a member of the business community
- at the *bank* or *building society* where the money is held.

(3) If the money, or part of it, is held successively or concurrently in accounts at different *banks* or *building societies*, the relevant *bank* or *building society* for the purpose of paragraph (2) will be whichever of those *banks* or *building societies* offered the best rate on the date when the money was first held.

(4) If, contrary to the rules, the money is not held in a *client account*, the relevant *bank* or *building society* nominated by the *client* (or other person on whose behalf *client money* is held).

Interest on stakeholder money

26. When a *solicitor* holds money as stakeholder, the *solicitor* must pay interest, or a sum in lieu of interest, on the basis set out in rule 24 to the person to whom the stake is paid. **15C–12**

Contracting out

27.—(1) In appropriate circumstances a *client* and his or her *solicitor* may by a written agreement come to a different arrangement as to the matters dealt with in *rule 24* (payment of interest). **15C–13**

(2) A *solicitor* acting as stakeholder may, by a written agreement with his or her own *client* and the other party to the transaction, come to a different arrangement as to the matters dealt with in rule 24.

Interest certificates

28. Without prejudice to any other remedy: **15C–14**

(a) any *client*, including one of joint *clients*, or a person funding all or part of a *solicitor's fees*, may apply to the *Society* for a certificate as to whether or not interest, or a sum in lieu of interest, should have been paid and, if so, the amount; and

(b) if the *Society* certifies that interest, or a sum in lieu of interest, should have been paid, the *solicitor* must pay the certified sum.

Part G. COMMENCEMENT

Commencement

15C–15 **50.**—(1) These rules must be implemented not later than May 1, 2000; until a practice implements these rules, it must continue to operate the Solicitors' Accounts Rules 1991.

(2) Practices opting to implement these rules before May 1, 2000 must implement them in their entirety, and not selectively.

(3) Part F of the rules (accountants' reports) will apply to:

(a) reports covering any period of time after April 30, 2000; and also

(b) reports covering any earlier period of time for which a practice has opted to operate these rules.

(4) The Accountant's Report Rules 1991 will continue to apply to:

(a) reports covering any period of time before July 22, 1998; and also

(b) reports covering any period of time after July 21, 1998 and before May 1, 2000 during which a practice continued to operate the Solicitors' Accounts Rules 1991.

(5) If a practice operated the Solicitors' Accounts Rules 1991 for part of an *accounting period*, and these rules for the rest of the *accounting period*, the practice may, in respect of that *accounting period* ("the transitional accounting period") either:

(a) deliver a single accountant's report covering the whole of the transitional accounting period, made partly under the Accountant's Report Rules 1991 and partly under Part F of these rules, as appropriate; or

(b) deliver a separate accountant's report for each part of the transitional accounting period, one under the Accountant's Report Rules 1991 and the other under Part F of these rules; or

(c) deliver a report under the Accountant's Report Rules 1991 to cover that part of the transitional accounting period during which the practice operated the Solicitors' Accounts Rules 1991; and subsequently a report under Part F of these rules to cover the remaining part of the transitional accounting period plus the whole of the next *accounting period*; or

(d) deliver a report under the Accountant's Report Rules 1991 to cover the last complete *accounting period* during which the practice operated the Solicitors' Accounts Rules 1991 plus that part of the transitional accounting period during which the practice continued to operate those rules; and subsequently a report under Part F of these rules to cover the remaining part of the transitional accounting period.

E. CONDITIONAL FEE AGREEMENTS ORDER 1995

Delete Conditional Fee Agreements Order 1995, and replace with Conditional Fee Agreements Order 1998: **15E–1** [p.1300]

E. THE CONDITIONAL FEE AGREEMENTS ORDER 1998 (S.I. 1998 NO. 1860)

Citation, commencement and interpretation

1.—(1) This Order may be cited as the Conditional Fee Agreements Order 1998 and shall come into force on the day after the day on which it is made.

(2) In this Order "the Act" means the Courts and Legal Services Act 1990.

2. The Conditional Fee Agreements Order 1995 is revoked. **15E–2**

Specified proceedings

3.—(1) All proceedings are proceedings specified for the purposes of **15E–3** section 58(3) of the Act (conditional fee agreements in respect of specified proceedings not to be unenforceable).

(2) Proceedings specified in paragraph (1) shall be specified proceedings notwithstanding that they are concluded without the commencement of court proceedings.

Maximum permitted percentage increase on fees

4. For the purposes of section 58(5) of the Act the maximum permitted **15E–4** percentage by which fees may be increased in respect of any proceedings designated by article 3 as proceedings specified for the purposes of section 58(3) of the Act is 100%.

F. CONDITIONAL FEE AGREEMENTS

REGULATIONS 1995, REGS 1–7

Note **15F–8**

Insert new note: [p.1302]

For a note on the indemnity principle and conditional fee arragements in arbitrations see **15F–9** 62/A2/27A and *Bevan Ashford v. Geoff Yeandle (Contractors) Ltd (in liquidation),* [1998] 3 W.L.R. * 172, Sir Richard Scott V.-C.

An agreement between solicitors and a non-solicitor party to share the fees earned by the * former in consideration for the introduction of clients by the latter, who would also provide associated services, is contrary to the Solicitors Practice Rules 1990, rr.3 & 7 made under the Solicitors Act 1974, s.31 and is illegal and unenforceable; however, although no claim in restitution can be made by the non-solicitor party for recovery of the shared fees, he may bring a *quantum meruit* claim in respect of the services he had performed (*Mohamed v. Alaga & Co.* [1999] 3 All E.R. 699, CA, *sub. nom. Mohammed v. Alaga & Co., The Times,* July 29, 1999, CA).

For a Scottish case where a contingency fee agreement was found to be valid see *Quantum Claims Compensation Specialist Ltd v. Powell, The Times,* February 26, 1998, OHCS.

The signature of the bill of costs under the rules is effectively the certificate of an officer of the Court that the receiving party's solicitors are not seeking to recover, in relation to any item more than they have agreed to charge their client. *Per* Henry L.J., *Bailey v. IBC Vehicles Ltd,* [1998] 3 All E.R. 570, CA.

G. NOTES ON THE GENERAL LAW RELATING TO SOLICITORS

15G–107 [p.1308]

Rights of Audience of Solicitors in the Supreme Court

Add:

As to the rights of audience in Chambers under section 27(2)(e) of the Courts and Legal Services Act 1990 the Court has no discretion to exclude an individual without legal qualifications who falls within the ambit of the section: *Re H-S (Minors) (Chambers proceedings rights of audience) The Times,* February 20, 1998, CA.

15G–109 [p.1309] *

Conflict of interests

Add at end:

It is not for the judge to take a point about conflict of interest of his own motion. The essential starting point was an objection taken by another party whose interests and confidentiality needed to be protected. See *Bolkiah v. KPMG* [1992] 2 W.L.R. 215. *Hood Sail Makers Ltd v. Berthom Boat Co. Ltd,* 149 New L.J. 529 (1999), CA.

SECTION 16

LEGAL AID

A. LEGAL AID ACT 1988

Scope of advice and assistance 16A–16/1
Add new note: [p.1320]

"legally assisted person"

A person ceases to be a "legally assisted person" within s.2(11) when he starts to act in person; therefore, from that date (a) his liability for costs is not limited by s.17, and (b) the Legal Aid Board is not liable for his costs under s.18 (*Burridge v. Stafford* [1999] 4 All E.R. 660, CA). 16A–16/2 *

Section 2(10) "Person" 16A–21
Delete reference to "R. v. Chester and North Wales Legal Aid Area Office, ex p. Floods of Queensbury Ltd". Insert "R. v. Chester and North Wales Legal Aid Area Office (No. 12), ex p. Floods of Queensferry Ltd [1998] 1 W.L.R. 1496, CA." [p.1321]

Circumstances in which an order will be made 16A–72
Add at end: [p.1340] *

An application for costs against LAB by a successful unassisted party should be made at the conclusion of judgment but may be made later after the applicant has failed in his effort to recover costs (*Lancashire Fires Ltd v. S.A. Lyons and Co. Ltd (No. 2), The Times,* July 24, 1999, CA).

Subs. (4)—"just and equitable"; "severe financial hardship" 16A–75
Add at end: [p.1342] *

For an example of a case in which an order for costs to be paid by the Board was made by the Court of Appeal in favour of a defendant local authority where an appeal by a legally aided plaintiff was dismissed, see *Stretch v. West Dorset District Council (No. 2), The Times,* May 20, 1999, CA.

Section 31(1)(b)—The exercise of the court's discretion—general principle 16A–86
Add at end: [p.1344]

In a case where a legally aided defendant was successful on a counterclaim the judge took into account the fact of the successful party being legally aided in deciding to make no order as to costs. The Court of Appeal decided that the defendant having been successful on a counterclaim was, under normal principles, entitled to costs. The court went on to award 50 per cent of the costs of the counterclaim since the defendant was only successful in one of three allegations. *Tobin v. Gwyther,* February 8, 1999, CA (unreported).

Subs. (1) 16A–93
Add at beginning of paragraph: [p.1346]

The right to select a legal representative in respect of any claim for:

(a) clinical negligence;
(b) claims for damages in respect of trespass to the person committed in the course of the provision of clinical or medical services;
(c) claims for damages in respect of professional negligence in the conduct of a claim falling within (a) or (b) above; or
(d) claims including any of the above claims;

is exercisable only in relation to authorised litigators who are for the time being members of the clinical negligence franchise panel. See Legal Aid (Prescribed Panels) Regulations 1999 (S.I. 1999 No. 166).

D. CIVIL LEGAL AID (GENERAL) REGULATIONS 1989

Note 16D–34
Delete note and substitute: [p.1376]

See para. 16D–99, *Scarth v. Jacobs-Paton,* as to notification of limitation in a legal aid certificate.

16D–45 **Note**
[p.1379] *Add to note:*

Amended by the Civil Legal Aid (General) (Amendment) Regulations 1999 (S.I. 1999 No. 1113).

16D–46 Power to transfer application to another area office

[p.1379] *Delete regulation 17 and substitute:*

17. (1) If it appears to an Area Director that an application or certificate could be more conveniently or appropriately dealt with in another Area Office, he may transfer the application or certificate to that other office.

(2) Where a certificate is transferred under this regulation to another Area Office the certificate shall, for all purposes, including any obligation by the assisted person to continue to pay a contribution, continue as if it were a certificate issued by that Area Office.

16D–91 **Paras (1)(2) and (3)**
[p.1389] *Add new paragraph:*

Where a claimant was granted legal aid to take proceedings for damages for personal injuries arising out of an accident and the nominated solicitors commenced proceedings but failed to serve the writ which subsequently expired and the solicitors issued a second writ which was properly served and the action proceeded to a successful conclusion (with new solicitors) the defendants argued that the claimant's solicitors had no entitlement to payment out of the legal aid fund since they had proceeded in breach of reg. 43(3). The court reluctantly came to the view that although the second solicitors were entirely blameless, the meaning of the regulation was plain and there was no entitlement to any costs, *Bridgewater v. Griffiths, Review of Taxation*, April 29, 1999, Burton J. (unreported).

16D–115 **Para. (1)**
[p.1394] *Add:*

The Legal Aid Board has power to give authority to enable solicitors to incur the expense of an assisted person attending upon a medical expert. Regulation 33 (16D–24) provides that "costs" are to be construed as including references to fees, charges, disbursements, expenses and remuneration. The Court held that the definition is illustrative and not exhaustive it expressly includes disbursements and there is no prior reason why, in the case of an impecunious client, the costs of getting him to a specialist should not be a proper disbursement. *Per* Sedley J. in *R. v. Legal Aid No. 15 Area (Merseyside), ex p. Eccleston* [1998] 1 W.L.R. 1279.

16D–129 Duty to report progress of proceedings

[p.1397] *In reg. 70(1) after* "these Regulations" *insert:*
whether in relation to the assisted person's case or any other application, certificate or contract.

Insert after sub-para. (b):

(c) notify the Area Director of any information which comes to his knowledge and which he considers may be relevant to the determination of any application or the continuance of any certificate or contract.

Add new note:

16D–129/1 **Note**

Amended by the Civil Legal Aid (General) (Amendment) Regulations 1999 (S.I. 1999 No. 1113).

16D–132 Privilege, etc., not to prevent disclosure

[p.1398] *At the end of reg. 73(1) insert:*
in relation to any application, certificate or contract.

In reg. 73(2) insert: "in relation to any application, certificate or contract" *before the words* "any party".

Add new note:

Note 16D–132/1

Amended by the Civil Legal Aid (General) (Amended) Regulations 1999 (S.I. 1999 No. 1113).

Note 16D–140 [p.1400]

Add new note:

Regulation 78(1) 16D–140/1

The relationship between an applicant for legal aid and the Legal Aid Board is one requiring the utmost good faith on the applicant's part. The Board is being asked to underwrite the costs of litigation on behalf of the applicant and is dependent on the applicant making full disclosure of all his assets. The Area Director may revoke or discharge a certificate both where an untrue statement has been made as to financial resources and where there has been a failure to disclose any material fact concerning them. *R. v. Legal Aid Board, ex p. Parsons, The Times,* April 1, 1999, CA.

The statutory charge 16D–155 [p.1403]

Delete final paragraph of note and substitute:

The position of unmarried co-owners is regulated solely by their legal status as beneficiaries under the trust for sale imposed by the Law of Property Act 1925. Where the parties agreed to a consent order postponing sale, each party's rights under the trust for sale of the house were preserved to the extent that the statutory charge attached: *Parkes v. Legal Aid Board,* [1996], 4 All E.R. 271, CA.

Note 16D–164 [p.1406]

Add new note:

Regulation 91(2) 16D–164/1

Where an order is made in favour of a party to proceedings who is an assisted person, that order and any subsequent assessment of costs creates a debt in respect of which the assisted person has the standing to serve a statutory demand notwithstanding being an assisted person. For the purposes of reg. 87(1)(a) costs are "monies payable to an assisted person by virtue" of an order made for the payment of costs. Bankruptcy proceedings, including the service of a statutory demand, are to be treated as giving effect to such an order for the purposes of reg. 91(2), *Re A Debtor (No. 68/SD/97)* [1998] 4 All E.R. 779, Jonathan Parker J.

Exemptions from the statutory charge 16D–169 [p.1407] *

Regulation 94 becomes paragraph (1), and add at end:

(2) The charge created by section 16(6) of the Act shall not apply in relation to any increase in the net liability of the fund arising out of the cost of giving advice or assistance under Part III of the Act which is mediation-related advice or assistance, as defined in regulation 32(2) of the Legal Advice and Assistance Regulations 1989.

Note 16D–169/1 *

Add new note:

Amended by The Civil Legal Aid (General) (Amendment) (No. 2) Regulations 1999.

Note 16D–192 [p.1415] *

Add at end:

The making of reg. 103 by the Lord Chancellor was authorised by the Legal Aid Act 1988, s.34(3) (*Microsoft Corporation v. Backslash Distribution Ltd, The Times,* March 15, 1999).

Basis of taxation 16D–208 [p.1418]

After reg. 107A(3)(b) insert:

(c) be conducted in accordance with any conditions or limitations on the relevant certificate, where the rest of the work authorised under the certificate, the maximum costs payable or otherwise;

(d) ensure that any limitation as to costs on the relevant certificate will not reduce any sums payable in respect of counsel's fees except where counsel's fees alone exceed such limitation, when paragraph (4) below will apply.

(4) Where counsel's fees alone exceed any limitation as to costs on the relevant certificate, the excess shall be borne by the assisted person's solicitor except where he has sent counsel a copy of the certificate and any amendments in accordance with regulation 59(2).

16D–210 **Note**
[p.1419] *Add to note:*

Amended by the Civil Legal Aid (General) (Amendment) Regulations 1999 (S.I. 1999 No. 1113).

16D–211 **Recovery of costs**
[p.1373] *In regulation 107B(3)(a) insert:*

including, without limitation, with respect to the rates for the basis of taxation set out in regulation 107A or any limitation as to costs on the relevant certificate or contract.

Add to note:

Amended by the Civil Legal Aid (General) (Amendment) Regulations 1999 (S.I. 1999 No. 1113).

16D–221 **Authority to carry in objections**
[p.1421] *Add:*

Although an assisted person, if dissatisfied with any decision of a taxing officer in respect of an amount which he is entitled to recover or in respect of which he is liable under an order for costs made against him, may, through his solicitor apply for authority to carry in objections, there is no provision for the assisted person himself to make that application, nor, if the taxation relates only to the legal aid costs, is there any right to do so. In *B v. B (Taxation of Costs)* [1991], 1 F.L.R. 156Anthony Lincoln J., held that there was no provision under the then current Matrimonial Causes (Costs) Rules 1979 or the Legal Aid (General) Regulations 1980 for a legally aided litigant to be heard on or to take objections to the taxation of his own solicitor's bills. Legal aid taxation is inquisitorial rather than adversarial, it is for the taxing officer to investigate the bill of costs presented by the solicitor. The taxing officer might at a glance request to hear him at the taxation if he chose to do so in the public interest. The client would not have become a party to the taxation as between himself and the solicitor merely because the client had been heard. The position under the Matrimonial Causes (Costs) Rules 1988 and the Civil Legal Aid (General) Regulations 1989 was expressly left open.

16D–241 **Note**
[p.1424] *Add at end:*
*

The making of reg. 124 by the Lord Chancellor was authorised by the Legal Aid Act 1988, s.34(3) (*Microsoft Corporation v. Backslash Distribution Ltd, The Times,* March 15, 1999).

16D–244 **Determination of liability for costs**
[p.1425] *Add new note:*

16D–244/1 **Assisted person's liability for costs**

Section 17 of the Legal Aid Act 1988 makes no provision for the consideration of assets belonging to an assisted person's spouse. Therefore the value of any interest which the assisted person might have in his dwelling house was not to be aggregated with that of his spouse or any third party, *Waterford Wedgwood plc v. David Nagli Ltd (in liquidation), The Times,* January 4, 1999, Mr Charles Aldous, Q.C.

16D–246 **"Postpone"**
[p.1425] *Add:*

Where the Court of Appeal makes an order for costs not to be enforced without leave, on an appeal from the County Court, an application to enforce the order may be made to the County Court rather than the Court of Appeal: *Ager v. Ager* [1998] 1 All E.R. 703, CA.

Add reference for Ager v. Ager [1998] 1 W.L.R. 1074, CA.

16D–251 **"On any such application the order may be varied"**
[p.1426] *Add:*

Wraith v. Wraith is now reported at [1997], 1 W.L.R. 1540, CA.

F. LEGAL AID IN CIVIL PROCEEDINGS (REMUNERATION) REGULATIONS 1994

Interpretation

16F–2 [p.1445] *

Delete the definition of "C.C.R. Order 38" *and substitute:*

"CPR" means the Civil Procedure Rules 1998, and a reference to a rule or a Part, prefixed by "CPR", means the rule or (as the case may be) Part so numbered in the CPR;

Delete the definition of "RSC Order 62". *In regulation 2(2), delete* "RSC Order 62, CCR Order 38" *and substitute* "CPR Parts 43 to 48". *

Note

16F–2/1 [p.1445] *

Add at end:

Amended by The Legal Aid in Civil Proceedings (Remuneration) (Amendment) Regulations 1999.

Remuneration

16F–4 [p.1446] *

In regulation 4(1) delete "The amounts" *and substitute* "Subject to paragraphs (3A) to (3D), the amounts". *In regulation 4(1)(b), delete* "paragraph (2) of RSC Order 62, rule 17" *and substitute* "CPR rule 44.4(b)". *In regulation 4(1)(c), delete from* "paragraph 1(1)" *to* "whichever is applicable" *and substitute* "CPR rules 44.3 to 44.5". *In regulation 4(3), delete from* "RSC Order 62" *to* "applicable" *and substitute* "CPR Parts 43 to 48". *Also in regulation 4(3) delete* "The relevant authority" *and substitute* "Subject to paragraphs (3A) to (3D), the relevant authority". *After regulation 4(3) insert:*

(3A) Paragraphs (3B) to (3D) apply where proceedings are allocated to the fast track, and in those paragraphs "advocate's costs" means the costs of an advocate for preparing for the trial and, if the claim proceeds to trial, for appearing at the trial, and "fixed fast track trial costs" means the amount of fast track trial costs which could be awarded under CPR rule 46.2(1) in respect of a claim.

(3B) Where, but for this paragraph, the amount to be allowed in respect of advocate's costs would have exceeded the fixed fast track trial costs, the amount to be allowed in respect of advocate's costs shall be equal to the fixed fast track trial costs.

(3C) Where, but for this paragraph, the amount to be allowed in respect of the costs of a legal representative's attendance at the trial to assist the advocate would have exceeded the amount prescribed by CPR rule 46.3(2), the amount to be allowed in respect of those costs shall be equal to the amount prescribed by CPR rule 46.3(2).

(3D) Paragraphs (3B) and (3C) shall have effect regardless of the awards actually made by the court under CPR Part 46.

In regulation 4(4) delete "Part XII of the General Regulations, RSC Order 62 * and CCR Order 38" *and substitute* "Part XII of the General Regulations and CPR Parts 43 to 48".

16F–5 [p.1446] * **Note**

Add at end:

Amended by The Legal Aid in Civil Proceedings (Remuneration) (Amendment) Regulations 1999.

SECTION 17

MISCELLANEOUS PARTIES AND PROCEEDINGS

A. PROCEDURE

2. Recall of orders 17A–12 [p.1460] *

After first paragraph insert:

In principle, before an order recording his judgment is drawn up, a judge retains control of the case and may hear further argument on a point which he had decided; in so doing he may permit pleadings to be amended and admit further evidence (*Charlesworth v. Relay Road Ltd* [1999] 4 All E.R. 397, CA).

Tomlin order 17A–32 [p.1465]

Add:

As a notice of motion to enforce a Tomlin order, after the staying of an action on agreed terms scheduled to the order, did not constitute "proceedings", the court had no power, pursuant to s.35A of the Supreme Court Act 1981, as inserted by s.15 of the Administration of Justice Act 1982, to award interest in respect of the late payment of a sum owed under the terms of the order: *Darby v. Meehan and Another, The Times,* November 25, 1998.

B. PARTIES GENERALLY

Introductory note 17B–1 [p.1474]

Add new paragraphs at end:

In the following section, substitute all references to "plaintiff" with "claimant", "summons" with "application notice", and "on motion" with "by an interim remedy".

In accordance with the table below, in lieu of the RSC provision mentioned, refer to the relevant CPR provision or Practice Direction.

Paragraph number	RSC provision	CPR provision
17B–1	O.15, r.6(2)	r.19.1
17B–3	O.77, r.18(1)	r.50.1.10, R77.18(1)
17B–5	O.20, r.5(4)	r.19.3
17B–6	O.10, r.2	r.6.16
17B–9	O.15, r.11	r.50.1.2, R15.11
17B–13	O.15, r.4(2) O.81	r.18.2 r.50.1.10, R81
17B–15	O.5, r.6 O.12, r.1(2)	r.39.6 None
17B–16	O.23	r.50.1.10, R23.1

Paragraph number	RSC provision	CPR provision
17B–17	O.103	None
17B–42	O.80	Pt 21
17B–47	O.81	r.50.1.10, R81
17B–48	O.104	None
17B–49	O.80	Pt 21
17B–58	O.4, r.10	r.3.1
17B–60	O.15, r.14	r.50.1.10, R15.14
17B–62	O.15, r.12	r.50.1.10, R15.12
17B–65	O.15, r.14	r.50.1.10, R15.14
17B–66	O.75 O.15 O.81 O.15, r.6	PD 49F r.19, r.50.1.10, R15 r.50.1.10, R81 r.19.3
17B–66/5	O.75, r.17	PD 49F
17B–74	O.87 O.15, r.12	r.50.1.10, R87 r.50.1.10, R15.12
17B–76	O.32, r.9(1)	None
17B–77	O.17	r.50.1.10, R17
17B–80	O.104	None
17B–82	O.104	None
17B–83	O.6, r.2(1) O.10, r.4 O.15, r.10	None r.50.1.10, R10.4 Pt 19

17B–19 **Directors of companies**

[p.1478] *Add at end:*

CPR r.39.6 allows, with permission of the court, a company or other corporation to be represented by an authorised employee. It is anticipated that, at any rate in the High Court, such permission will be sparingly given. No party is obliged to conduct business as a corporate entity and the obligation in the overriding objective to allot a fair share of the court's resources will militate against allowing non-professional representation.

SECTION 18

MISCELLANEOUS MATTERS OF PRACTICE

B. CIRCUIT ARRANGEMENTS

Introduction **18B–1**
Add note: [p.1496]

Amendments to Circuit Arrangements **18B–1/1**

Amend postcode for Wales and Chester Circuit Administrator to read CF10 2HH. The new telephone number is 01222 415 505. The new fax number is 01222 415511. In third column, amend Group Manager's telephone number to read (029) 20 344 381/344 239.

Amend address of Exmouth and Truro Trial Centre to read:

5th Floor,
Northernhay House,
Northernhay Place,
Exeter, EX4 3TH
Tel: 01392 455900
Fax: 01392 455909

C. LIST OF DISTRICT REGISTRIES

Note **18C–2**
Add new paragraph at end: [p.1501] *

The Civil Courts Order 1983 has since been amended by the Civil Courts (Amendment No. 3) Order 1997 (S.I. 1997 No. 2310), the Civil Courts (Amendment No. 4) Order 1997 (S.I. 1997 No. 2762), the Civil Courts (Amendment) Order 1998 (S.I. 1998 No. 1880), the Civil Courts (Amendment) Order 1999 (S.I. 1999 No. 216), the Civil Courts (Amendment) (No. 2) Order 1999 (S.I. 1999 No. 1011), the Civil Courts (Amendment) (No. 3) Order 1999 (S.I. 1999 No. 3187). The Civil Courts (Amendment) (No. 2) Order 1999 removed all Admiralty jurisdiction from county courts after April 26, 1999; since then all Admiralty proceedings have been commenced in the High Court.

D. COUNTY COURT DIRECTORY

Amendments to Directory **18D–1**
Add note: [p.1502]

In text preceding table, delete "(Amendment No. 4) Order 1997 (S.I. 1997 No. 2762)" and substitute "(Amendment No. 2) Order 1998 (S.I. 1998 No. 2910)".

The telephone number for Melton Mowbray County Court has changed by adding "5" as a prefix. The new number is 01644–568336.

Scarborough County Court has moved. The new address is Pavilion House, Valley Bridge Road, Scarborough, YO11 2JS. The telephone, fax and DX numbers have not changed.

The telephone number for Croydon County Court has changed. The new number is 0181–410 4700.

The postcode at York County Court has changed. The new code is YO1 9WL.

The telephone number for Northampton County Court has changed. The new number is 01604–470400.

Holywell County Court has now closed. (Civil Courts (Amendment) Order 1998 (S.I. 1998 No. 1880)).

Rochdale County Court has now closed. (Civil Courts (Amendment) Order 1998 (S.I. 1998 No. 1880)).

West Bromwich County Court has now closed. (Civil Courts (Amendment) (No. 2) Order 1998 (S.I. 1998 No. 2910)).

Camborne and Redruth County Court has now closed. (Civil Courts (Amendment) (No. 2) Order 1998 (S.I. 1998 No. 2910)).

Hemel Hempstead County Court has now closed. (Civil Courts (Amendment) (No. 2) Order 1998 (S.I. 1998 No. 2910)).

Loughborough County Court has now closed. (Civil Courts (Amendment) (No. 2) Order 1998 (S.I. 1998 No. 2910)).

The contact numbers for Barnet County Court are now prefixed by (020) 8 rather than 0181.

The new contact numbers for Basingstoke County Court are: tel: 01256 318200 and fax: 01256 318225.

The new telephone number for Bow County Court is (020) 8536 5200.

The contact numbers for Brentford County Court are now prefixed by (020) 8 rather than 0181.

The contact numbers for Bromley County Court are now prefixed by the code (020) 8 rather than 0181.

The contact numbers for Cardiff County Court are now prefixed by (029) 20 rather than 01222.

The contact numbers for the Central London Patents County Court and Business List are now prefixed by (020) 7 rather than 0171.

The contact numbers for Clerkenwell County Court are now prefixed by (020) 7 rather than 0171.

Corby County Court has now closed.

The contact numbers for the Coventry County Court are now prefixed by (024) 76 rather than 01203.

The telephone number for Croydon County Court has changed to (020) 8410 4700. The fax numbers are now prefixed by (020) 8 rather than 0181.

The contact numbers for Edmonton County Court are now prefixed by (020) 8 rather than 0181. The DX number has changed to 136686 Edmonton-3.

The contact numbers for Ilford County Court are now prefixed by (020) 8 rather than 0181.

The contact numbers for Kingston-upon-Thames County Court are now prefixed by (020) 8 rather than 0181.

The contact numbers for Lambeth County Court are now prefixed by (020) 7 rather than 0171.

The address for the Mayor's and City of London County Court has changed to The Guildhall Building, Basinghall Street, London EC2V 5AR. The new telephone number is (020) 7796 5400. The new fax number is (020) 7796 5424. The new DX number is 97520 Moorgate-2.

The contact numbers for Portsmouth County Court are now prefixed by (023) 92 rather than 01705.

The Runcorn County Court address now reads Halton Lea rather than Shopping City.

The contact numbers for Shoreditch County Court are now prefixed by (020) 7 rather than 0171.

The contact numbers for Southampton County Court are now prefixed by (023) 80 rather than 01703.

The contact numbers for West London County Court are now prefixed by (020) 7 rather than 0171.

The contact numbers for Wandsworth, Willesden and Woolwich County Courts are now prefixed by (020) 8 rather than 0181.

SECTION 19

HOUSE OF LORDS APPEALS

A. CIVIL APPEALS

General introduction to the House of Lords

19A–1 [p.1523]

In fourth line of first paragraph, following "the Administration of Justice Act 1969", *delete* "and" *and insert comma. After* "the Judicature (Northern Ireland) Act 1978" *add* "and the Judicial Pensions and Retirement Act 1993".

Admissibility of Petitions

19A–7 [p.1524] *

Delete direction 1.6(b). Add new note:

Note

19A–7/1 *

Direction 1.6(b) was repealed by *Practice Direction (House of Lords: Civil Procedure Amendments)* [1999] 1 W.L.R. 1833, HL.

Form of petition

19A–14 [p.1526]

In 3.2 delete "Court" *and substitute* "Office".

Preliminary procedure

19A–21 [p.1528]

Delete final sentence of 4.5.

Add at end of 4.6:

In certain circumstances the Appeal Committee may decide that leave to appeal should be given without the need for further submissions or argument.

Respondents' objections

19A–22 [p.1528] *

At beginning of direction 4.7 insert the words "If the Appeal Committee is satisfied that leave to appeal should be given, the House may grant leave, with or without terms.". *Add new note:*

Note

19A–22/1 *

Amended by *Practice Direction (House of Lords: Civil Procedure Amendments)* [1999] 1 W.L.R. 1833, HL.

Statement of facts and issues

19A–43 [p.1533] *

Delete directions 12.1 and 12.2 and insert:

12.1 The appellants must prepare a statement of the facts and issues involved in the appeal. The appellants should draw up the statement and submit it to the respondents for discussion. The statement lodged must be a single document agreed between the parties. It should not contain material more appropriately included in a case. Should there be any disagreement, disputed material should be included in each party's case.

Note

19A–43/1 *

Add new note:

Amended by *Practice Direction (House of Lords: Civil Procedure Amendments)* [1999] 1 W.L.R. 1833, HL.

19A–53 **Petitions for extension of time**
[p.1535] *Delete direction 14.5 and insert:*
* **14.5** Up to three extensions of time will ordinarily be granted, provided that they do not prejudice the proper preparation for the hearing or its proposed date. Subsequent petitions may, at the direction of the Principal Clerk, be referred to an Appeal Committee.

19A–53/1 **Note**
* *Add new note:*
Amended by *Practice Direction (House of Lords: Civil Procedure Amendments)* [1999] 1 W.L.R. 1833, HL.

19A–57 **Appellants' and respondents' cases**
[p.1536] *Delete text of direction 16.1 and insert* "[Repealed]".
*

19A–57/1 **Note**
* *Add new note:*
Amended by *Practice Direction (House of Lords: Civil Procedure Amendments)* [1999] 1 W.L.R. 1833, HL.

19A–58 **Appellants' and respondents' cases**
[p.1536] *Delete direction 16.6 and insert:*
* **16.6** Transcripts of unreported judgments should only be cited when they contain an authoritative statement of a relevant principle law not to be found in a reported case or are necessary for the understanding of some other authority.

19A–58/1 **Note**
* *Add new note:*
Amended by *Practice Direction (House of Lords: Civil Procedure Amendments)* [1999] 1 W.L.R. 1833, HL.

19A–60 **Joint cases**
[p.1537] *Delete direction 16.12 and insert:*
* **16.12** As soon as the cases have been prepared, in any event no later than *three weeks* before the proposed date of the hearing, each party must lodge in the Judicial Office three copies of its case and all parties must exchange cases. The number of copies of cases exchanged should be sufficient to meet the requirements of counsel and agents but should not usually exceed eight. The respondents must also (where applicable) lodge a copy of their additional documents if supplementary to Part I of the appendix (15 copies if supplementary to any other part of the appendix). To enable the appellants to lodge the bound volumes, the respondents must provide them with 15 further copies of their case and, where applicable, with 15 further copies of their additional documents (if any).

19A–60/1 **Note**
* *Add new note:*
Amended by *Practice Direction (House of Lords: Civil Procedure Amendments)* [1999] 1 W.L.R. 1833, HL.

19A–61 **Lodgment of cases**
[p.1537] Delete *direction 16.13 and insert* "[Repealed]".

Note 19A–61/1 *

Add new note:

Amended by *Practice Direction (House of Lords: Civil Procedure Amendments)* [1999] 1 W.L.R. 1833, HL.

Bound volumes

19A–63 [p.1537] *

Delete direction 17.1 and insert:

17.1 No later than *two weeks* before the proposed date of hearing, the appellants must lodge (in, addition to the documents earlier lodged) 15 bound volumes. Each should contain: (a) the petition(s) of appeal; (b) the petition(s) of cross appeal (if any); (c) the statement of facts and issues; (d) the appellants' and respondents' cases, with cross-references to the appendices and authorities volumes; (e) Part I of the appendix; (f) respondents' additional documents (if any and if supplementary to Part I of the appendix); (g) the index to the authorities volumes.

Note 19A–63/1 *

Add new note:

Amended by *Practice Direction (House of Lords: Civil Procedure Amendments)* [1999] 1 W.L.R. 1833, HL.

Authorities

19A–65 to 19A–66 [p.1538] *

Delete direction 19 and insert:

19.1 Seven copies of all authorities which may be needed during the hearing must be lodged at the same time as the bound volume. The authorities volumes should be bound in green covers. They should be lodged in separate containers from the bound volumes. The binding and lodging of the volumes is the duty of the appellants. To enable the appellants to lodge the volumes, the respondents must provide them with seven copies of any authorities which they require but which the appellants do not, or arrange with the appellants for their photocopying. Respondents should arrange with the appellants for the binding of such volumes as the respondents' counsel and agents may require.

19.2 Small, flexible covers should be used in preference to heavy binders, and no volume should be more than one inch thick. The volumes should be numbered consecutively, with large Roman numerals on the spine and cover. The first volume(s) should contain citations from the C and L series of the Official Journal of the European Union; the Law Reports; the All England Law Reports; the Weekly Law Reports; Session Cases; the Scots Law Times; and the current edition of *Halsbury's Laws of England and Wales*. Subsequent volumes should contain all other material. The first volume must contain an index to the authorities volumes and a separate index to the first volume. Each subsequent volume must contain an index to that volume. The authorities themselves should be separated by numbered dividers.

19.3 Where a case is not reported in the Law Reports or Session Cases, references to other recognised reports should be given. In revenue appeals, Tax Cases may be cited but, wherever possible, references to the case in the Law Reports or Session Cases should also be given.

19.4 In emergencies (for the convenience of the House or Committee), the House of Lords Library can arrange for photocopies of certain authorities to be made available at the hearing. Parties must themselves provide seven copies of any other authority or of unreported cases. They must similarly provide copies of any authority of which adequate notice has not been given.

19.5 The cost of preparing the volumes is borne in the first instance by the appellants, though it will ultimately be subject to the decision of the House as to the costs of the appeal.

19A–66/1 **Note**

* *Add new note:*

Amended by *Practice Direction (House of Lords: Civil Procedure Amendments)* [1999] 1 W.L.R. 1833, HL.

19A–67 Submissions at the hearing

[p.1538] *Add at end:*

* Any such submission, whether heard or not, should also be made in writing no more than 14 days after the conclusion of the hearing.

19A–67/1 **Note**

* *Add new note:*

Amended by *Practice Direction (House of Lords: Civil Procedure Amendments)* [1999] 1 W.L.R. 1833, HL.

19A–76 Legal aid

[p.1541] *In direction 25.3, between the words* "writing" *and* "within", *insert the words* "of

* the date on which the application was made".

19A–76/1 **Note**

* *Add new note:*

Amended by *Practice Direction (House of Lords: Civil Procedure Amendments)* [1999] 1 W.L.R. 1833, HL.

19A–99 Dispute between parties disposed of

[p.1546] *Delete reference to Ainsbury v. Millington.*

*

19A–99/A **Note**

* *Add new note:*

Amended by *Practice Direction (House of Lords: Civil Procedure Amendments)* [1999] 1 W.L.R. 1833, HL.

19A–107 Security for costs

[p.1548] *In first line of Standing Order V, after* "that" *insert* "unless otherwise ordered by

* the House,".

19A–107/1 **Note**

* *Add new note:*

Amended by *Practice Direction (House of Lords: Civil Procedure Amendments)* [1999] 1 W.L.R. 1833, HL.

B. CRIMINAL APPEALS

19B–4 3. Time limits

[p.1562] *Add at end of second sentence in 3.1:*

* (the first of the fourteen days is the day on which the decision was made)

* *In direction 3.1, after* "that court", *insert the words* "beginning with the date of the decision and not the following day". *In direction 3.2, after* "court below", *insert the words* "beginning with the date on which the application is refused and not the following day".

19B–4/1 **Note**

* *Add new note:*

Amended by *Practice Direction (House of Lords: Civil Procedure Amendments)* [1999] 1 W.L.R. 1830, HL.

Respondents' objections **19B–16** [p.1564] *

Insert at the beginning of direction 5.5 the words "If the Appeal Committee is satisfied that leave to appeal should be given, the House may grant leave, with or without terms.".

Note **19B–16/1** *

Add new note:

Amended by *Practice Direction (House of Lords: Civil Procedure Amendments)* [1999] 1 W.L.R. 1830, HL.

6. Costs **19B–20** [p.1565] *

Add new note:

Note **19B–20/1** *

Practice Direction (Taxation Procedure Amendment) [1999] 1 W.L.R. 1860, HL has amended the Form of Bills of Costs Applicable to Judicial Taxations (1997) (see para. 6.6 of the practice direction above) by inserting in Part I a new direction 9(A) relating to criminal legal aid.

12. Statement of facts and issues **19B–31** [p.1567] *

Delete directions 12.1 and 12.2 and insert:

12.1 The appellants must prepare a statement of the facts and issues involved in the appeal. The appellants should draw up the statement and submit it to the respondents for discussion. The statement lodged must be a single document agreed between the parties. It should not contain material more appropriately included in a case. Should there by any disagreement, disputed material should be included in each party's case.

Note **19B–32/1** *

Add new note:

Amended by *Practice Direction (House of Lords: Criminal Procedure Amendments)* [1999] 1 W.L.R. 1830, HL.

15. Appellants' and respondents' cases **19B–39** [p.1568] *

Delete text of direction 15.1 and insert "[Repealed]".

15. Appellants' and respondents' cases **19B–40** [p.1569] *

Delete direction 15.7 and insert:

15.7 Transcripts of unreported judgments should only be cited when they contain an authoritative statement of a relevant principle of law not to be found in a reported case or are necessry for the understanding of some other authority.

Note **19B–40/1** *

Add new note:

Amended by *Practice Direction (House of Lords: Criminal Procedure Amendments)* [1999] 1 W.L.R. 1830, HL.

Lodgment of cases **19B–43** [p.1570] *

Delete direction 15.12 and insert:

15.12 As soon as the cases have been prepared, in any event no later than *three weeks* before the proposed date of the hearing, each party must lodge in the Judicial Office three copies of its case and all parties must exchange cases. The number of copies of cases exchanged should be sufficient to meet the requirements of counsel and agents but should not usually exceed eight. The respondents must also (where applicable) lodge a copy of their additional documents if supplementary to Part I of the appendix (15 copies if supplementary to any other part of the appendix). To enable the appellants to lodge the bound volumes, the respondents must provide them with 15 further copies of their case and, where applicable, with 15 further copies of their additional documents (if any).

19B–43/1 **Note**
*
Add new note:
Amended by *Practice Direction (House of Lords: Criminal Procedure Amendments)* [1999] 1 W.L.R. 1830, HL.

19B–44 **Exchange of cases**
[p.1570] *Delete direction 15.13 and insert* "[Repealed]".
*

19B–44/1 **Note**
*
Add new note:
Amended by *Practice Direction (House of Lords: Criminal Procedure Amendments)* [1999] 1 W.L.R. 1830, HL.

19B–45 **16. Bound Volumes**
[p.1570] *Delete direction 16.1 and insert:*
*
16.1 No later than *two weeks* before the proposed date of hearing, the appellants must lodge (in addition to the documents earlier lodged) 15 bound volumes. Each should contain: (a) the petition(s) of appeal; (b) the petition(s) of cross appeal (if any); (c) the statement of facts and issues; (d) the appellants' and respondents' cases, with cross-references to the appendices and authorities volumes; (e) Part I of the appendix; (f) respondents' additional documents (if any and if supplementary to Part I of the appendix); (g) the index to the authorities volumes.

19B–45/1 **Note**
*
Add new note:
Amended by *Practice Direction (House of Lords: Criminal Procedure Amendments)* [1999] 1 W.L.R. 1830, HL.

19B–49 and **19. Authorities**
19B–50 *Delete direction 19 and insert:*
[p.1571]
*
19.1 Seven copies of all authorities which may be needed during the hearing must be lodged at the same time as the bound volume. The authorities volumes should be bound in green covers. They should be lodged in separate containers from the bound volumes. The binding and lodging of the volumes is the duty of the appellants. To enable the appellants to lodge the volumes, the respondents must provide them with seven copies of any authorities which they require but which the appellants, do not, or arrange with the appellants for their photocopying. Respondents should arrange with the appellants for the binding of such volumes as the respondents' counsel and agents may require.

19.2 Small, flexible covers should be used in preference to heavy binders, and no volume should be more than one inch thick. The volumes should be numbered consecutively, with large Roman numerals on the spine and cover. The first volume(s) should contain; citations from the C and L series of the Official Journal of the E.U.; the Law Reports; the All England Law Reports; the Weekly Law Reports; the Scots Law Times; and the current edition of *Halsbury's Laws of England and Wales.* Subsequent volumes should contain all other material. The first volume must contain an index to the authorities volumes and a separate index to the first volume. Each subsequent volume must contain an index to that volume. The authorities themselves should be separated by numbered dividers.

19.3 Where a case is not reported in the Law Reports or Session Cases, references to other recognised reports should be given.

19.4 In emergencies (for the convenience of the House or Committee), the House of Lords Library can arrange for photocopies of certain authorities to be made available at the hearing. Parties must themselves provide seven copies of any other authority or of unreported cases. They must similarly provide copies of any authority of which adequate notice has not been given.

19.5 The cost of preparing the volumes is borne in the first instances by the appellants, though it will ultimately be subject to the decision of the House as to the costs of the appeal.

Note **19B–50/1** *

Add new note:

Amended by *Practice Direction (House of Lords: Criminal Procedure Amendments)* [1999] 1 W.L.R. 1830, HL.

Submissions at the hearing **19B–51**

Add at end the words "Any such submission, whether heard or not, should also be made in writing no more than 14 days after the conclusion of the hearing.". [p.1571] *

Note **19B–51/1** *

Add new note:

Amended by *Practice Direction (House of Lords: Criminal Procedure Amendments)* [1999] 1 W.L.R. 1830, HL.

Insert new note: **19B–56**

23.3 Where a party has been granted criminal legal aid, attention is drawn to the report of the Appeal Committee of October 14, 1998.[1] The guidelines and criteria there set out will be followed in all subsequent taxations in the House of Lords. [p.1572]

[1] HL 145.

SECTION 20

JURISDICTIONAL STATUTES AND REGULATIONS

A. MAIN STATUTES

CIVIL PROCEDURE ACT 1997

20A–2 [p.1585] * **Introductory note**

At end of second paragraph add:

The Civil Procedure Act 1997 (Commencement No. 2) Order 1999 (S.I. 1999 No. 1009) brought into force on April 26, 1999, those provisions of the Act which were not already in force.

20A–8/2 [p.1592] * **Effect of section**

After second sentence of this note insert:

Amendments to s.33(2) and s.52(2), sufficient to carry into effect the first (but not the second) of these recommendations, were made by the Civil Procedure (Modification of Enactments) Order 1998 (S.I. 1998 No. 2940), paras 5(a) and 6(b). (It may be noted that this Order was made not under s.8, but under s.4(2) of this Act.)

At end of this note add:

As explained above, once proceedings are commenced, the court has power under s.34 of the 1981 Act and s.53 of the 1984 Act, in accordance with rules of court, to make an order requiring a person who is not a party to the proceedings to give disclosure of documents (and to permit inspection of property and the taking of samples). It is convenient to note here that, as a result of amendments to these sections made by the Civil Procedure (Modification of Enactments) Order 1998 (S.I. 1998 No. 2940), paras 5(b) and 6(c), that power is not restricted to proceedings in respect of personal injuries or wrongful death.

SUPREME COURT ACT 1981

20A–139 [p.1601] * **The High Court**

In subs. (1) add "(ddd) the vice-president of the Queen's Bench Division;". *At end of subs. (6) add* "and whether or not an appointment has been made to the office of vice-president of the Queen's Bench Division.

20A–140 [p.1601] * **Note**

Replace after "s.72;" with the following:

and Access to Justice Act 1999, s.69(2); note also Maximum Number of Judges Order 1999 (S.I. 1999 No. 3138), Art. 2.

20A–142 [p.1602] * **Divisions of High Court**

In subs. (1)(b), after "thereof" insert "the vice-president of the Queen's Bench Division".

20A–143 [p.1602] * **Note**

Add at end:

Further amended by the Access to Justice Act 1999, s.69(3).

20A–169 [p.1609] * *Add new note:*

"incapable of acting"

20A–169/1 [p.1609] * As to circumstances in which a judge should disqualify himself on grounds of partiality or prejudice, see *Locabail (U.K.) Ltd v. Bayfield Properties Ltd, The Times*, November 19, 1999, CA.

Add new note: *

Application of High Court enforcement provisions to Court of Appeal judgments **20A–172** [p.1609] *

The purpose of the declaration in s.15(4) to the effect that provisions for the enforcement of High Court judgment or orders (which are legion) apply to the enforcement by the High Court of judgments and orders of the Court of Appeal (Civil Division) is obvious. The County Courts Act 1984 contains no similar provision. However, in *Ager v. Ager* (1998) *The Times*, January 6, CA, it was held that the jurisdiction conferred on the High Court by s.15(4) constituted a "general principal of practice" within the meaning of s.76 of the 1984 Act which could be adopted and applied in proceedings in a county court. **20A–172/1** [p.1610] *

Restrictions on appeals to Court of Appeal **20A–177** [p.1611] *

In s.18(1)(d) omit "divorce or". *In s.18(1)(g) substitute* "Part" *for* "part". *Delete subss.(1A) and (1B).*

Note **20A–178** [p.1611] *

Add at end:

Amended also by the Family Law Act 1996 and the Access to Justice Act 1999, c.22, s.106 and Sched. 15, Pt III.

Ouster of jurisdiction **20A–185** [p.1613] *

Add at end:

As to effect on court's jurisdiction of mediation clause in contract, see *Halifax Financial Services Ltd v. Intuitive Systems Ltd*, December 21, 1998, unrep. (McKinnon J.).

Hypothetical case **20A–191/1** [p.1614] *

Add at end:

However, in modern times, the appellate courts have indicated a greater willingness to entertain proceedings which raise points of law which, although "academic" or "hypothetical", are points of general public interest (see cases cited arguendo in *R. v. Canons Park Mental Health Tribunal, ex p. A* [1995] Q.B. 60, CA, at 63) but no general principle to this effect has emerged. The law is not settled. Note also *R. v. Inland Revenue Commissioners, ex parte Bishopp, The Times*, May 18, 1999 (court should not answer abstract tax question). In *R. v. Secretary of State for the Home Department, ex p. Salem* [1999] 2 W.L.R. 483, HL, it was held that the House of Lords has a discretion, to be exercised sparingly, to hear an appeal on an "academic" issue of public law involving a public authority where there was good reason in the public interest for doing so (see further Practice Directions and Standing Orders Applicable to Civil Appeals No. 42, as amended (para. 19A–99 above)).

Appeals from Crown Court and inferior courts **20A–198** [p.1615] *

After subs. (3) add:

(4) In subsection (2)(a) the reference to a decision of the Crown Court relating to trial on indictment does not include a decision relating to an order under section 17 of the Access to Justice Act 1999.

Note **20A–199** [p.1615] *

Add at end:

Further amended by the Access to Justice Act 1999, s.24 and Sched. 4, para. 22.

Proceedings on case stated by magistrates' court **20A–201** [p.1615] *

For subs. (1) of s.28A substitute the following:

(1) This section applies where a case is stated for the opinion of the High Court—

(a) by a magistrates' court under section 111 of the Magistrates' Courts Act 1980; or

(b) by the Crown Court under section 28(1) of this Act.

In subs. (2) for "amendment, whereupon it" *substitute* "amendment and, where it does so, the case". *For para. (b) of subs. (3) substitute:*

(b) remit the matter to the magistrates' court, or the Crown court, with the opinion of the High Court,"

In subs. (4) delete "and conclusive on all parties".

20A–202 **Note**
[p.1616] *Add at end:*
* Substituted by the Access to Justice Act 1999, s.61.

20A–203 **Orders of mandamus, prohibition and certiorari**
[p.1616] *After subs. (5) add:*
* (6) In subsection (3) the reference to the Crown Court jurisdiction relating to trial on indictment does not include a decision relating to an order under section 17 of the Access to Justice Act 1999.

20A–204 **Note**
[p.1616] *Add at end:*
* Amended by the Access to Justice Act 1999, s.24 and Sched. 4, para. 32.

20A–215 **Powers of High Court before commencement of action**
[p.1619] *In s.33(2), delete* "in which a claim in respect of personal injuries to a person, or in respect of a person's death, is likely to be made,".

20A–216 **Note**
[p.1619] *Add at end:*
Subs. (2) amended by The Civil Procedure (Modification of Enactments) Order 1998 (S.I. 1998 No. 2940), art. 5.

20A–219 **Power of High Court to order disclosure of documents, etc.**
[p.1619] *Delete subs. (1); and in each of subss. (2) and (3), delete* "to which this subsection applies".

20A–220 **Note**
[p.1620] *Add at end:*
Subss. (1), (2) and (3) amended by The Civil Procedure (Modification of Enactments) Order 1998 (S.I. 1998 No. 2940), art. 5.

20A–255 **Applications for order**
[p.1629] *After reference to Re Hutchinson add:*
* Where, by a High Court order, a person who is subject to a civil proceedings order is given leave to institute proceedings, such order does not give him leave to appeal to the Court of Appeal from the judgment resulting from those proceedings (*Johnson v. Valks, The Times*, November 23, 1999, CA).

At end add:
The inherent jurisdiction of the court to prevent its procedures being abused is extensive and includes the power to restrain not only the continuation of, but also the initiation of, proceedings which are likely to constitute such abuse (*Ebert v. Venvil* [1999] 3 W.L.R. 670, CA, *sub. nom. Ebert v. Birch* 149 New L.J. 608 (1999), CA).

20A–259 **Effect of this section**
[p.1630] *Add new rule:*
*

20A–259/1 **Power of High Court to vary committal in default**

* **43ZA.**—(1) Where the High Court quashes the committal of a person to prison or detention by a magistrates' court or the Crown Court for—

(a) a default in paying a sum adjudged to be paid by a conviction, or

(b) want of sufficient distress to satisfy such a sum,

the High Court may deal with the person for the default or want of sufficient distress in any way in which the magistrates' court or Crown Court would have power to deal with him if it were dealing with him at the time when the committal is quashed.

(2) If the High Court commits him to prison or detention, the period of imprisonment or detention shall, unless the High Court otherwise directs, be treated as having begun when the person was committed by the magistrates' court or the Crown Court (except that any time during which he was released on bail shall not be counted as part of the period)."

Note **20A–259/2** *

Add new note:

This section was inserted after s.43 by the Access to Justice Act 1999, s.62. The section extends the powers of the High Court in the circumstances referred to in the section in a manner which avoids the necessity of proceedings being remitted to the Crown Court or a magistrates' court.

Sentences and other orders of Crown Court when dealing with offenders **20A–263/5**

After subs. (1), insert the following subsection: [p.1631]

(1A) The power to give a direction under subsection (1) above has effect subject to section 102 of the Crime and Disorder Act 1998.

In subs. (7) for "a contribution order made under section 23 of the Legal Aid Act 1988" *substitute* "an order under section 17(2) of the Access to Justice Act 1999". *

Note **20A–263/6** [p.1632] *

At end add:

Further amended by the Access to Justice Act 1999, s.24 and Sched. 4, para. 24.

Note **20A–402** *

Add at end:

Order 51 has been amended by Access to Justice Act 1999.

Effect of this section **20A–403** [p.1649] *

Add at end:

The jurisdiction to make an order for costs against a non-party in favour of a party is not dependent on that party first obtaining an order for costs against his opponent in the proceedings (*Nordstern Allgemeine Versicherungs A.G. v. Internav Ltd* [1999] 2 Lloyd's Rep. 139, CA). It is not a pre-condition for the exercise of the power that the circumstances should be exceptional (*Globe Equities Ltd v. Globe Legal Services Ltd, The Times,* April 14, 1999, CA).

For jurisdiction of court where non-party domiciled outside the jurisdiction in a Convention State and observations on appropriate procedure under Civil Procedure Rules for joinder of non-party for purposes of costs, see *National Justice Compania Naviera S.A. v. Prudential Assurance Co. Ltd (No. 2), The Times,* October 15, 1999, CA, *sub. nom. Comninos v. Prudential Assurance Co. Ltd,* 149 New L.J. 1561 (1999), CA.

Court of civil division **20A–406**

For s.54 substitute: [p.1651]

(1) This section relates to the civil division of the Court of Appeal; and in this section "court", except where the context otherwise requires, means a court of that division. *

(2) Subject as follows, a court shall be duly constituted for the purpose of exercising any of its jurisdiction if it consists of one or more judges.

(3) The Master of the Rolls may, with the concurrence of the Lord Chancellor, give (or vary or revoke) directions about the minimum number of judges of which a court must consist if it is to be duly constituted for the purpose of any description of proceedings.

(4) The Master of the Rolls, or any Lord Justice designated by him, may (subject to any directions under subsection (3)) determine the number of judges of which a court is to consist for the purpose of any particular proceedings.

(4A) The Master of the Rolls may give directions as to what is to happen in any particular case where one or more members of a court which has partly heard proceedings are unable to continue.

(5) Where—

(a) an appeal has been heard by a court consisting of an even number of judges; and

(b) the members of the court are equally divided,

the case shall, on the application of any party to the appeal, be re-argued before and determined by an uneven number of judges not less than three, before any appeal to the House of Lords.

(6) [Repealed]

(7) [Repealed]

(8) Subsections (1) and (2) of section 70 (assessors in the High Court) shall apply in relation to causes and matters before the civil division of the Court of Appeal as they apply in relation to causes and matters before the High Court.

(9) Subsections (3) and (4) of section 60 (scientific advisers to assist the Patents Court in proceedings under the Patents Act 1949 and the Patents Act 1977) shall apply in relation to the civil division of the Court of Appeal and proceedings on appeal from any decision of the Patents Court in proceedings under those Acts as they apply in relation to the Patents Court and proceedings under those Acts.

(10) [Repealed]

20A–407 **Note**

[p.1652] *Add at end:*

* Further amended by the Access to Justice Act 1999, c.22, s.59 and s.106, Sched. 15, Pt III.

20A–422 **Exercise of incidental jurisdiction in civil division**

[p.1655] *Delete s.58 and substitute:*

*

20A–422 **Calling into question of incidental decisions in civil division**

* (1) Rules of court may provide that decisions of the Court of Appeal which—

(a) are taken by a single judge or any officer or member of staff of that court in proceedings incidental to any cause or matter pending before the civil division of that court; and

(b) do not involve the determination of an appeal or of an application for permission to appeal,

may be called into question in such manner as may be prescribed.

(2) No appeal shall lie to the House of Lords from a decision which may be called into question pursuant to rules under subsection (1).

20A–422/1 **Note**

* *Add new notes:*

Substituted by the Access to Justice Act 1999, s.60.

20A–422/2 **Jurisdiction of a single judge or any officer or member of court staff to hear incidental applications**

* Subsection (1) makes provision for any application incidental to any cause or matter pending before the Civil Division of the Court of Appeal to be heard by a single judge, or any officer or member of court staff, so far as provided in rules of court. (The office of Registrar of Civil Appeals, formerly referred to in s.58, was abolished by the Access to Justice Act 1999, s.70.)

20A–263/6 **Note**

[p.1633] *Add at end:*

* ; and the Crime and Disorder Act 1998 (c.37), s.119, Sched. 8, paras 47 and 48. Further amended by the Access to Justice Act 1999, s.24 and Sched. 4, para. 24.

20A–465/11 **Bail**

[p.1669] *In subs. (1)(a), after the words* "Criminal Justice Act 1987" *insert the words* "or who has been sent in custody to the Crown Court for trial under section 51 of the Crime and Disorder Act 1998".

Note 20A–465/12
Add at end: [p.1671]
; and the Crime and Disorder Act 1998 (c.37), s.119, Sched. 8, paras 47 and 48.

Right of audience for solicitors in certain Crown Court centres 20A–465/14

Delete the whole of s.83. [p.1671]
*

Note 20A–465/15
Add at end: [p.1671]
Repealed by the Access to Justice Act 1999, s.106 and Sched. 15, Pt II. *

Schedule 2 20A–572/1
Delete item no. 10. Add new note: *

Note 20A–572/2
Amended by the Access to Justice Act 1999, Sched. 15, Pt III. *

COUNTY COURTS ACT 1984

County courts to be held for districts 20A–650

In subs. (1) for "throughout the whole of each district the court so held for the district" *substitute* "each court". [p.1703]
*

Note 20A–650/1
Add new note: *
Amended by the Civil Procedure Act 1997, Sched. 2, para. 2(4).

Places and times of sittings 20A–652

Delete subs. (3). [p.1704]
*

Note 20A–652/1
Add new note: *
Amended by the Civil Procedure Act 1997, Sched. 2, para. 2(5).

Note 20A–655/1
Add new note: [p.1705]
*

Office of district judge and deputy district judge 20A–655/2
By the Courts and Legal Services Act 1990, s.74(1), the offices of registrar, assistant registrar and deputy registrar became the offices of district judge. Section 74(2) of the Act states that any reference in any enactment to the offices of registrar, etc., shall be construed as a reference to that office by its new name. *

"any order which could be made by the High Court" 20A–700
Add at end: [p.1717]
For powers of county court to make order under Mental Health Act 1983, see *R. v. Central London County Court, ex p. London* [1999] 3 W.L.R. 1; [1999] 3 All E.R. 991, CA. For powers of county court to grant interlocutory injunctions, see generally *Ali v. Westminster City Council* [1999] 1 W.L.R. 384, CA. *

Minors 20A–720

Delete s.47. [p.1721]

Minors 20A–720/1
Add new note: [p.1721]

Note 20A–720/2
Section 47 is deleted by The Civil Procedure (Modification of Enactments) Order 1998 (S.I. 1998 No. 2940), art. 6.

20A–725 Powers of court exercisable before commencement of action

[p.1724] *In s.52(2), delete* "in which a claim in respect of personal injuries to a person, or in respect of a person's death, is likely to be made,".

20A–725/1 Note

[p.1724] *Add at end:*

Subs. (2) is amended by The Civil Procedure (Modification of Enactments) Order 1998 (S.I. 1998 No. 2940), art. 6.

20A–726 Power of court to order disclosure of documents, etc.

[p.1724] *Delete subs. (1) and in each of subss. (2) and (3), delete* "to which this section applies".

20A–726/1 Note

[p.1725] *Add at end:*

Subss. (1), (2) and (3) are amended by The Civil Procedure (Modification of Enactments) Order 1998 (S.I. 1998 No. 2940), art. 6.

20A–735/1 General power of judge to determine questions of law and fact

[p.1729] *Substitute last two sentences with the following:*

* Where the rules found in the Civil Procedure Rules provide for a county court to "perform any act", that act may be performed, not only by any judge, but also by any district judge. In terms, CPR r.3.4 is subject to any enactment, rule or practice direction that provides otherwise. What is meant in this context by "perform any act" provided for by the CPR is not free from doubt. Practice Direction (Allocation of Cases to Levels of Judiciary) sets out the matters over which district judges do not have jurisdiction or which they may deal with only on certain conditions (see *Civil Procedure* (2nd ed.), para. 2BPD–001). Circuit judges and district judges have concurrent jurisdiction to hear trials of cases allocated to the fast track. For the jurisdiction of district judges to deal with trials and assessments of damages in multi-track cases, see Practice Direction (Allocation of Cases to Levels of Judiciary) *op. cit.*, para. 4.1.

20A–736 Assessors

[p.1730] *In s.63(1), delete* "on the application of any party". *Delete subs. (2). In subs. (3), for* "at such rate as may be prescribed" *substitute* "determined by the judge". *In subs. (4), for* "subsection (2) (otherwise than on the application of a party to the proceedings)" *substitute* "assisting the judge in reviewing the taxation by the district judge of the costs of any proceedings".

20A–736/1 Assessors

[p.1730] *Add new note:*

20A–736/2 Note

Subss. (1), (2), (3) and (4) are amended by The Civil Procedure (Modification of Enactments) Order 1998 (S.I. 1998 No. 2940), art. 6.

20A–737/2 Reference to arbitration

[p.1731] *Replace this note with the following:*

* Before the Civil Procedure Rules came into force, rules of court found in CCR, O.19, Pt I and made under s.64 provided for two forms of reference to arbitration by the court. They were (1) reference on application by a party to proceedings, and (2) automatic reference by rule of proceedings falling within the "small claims" jurisdiction of the court. Under the CPR, the second form of reference has been replaced by the procedure for the allocation to the small claims track of minor claims. The relevant rules of court are found in CPR Pts 26 and 27. In these provisions, no use is made of the words "arbitration" for the purpose of describing the summary procedures used by the court for the handling and trial of small claims. It would seem that it would be appropriate to describe the allocation of a claim to the small claims track as a reference to a form of statutory arbitration. Consequently, the significance of the Arbitration Act 1996, s.92, which states that nothing in Pt I of that Act applies to arbitrations under s.64 is diminished.

There are no express provisions in the CPR comparable to those formerly found in CPR, O.19, Pt I for the first form of reference of county court proceedings to arbitration mentioned above, that is to say, a reference on the application of a party. However, r.1.4(2) (e) states that the court's duty to manage cases includes encouraging the parties "to use an alternative dispute resolution procedure if the court considers that appropriate and facilitating the use of such procedure". (In the Glossary attached to the CPR, "alternative dispute resolution" is described in terms sufficiently wide to include arbitration.) Further, r.26.4 states that, in certain circumstances, the court may stay proceedings whilst parties try to settle the case "by alternative dispute resolution or other means". It would seem, therefore, that the court has power under the CPR to refer proceedings to arbitration on the application of a party. However, it is doubtful whether the rules from which such power may be derived are rules of court of the express type envisaged by s.64. Further, it is doubtful whether a reference to arbitration on the application of a party (if it is permissible) could be described as a reference under s.64 (see above observations on the Arbitration Act 1996, s.92).

Note **20A–738/1** [p.1731] *

Add new paragraph:

Amended by Civil Procedure Act 1997, Sched. 2, para. 2(2). The Courts and Legal Services Act 1999, s.74 states that any reference in any enactment to the offices of registrar, etc., shall be construed as a reference to the office of district judge.

Add new note:

Reference for inquiry and report **20A–738/2** [p.1731] *

This section is comparable to the Supreme Court Act 1981, s.68, the provision upon which what was once called "official referees' business" was based. Before the Civil Procedure Rules came into force, rules of court made in pursuance of s.65 were found in CCR, O.19, Pt II (reference for inquiry and report). No comparable rules are found under the CPR. However, under the CPR, official referees' business, which is now described as "Technology and Construction Court Business" is treated as a form of "specialist proceedings" under CPR Pt 49. The provisions of the CPR apply to such business subject to the provisions of the relevant practice direction.

Trial by jury **20A–739/2** [p.1732] *

Add new note:

Application made in such manner and within such time "as may be prescribed" **20A–739/3** *

Section 66(2) states that the trial of certain proceedings shall be without jury and that in all other proceedings trial should be without a jury unless the court otherwise orders "on an application made in that behalf by any party to the proceedings in such manner and within such time before the trial *as may be prescribed*", which means, as prescribed by rules of court (see County Court Act 1984, s.147(1)) (see also Supreme Court Act 1981, s.69(2)). Before the Civil Procedure Rules came into force "as may be prescribed" means as prescribed by CCR, O.13, r.10 (see also former RSC, O.33, rr.4 and 5). Rule 10 stated that application should be made "on notice stating the grounds of the application" and that notice had to be given not less than 10 days before the return day and where notice was given later, or where for that or any other reason the application could not be heard in time for a jury to be summoned, the court could postpone the trial so as to allow time for a jury to be summoned. This rule is not replicated in the CPR. In *Oliver v. Calderdale Metropolitan Borough Council, The Times,* July 7, 1999, CA, a case decided under the old rules, it was held that an application for jury trial should be made at the earliest pre-trial directions hearing and that an application made wholly out of time could be rejected on the ground that it was unreasonable.

Set-off in cases of cross judgments in county courts and High Court **20A–745/2** [p.1736] *

Substitute entire note with the following:

The section states that where, in High Court proceedings or in county court proceedings, X has obtained judgment against Y for (say) £10,000, and Y has obtained judgment against X in other proceedings, either in the same or a different county court or in the High Court, for (say) £5,000, Y may apply for leave to set off his judgment against P's.

It may be noted that the section further states that Y may make such application "to the court or any of the said courts" and should do so "in accordance with rules of court".

Where the several judgments have been obtained in a county court (or several county courts), CPR, Sched. 2, CCR, O.22, r.11 applies and Y should make his application to a county court in accordance with the provisions of that rule. Where the several judgments have been obtained in the High Court it would seem that application should be made to the High Court, but no rules of court expressly dedicated to such applications are contained in the CPR.

Where X has obtained judgment against Y for (say) £10,000 in county court proceedings, and Y has obtained judgment against X in High Court proceedings for (say) £5,000, and Y wishes to apply for permission to set off his High Court judgment against Y's county court judgment, the provisions of CPR, Sched. 2, CCR, O.22, r.11 do not apply. Before the Civil Procedure Rules came into force, such applications were made to the High Court and fell within the procedure stipulated by RSC, O.107, r.4. Rule 4 was not replicated in the CPR; consequently, the appropriate procedure is now a matter for doubt.

Where an order is made by the High Court giving permission to set off sums payable under several judgments and orders obtained respectively in the High Court and a county court, the court officer of the county court shall, on receipt of a copy of the order, proceed in accordance with r.11(7) (see CPR, Sched. 1, CCR, O.22, r.11(8)).

A party is not entitled as of right to set off one judgment against another. The relevant considerations need not be explained here. However, it should be noted that s.72(2) states that, where an application for permission to set off one judgment against another is made to a county court, the county court should approach the matter in accordance with the practice for the time being in force in the High Court as to the circumstances in which set off should be allowed and, in particular, in accordance with the practice relating to solicitors' liens for costs (s.72(2)) (see para. 20A–464).

20A–748 County court rules

[p.1738] *Omit s.75:*

*

20A–748/1 Note

[p.1740] *Add at end:*

* Omitted by the Civil Procedure Act 1997, Sched. 2, para. 2(6).

20A–749/1 Application of practice of High Court

[p.1740] *Substitute entire note with the following:*

* This section says that the general principles of High Court practice may be adopted and applied to proceedings in a county court where there is, as it were, a "gap" in county court practice and procedure because the matter is "not expressly provided for by or in pursuance of this Act", that is to say, provided for by sections in the Act or in delegated legislation made under the Act, including, principally, rules of court. Before the Civil Procedure Rules came into force, the CCR were made under s.75 of the Act (now omitted) and the rules found therein were significantly different in many respects to those found in the RSC and, generally, much simpler. In these circumstances, s.76 was occasionally brought into play to deal with "gaps" apparent in the CCR (see cases referred to in *SCP 1999*, Vol. 2, para. 20A–749/1). The CPR govern county court and High Court proceedings and, in the main, the procedures for both levels of court are the same. Nevertheless, some differences do remain and this leaves open the possibility that "gaps" in county court practice will continue to emerge and that s.76 may still have a role to play (*e.g. Ager v. Ager* (1998) *The Times*, January 6, CA, where it was held that the jurisdiction conferred on the High Court by the Supreme Court Act 1981, s.15(4) could be conferred on county courts by operation of s.76). However, it should be noted that, as explained above, the section takes effect where a particular matter of practice or procedure is "not expressly provided for by or in pursuance of this Act" and that would not include a matter not expressly provided for by the CPR, because the CPR are not made "in pursuance of this Act". If this analysis is correct, the meaning of s.76 becomes obscure.

20A–808 Proof of service of summonses, etc.

[p.1763] *In s.133(1), delete* "under the hand of that officer".

20A–808/1 Proof of service of summonses, etc.

[p.1764] *Add new note:*

20A–808/2 Note

Subs. (1) is amended by The Civil Procedure (Modification of Enactments) Order 1998 (S.I. 1998 No. 2940), art. 6.

20A–809 Summonses and other process to be under seal

[p.1764] *Delete s.134. Add new note:*

20A–809/1 Note

Section 134 is deleted by The Civil Procedure (Modification of Enactments) Order 1998 (S.I. 1998 No. 2940), art. 6.

20A–814/4 Relief from forfeiture where re-entry without action (subss. (2) & (3))

[p.1769] *Add at end:*

* See also *Croydon (Unique) Ltd v. Wright* [1999] 4 All E.R. 257, CA (whether person having the benefit of a charge had "an interest under a lease derived from the lessee's interests therein" within s.138(9C) and was thus entitled to apply for relief from forfeiture in possession proceedings).

20A–823 Interpretation

[p.1771] *Delete definition of* "county court rules".

*

Note 20A–823/1 [p.1772] *

Add at end of first paragraph:

Further amended by the Civil Procedure Act 1997, Sched. 2, para. 2(9).

B. OTHER STATUTES AND REGULATIONS

Introductory note 20B–240 [p.1852] *

At end of first paragraph add:

This Order was amended by the High Court and County Courts Jurisdiction (Amendment) Order 1999 (S.I. 1999 No. 1014) with effect from April 26, 1999. The 1999 Order provides, amongst other things, that for the word "plaintiff", wherever it appears in the 1991 Order, there should be substituted the word "claimant".

Allocation—Commencement of proceedings 20B–247 [p.1853] *

In art. 4, after "articles", *insert* "4A,". *After art. 4, insert the following new rule:*

4A. Except for proceedings to which article 5 applies, a claim for money in which county courts have jurisdiction may only be commenced in the High Court if the financial value of the claim is more than £15,000.

The following amendments should be made to art. 5. For paragraph (1), substitute:

(1) Proceedings which include a claim for damages in respect of personal injuries may only be commenced in the High Court if the financial value of the claim is £50,000 or more.

After paragraph (2), insert:

(3) This article does not apply to proceedings which include a claim for damages in respect of an alleged breach of duty of care committed in the course of the provision of clinical or medical services (including dental or nursing services).

Allocation—trial 20B–249 [p.1854] *

Article 7 is omitted as comparable provisions are now made in the Civil Procedure Rules.

Enforcement 20B–252 [p.1855] *

In sub-para. (1)(b), for "£1,000", *substitute* "£600".

Definition of value of action 20B–261 [p.1856] *

For art. 9 substitute:

Financial value of claim

9. For the purposes of Articles 4A, and 5, the financial value of the claim shall be calculated in accordance with rule 16.3(6) of the Civil Procedure Rules 1998.

Omit art. 10.

Savings 20B–265 [p.1857] *

Omit art. 12(b).

SECTION 21

MISCELLANEOUS STATUTES

A. ARBITRATION ACT 1950

21A–8 [p.1865] **Illegal agreement**

Add:

In *O'Callaghan v. Coral Racing Ltd, The Times,* November 26, 1998, the Court of Appeal held that a clause in a gaming agreement under which disagreements could be referred to the editor of *The Sporting Life* was part and parcel of a void agreement and could not survive independently. The Court further held that the clause was not an arbitration clause since the hall-mark of arbitration was a procedure to determine the legal rights and obligations of the parties which was enforceable in law, such hall-mark being absent.

21A–41 [p.1869] **Taking a step in the section**

In title, alter "section" *to* "action".

In the last paragraph delete reference to Northern Regional Health Authority v. Derek Crouch Construction Co. Ltd.

21A–85 [p.1877] **Injunction restraining arbitration**

In fourth paragraph delete reference to Northern Regional Health Authority v. Derek Crouch Construction Co. Ltd.

21A–206 [p.1896] **"May remit the matters referred"**

Add:

It is the duty of an arbitrator to take steps to ensure that, so far as is reasonably possible before making his award, each of the parties knew the case which had been put against them: *Mirpuri v. Jass* (1998) 56 Con. L.R. 31.

* *Add new paragraph:*

A final costs award made by an arbitrator as a result of a simple mathematical error neither accidental nor admitted either by the arbitrator or the party benefiting from the error comes within the jurisdiction of the court to remit to arbitrators conferred by s.22 (*Danae Air Transport S.A. v. Air Canada* [1999] 2 Lloyd's Rep. 547, CA, allowing appeal from [1999] 1 Lloyd's Rep. 105).

* *Add at end:*

Where an award is remitted the remission is parasitic to the granting of leave to appeal against the original award and exactly the same policy considerations apply to the need to process the remission timeously as apply to the need to process an appeal timeously (*Huyton S.A. v. Jakil S.P.A.* [1999] 2 Lloyd's Rep. 83, CA). The arbitrator only has power on the remission to reconsider the matter or matters mentioned in the court's directions pursuant to s.22(1) (*ibid.*).

21A–248 [p.1903] * **"By leave of the Court or a Judge"**

Delete at end of second paragraph "(1998) *The Times,* March 4" *and substitute* "*Soleimany v. Soleimany* [1999] Q.B. 785; [1998] 3 W.L.R. 811; [1999] 3 All E.R. 847, CA".

Add at end of second paragraph:

See too *Westacre Investments Inc. v. Jugoimport—SPDR Holding Co. Ltd* [1999] 3 W.L.R. 811; [1999] 3 All E.R. 864; [1999] 2 Lloyd's Rep. 64, CA, pet. dis. [1999] 1 W.L.R. 1999, HL under para. 21B–23 of this Supplement in which some *obiter dicta* in *Soleimany v. Soleimany* is commented upon.

Appeal from order to enforce award 21A–254 [p.1904]

The case of Soinco Saci v. Novokuznetsk Aluminium is now reported at [1998] 2 Lloyd's Rep. 337, CA.

B. ARBITRATION ACT 1975

Grounds of refusal 21B–23 [p.1922] *

Add:

In *Westacre Investments Inc. v. Jugoimport-SPDR Holding Co. Ltd* [1999] 3 W.L.R. 811; [1999] 3 All E.R. 864; [1999] 2 Lloyd's Rep. 64, CA, pet. dis. [1999] 1 W.L.R. 1999, HL, the Court held that two separate questions were raised. First, was it open to the appellants in the enforcement proceedings to challenge the arbitrator's findings of fact on the bribery issue and, secondly, if it was and they succeeded in proving the facts alleged, should the English Court enforce the award. As to the first, the majority held of crucial importance to evaluate both the majority decision in the arbitration and the ruling of the Swiss Federal Court, Swiss Law being both the proper law of the contract and the curial law of the arbitration and Switzerland, like the United Kingdom, being a party to the 1958 New York Convention. From the award itself it is clear that bribery was a central issue. The allegation was made, entertained and rejected. Had it not been rejected the claim would have failed, Swiss and English public policy being indistinguishable in this respect. Authority apart, in those circumstances and without fresh evidence there could be no justification for refusing to enforce the award. The majority also considered an obiter passage in *Soleimany v. Soleimany* [1998] 3 W.L.R. 811, CA at 824E to the effect that some kind of preliminary inquiry short of a full scale trial should be embarked upon whenever "there is prima facie evidence from one side that the award is based on an illegal contract". As to such Mantell L.J. with whom Sir David Hust agreed said: "For my part I have some difficulty with the concept and even greater concerns about its application in practice, but, for the moment and uncritically accepting the guidelines offered, it seems to me that any such preliminary inquiry in the circumstances of the present case must inevitably lead to the same conclusion, namely, that the attempt to re-open the facts should be rebuffed. I so conclude by reference to the criteria given by way of example in *Soleimany* itself. First, there was evidence before the Tribunal that this was a straightforward, commercial contract. Secondly, the arbitrators specifically found that the underlying contract was not illegal. Thirdly, there is nothing to suggest incompetence on the part of the arbitrators. Finally, there is no reason to suspect collusion or bad faith in the obtaining of the award. The seriousness of the alleged illegality to which Waller L.J. gives weight is not, in my judgment, a factor to be considered at the stage of deciding whether or not to mount a full scale inquiry. It is something to be taken into account as part of the balancing exercise between the competing public policy considerations of finality and illegality which can only be performed in response to the second question, if it arises, namely, should the award be enforced."

D. ARBITRATION ACT 1996

Agreement to submit to arbitration 21D–15 [p.1943]

Add:

The words in sub-clause (2) "if the reference is such as to make that clause part of the agreement" were held in *Trygg Hansa Insurance Co. v. Equitas Ltd* [1998] 2 Lloyd's Rep. 439, to preserve the pre-existing law that general words of incorporation in an agreement were not appropriate to incorporate an arbitration clause.

Note 21D–20 [p.1944]

Add:

There is a right of appeal to the Court of Appeal, see *INCO Europe Ltd v. First Choice Distribution* [1999] 1 W.L.R. 270; [1999] 1 All E.R. 820; [1999] C.L.C. 165, CA. The court held that the general terms of s.107 and Schedule 3 of the 1996 Act (*q.v.*) were not to be construed as removing the right of appeal which had existed under earlier legislation.

21D–23 **The Application**
[p.1944] *Add new note:*

21D–23/1 **Form of Order**

See Queen's Bench Masters' Practice Forms, Form No. 167, *Main Work*, Vol. 2, para. 1B–128.

21D–24 **"... or after he has taken any step in those proceedings to answer the substantive claim"**
[p.1944] *Add new paragraph:*

A defendant did not take any step to answer the substantive claim so as to lose his right to apply for a stay by applying for relief which was otiose to the relief he needed in addition to the relief he did need, see *Patel v. Patel*, [1999] 3 W.L.R. 322, CA. In this case the defendant asked for the default judgment to be set aside (the relief he needed) but in addition and unnecessarily for leave to defend and counterclaim which he was entitled to do once default judgment was set aside.

21D–25 **Onus of showing that action should proceed**
[p.1945] *The Court of Appeal decision in Halki Shipping Corporation v. Sopex Gils Ltd is now reported at:* [1998] 1 W.L.R. 726; [1998] 2 All E.R. 23; [1998] 1 Lloyd's Rep. 465.

Add:

In *Wealands v. C.L.C. Contractors Ltd* [1998] C.L.C. 808, the Court held on an application by a sub-contractor for third party proceedings against it by the contractor to be stayed under s.9 of the Arbitration Act 1996 that despite the disadvantages of the claim against the third party going to arbitration (if the plaintiff did not join the third party as a defendant) the 1996 Act gave priority to party autonomy and entitled the third party as of right to the stay which it sought.

Where a party objected under s.9 of the 1996 Act to a matter being considered other than by arbitrators then a dispute as to whether or not an arbitration agreement was time barred by limitation should be considered by the arbitrators even though the claimant might if he failed on such issue need to seek the exercise of the Court's discretion under s.12 of the 1996 Act: *Grimaldi Compagnia di Navigazione SpA v. Sekihyo Line Ltd* [1999] 1 W.L.R. 708; [1998] 3 All E.R. 943.

21D–34 **"... the Court may by order extend the time for taking that step"**
[p.1946] *Add:*

Section 12 of the 1996 Act is markedly more restricted than its predecessor, s.27 of the 1950 Act. See in particular sub-section 3. It is now not possible to extend time because the court concludes in general terms that it would be just to do so (*Cathiship SA v. Allanasons Ltd, The Catherine Helen* [1998] 3 All E.R. 714).

* *Add at end:*

The failure of a party to contract to read term no reason for extending time for bringing arbitral proceedings (*Harbour and General Works Ltd v. Environment Agency, The Times*, October 22, 1999, CA).

21D–38 **"... when on party serves ... a notice in writing requiring him ... to appoint an arbitrator"**
[p.1947] *The case of Vosnoc Ltd v. Transglobal Projects Ltd* is also reported at [1998] 2 All E.R. 990; [1998] 1
* Lloyd's Rep. 711. But this case was not followed in *Allianz Versicherungs-Aktiengesellschaft v. Fortuna Inc. (The Baltic Universal)* [1999] 1 W.L.R. 2117; [1999] 2 All E.R. 625[1999] 1 Lloyd's Rep. 497, nor in *Charles M. Willie & Co. (Shipping) Ltd v. Ocean Laser Shipping Ltd* [1999] 1 Lloyd's Rep. 225 which held that it was sufficient that an intention to commence arbitration/invoke the arbitration agreement was clear in the notice even though it did not as such request the appointment of an arbitrator. See also *Seabridge Shipping A.B. v. A.C. Orssleff's Eftf's A/S* [1999] 2 Lloyd's Rep. 685 (whether notice given before expiry of time limit satisfied).

21D–41 Procedure for appointment of arbitrators

[p.1948] *Add new note:*
*

21D–41/1 **Agreement as to time for appointing arbitrator**

Section 27(3) of this Act provides that the provisions of s.16 apply in relation to the filling of a vacancy on an arbitral tribunal as in relation to an original appointment. Where the parties have agreed that arbitrators should be appointed, not within the 14 days provided by s.16(5), but within 30 days of a request in writing, and it subsequently becomes necessary for a vacancy on the arbitral tribunal to be filled, the party required to reappoint has 30 days in which to do so and not merely the 14 days stipulated by s.16(5), (*Federal Insurance Co. and Chubb Insurance Co. of Europe S.A. v. Transamerica Occidental Life Insurance Co.* [1999] 2 Lloyd's Rep. 286).

21D–59 **"(a) circumstances exist that give rise to justifiable doubts as to his impartiality", etc.**
[p.1951] *Add at end:*
*
See also *Andrews v. Bradshaw, The Times*, October 11, 1999, CA (whether arbitrator showing irritation should be removed), and *Laker Airways Inc. v. F.L.S. Aerospace Ltd, The Times*, May 21, 1999 (judge refusing application to remove barrister appointed arbitrator who belonged to same set of chambers as counsel acting for one of the parties).

Enforcement of peremptory orders of tribunal

The text of s.42 of the Arithration Act 1996 is amended by S.I. 1998 No. 649, Sched., Pt I, Art. 24 as follows: 21D–93 [p.1958]

(a) in subs. (2) for the word "tribunal" wherever it appears there shall be substituted the word "adjudicator",
(b) in sub-para. (b) of subs. (2) for the words "arbitral proceedings" there shall be substituted the word "adjudication",
(c) sub-para. (c) of subs. (2) shall be deleted, and
(d) subs. (3) shall be deleted.

Interim injunctions 21D–101

Add at end: [p.1959] *

On question whether parties had "otherwise agreed" that court should have power to grant *Mareva* injunction where arbitral tribunal was to have "exclusive jurisdiction" over the dispute, see *Re Q.'s Estate* [1999] 1 Lloyd's Rep. 931 (Rix J.).

Add new note:

Time when powers exercisable 21D–101/1

It is doubtful that there is jurisdiction under this provision to order pre-delivery tests and inspection of a vessel before a cause of action had arisen for defective condition upon delivery or circumstances giving rise to an injunction under RSC, O.29, r.1: see *Tsakos Shipping & Trading SA v. Orizon Tanker Co. Ltd (The Centaurus Mar)* [1998] C.L.C. 1003.

Note 21D–127

Add new note: [p.1964]

Form of Order 21D–127/1

See Queen's Bench Masters' Practice Forms, Form 166, Main Work, Vol. 2, para. 1B–127.

Appeal from order to enforce award 21D–145

Add reference for Soinco Savi v. Novokuznetsk Aluminium Plant: [1998] 2 Lloyd's Rep. 337, CA. [p.1967]

"On the ground of serious irregularity" 21D–157

Add at end: [p.1969] *

Where it is alleged that the arbitrators were wrong on a question of law going to the construction of a contract the test to be applied by the court is whether the arbitrators were obviously wrong; it is not enough to say maybe the arbitrators were wrong or even that there was only a possibility that they were right (*Egmatra A.G. v. Marco Trading Corporation* [1999] 1 Lloyd's Rep. 862).

Note 21D–213/1

Add at end: [p.1981] *

With effect from January 1, 2000, the Unfair Arbitration Agreements (Specified Amount) Order 1999 (S.I. 1999 No. 2167) raises to £5,000 (from £3,000) the amount specified for the purposes of s.91 of the 1996 Act (agreements unfair under Unfair Terms in Consumer Contracts Regulations 1994) for England and Wales and Scotland.

Enforcing court and curial court the same 21D–243

Add at end: [p.1986]

In *Minmetals Germany GmbH v. Ferco Steel Ltd, The Times,* March 1, 1999 it was held that by agreeing the place of a foreign arbitration, a party not only agreed to submit all contractual disputes to arbitration but also agreed that the conduct of the arbitration should be subject to the supervisory jurisdiction of the courts of that place. Further the Court stated that in a case where a party against whom enforcement was sought alleged that a New York Convention award should not be enforced on the ground that such enforcement would lead to substantial injustice and therefore be contrary to English public policy the following must normally be included among the relevant considerations:

1. The nature of the procedural injustice.
2. Whether that party had invoked the supervisory jurisdiction of the seat of the arbitration.
3. Whether a remedy was available under that jurisdiction.
4. Whether the courts of that jurisdiction had conclusively determined the enforcee's complaint in favour of upholding the award.
5. If that party had failed to invoke that remedial jurisdiction, what reason had he and, in particular, whether he was acting, unreasonably in failing to do so.

21D–258/1 **Schedule 3**
[p.1990] *Schedule 3, para. 51 is repealed by S.I. 1998 No. 3162 (N.I. 21), art. 105, Sched. 5. Para. 54 is repealed by 1998 c.14, s.86, Sched. 8. Para. 55 is repealed by S.I. 1998 No. 150 (N.I. 10), art. 78, Sched. 7.*

21D–259 **High Court and County Courts (Allocation of Arbitration Proceedings) Order 1996**
[p.1999] *Delete text of art. 5(5) and substitute:*

(5) The value of any claim or counterclaim shall be calculated in accordance with rule 16.3(6) of the Civil Procedure Rules 1998.

21D–260 **Note**
[p.2000] *Add new para. at end:*

Article 5(5) is amended by The High Court and County Courts (Allocation of Arbitration Proceedings) (Amendment) Order 1999 (S.I. 1999 No. 1010).

E. ATTACHMENT OF EARNINGS ACT 1971

21E–42 **Meaning of "earnings"**
[p.2016] *In s.24(2), at the end of para. (b) insert:*

other than pay or allowances payable by his employer to him as a special member of a reserve force (within the meaning of the Reserve Forces Act 1996).

21E–43 **Note**
[p.2016] *Add at end:*

Section 24(2) is amended by The Reserve Forces Act 1996 (Consequential Provisions, etc.) Regulations 1998 (S.I. 1998 No. 3086), reg. 6.

F. CHARGING ORDERS ACT 1979

21F–7 **Provisions supplementing sections 1 and 2**
[p.2024] *Add new note:*
*

21F–7/1 **"interested in any property"**

To be "interested" in the property subject to a charging order for the purposes of *locus standi* under s.3(5) a person (a) has to be directly affected by the order and (b) has to have a proprietary interest or something similar to a proprietary interest in the property (*Banque National de Paris Plc. v. Montman Ltd, The Times,* September 7, 1999).

G. CIVIL EVIDENCE ACT 1968

21G–31 **Findings of adultery and paternity as evidence in civil proceedings**
[p.2029] *Add new note:*
*

21G–31/1 **"unless the contrary is proved"**

Where a party against whom a conviction is admissible has good cause for doing so, he may seek to rebut the presumption raised by proof of the conviction; such attempted rebuttal is not an abuse of process (*McCauley v. Vine* [1999] 1 W.L.R. 1977, CA).

H. CIVIL EVIDENCE ACT 1972

General
Delete existing note and add new note: 21H–3 [p.2035] *

Note
21H–3 This Act is concerned with (1) evidence of opinion, and (2) foreign evidence. Initially, s.5 (Interpretation, application to arbitration, etc.) stated that the provisions of the Act applied to "civil proceedings" and in "courts" as defined in the Civil Evidence Act 1968, s.18 (see para. 9B–249 above). This provision, in combination with Commencement Orders issued in 1973 and 1974, restricted the application of the Act to certain civil proceedings in certain courts (see SCP 1999, Vol. 2, para. 21H–3). However, s.5(1) was amended by the Civil Evidence Act 1995 and now states (see para. 9B–264 below) that "civil proceedings" means civil proceedings "before any tribunal in relation to which the strict rules of evidence apply, whether as a matter of law or by agreement between the parties" (*e.g.* an arbitration agreement); references to "court" should be construed accordingly (note also s.5(2)).

J. CIVIL LIABILITY (CONSTRUCTION) ACT 1978

"any person liable ... in respect of the same damage, ..."
Add new note: 21J–4 [p.2052] *

Contribution in arbitration
21J–4/1 Where parties refer a dispute between them to arbitration in England, they impliedly agree that the arbitration is to be conducted in accordance in all respects with the law of England, unless the agreement of reference provides otherwise. Accordingly, under the terms of an arbitration agreement in standard form between a contractor and a sub-contractor, the arbitrator has jurisdiction to make an award for contribution under this Act (*Wealands v. C.L.C. Contractors Ltd* [1999] 2 Lloyd's Rep. 739, CA).

K. COMPANIES ACT 1985

Power of court to declare dissolution of company void
21K–39 [p.2073] *In subs. (2) delete words* "may have been" *and substitute words* "may be".

L. CROWN PROCEEDINGS ACT 1947

Interpretation
21L–94 [p.2098] *In s.38(2), in the definition of* "His Majesty's aircraft", *after* "Kingdom" *there is inserted* "or the Scottish Administration". *In the definition of* "His Majesty's ships", *after* "Kingdom" *there is inserted* "or the Scottish Administration" *and after* "said Government" *there is inserted* "or Administration". *In the definition of* "officer", *after* "Minister of the Crown" *there is inserted* "and a member of the Scottish Executive".

Note
21L–94/1 [p.2098] *Add at end:*

Section 38(2) is amended by the Scotland Act 1998 (c.46), s.125, Sched. 8, para. 7.

21L–97 **Savings**
[p.2099] *In subs. (2), after* "in the United Kingdom", *in each place where those words appear, there is inserted* "or the Scottish Administration", *and after subs. (3) there is inserted:*

(3A) A certificate of the Scottish Ministers to the effect that—
(a) any alleged liability of the Crown arises otherwise than in respect of the Scottish Administration,
(b) any proceedings by the Crown are proceedings otherwise than in right of the Scottish Administration,
shall, for the purposes of this Act, be conclusive as to that matter.

21L–97/1 **Note**
[p.2099] *Add at end:*
Section 40 is amended by the Scotland Act 1998 (c.46), s.125, Sched. 8, para. 7.

R. LITIGANTS IN PERSON (COSTS AND EXPENSES) ACT 1975

21R–4 **Note**
[p.2117] *Delete note.*

21R–5 **Litigants in person—rights of audience**
[p.2117] *Add new note:*

21R–6 **Official Receiver**
In a case in which the Official Receiver obtained disqualification orders in the High Court against three respondents, together with an order for the Official Receiver's costs, the issue arose, in respect of work done by the Official Receiver himself, whether he was entitled to be treated as a litigant in person or whether recovery was limited to out of pocket expenses. The Court of Appeal found that the Official Receiver, if unrepresented in the conduct of an application to disqualify a director, was himself a litigant in person for the purpose of assessing and recovering costs. The court also considered whether or not the Official Receiver had suffered financial loss. The Court referred with approval to *Re Eastwood (dec'd) Lloyds Bank Ltd v. Eastwood* [1974] 3 All E.R. 603. The Court found that the Official Receiver worked upon the case like the Treasury Solicitor and an employed solicitor. The costs, like the costs of the Treasury Solicitor in *Re Eastwood* were pecuniary in nature and therefore the amount recoverable should be that provided for by the
* rules, *Re Minotaur Data Systems Ltd: The Official Receiver v. Brunt* [1999] 1 W.L.R. 1129, CA [1999] 3 All E.R. 122, CA; *The Times*, March 18, 1999, CA.

S. OATHS ACT 1978

21S–11 **Short title, extent and commencement**
[p.2120] *Add new sections at end:*

T. HUMAN RIGHTS ACT 1998

(c.42)

21T–1 An Act to give further effect to rights and freedoms guaranteed under the European Convention on Human Rights; to make provision with respect to holders of certain judicial offices who become judges of the European Court of Human Rights; and for connected purposes. [November 9, 1998]

Be it enacted by the Queen's most Excellent Majesty, by and with the advice and consent of the Lords Spiritual and Temporal, and Commons, in this present Parliament assembled, and by the authority of the same, as follows:

Introduction

The Convention rights

1.—(1) In this Act, "the convention rights" means the rights and fundamental freedoms set out in— **21T–2**

(a) Articles 2 to 12 and 14 of the Convention,
(b) Articles 1 to 3 of the First Protocol, and
(c) Articles 1 and 2 of the Sixth Protocol.

as read with Articles 16 to 18 of the Convention.

(2) Those Articles are to have effect for the purposes of this Act subject to any designated derogation or reservation (as to which see sections 14 and 15).

(3) The Articles are set out in Schedule 1.

(4) The Secretary of State may by order make such amendments to this Act as he considers appropriate to reflect the effect, in relation to the United Kingdom, of a protocol.

(5) In subsection (4) "protocol" means a protocol to the Convention—

(a) which the United Kingdom has ratified; or
(b) which the United Kingdom has signed with a view to ratification.

(6) No amendment may be made by an order under subsection (4) so as to come into force before the protocol concerned is in force in relation to the United Kingdom.

Section 2(1) **21T–2/1**

Unfocused recourse to generalised propositions in Strasbourg jurisprudence, whether before or after the incorporation of the Convention into English law, is positively unhelpful, cluttering up the court's consideration of adequate and more precise domestic principles and authorities governing the issues in play: *R. v. North West Lancashire Health Authority, ex parte A, The Times*, August 24, 1999, CA.

Interpretation of Convention rights

2.—(1) A court or tribunal determining a question which has arisen under this Act in connection with a Convention right must take into account any— **21T–3**

(a) judgment, decision, declaration or advisory opinion of the European Court of Human Rights,
(b) opinion of the Commission given in a report adopted under Article 31 of the Convention,
(c) decision of the Commission in connection with Article 26 or 27(2) of the Convention, or
(d) decision of the Committee of Ministers taken under Article 46 of the Convention,

whenever made or given, so far as, in the opinion of the court or tribunal, it is relevant to the proceedings in which that question has arisen.

(2) Evidence of any judgment, decision, declaration or opinion of which account may have to be taken under this section is to be given in proceedings before any court or tribunal in such manner as may be provided by rules.

(3) In this section "rules" means rules of court or, in the case of proceedings before a tribunal, rules made for the purposes of this section—

(a) by the Lord Chancellor or the Secretary of State, in relation to any proceedings outside Scotland;
(b) by the Secretary of State, in relation to proceedings in Scotland; or
(c) by a Northern Ireland department, in relation to proceedings before a tribunal in Northern Ireland—
  (i) which deals with transferred matters; and

(ii) for which no rules made under paragraph (a) are in force.

21T–4 **section 2(1)(b)**

This refers to Art. 31 of the Convention before it was amended by the 11th Protocol, which dealt with the duty of the European Commission of Human Rights in the event that it did not secure a friendly settlement of an application which it had declared admissible. Article 31(1) provided "If a solution is not reached, the Commission shall draw up a Report on the facts and state its opinion as to whether the facts found disclose a breach by the State concerned of its obligations under the Convention. The opinions of all the members of the Commission on this point may be stated in the Report."

21T–4/1 **section 2(1)(c)**

This refers to Art. 26 of the Convention before it was amended by the 11th Protocol, which provided "The Commission may only deal with the matter [i.e. non-state applications] after all domestic remedies have been exhausted, according to the generally recognised rules of international law, and within a period of six months from the date on which the final decision was taken." Article 27(2) of the unamended Convention provided "3. The Commission shall declare inadmissible any individual application submitted under Art. 25 which it considers incompatible with the provisions of the present Convention, manifestly ill-founded, or an abuse of the right of petition". See now Art. 35 of the Convention as amended.

21T–4/2 **section 2(1)(d)**

"Article 46—Binding force and execution of judgments

1. The High Contracting Parties undertake to abide by the final judgment of the Court in any case to which they are parties.

2. The final judgment of the Court shall be transmitted to the Committee of Ministers, which shall supervise its execution."

The reference to Art. 46 includes a reference to Arts 32 and 54 of the Convention before it was amended by the 11th Protocol: see s.21(3). Article 32(1) provided that if, after the Commission had adopted a Report under Art. 31, the case was not referred to the European Court of Human Rights, "the Committee of Ministers [of the Council of Europe] shall decide by a majority of two-thirds of the members entitled to sit on the Committee whether there has been a violation of the Convention". Article 54 was virtually identical to the new Art. 46.

Legislation

Interpretation of legislation

21T–5 **3.**—(1) So far as it is possible to do so, primary legislation and subordinate legislation must be read and given effect in a way which is compatible with the Convention rights.

(2) This section—

(a) applies to primary legislation and subordinate legislation whenever enacted;

(b) does not affect the validity, continuing operation or enforcement of any incompatible primary legislation; and

(c) does not affect the validity, continuing operation or enforcement of any incompatible subordinate legislation if (disregarding any possibility of revocation) primary legislation prevents removal of the incompatibility.

Declaration of incompatibility

21T–6 **4.**—(1) Subsection (2) applies in any proceedings in which a court determines whether a provision of primary legislation is compatible with a Convention right.

(2) If the court is satisfied that the provision is incompatible with a Convention right, it may make a declaration of that incompatibility.

(3) Subsection (4) applies in any proceedings in which a court determines whether a provision of subordinate legislation, made in the exercise of a power conferred by primary legislation, is compatible with a Convention right.

(4) If the court is satisfied—

(a) that the provision is incompatible with a Convention right, and

(b) that (disregarding any possibility of revocation) the primary legislation concerned prevents removal of the incompatibility, it may make a declaration of that incompatibility.

(5) In this section "court" means—

(a) the House of Lords;
(b) the Judicial Committee of the Privy Council;
(c) the Courts-Martial Appeal Court;
(d) in Scotland, the High Court of Justiciary sitting otherwise than as a trial court or the Court of Session;
(e) in England and Wales or Northern Ireland, the High Court or the Court of Appeal.

(6) A declaration under this section ("a declaration of incompatibility")—

(a) does not affect the validity, continuing operation or enforcement of the provision in respect of which it is given; and
(b) is not binding on the parties to the proceedings in which it is made.

Right of Crown to intervene

5.—(1) Where a court is considering whether to make a declaration of incompatibility, the Crown is entitled to notice in accordance with rules of court. **21T–7**

(2) In any case to which subsection (1) applies—

(a) a Minister of the Crown (or a person nominated by him),
(b) a member of the Scottish Executive,
(c) a Northern Ireland Minister,
(d) a Northern Ireland department,

is entitled, on giving notice in accordance with rules of court, to be joined as a party to the proceedings.

(3) Notice under subsection (2) may be given at any time during the proceedings.

(4) A person who has been made a party to criminal proceedings (other than in Scotland) as the result of a notice under subsection (2) may, with leave, appeal to the House of Lords against any declaration of incompatibility made in the proceedings.

(5) In subsection (4)—

"criminal proceedings" includes all proceedings before the Courts-Martial Appeal Court; and

"leave" means leave granted by the court making the declaration of incompatibility or by the House of Lords.

Public authorities

Acts of public authorities

6.—(1) It is unlawful for a public authority to act in a way which is incompatible with a Convention right. **21T–8**

(2) Subsection (1) does not apply to an act if—

(a) as the result of one or more provisions of primary legislation, the authority could not have acted differently; or
(b) in the case of one or more provisions of, or made under, primary legislation which cannot be read or given effect in a way which is compatible with the Convention rights, the authority was acting so as to give effect to or enforce those provisions.

(3) In this section "public authority" includes—

(a) a court or tribunal, and
(b) any person certain of whose functions are functions of a public nature,

but does not include either House of Parliament or a person exercising functions in connection with proceedings in Parliament.

(4) In subsection (3) "Parliament" does not include the House of Lords in its judicial capacity.

(5) In relation to a particular act, a person is not a public authority by virtue only of subsection (3)(b) if the nature of the act is private.

(6) "An act" includes a failure to act but does not include a failure to—

(a) introduce in, or lay before, Parliament a proposal for legislation; or

(b) make any primary legislation or remedial order.

Proceedings

21T–9 **7.**—(1) A person who claims that a public authority has acted (or proposes to act) in a way which is made unlawful by section 6(1) may—

(a) bring proceedings against the authority under this Act in the appropriate court or tribunal, or

(b) rely on the Convention right or rights concerned in any legal proceedings,

but only if he is (or would be) a victim of the unlawful act.

(2) In subsection (1)(a) "appropriate court or tribunal" means such court or tribunal as may be determined in accordance with rules; and proceedings against an authority include a counterclaim or similar proceeding.

(3) If the proceedings are brought on an application for judicial review, the applicant is to be taken to have a sufficient interest in relation to the unlawful act only if he is, or would be, a victim of that act.

(4) If the proceedings are made by way of a petition for judicial review in Scotland, the applicant shall be taken to have title and interest to sue in relation to the unlawful act only is he is, or would be, a victim of that act.

(5) Proceedings under subsection (1)(a) must be brought before the end of—

(a) the period of one year beginning with the date on which the act complained of took place; or

(b) such longer period as the court or tribunal considers equitable having regard to all the circumstances,

but that is subject to any rule imposing a stricter time limit in relation to the procedure in question.

(6) In subsection (1)(b) "legal proceedings" includes—

(a) proceedings brought by or at the instigation of a public authority; and

(b) an appeal against the decision of a court or tribunal.

(7) For the purposes of this section, a person is a victim of an unlawful act only if he would be a victim for the purposes of Article 34 of the Convention if proceedings were brought in the European Court of Human Rights in respect of that act.

(8) Nothing in this Act creates a criminal offence.

(9) In this section "rules" means—

(a) in relation to proceedings before a court or tribunal outside Scotland, rules made by the Lord Chancellor or the Secretary of State for the purposes of this section or rules of court,

(b) in relation to proceedings before a court or tribunal in Scotland, rules made by the Secretary of State for those purposes,

(c) in relation to proceedings before a tribunal in Northern Ireland—

(i) which deals with transferred matters; and

(ii) for which no rules made under paragraph (a) are in force,

rules made by a Northern Ireland department for those purposes,

and includes provision made by order under section 1 of the Courts and Legal Services Act 1990.

(10) In making rules regard must be had to section 9.

(11) The Minister who has power to make rules in relation to a particular tribunal may, to the extent he considers it necessary to ensure that the tribunal can provide an appropriate remedy in relation to an act (or proposed act) of a public authority which is (or would be) unlawful as a result of section 6(1), by order add to—

(a) the relief or remedies which the tribunal may grant; or
(b) the grounds on which it may grant any of them.

(12) An order made under subsection (11) may contain such incidental, supplemental, consequential or transitional provision as the Minister making it considers appropriate.

Judicial remedies

8.—(1) In relation to any act (or proposed act) of a public authority which the court finds is (or would be) unlawful, it may grant such relief or remedy, or make such order, within its powers as it considers just and appropriate. **21T–10**

(2) But damages may be awarded only by a court which has power to award damages, or to order the payment of compensation, in civil proceedings.

(3) No award of damages is to be made unless, taking account of all the circumstances of the case, including—

(a) any other relief or remedy granted, or order made, in relation to the act in question (by that or any other court), and
(b) the consequences of any decision (of that or any other court) in respect of that act,

the court is satisfied that the award is necessary to afford just satisfaction to the person in whose favour it is made.

(4) In determining—

(a) whether to award damages, or
(b) the amount of an award,

the court must take into account the principles applied by the European Court of Human Rights in relation to the award of compensation under Article 41 of the Convention.

(5) A public authority against which damages are awarded is to be treated—

(a) in Scotland, for the purposes of section 3 of the Law Reform (Miscellaneous Provisions) (Scotland) Act 1940 as if the award were made in an action of damages in which the authority has been found liable in respect of loss or damage to the person to whom the award is made;
(b) for the purposes of the Civil Liability (Contribution) Act 1978 as liable in respect of damage suffered by the person to whom the award is made.

(6) In this section—

"court" includes a tribunal;
"damages" means damages for an unlawful act of a public authority; and
"unlawful" means unlawful under section 6(1).

Judicial acts

9.—(1) Proceedings under section 7(1)(a) in respect of a judicial act may be brought only— **21T–11**

(a) by exercising a right of appeal;
(b) on any application (in Scotland a petition) for judicial review; or
(c) in such other forum as may be prescribed by rules.

(2) That does not affect any rule of law which prevents a court from being the subject of judicial review.

(3) In proceedings under this Act in respect of a judicial act done in good faith, damages may not be awarded otherwise than to compensate a person to the extent required by Article 5(5) of the Convention.

(4) An award of damages permitted by subsection (3) is to be made against the Crown, but no award may be made unless the appropriate person, if not a party to the proceedings, is joined.

(5) In this section—

"appropriate person" means the Minister responsible for the court concerned, or a person or government department nominated by him;

"court" includes a tribunal;
"judge" includes a member of a tribunal, a justice of the peace and a clerk or other officer entitled to exercise the jurisdiction of a court;
"judicial act" means a judicial act of a court and includes an act done on the instructions, or on behalf, of a judge; and
"rules" has the same meaning as in section 7(9).

Remedial action

Power to take remedial action

21T–12 **10.**—(1) This section applies if—

(a) a provision of legislation has been declared under section 4 to be incompatible with a Convention right and, if an appeal lies—
   (i) all persons who may appeal have stated in writing that they do not intended to do so;
   (ii) the time for bringing an appeal has expired and no appeal has been brought within that time; or
   (iii) an appeal brought within that time has been determined or abandoned; or
(b) it appears to a Minister of the Crown or Her Majesty in Council that, having regard to a finding of the European Court of Human Rights made after the coming into force of this section in proceedings against the United Kingdom, a provision of legislation is incompatible with an obligation of the United Kingdom arising from the Convention.

(2) If a Minister of the Crown considers that there are compelling reasons for proceeding under this section, he may by order make such amendments to the legislation as he considers necessary to remove the incompatibility.

(3) If, in the case of subordinate legislation, a Minister of the Crown considers—

(a) that it is necessary to amend the primary legislation under which the subordinate legislation in question was made, in order to enable the incompatibility to be removed; and
(b) that there are compelling reasons for proceeding under this section,

he may by order make such amendments to the primary legislation as he considers necessary.

(4) This section also applies where the provision in question is in subordinate legislation and has been quashed, or declared invalid, by reason of incompatibility with a Convention right and the Minister proposes to proceed under paragraph 2(b) of Schedule 2.

(5) If the legislation is an Order in Council, the power conferred by subsection (2) or (3) is exercisable by Her Majesty in Council.

(6) In this section "legislation" does not include a Measure of the Church Assembly or of the General Synod of the Church of England.

(7) Schedule 2 makes further provision about remedial orders.

Other rights and proceedings

Safeguard for existing human rights

21T–13 **11.** A person's reliance on a Convention right does not restrict—

(a) any other right or freedom conferred on him by or under any law having effect in any part of the United Kingdom; or
(b) his right to make any claim or bring any proceedings which he could make or bring apart from sections 7 to 9.

Freedom of expression

12.—(1) This section applies if a court is considering whether to grant any relief which, if granted might affect the exercise of the Convention right to freedom of expression. **21T–14**

(2) If the person against whom the application for relief is made ("the respondent") is neither present nor represented, no such relief is to be granted unless the court is satisfied—

(a) that the applicant has taken all practicable steps to notify the respondent; or

(b) that there are compelling reasons why the respondent should not be notified.

(3) No such relief is to be granted so as to restrain publication before trial unless the court is satisfied that the applicant is likely to establish that publication should not be allowed.

(4) The court must have particular regard to the importance of the Convention right to freedom of expression and, where the proceedings relate to material which the respondent claims, or which appears to the court, to be journalistic, literary or artistic material (or to conduct connected with such material), to—

(a) the extent to which—

(i) the material has, or is about to, become available to the public; or

(ii) it is, or would be, in the public interest for the material to be published;

(b) any relevant privacy code.

(5) In this section—

"court" includes a tribunal; and

"relief" includes any remedy or order (other than in criminal proceedings).

Freedom of thought, conscience and religion

13.—(1) If a court's determination of any question arising under this Act might affect the exercise by a religious organisation (itself or its members collectively) of the Convention right to freedom of thought, conscience and religion, it must have particular regard to the importance of that right. **21T–15**

(2) In this section, "court" includes a tribunal.

Derogations and reservations

Derogations

14.—(1) In this Act, "designated derogation" means— **21T–16**

(a) the United Kingdom's derogation from Article 5(3) of the Convention; and

(b) any derogation by the United Kingdom from an Article of the Convention, or of any protocol to the Convention, which is designated for the purposes of this Act in an order made by the Secretary of State.

(2) The derogation referred to in subsection (1)(a) is set out in Part I of Schedule 3.

(3) If a designated derogation is amended or replaced it ceases to be a designated derogation.

(4) But subsection (3) does not prevent the Secretary of State from exercising his power under subsection (1)(b) to make a fresh designation order in respect of the Article concerned.

(5) The Secretary of State must by order make such amendments to Schedule 3 as he considers appropriate to reflect—

(a) any designation order; or

(b) the effect of subsection (3).

(6) A designation order may be made in anticipation of the making by the United Kingdom of a proposed derogation.

Reservations

21T–17 **15.**—(1) In this Act, "designated reservation" means—

(a) the United Kingdom's reservation to Article 2 of the First Protocol to the Convention; and

(b) any other reservation by the United Kingdom to an Article of the Convention, or of any protocol to the Convention, which is designated for the purposes of this Act in an order made by the Secretary of State.

(2) The text of the reservation referred to in subsection (1)(a) is set out in Part II of Schedule 3.

(3) If a designated reservation is withdrawn wholly or in part it ceases to be a designated reservation.

(4) But subsection (3) does not prevent the Secretary of State from exercising his power under subsection (1)(b) to make a fresh designation order in respect of the Article concerned.

(5) The Secretary of State must by order make such amendments to this Act as he considers appropriate to reflect—

(a) any designation order; or

(b) the effect of subsection (3).

Period for which designated derogations have effect

21T–18 **16.**—(1) If it has not already been withdrawn by the United Kingdom, a designated derogation ceases to have effect for the purposes of this Act—

(a) in the case of the derogation referred to in section 14(1)(a), at the end of the period of five years beginning with the date on which section 1(2) came into force;

(b) in the case of any other derogation, at the end of the period of five years beginning with the date on which the order designating it was made.

(2) At any time before the period—

(a) fixed by subsection (1)(a) or (b), or

(b) extended by an order under this subsection,

comes to an end, the Secretary of State may by order extend it by a further period of five years.

(3) An order under section 14(1)(b) ceases to have effect at the end of the period for consideration, unless a resolution has been passed by each House approving the order.

(4) Subsection (3) does not affect—

(a) anything done in reliance on the order; or

(b) the power to make a fresh order under section 14(1)(b).

(5) In subsection (3) "period for consideration" means the period of forty days beginning with the day on which the order was made.

(6) In calculating the period for consideration, no account is to be taken of any time during which—

(a) Parliament is dissolved or prorogued; or

(b) both Houses are adjourned for more than four days.

(7) If a designated derogation is withdrawn by the United Kingdom, the

Secretary of State must by order make such amendments to this Act as he considers are required to reflect that withdrawal.

Periodic review of designated reservations

17.—(1) The appropriate Minister must review the designated reservation referred to in section 15(1)(a)— **21T–19**

(a) before the end of the period of five years beginning with the date on which section 1(2) came into force; and

(b) if that designation is still in force, before the end of the period of five years beginning with the date on which the last report relating to it was laid under subsection (3).

(2) The appropriate Minister must review each of the other designated reservations (if any)—

(a) before the end of the period of five years beginning with the date on which the order designating the reservation first came into force; and

(b) if the designation is still in force, before the end of the period of five years beginning with the date on which the last report relating to it was laid under subsection (3).

(3) The Minister conducting a review under this section must prepare a report on the result of the review and lay a copy of it before each House of Parliament.

Judges of the European Court of Human Rights

Appointment to European Court of Human Rights

18.—(1) In this section "judicial office" means the office of— **21T–20**

(a) Lord Judstice of Appeal, Justice of the High Court or Circuit judge, in England and Wales;

(b) judge of the Court of Session or sheriff, in Scotland;

(c) Lord Justice of Appeal, judge of the High Court or county court judge, in Northern Ireland.

(2) The holder of a judicial office may become a judge of the European Court of Human Rights ("the Court") without being required to relinquish his office.

(3) But he is not required to perform the duties of his judicial office while he is a judge of the Court.

(4) In respect of any period during which he is a judge of the Court—

(a) a Lord Justice of Appeal or Justice of the High Court is not to count as a judge of the relevant court for the purposes of section 2(1) or 4(1) of the Supreme Court Act 1981 (maximum number of judges) nor as a judge of the Supreme Court for the purposes of section 12(1) to (6) of that Act (salaries etc.);

(b) a judge of the Court of Session is not to count as a judge of that court for the purposes of section 1(1) of the Court of Session Act 1988 (maximum number of judges) or of section 9(1)(c) of the Administration of Justice Act 1973 ("the 1973 Act") (salaries etc.);

(c) a Lord Justice of Appeal or judge of the High Court in Northern Ireland is not to count as a judge of the relevant court for the purposes of section 2(1) or 3(1) of the Judicature (Northern Ireland) Act 1978 (maximum number of judges) nor as a judge of the Supreme Court of Northern Ireland for the purposes of section 9(1)(d) of the 1973 Act (salaries etc.);

(d) a Circuit judge is not to count as such for the purposes of section 18 of the Courts Act 1971 (salaries etc.);

(e) a sheriff is not to count as such for the purposes of section 14 of the Sheriff Courts (Scotland) Act 1907 (salaries etc.);

(f) a county court judge of Northern Ireland is not to count as such for the purposes of section 106 of the County Courts Act (Northern Ireland) 1959 (salaries etc.).

(5) If a sheriff principal is appointed a judge of the Court, section 11(1) of the Sheriff Courts (Scotland) Act 1971 (temporary appointment of sheriff principal) applies, while he holds that appointment, as if his office is vacant.

(6) Schedule 4 makes provision about judicial pensions in relation to the holder of a judicial office who serves as a judge of the Court.

(7) The Lord Chancellor or the Secretary of State may by order make such transitional provision (including, in particular, provision for a temporary increase in the maximum number of judges) as he considers appropriate in relation to any holder of a judicial office who has completed his service as a judge of the Court.

Parliamentary procedure

Statements of compatibility

21T–21 **19.**—(1) A Minister of the Crown in charge of a Bill in either House of Parliament must, before Second Reading of the Bill—

(a) make a statement to the effect that in his view the provisions of the Bill are compatible with the Convention rights ("a statement of compatibility"); or

(b) make a statement to the effect that although he is unable to make a statement of compatibility the government nevertheless wishes the House to proceed with the Bill.

(2) The statement must be in writing and be published in such manner as the Minister making it considers appropriate.

Supplemental

Orders, etc., under this Act

21T–22 **20.**—(1) Any power of a Minister of the Crown to make an order under this Act is exercisable by statutory instrument.

(2) The power of the Lord Chancellor or the Secretary of State to make rules (other than rules of court) under section 2(3) or 7(9) is exercisable by statutory instrument.

(3) Any statutory instrument made under section 14, 15 or 16(7) must be laid before Parliament.

(4) No order may be made by the Lord Chancellor or the secretary of State under section 1(4), 7(11) or 16(2) unless a draft of the order has been laid before, and approved by, each House of Parliament.

(5) Any statutory instrument made under section 18(7) or Schedule 4, or to which subsection (2) applies, shall be subject to annulment in pursuance of a resolution of either House of Parliament.

(6) The power of a Northern Ireland department to make—

(a) rules under section 2(3)(c) or 7(9)(c), or

(b) an order under section 7(11),

is exercisable by statutory rule for the purposes of the Statutory Rules (Northern Ireland) Order 1979.

(7) Any rules made under section 2(3)(c) or 7(9)(c) shall be subject to negative resolution; and section 41(6) of the Interpretation Act (Northern Ireland) 1954 (meaning of "subject to negative resolution") shall apply as if the power to make the rules were conferred by an Act of the Northern Ireland Assembly.

(8) No order may be made by a Northern Ireland department under section 7(11) unless a draft of the order has been laid before, and approved by, the Northern Ireland Assembly.

Interpretation, etc.

21.—(1) In this Act—

"amend" includes repeal and apply (with or without modification); **21T–23**

"the appropriate Minister" means the Minister of the Crown having charge of the appropriate authorised government department (within the meaning of the Crown Proceedings Act 1947);

"the Commission" means the European Commission of Human Rights;

"the Convention" means the Convention for the Protection of Human Rights and Fundamental Freedoms, agreed by the Council of Europe at Rome on November 4, 1950 as it has effect for the time being in relation to the United Kingdom;

"declaration of incompatibility" means a declaration under section 4;

"Minister of the Crown" has the same meaning as in the Ministers of the Crown Act 1975;

"Northern Ireland Minister" includes the First Minister and the deputy First Minister in Northern Ireland;

"primary legislation" means any—

(a) public general Act;
(b) local and personal Act;
(c) private Act;
(d) Measure of the Church Assembly;
(e) Measure of the General Synod of the Church of England;
(f) Order in Council—
  (i) made in exercise of Her Majesty's Royal Prerogative;
  (ii) made under section 38(1)(a) of the Northern Ireland Constitution Act 1973 of the corresponding provision of the Northern Ireland Act 1998; or
  (iii) amending an Act of a kind mentioned in paragraph (a), (b) or (c);

and includes an order or other instrument made under primary legislation (otherwise than by the National Assembly for Wales, a member of the Scottish Executive, a Northern Ireland Minister or a Northern Ireland department) to the extent to which it operates to bring one or more provisions of that legislation into force or amends any primary legislation;

"the First Protocol" means the protocol to the Convention agreed at Paris on March 20, 1952;

"the Sixth Protocol" means the protocol to the Convention agreed at Strasbourg on April 28, 1983;

"11th Protocol" means the protocol to the Convention (restructuring the control machinery established by the Convention) agreed at Strasbourg on May 11, 1994;

"remedial order" means an order under section 10;

"subordinate legislation" means any—

(a) Order in Council other than one—
  (i) made in exercise of Her Majesty's Royal Prerogative;
  (ii) made under section 38(1)(a) of the Northern Ireland Constitution Act 1973 or the corresponding provision of the Northern Ireland Act 1998; or;
  (iii) amending an Act of a kind mentioned in the definition of primary legislation;
(b) Act of the Scottish Parliament;
(c) Act of the Parliament of Northern Ireland;
(d) Measure of the Assembly established under section 1 of the Northern Ireland Assembly Act 1973;
(e) Act of the Northern Ireland Assembly;
(f) order, rules, regulations, scheme, warrant, byelaw or other

instrument made under primary legislation (except to the extent to which it operates to bring one or more provisions of that legislation into force or amends any primary legislation);

(g) order, rules, regulations, scheme, warrant, byelaw or other instrument made under legislation mentioned in paragraph (b), (c), (d) or (e) or made under an Order in Council applying only to Northern Ireland;

(h) order, rules, regulations, scheme, warrant, byelaw or other instrument made by a member of the Scottish Executive, a Northern Ireland Minister or Northern Ireland department in exercise of prerogative or other executive functions of Her Majesty which are exercisable by such a person on behalf of Her Majesty;

"transferred matters" has the same meaning as in the Northern Ireland Act 1998; and

"tribunal" means any tribunal in which legal proceedings may be brought.

(2) The references in paragraphs (b) and (c) of section 2(1) to Articles are to Articles of the Convention as they had effect immediately before the coming into force of the 11th Protocol.

(3) The reference in paragraph (d) of section 2(1) to Article 46 includes a reference to Articles 32 and 54 of the Convention as they had effect immediately before the coming into force of the 11th Protocol.

(4) The references in section 2(1) to a report or decision of the Commission or a decision of the Committee of Ministers include references to a report or decision made as provided by paragraphs 3, 4 and 6 of Article 5 of the 11th Protocol (transitional provisions).

(5) Any liability under the Army Act 1955, the Air Force Act 1955 or the Naval Discipline Act 1957 to suffer death for an offence is replaced by a liability to imprisonment for life or any less punishment authorised by those Acts; and those Acts shall accordingly have effect with the necessary modifications.

Short title, commencement, application and extent

21T–24 **22.**—(1) This Act may be cited as the Human Rights Act 1998.

(2) Sections 18, 20 and 21(5) and this section come into force on the passing of this Act.

(3) The other provisions of this Act come into force on such day as the Secretary of State may by order appoint; and different days may be appointed for different purposes.

(4) Paragraph (b) of subsection (1) of section 7 applies to proceedings brought by or at the instigation of a public authority whenever the act in question took place; but otherwise that subsection does not apply to an act taking place before the coming into force of that section.

(5) This Act binds the Crown.

(6) This Act extends to Northern Ireland.

(7) Section 21(5), so far as it relates to any provision contained in the Army Act 1955, the Air Force Act 1955 or the Naval Discipline Act 1957, extends to any place to which that provision extends.

21T–25 **Section 22(4)**

A public authority instituting proceedings before the Act is brought into force is obliged to take account of the likely effect of the Act and the Convention on those proceedings, for example if it is likely that the substantive hearing or any appeal will be heard after the coming into force of the Act: *R. v. DPP, ex p. Kebilene, The Times,* March 31, 1999, DC.

SCHEDULE 1

THE ARTICLES

PART 1

THE CONVENTION

RIGHTS AND FREEDOMS

Article 2—Right to life

1. Everyone's right to life shall be protected by law. No one shall be deprived of his life **21T–26**
intentionally save in the execution of a sentence of a court following his conviction of a crime for which this penalty is provided by law.

2. Deprivation of life shall not be regarded as inflicted in contravention of this Article when it results from the use of force which is no more than absolutely necessary:
(a) in defence of any person from unlawful violence;
(b) in order to effect a lawful arrest or to prevent the escape of a person lawfully detained;
(c) in action lawfully taken for the purpose of quelling a riot or insurrection.

Article 3—Prohibition of torture

No one shall be subjected to torture or to inhuman or degrading treatment or punishment. **21T–27**

Article 4—Prohibition of slavery and forced labour

1. No one shall be held in slavery or servitude. **21T–28**
2. No one shall be required to perform forced or compulsory labour.
3. For the purpose of this Article the term "forced or compulsory labour" shall not include:
(a) any work required to be done in the ordinary course of detention imposed according to the provisions of Article 5 of this Convention or during conditional release from such detention;
(b) any service of a military character or, in case of conscientious objectors in countries where they are recognised, service exacted instead of compulsory military service;
(c) any service exacted in case of an emergency or calamity threatening the life or well-being of the community;
(d) any work or service which forms part of normal civic obligations.

Article 5—Right to liberty and security

1. Everyone has the right to liberty and security of person. No one shall be deprived of his **21T–29**
liberty save in the following cases and in accordance with a procedure prescribed by law:
(a) the lawful detention of a person after conviction by a competent court;
(b) the lawful arrest or detention of a person for non-compliance with the lawful order of a court or in order to secure the fulfilment of any obligation prescribed by law;
(c) the lawful arrest or detention of a person effected for the purpose of bringing him before the competent legal authority on reasonable suspicion of having committed an offence or when it is reasonably considered necessary to prevent his committing an offence or fleeing after having done so;
(d) the detention of a minor by lawful order for the purpose of educational supervision or his lawful detention for the purpose of bringing him before the competent legal authority;
(e) the lawful detention of persons for the prevention of the spreading of infectious diseases, of persons of unsound mind, alcoholics or drug addicts or vagrants;
(f) the lawful arrest or detention of a person to prevent his effecting an unauthorised entry into the country or of a person against whom action is being taken with a view to deportation or extradition.

2. Everyone who is arrested shall be informed promptly, in a language which he understands, of the reasons for his arrest and of any charge against him.

3. Everyone arrested or detained in accordance with the provisions of paragraph 1(c) of this Article shall be brought promptly before a judge or other officer authorised by law to exercise judicial power and shall be entitled to trial within a reasonable time or to release pending trial. Release may be conditioned by guarantees to appear for trial.

4. Everyone who is deprived of his liberty by arrest or detention shall be entitled to take proceedings by which the lawfulness of his detention shall be decided speedily by a court and his release ordered if the detention is not lawful.

5. Everyone who has been the victim of arrest or detention in contravention of the provisions of this Article shall have an enforceable right to compensation.

Article 6—Right to a fair trial

1. In the determination of his civil rights and obligations or of any criminal charge against him, **21T–30**
everyone is entitled to a fair and public hearing within a reasonable time by an independent and impartial tribunal established by law. Judgment shall be pronounced publicly but the press and public may be excluded from all or part of the trial in the interest of morals, public order or

national security in a democratic society, where the interests of juveniles or the protection of the private life of the parties so require, or to the extent strictly necessary in the opinion of the court in special circumstances where publicity would prejudice the interests of justice.

2. Everyone charged with a criminal offence shall be presumed innocent until proved guilty according to law.

3. Everyone charged with a criminal offence has the following minimum rights:

(a) to be informed promptly, in a language which he understands and in detail, of the nature and cause of the accusation against him;
(b) to have adequate time and facilities for the preparation of his defence;
(c) to defend himself in person or through legal assistance of his own choosing or, if he has not sufficient means to pay for legal assistance, to be given it free when the interest of justice so require;
(d) to examine or have examined witnesses against him and to obtain the attendance and examination of witnesses on his behalf under the same conditions as witnesses against him;
(e) to have the free assistance of an interpreter if he cannot understand or speak the language used in court.

Article 7—No punishment without law

21T–31 1. No one shall be held guilty of any criminal offence on account of any act or omission which did not constitute a criminal offence under national or international law at the time when it was committed. Nor shall a heavier penalty be imposed than the one that was applicable at the time the criminal offence was committed.

2. The Article shall not prejudice the trial and punishment of any person for any act or omission which, at the time when it was committed, was criminal according to the general principles of law recognised by civilised nations.

Article 8—Right to respect for private and family life

21T–32 1. Everyone has the right to respect for his private and family life, his home and his correspondence.

2. There shall be no interference by a public authority with the exercise of this right except such as is in accordance with the law and is necessary in a democratic society in the interests of national security, public safety or the economic well-being of the country, for the prevention of disorder or crime, for the protection of health or morals, or for the protection of the rights and freedoms of others.

Article 9—Freedom of thought, conscience and religion

21T–33 1. Everyone has the right to freedom of thought, conscience and religion; this right includes freedom to change his religion or belief and freedom, either alone or in community with others and in public or private, to manifest his religion or belief, in worship, teaching, practice and observance.

2. Freedom to manifest one's religion or beliefs shall be subject only to such limitations as are prescribed by law and are necessary in a democratic society in the interests of public safety, for the protection of public order, health or morals, or for the protection of the rights and freedoms of others.

Article 10—Freedom of expression

21T–34 1. Everyone has the right to freedom of expression. This right shall include freedom to hold opinions and to receive and impart information and ideas without interference by public authority and regardless of frontiers. This Article shall not prevent States from requiring the licensing of broadcasting, television or cinema enterprises.

2. The exercise of these freedoms, since it carries with it duties and responsibilities, may be subject to such formalities, conditions, restrictions or penalties as are prescribed by law and are necessary in a democratic society, in the interests of national security, territorial integrity or public safety, for the prevention of disorder or crime, for the protection of health or morals, for the protection of the reputation or rights of others, for preventing the disclosure of information received in confidence, or for maintaining the authority and impartiality of the judiciary.

Article 11—Freedom of assembly and association

21T–35 1. Everyone has the right to freedom of peaceful assembly and to freedom of association with others, including the right to form and to join trade unions for the protection of his interests.

2. No restrictions shall be placed on the exercise of these rights other than such as are prescribed by law and are necessary in a democratic society in the interests of national security or public safety, for the prevention of disorder or crime, for the protection of health or morals or for the protection of the rights and freedoms of others. This Article shall not prevent the imposition of lawful restrictions on the exercise of these rights by members of the armed forces, of the police or of the administration of the State.

Article 12—Right to marry

21T–36 Men and women of marriageable age have the right to marry and to found a family, according to the national laws governing the exercise of this right.

Article 14—Prohibition of discrimination

The enjoyment of the rights and freedoms set forth in this Convention shall be secured without discrimination on any ground such as sex, race, colour, language, religion, political or other opinion, national or social origin, association with a national minority, property, birth or other status. 21T–37

Article 16—Restrictions on political activity of aliens

Nothing in Articles 10, 11 and 14 shall be regarded as preventing the High Contracting Parties from imposing restrictions on the political activity of aliens. 21T–38

Article 17—Prohibition of abuse of rights

Nothing in this Convention may be interpreted as implying for any State, group or person any right to engage in any activity or perform any act aimed at the destruction of any of the rights and freedoms set forth herein or at their limitation to a greater extent than is provided for in the Convention. 21T–39

Article 18—Limitation on use of restrictions on rights

The restrictions permitted under this Convention to the said rights and freedoms shall not be applied for any purpose other than those for which they have been prescribed. 21T–40

PART II

THE FIRST PROTOCOL

Article 1—Protection of property

Every natural or legal person is entitled to the peaceful enjoyment of his possessions. No one shall be deprived of his possessions except in the public interest and subject to the conditions provided for by law and by the general principles of international law. 21T–41

The preceding provisions shall not, however, in any way impair the right of a State to enforce such laws as it deems necessary to control the use of property in accordance with the general interest or to secure the payment of taxes or other contributions or penalties.

Article 2—Right to education

No person shall be denied the right to education. In the exercise of any functions which it assumes in relation to education and to teaching, the State shall respect the right of parents to ensure such education and teaching in conformity with their own religious and philosophical convictions. 21T–42

Article 3—Right to free elections

The High Contracting Parties undertake to hold free elections at reasonable intervals by secret ballot, under conditions which will ensure the free expression of the opinion of the people in the choice of the legislature. 21T–43

PART III

THE SIXTH PROTOCOL

Article 1—Abolition of the death penalty

The death penalty shall be abolished. No one shall be condemned to such penalty or executed. 21T–44

Article 2—Death penalty in time of war

A State may make provision in its law for the death penalty in respect of acts committed in time of war or of imminent threat of war; such penalty shall be applied only in the instances laid down in the law and in accordance with its provisions. The State shall communicate to the Secretary General of the Council of Europe the relevant provisions of that law. 21T–45

U. EUROPEAN CONVENTION ON HUMAN RIGHTS

Introduction 21U–1

Although not among the Convention rights to which s.1(2) of the Human Rights Act 1998 gives effect, Articles 1 and 13 of the Convention are also of significance. Their text is set out below.

21U–2 **Article 1—Obligation to respect human rights**

The High Contracting Parties shall secure to everyone within their jurisdiction the rights and freedoms defined in Section I of this Convention.

* * * *

21U–3 **Article 13—Right to an effective remedy**

Everyone whose rights and freedoms as set forth in this Convention are violated shall have an effective remedy before a national authority notwithstanding that the violation has been committed by persons acting in an official capacity.

INDEX

References to paragraph numbers in square brackets are to Volume 2

References to paragraph numbers with prefix "C" are to County Court Rules Supplement

Abatement
death, on 15/7/3

Acceptance of payment in
timetable for
RSC [3D–1]

Accountant General, Office of
generally [5B–1], [5C–2]—[5C–2/1], [5C–5]—[5C–6], [5C–18]—[5C–19], [5C–26]—[5C–27], [5C–33]—[5C–34], [5C–37], [5C–41]—[5C–42], [5C–46]—[5C–46/1], [5C–48]—[5C–48/1], [5C–49]—[5C–50], [5C–53]—[5C–55/1], [5C–58]—[5C–60/1], [5C–66], [5C–71], [5C–73], [5C–82], [5C–84/1], [5C–85]—[5C–85/1], [5C–92]—[5C–92/1], [5D–2]
investment [5D–2]
rules [5C–2]—[5C–2/1], [5C–5]—[5C–6], [5C–18]—[5C–19], [5C–26]—[5C–27], [5C–33]—[5C–34], [5C–37], [5C–41]—[5C–42], [5C–46]—[5C–46/1], [5C–48]—[5C–48/1], [5C–49]—[5C–50], [5C–53]—[5C–55/1], [5C–58]—[5C–60/1], [5C–66], [5C–71], [5C–73], [5C–82], [5C–84/1], [5C–85]—[5C–85/1], [5C–92]—[5C–92/1]
statutory provisions [5B–1]

Acknowledgment of service
Admiralty direction [6B–3]
time for
generally [3D–1]

Act to be done, judgment requiring
penal notice, indorsement of 45/7/7
requirements
penal notice 45/7/7
service of order
dispensing with 45/7/8

Addition of parties
application 15/6/17—15/6/18

Adjournment to court
chambers, proceedings in
Family Division 32/13/23
QBD 32/13/23

Administration actions
applications
costs from estate in any event 85/2/3

Administration of Justice Act 1970
housing [8C–3]—[8C–4/1]
mortgage actions [8C–3]—[8C–4/1]

Administration of Justice Act 1982
Funds Office [5B–1]

Admiralty claims
goods and materials supplied [6D–38]
ownership [6D–11]
possession [6D–11]

Admiralty Court
directions [6B–1]—[6B–15]
forms
list of [6A–1A]
precedents [6A–3]—[6A–28]
jurisdiction
generally [6D–1], [6D–3], [6D–11], [6D–60], [6D–73]

Admiralty directions
acknowledgment of service [6B–3]
affidavits, exhibits to [6B–11]
amendment [6B–7]
Anton Piller injunctions [6B–7]
application of [6B–2]
arbitration [6B–7]
cargo, discharge of [6B–9]
court practice [6B–4]—[6B–8]
discovery [6B–7]
documents [6B–7]
evidence, exchange of [6B–7]
ex parte applications [6B–7]
foreign currency [6B–14]
generally [6B–1]
interlocutory applications [6B–5]
inter partes summons [6B–7]
interrogatories [6B–7]
Mareva injunctions [6B–7]
persons under disability
compromise by [6B–12]
pleadings [6B–7]
postal issue [6B–10]
preliminary issues [6B–7]
pre-trial checklist [6B–7]
schedules, form of [6B–13]
security for costs [6B–7]
service out of the jurisdiction [6B–7]
summons for directions [6B–7]
taxation [6B–15]
trial procedure [6B–7]
trials [6B–6]
writ of summons [6B–3]

Admiralty forms
affidavit in support
arrest and custody [6A–7]

Admiralty forms—*cont.*
application for arrest and custody [6A–6]
arrest and custody
application [6A–6]
declaration in support [6A–7]
notice to Consular Officer [6A–8]
requests for caveat against [6A–9]—[6A–10]
warrant [6A–11]
claim form
claim *in personam* [6A–2]
claim *in rem* [6A–1]
limitation claim [6A–17]
claim *in personam* [6A–2]
claim *in rem*
claim form [6A–1]
notes for claimant [6A–3]
notes for defendant [6A–3/1]
response pack [6A–4]
declaration in support
arrest and custody [6A–7]
inability to file statement in limitation claim [6A–27]
decree of limitation
order [6A–25]
restricted [6A–23]—[6A–24]
defence
limitation claim [6A–21]
directions to Admiralty Marshal [6A–12]
judgment in default [6A–15]
limitation claim
application for restricted decree of limitation [6A–23]
claim form [6A–17]
declaration of inability of defendant to file statement of claim [6A–27]
decree of limitation [6A–25]
defence [6A–21]
defendant's claim [6A–26]
notes for claimant [6A–18]
notes for defendant [6A–19]
notice of admission of right of claimant to limit liability [6A–20]
response pack [6A–22]
restricted decree of limitation [6A–24]
list of [6A–1A]
notice of appeal [6A–28]
restricted decree of limitation
application [6A–23]
order [6A–24]
notes for claimant
claim *in rem* [6A–3]
limitation claim [6A–18]
notes for defendant
claim *in rem* [6A–3/1]
limitation claim [6A–19]
notice to Consular Officer [6A–8]
preliminary act
generally [6A–5]
judgment in default [6A–15]
release
application and undertaking [6A–14]
request for caveat against [6A–13]
request for caveat against arrest
generally [6A–9]
Limitation Fund, after constitution of [6A–10]
request for caveat against release [6A–13]

Admiralty forms—*cont.*
response pack
claim *in rem* [6A–4]
limitation claim [6A–22]
sale of ship, order for [6A–16]
undertaking for arrest and custody [6A–6]
warrant for arrest
application [6A–6]
declaration in support [6A–7]
notice to Consular Officer [6A–8]
order [6A–11]
requests for caveat against [6A–9]—[6A–10]

Admiralty jurisdiction
county court
generally [6D–301]
Merchant Shipping Act 1995
insurance [6D–262]
liability [6D–209]
limitation period [6D–252], [6D–258]
multiple fault [6D–235]
time limits [6D–252], [6D–258]
Supreme Court Act 1981
generally [6D–1], [6D–3], [6D–11], [6D–60], [6D–73]

Admiralty proceedings
acknowledgment of service
direction [6B–3]
arrest, warrant of
generally 75/5/10
arrested property
directions 75/12/3
assessment of damages
disruption of business 75/42/8
county court
generally [6D–301]
statutory basis [6D–301]
duration of writ 75/4/3
forms
list of [6A–1A]
precedents [6A–3]—[6A–28]
limitation actions
parties 75/37/2
limitation fund
generally 75/37/5
parties
limitation actions 75/37/2
practice directions [6B–1]—[6B–15]
references
disruption of business 75/42/8
setting down
generally 72/2/5
statutory basis
County Courts Act 1984 [6D–301]
Merchant Shipping Act 1995 [6D–209], [6D–235], [6D–252], [6D–258], [6D–262]
Supreme Court Act 1981 [6D–1], [6D–3], [6D–11], [6D–60], [6D–73]
undertakings, solicitor, by
expenses 75/23A/2
wages action 75/1/23
warrant of arrest
generally 75/5/10
writ
direction [6B–3]
generally 75/4/3

Admissions
patent actions 104/0/17
timetable for
RSC [3D–1]

Adultery
evidence of [21G–31]—[21G–31/1]

Affidavits
Admiralty directions [6B–11]
default judgment
service of writ 13/7/3
interim payments
generally 29/10/6
judgment in default
service of writ 13/7/3
summary judgment
plaintiff in reply 14/4/7
timetable for
RSC [3D–1]

Affidavits of service
default judgment 13/7/3
judgment in default 13/7/3

Agent of overseas principal
service
generally 10/2/2

Allocation of business
Chancery direction [2B–123]
county court
arbitration [21D–259]—[21D–260]
county court
commencement [20B–247]
enforcement
generally [20B–252]
trial [20B–249]
value of actions [20B–261]

Allocation of jurisdiction
E.C., within
exclusive jurisdiction [7B–67]
prorogation [7B–69]—[7B–69/1]
special jurisdiction [7B–49]
U.K., within
generally [7A–3]
special jurisdiction [7B–139]

Amendment
Admiralty directions [6B–7]
limitation period, after expiry of
time limits [14–42/5]—[14–42/6]
time limits
limitation period, after expiry of
[14–42/5]—[14–42/6]
parties, of
application 15/6/17
generally 15/6/16
terms 15/6/18
statement of claim
timetable for
RSC [3D–1]
time limits
limitation period, after expiry of
[14–42/6]
timetable for
RSC [3D–1]

***American Cyanamid* principles**
generally 29/L/2

Antecedent negotiations [9A–62/2]

Anti-social behaviour
injunctions
generally [8Q–66], [8Q–70]
power of arrest [8Q–85], [8Q–88]
power of arrest
remand [8Q–88]
remand
generally [8Q–85]
medical examination and report
[8Q–88]

***Anton Piller* order**
Admiralty direction [6B–7]
forms [2C–66]
forms
standard terms [2C–66]
QBD direction
form [2C–66]
QBD directions [2C–66]

Appeal Committee
House of Lords civil appeal
objections [19A–22]
preliminary steps [19A–21]
House of Lords criminal appeal
objections [19B–16]—[19B–16/1]

Appeals
arbitration
enforcement, against [21D–145]
committal for contempt of court
generally 52/1/41
Crown Court, from
statutory basis [20A–198]—[20A–199]
High Court, to
QBD, in 94/15/4
House of Lords
civil cases
practice directions [19A–43],
[19A–76]—[19A–76/1],
[19A–99]—[19A–99/A]
criminal cases
practice directions [19B–4]—
[19B–4/1], [19B–16]—
[19B–16/1], [19B–20]—
[19B–20/1], [19B–31],
[19B–32/1], [19B–39]—
[19B–40/1], [19B–43]—
[19B–45/1], [19B–49]—
[19B–51/1], [19B–56]
generally [19A–1]
receiver, court appointed 30/1/12
revenue proceedings
VAT Tribunals, from 91/6—91/6/1
statute, under
QBD, in 94/15/4
timetable for
RSC [3D–1]

Appeals to High Court
application
service 55/4/2
court's powers
other 55/7/3

Appeals to High Court—*cont.*
hearing
court's powers 55/7/3
notice of motion
service 55/4/2
procedure
service 55/4/2

Appendix
House of Lords civil appeal
time limits [19A–53]—[19A–53/1]

Applications
administration actions
costs from estate in any event 85/2/3
appeals to High Court
service 55/4/2
Banking Act 1987, under 93/23—93/23/1
Court of Appeal, to
leave to appeal 59/14/18, 59/14/18A, 59/14/21, 59/14/24, 59/14/25, 59/14/26, 59/14/26A—59/14/26C, 59/14/31, 59/14/35—59/14/35L
procedure 59/14/10
Court of Protection Rules
short order [10C–10]—[10C–10/1]
habeas corpus, writ of
generally 54/1/3
interim payments
affidavit 29/10/6—29/10/8
quash governmental decisions, etc., to
notice of motion 94/2/2
statute, under
QBD, in 94/15/4
summary judgment
relevant actions 14/1/2
Supreme Court Act 1981, under 94/15/4
wasted costs order
procedure 62/11/14

Arbitration
Admiralty directions [6B–7]
allocation of business
post-31.1.97 [21D–259]—[21D–260]
costs
references 62/B/12
proceedings
generally [21D–34], [21D–38]
timetable for
RSC [3D–1]

Arbitration (post-31.1.97)
agreements
consumer [21D–213/1]
generally [21D–15]
allocation of business [21D–259]—[21D–260]
arbitrators
generally [21D–41]
award
challenges to [21D–157]
generally [21D–127/1]
consumer agreements
generally [21D–213/1]
enforcement of award
generally [21D–145], [21B–23]
New York Convention [21D–243]
extension of time
proceedings [21D–34]

Arbitration (post-31.1.97)—*cont.*
New York Convention
generally [21D–243]
peremptory orders [21D–93]
proceedings
court powers [21D–101/1]
generally [21D–34], [21D–38]
stay of proceedings
application [21D–24]
burden of proof [21D–25]
generally [21D–20], [21D–23]
proceedings
generally [21D–38]

Arbitration (pre-1.2.97)
agreements
generally [21A–8]
award
enforcement [21A–248], [21A–254], [21B–23]
remission [21A–206]
enforcement of award
generally [21A–248], [21A–254]
New York Convention [21B–23]
New York Convention
generally [21B–23]
remission of award
generally [21A–206]
stay of proceedings
procedure [21A–41], [21A–85]
refusal [21A–85]

Arbitration Act 1950
agreements
generally [21A–8]
award
remission [21A–206]
enforcement [21A–248], [21A–254]
enforcement of award
generally [21A–248], [21A–254]
generally [21A–8], [21A–41], [21A–85], [21A–206], [21A–248], [21A–254]
stay of proceedings [21A–41], [21A–85]

Arbitration Act 1975
enforcement of award [21B–23]

Arbitration Act 1996
agreements
consumer [21D–213/1]
generally [21D–15]
arbitrators
generally [21D–41], [21D–59]
award
challenges to [21D–157]
generally [21D–127/1]
consequential amendments [21D–258/1]
enforcement
generally [21D–145]
New York Convention [21D–243]
generally [21D–15], [21D–20], [21D–23]—[21D–25], [21D–34], [21D–41], [21D–93], [21D–101/1], [21D–127/1], [21D–145], [21D–243], [21D–258/1]
proceedings
actions
generally [21D–41]
court powers [21D–101/1]
generally [21D–34]
generally [21D–38]

Arbitration Act 1996—*cont.*
- schedules [21D–258/1]
- stay of proceedings
  - generally [21D–20], [21D–23]—[21D–25]
- tribunal
  - powers [21D–93]

Arbitration agreements (post-31.1.97)
- consumer agreements
  - unfair terms [21D–213/1]
- definition [21D–15]

Arbitration agreements (pre-1.2.97)
- illegality [21A–8]

Arbitration appeals
- enforcement, against [21D–145]

Arbitration award
- enforcement
  - generally 73/31, 73/31/3
- post-31.1.97
  - enforcement [21D–145]
  - generally [21D–127/1]
- pre-1.2.97
  - enforcement [21A–248], [21A–254], [21B–23]
  - remission [21A–206]

Arbitration award (post-31.1.97)
- challenging
  - serious irregularity [21D–157]
- enforcement
  - appeals [21D–145]
  - peremptory orders [21D–93]
  - New York Convention [21D–243]
- form [21D–127/1]

Arbitration award (pre-1.2.97)
- enforcement
  - generally [21A–248], [21A–254]
  - New York Convention [21B–23]
- remission
  - generally [21A–206]

Arbitration proceedings
- commencement [21D–38]
- costs
  - references 62/B/12
- court powers [21D–101/1]
- extension of time [21D–34]
- interlocutory applications [21D–99]—[21D–101/1]
- timetable for
  - RSC [3D–1]

Arbitration tribunal
- membership [21D–41]
- powers
  - ancillary powers [21D–101/1]

Arbitration proceedings
- commencement [21D–38]
- costs
  - references 62/B/12
- court powers [21D–101/1]
- extension of time [21D–34]
- interlocutory applications [21D–99]—[21D–101/1]

Arbitration tribunal
- powers
  - ancillary powers [21D–101/1]

Arbitrators (post-31.1.97)
- appointment
  - generally [21D–41], [21D–59]
- removal [21D–59]

Arrest
- admiralty proceedings, in
  - generally 75/5/10
- power of
  - timetable for
    - RSC [3D–1]
- warrant of
  - generally 75/5/10

Assessment of costs
- interpleader proceedings 62/13/5
- patent actions 104/0/32
- QBD direction [2C–259]

Assessment of damages
- admiralty proceedings
  - disruption of business 75/42/8

Assessors
- generally 33/6—33/6/2

Assignment
- secure tenancy
  - exchange, by [8L–80]—[8L–81], [8L–85]
  - general prohibition [8L–76/1]

Assignment of business
- Chancery direction [2B–123]
- county court
  - arbitration [21D–259]—[21D–260]
- county court
  - commencement [20B–247]
  - enforcement
    - generally [20B–252]
  - trial [20B–249]
  - value of actions [20B–261]
- statute, under
  - QBD, in 94/15/4

Assistance at sea
- distress [6D–204]—[6D–205]

Assisted party, costs against
- determination
  - generally [16D–244]—[16D–244/1]
- liability
  - determination [16D–244]—[16D–244/1], [16D–246]
  - generally [16D–241]
- order for
  - variation [16D–251]

Assisted party, costs of
- pre-certificate costs [16D–192]
- taxation
  - basis [16D–208]
  - objections
    - generally [16D–221]
  - recovery [16D–210]—[16D–211]

Assured shorthold tenancy
county court C49/6A
generally [8O–137]
possession [8O–147]

Assured tenancy
county court C49/6
exempt tenancy
Crown let [8O–201]—[8O–201/1]
local authority let [8O–202]
resident landlord [8O–217]—[8O–217/1]
student lets [8O–215]
grounds for possession
Ground 4 [8O–243]
Ground 14 [8O–253]
meaning
generally [8O–8]
sharing accommodation [8O–19]
notice of possession [8O–243], [8O–253]
notice of proceedings
dispensation [8O–60]
periodic tenancy
succession [8O–118]
possession
court's discretion [8O–72]—[8O–72/1]
notice of proceedings [8O–243], [8O–253]
order for [8O–49]—[8O–49/1]
rent increase
determination of
generally [8O–99]
generally [8O–93]—[8O–93/1]
security of tenure
possession [8O–49]—[8O–49/1]
succession [8O–118]

Asylum-seekers
homelessness
eligibility for assistance [8Q–141]

Attachment of earnings
relevant earnings
meaning [21E–42]—[21E–43]

Attachment of Earnings Act 1971
definitions [21E–42]—[21E–43]

Attorney, powers of
rules [10G–38]—[10G–39]

Audience, rights of
chambers, proceedings in
generally 32/6/31
Crown Court [20A–465/14]—[20A–465/15]
generally [15G–107]
litigants in person [21R–5]
patent actions 104/0/26
QBD direction 104/0/26
taxation of costs 62/A2/38

Authorities
list of
House of Lords civil appeal [19A–65]—[19A–66/1]
House of Lords criminal appeal [19B–49]—[19B–50/1]

Automatic directions
timetable for
RSC [3D–1]

Automatic discovery
relevant issues 24/2/11

Award
timetable for
RSC [3D–1]

Bail
Crown Court
generally [20A–465/11]—[20A–465/12]

Banking Act 1987 92/3A—92/3A/1, 93/23—93/23/1

Banking Act 1987
applications 93/23—93/23/1
payment into court
generally 92/3A—92/3A/1

Bankrupt
costs
generally 62/B/120

Bankruptcy
fieri facias, writ of
stay of execution 47/1/10—47/1/11

Bill of costs
amendment 62/A2/37
costs of preparation 62/A2/37
enforcement
generally [15A–58/54]
form of [15A–58/40]
House of Lords criminal appeal [19B–56]
taxation
client, application by
expiry of 12 months [15A–58/71]
generally [15A–58/71], [15A–58/74]
solicitor, application by
expiry of 12 months [15A–58/71]
generally [15A–58/71], [15A–58/74]

Blood tests
procedure
list of testers 112/6/10

Bound volumes
House of Lords civil appeal
generally [19A–63]—[19A–63/1]
House of Lords criminal appeal
generally [19B–45]—[19B–45/1]

Brief fees
written submissions 62/A2/15/1

Brussels Convention 1968
generally [7A–1], [7B–42]
implementation [7A–3]—[7A–4]
jurisdiction
exclusive jurisdiction [7B–67]
prorogation [7B–69]—[7B–69/1]
special jurisdiction [7B–49]
modified version of
generally [7A–3]

Bundles
Court of Appeal, appeals to
copy for respondent 59/9/13
Practice Directions 59/9/71—59/9/75
skeleton arguments 59/9/2A
transcripts 59/9/13
Court of Appeal, applications to
single Lord Justice, before 59/14/10
skeleton arguments 59/9/2A
transcripts
copy for respondent 59/9/13

Cargo
discharge of
Admiralty directions [6B–9]
insurance [6D–262]
limitation period [6D–252], [6D–258]

Case stated, appeals by
Crown Court, from
generally 56/1/2
jurisdiction [20A–198]—[20A–199]
procedure 56/1/9
procedure
generally 56/1/9
magistrates' court, from
generally 56/5/3
jurisdiction [20A–201]—[20A–202]
statutory basis
Crown Court [20A–198]—[20A–199]
magistrates' court [20A–201]—
[20A–202]

Causes of action
abatement of 15/7/3
county court C5/1
county court
joinder C5/1/1
joinder
county court C5/1/1
separate trials
generally 15/5/1

Caveats
generally 76/1/2, [11B–90]

Certificate of deduction of benefits
payment into court 22/1/18, 22/5/2

Certificate for counsel
three counsel 62/A2/13

Certiorari
jurisdiction [20A–203]—[20A–204]
timetable for
RSC [3D–1]

Chambers, proceedings in
adjournment to court
Family Division 32/13/23
QBD 32/13/23
audience, rights of 32/6/31
Family Division
adjournment to court 32/13/23
hearing
audience, rights of 32/6/31
QBD
adjournment to court 32/13/23

Chambers, proceedings in—*cont.*
QBD direction
Anton Piller order [2C–66]
interlocutory injunctions [2C–148]
Mareva injunctions [2C–81], [2C–96]
QBD directions [2C–66], [2C–81],
[2C–96], [2C–148]

Chancery directions
assignment of business [2B–123]
distribution of business [2B–123]
generally [2B–1]—[2B–179]

Chancery Division
Guide [2B–201]—[2B–332]
practice directions [2B–1]—[2B–179]

Chancery Guide
generally [2B–201]—[2B–332]

Change of parties
death, on
generally 15/7/3

Charging orders
statutory basis
supplementary provision [21F–7]—
[21F–7/1]
timetable for
RSC [3D–1]

Charging Orders Act 1979
charging orders [21F–7]—[21F–7/1]

Circuit
administration
generally [18B–1]—[18B–1/1]

Citations
generally [11B–95]

Civil Evidence Act 1968
convictions [21G–31]—[21G–31/1]

Civil Jurisdiction and Judgments Act 1982
Brussels Convention
generally [7B-42]
generally [7A–3]
jurisdiction
Brussels Convention [7B–42], [7B–49],
[7B–67], [7B–69]—[7B–69/1]
schedules
Brussels Convention [7B-42], [7B-49],
[7B-67], [7B-69]—[7B-69/1]

Civil legal aid
certificates
scope [16D–91]
effect
generally [16A–86]
selection of representatives [16A–93]
general regulations
generally [16D–45], [16D–46],
[16D–91], [16D–129]—
[16D–129/1], [16D–132]—
[16D–132/1], [16D–140]—
[16D–140/1], [16D–164]—
[16D–164/1], [16D–169]—
[16D–169/1], [16D–192],
[16D–208], [16D–210], [16D–211],
[16D–221], [16D–241],
[16D–244]—[16D–244/1]

Civil legal aid—*cont.*
House of Lords civil appeal
generally [19A–76]—[19A–76/1]
regulations
general [16D–45], [16D–46], [16D–91], [16D–129]—[16D–129/1], [16D–132]—[16D–132/1], [16D–140]—[16D–140/1], [16D–164]—[16D–164/1], [16D–169]—[16D–169/1], [16D–192], [16D–208], [16D–210], [16D–211], [16D–221], [16D–241], [16D–244]—[16D–244/1]
remuneration
generally [16F–1]—[16F–2], [16F–4]—[16F–5]
statutory basis
generally [16A–72], [16A–75]
successful unassisted party's costs [16A–72], [16A–75]

Civil Liability (Contribution) Act 1978
general provisions [21J–4]—[21J–4/1]

Civil Procedure Act 1997
introductory note [20A–2]
pre-action discovery [20A–8/2]

Close of pleadings
timetable for
RSC [3D–1]

Commercial actions
setting down 72/2/5

Commercial Court forms
timetable for heavy summons 72/A49

Commercial Court Guide
inter partes applications 72/A9

Committal for contempt of court
appeal
generally 52/1/41
criminal
prejudice due course of justice, acts calculated to 52/1/23
Divisional Court, order by
generally 52/1/34
order
Divisional Court, by 52/1/34
types
criminal 52/1/23

Committal for failure to do or abstain from act
penal notice, indorsement of 45/7/7
requirements
penal notice 45/7/7
service of order
dispensing with 45/7/8

Common investment schemes
generally [5D–2]

Communications in contemplation of litigation
medical advisers 24/5/22

Community judgment
generally 71/15/1

Companies Act 1985
court powers
declaring dissolution void [21K–39]

Company
court powers
declaring dissolution void [21K–39]
dissolution void [21K–39]
party as
directors [17B–19]
security for costs
plaintiff 23/3/21

Composition of court
Court of Appeal
civil division
generally [20A–406]—[20A–408]

Conditional fee agreements
legal representatives 62/15A/3
maximum increase
1995 Order [15E–3]
1998 Order [15E–4]
relevant actions
1995 Order [15E–2]
1998 Order [15E–3]
taxation of costs [15F–9]

Conditional Fee Agreements Order 1998 [15E–1]—[15E–4]

Conditional Fee Agreements Regulations 1995 [15F–9]

Conditional Fee Agreements Regulations 1995
general provisions [15F–9]

Conflict of interest
solicitors [15G–109]

Conflict of jurisdiction
service out of the jurisdiction 11/1/70

Consent orders
patent actions 104/0/23
Tomlin [17A–32]

Constitution of courts
High Court [20A–139]—[20A–140]

Consumer credit
antecedent negotiations [9A–62/2]
credit
definition [9A–45/1]
fixed-sum [9A–46/1]
restricted-use [9A–47/1]
running-account [9A–46/1]
unrestricted-use [9A–47/1]
debtor-creditor-supplier agreement [9A–48/1]
default notice
contents [9A–99/1]
effect [9A–99/1]

Consumer credit—*cont.*
entry into agreement
antecedent negotiations [9A–62/2]
exempt agreement [9A–53]—[9A–54/1]
extortionate credit bargains
relevant agreements [9A–159/3]
reopening [9A–161/1]
fixed-sum agreement
generally [9A–46/1]
judicial control
extortionate credit bargains [9A–161/1]
multiple agreement [9A–57/1]
restricted-use agreement [9A–47/1]
running-account agreement
generally [9A–46/1]
time orders
generally [8F–6]
unrestricted-use agreement [9A–47/1]
types of agreement [9A–45/1], [9A–46/1], [9A–47/1], [9A–48/1], [9A–53], [9A–54]—[9A–54/1], [9A–57/1]

Consumer Credit Act 1974
generally [9A–45/1], [9A–46/1], [9A–47/1],[9A–48/1], [9A–53], [9A–54], [9A–57/1], [9A–62/2], [9A–159/3], [9A–161/1]
entry into agreements [9A–62/2]
housing [8F–6]
judicial control [9A–159/3], [9A–161/1]
introductory note
generally [92–42/1]
goods [92–42/3]
land [92–42/2]
money claims [92–42/4]
types of agreement [9A–45/1], [9A–46/1], [9A–47/1], [9A–48/1], [9A–53], [9A–54], [9A–57/1]

Contempt of court
committal for
generally 52/1/23, 52/1/37, 52/1/41

Contentious business agreements
effect of [15A–58/28/1]
generally [15A–58/23/1]

Contentious business remuneration
agreements
effect [15A–58/28/1]
generally [15A–58/23/1]

Contribution
generally [21J–4]—[21J–4/1]
jointly liable parties
successive actions [21J–4]—[21J–4/1]

Contumelious default 25/L/3

Convention judgment
statutory basis
Civil Jurisdiction and Judgments Act 1982 [7B–37]—[7B–38]
generally [7A–1]—[7A–4]

Costs
amount
discretionary sums 62/A2/5, 62/A2/27A, 62/A2/28, 62/2A/37, 62/A2/38
arbitration proceedings
references 62/B/12
assessment of
interpleader proceedings 62/13/5
QBD direction [2C–259]
assisted party, against
generally [16D–244]—[16D–244/1], [16D–246], [16D–251]
assisted party, of
generally [16D–208], [16D–210]—[16D–211], [16D–221]
bankrupt
generally 62/B/120
bill of costs, of 62/A2/37
chargeable items
hourly rate 62/A2/28
indemnity principle 62/A2/27A
taxation 62/A2/37, 62/A2/38
conditional fee agreements
generally 62/15A/3
statutory basis [15E–1]—[15E–4]
counsel's fees
brief fee 62/A2/15/1
matrimonial proceedings 62/A2/19
three counsel 62/A2/13
vouchers 62/A2/5
counterclaims 62/B/128
Court of Protection Rules
RSC Order 62 [10C–90]—[10C–90/1]
deemed order for
payment into court, acceptance of 62/5/7
discontinuance
costs in cause 62/5/4
discretion
generally 62/2/7
judicial review 62/3/6
legal representatives 62/2/9
written offers 62/9/4
discretionary sums
chargeable items 62/A2/37, 62/A2/38
entitlement to
considerations for discretion 62/9/4
deemed order for costs 62/5/7
exceptions to general rule 62/6/6
general principles 62/3/1, 62/3/3
misconduct 62/10/6—62/10/7
wasted costs order 62/11/2, 62/11/5, 62/11/6, 62/11/14, 62/11/20, 62/11/21, 62/11/25, 62/11/29 , 62/11/31
exceptions to general rule
mortgagees 62/6/6
follow the event, to
exceptions to rule 62/6/6
generally 62/3/3
judicial review 62/3/6
general principles
follow the event, costs to 62/3/3, 62/3/6
generally 62/3/1, 62/3/3
gross sum 62/7/14

Costs—*cont.*
group actions
generally 62/B/83
guarantor of action 62/10/7
House of Lords
civil appeal
appeal [19A–67]—[19A–67/1]
criminal appeal
appeal [19B–51]—[19B–51/1]
petition for leave [19B–20]—[19B–20/1]
interest on 62/35/12
judicial review
principles 62/3/6
Lands Tribunal 62/B/47
legal representatives
wasted costs order 62/2/9
liquidator
generally 62/B/132
litigants in person
generally 62/18/2
Official Receiver 62/18/2/1
Local Government Act 1972, under 62/B/55
maintainer of action 62/10/7
misconduct in proceedings
taxation 62/28/4
unreasonableness 62/10/6
mortgagees
heads 62/6/6
pre-emptive orders 62/B/151
pre-emptive orders
generally 62/B/151
neglect in proceedings
taxation 62/28/4
next friend
solicitor and own-client basis 62/16/4
Ombudsman 62/B/132/1
neglect in proceedings
unreasonableness 62/10/6
patent actions
assessment of 104/0/32
payment into court, acceptance of 62/5/7
payment into court, acceptance of
generally 62/5/7
payment into court
generally 62/9/4
personal representatives
pre-emptive orders 62/B/151
pre-emptive orders
generally 62/B/151
persons under mental disorder
fixed [10A–176]
post-judgment 62/B/137
practice directions 62/C/17, 62/C/35D
preparation
bill of costs, of 62/A2/37
hourly rate 62/A2/28
indemnity principle 62/A2/27A
principles
discretion 62/2/7
general 62/3/1
QBD direction [2C–259]
recovery of
generally [16D–155], [16D–164]—[16D–164/1]
references
arbitration proceedings 62/B/12
review of taxation of
generally 62/35/12

Costs—*cont.*
Rules of the Supreme Court
related sources 62/0/3
solicitor and own-client
conditional fee agreements 62/15A/3
generally 62/15/2/1
next friend 62/16/46/4
special circumstances
gross sum costs 62/7/14
statutory basis
generally [20A–403]
summary judgment
scale 14/7/8
taxation of
generally 62/12/1, 62/18/2
procedure 62/29/6, 62/29/8
review 62/35/12
taxing officers' powers 62/20/2, 62/28/4
third party proceedings
indemnity 62/B/150
trustees
pre-emptive orders 62/B/151
pre-emptive orders
generally 62/B/151
wasted costs order
application 62/11/14
examples 62/11/31
generally 62/2/9, 62/11/2, 62/11/20
grounds 62/11/5, 62/11/6
inherent jurisdiction 62/11/21, 62/11/25
SCTO direction 62/C/6
witness expenses 62/B/155
written offer
form of 62/9/9
payment into court 62/9/4

Costs in cause
discontinuance 62/5/4

Counsel
wasted costs order
relationship with solicitors 62/11/20

Counsel's fees
brief fee
written submissions 62/A2/15/1
certificate for counsel
three counsel 62/A2/13
matrimonial proceedings 62/A2/19
three counsel 62/A2/13
vouchers 62/A2/5

Counterclaim
amendment of
timetable for
RSC [3D–1]
costs 62/B/128
payment into court
taking into account 22/2—22/2/2
service of
timetable for
RSC [3D–1]

County court
allocation of business
commencement [20B–247]
enforcement
generally [20B–252]
trial [20B–249]
value of actions [20B–261]

County Court—*cont.*
constitution
generally [20A–650]—[20A–650/1]
Directory
list [18D–1]
district judges
generally [20A–655/1]—[20A–655/2]
forfeiture for non-payment of rent
procedure [20A–814/4]
Funds Office
lodgment [5C–48]—[5C–48/1]
judicial officers
district judges [20A–655/1]—[20A–655/2]
procedure
generally [20A–748]—[20A–748/1], [20A–749/1]
RSC, application of
generally [20A–749/1]
service [20A–808]—[20A–808/2]
sittings
place
generally [20A–652]—[20A–652/1]
time [20A–652]—[20A–652/1]
summons
sealing [20A–809]—[20A–809/1]
service [20A–808]—[20A–808/2]

County court forms
attachments to summonses [1C–3]
enforcement [1C–6]
housing [1C–10]
list [1C–1]

County court judgment
enforcement
Q.B. Masters' direction [2A–100]

County court jurisdiction
admiralty [6D–301]
admiralty
generally [6D–301]
exercise of
remedies [20A–700]
remedies [20A–700]

County court procedure
discovery
personal injury actions [20A–726]—[20A–726/1]
discovery
pre-action [20A–725]—[20A–725/1]
judgment
set-off [20A–745/2]
jury trial
generally [20A–739/2]—[20A–739/3]
mode of trial
arbitration, reference to [20A–737/2]
assessors [20A–736]—[20A–736/2]
generally [20A–735/1]
referee, to [20A–738/1]—[20A–738/2]
registrar, to [20A–738/1]—[20A–738/2]
order
set-off [20A–745/2]
parties
minors [20A–720]—[20A–720/2]
personal injury actions
discovery
generally [20A–726]—[20A–726/1]

County court procedure—*cont.*
pre-action discovery
generally [20A–725]—[20A–725/1]
rules
application of RSC [20A–749/1]
generally [20A–748]—[20A–748/1]

County Court Rules
statutory basis [20A–748]—[20A–748/1]

County Courts Act 1984
admiralty jurisdiction [6D–301]
constitution [20A–650]—[20A–650/1]
definitions
generally [20A–823]—[20A–823/1]
forfeiture for non-payment of rent [8K–3], [8K–4]—[8K–4/1], [20A–814/4]
judicial officers [20A–655/1]—[20A–655/2]
jurisdiction [20A–700]
procedure [20A–720]—[20A–720/2], [20A–725]—[20A–725/1], [20A–726]—[20A–726/1], [20A–735/1], [20A–736]—[20A–736/2], [20A–737/2], [20A–738/1]—[20A–738/2], [20A–739/2]—[20A–739/3], [20A–745/2], [20A–748]—[20A–748/1], [20A–749/1]
sittings [20A–652]—[20A–652/1]
summonses [20A–808]—[20A–809/1]

Court dress
QBD direction [2C–207]—[2C–208/1]

Court Funds Office
investment [5D–2]
rules [5C–2]—[5C–2/1], [5C–5]—[5C–6], [5C–18]—[5C–19], [5C–26]—[5C–27], [5C–33]—[5C–34], [5C–37], [5C–41]—[5C–42], [5C–46]—[5C–46/1], [5C–48]—[5C–48/1], [5C–49]—[5C–50], [5C–53]—[5C–55/1], [5C–58]—[5C–60/1], [5C–66], [5C–71], [5C–73], [5C–82], [5C–84/1], [5C–85]—[5C–85/1], [5C–92]—[5C–92/1]
statutory provisions [5B–1]

Court Funds Rules 1987
appropriation [5C–49]—[5C–50]
arrangement of rules [5C–2]—[5C–2/1]
authorities [5C–18]—[5C–19]
definitions [5C–5]—[5C–6]
deposit [5C–53]—[5C–55/1], [5C–58]—[5C–60/1]
foreign currency dealing [5C–71], [5C–73]
forms [5C–115]—[5C–139]
investment [5C–53]—[5C–55/1], [5C–58]—[5C–60/1], [5C–66]
lodgment [5C–26]—[5C–27], [5C–33]—[5C–34], [5C–37], [5C–41]—[5C–42], [5C–46]—[5C–46/1], [5C–48]—[5C–48/1]
payment out [5C–82], [5C–84/1], [5C–85]—[5C–85/1], [5C–92]—[5C–92/1]

Court of Appeal
appeals to
leave
exempt categories 59/1B/5—59/1B/8
generally 59/1/91, 59/1B—59/1B/4
person to grant 59/1B/9
applications to
leave to appeal
generally 59/14/18, 59/14/18A, 59/14/21, 59/14/24, 59/14/25, 59/14/26, 59/14/26A—59/14/26C

Court of Appeal, applications to
leave for appeal
procedure 59/14/31, 59/14/35—59/14/35L

Court of Appeal
applications to
procedure 59/14/10
composition
civil division
generally [20A–406]—[20A–408]
incidental actions [20A–422]—[20A–422/2]
jurisdiction
civil courts, appeals from [20A–172]—[20A–172/1]
restrictions on [20A–177]—[20A–178]
practice
incidental actions [20A–422]—[20A–422/2]

Court of Appeal, appeals to
bundles
copy for respondent 59/9/13
skeleton arguments 59/9/2A
transcripts 59/9/13
documents
bundles 59/9/13
skeleton arguments 59/9/24, 59/9/28—59/9/32
final orders
definition 59/1A/2
interlocutory orders
definition 59/1A/2
Practice Directions
appeals 59/9/50
applications 59/9/40
skeleton arguments 59/9/71—59/9/75
procedure
document lodgment 59/9/71—59/9/75
Practice Directions 59/9/40, 59/9/71—59/9/75
restrictions
leave required 59/1/91, 59/1/137—59/1/139
skeleton arguments
bundles 59/9/2A
generally 59/9/24
Practice Direction 59/9/50
time limits 59/9/28—59/9/32
transcripts
copy for respondent 59/9/13

Court of Appeal, applications to
bundles
single Lord Justice, before 59/14/10
leave for appeal
grounds 59/14/18—59/14/18A
procedure 59/14/21, 59/14/24—59/14/26C
Practice Direction
renewed 59/9/40
procedure
single Lord Justice, before 59/14/10
single Lord Justice, before
bundles 59/14/10

Court of Appeal direction
appeals
skeleton arguments 59/9/50
application for leave
renewed 59/9/40
skeleton arguments
case management 59/9/69
leave to appeal 59/9/71—59/9/75
time limits 59/9/50

Court of Protection
attorney, powers of
rules [10G–38]—[10G–39]
fees
administration [10C–81]—[10C–81/1]
commencement [10C–80]—[10C–80/1]
generally [10C–101]—[10C–104]
taxation [10C–83]—[10C–83/1]
rules
applications [10C–10]—[10C–10/1]
fees [10C–101]—[10C–104]
service [10C–22]—[10C–22/1]
statutory basis
supplementary provisions [10B–34]—[10B–34/1]

Court of Protection Rules
applications
short order [10C–10]—[10C–10/1]
costs
RSC Order 62 [10C–90]—[10C–90/1]
fees
administration [10C–81]—[10C–81/1]
commencement [10C–80]—[10C–80/1]
generally [10C–101]—[10C–104]
taxation [10C–83]—[10C–83/1]
service
generally [10C–22]—[10C–22/1]

Credit
definition [9A–45/1]
fixed-sum [9A–46/1]
restricted-use [9A–47/1]
running-account [9A–46/1]
unrestricted-use [9A–47/1]

Crown Court
bail [20A–465/11]—[20A–465/12]
appeals from
jurisdiction [20A–198]—[20A–199], [20A–201]—[20A–202]
audience, rights of [20A–465/14]—[20A–465/15]

Crown Court—*cont.*
case stated from, appeals by
generally 56/1/2
jurisdiction [20A–198]—[20A–199]
procedure 56/1/9
procedure
generally 56/1/9
jurisdiction
sentencing [20A–263/5]—[20A–263/6]
appeals from [20A–198]—[20A–199]

Crown Proceedings Act 1947
definitions
generally [21L–94]—[21L–94/1]
savings [21L–97]—[21L–97/1]

Damages
protection from eviction
generally [8O–162]
measure [8O–168]
repairing obligation [8M–13]

Date of knowledge
generally [14–17/6], [14–17/8]
personal injury [14–17/3]

Death
change of parties on
generally 15/7/3

Debt actions
interest
pleading 6/L/2

Debtor-creditor-supplier agreement
[9A–48/1]

Declaratory relief
jurisdiction [20A–203]—[20A–204]
timetable for
RSC [3D–1]

Default
notice
contents [9A–99/1]
effect [9A–99/1]
security for costs, in giving 23/3/40

Default judgment
foreign state, against
application 13/7A/3
procedure
proof of service 13/7/3
setting aside
discretion 13/9/18
irregular, where
application 13/9/9

Defence
service
timetable for
RSC [3D–1]

Delay
court, caused by 25/L/23
dismissal for want of prosecution
prejudicial 25/L/7

Deposition evidence
timetable for
RSC [3D–1]

Directions
summary judgment
trial by Master 14/6/5

Director
party, as [17B–19]

Discontinuance
costs
cause, in 62/5/4
timetable for
RSC [3D–1]

Discovery
Admiralty directions [6B–7]
automatic
relevant issues 24/2/11
county court
personal injury actions [20A–726]—[20A–726/1]
pre-action [20A–725]—[20A–725/1]
statutory basis [20A–725]—[20A–725/1], [20A–726]—[20A–726/1]
mutual
relevant issues 24/2/11
non-party
relevant actions 24/7A/3
statutory basis [20A–219]—[20A–220]
obligation of
continuing 24/2/17
pre-action
county court [20A–725]—[20A–725/1]
relevant actions 24/7A/3
statutory basis [20A–215]—[20A–216]
relevant issues 24/2/11
statutory basis
personal injury actions [20A–219]—[20A–220]
timetable for
RSC [3D–1]
without order
relevant issues 24/2/11

Discretion
costs
generally 62/2/7
judicial review 62/3/2A, 62/3/6
legal representatives 62/2/9
written offers 62/9/4

Dismissal for want of prosecution
contumelious default 25/L/3
delay
prejudicial 25/L/7
grounds
contumelious default 25/L/3
inordinate and inexcusable delay 25/L/7

Distribution of business
Chancery direction [2B–123]
county court
arbitration [21D–259]—[21D–260]
county court
commencement [20B–247]
enforcement
generally [20B–252]
trial [20B–249]
value of actions [20B–261]

District judges
county court
generally [20A–655/1]—[20A–655/2]
taxation of costs
supplementary powers 62/20/2

District registries
list of [18C–2]

***Distringas*, writ of**
timetable for
RSC [3D–1]

Divisional Court
committal for contempt of court
generally 52/1/34

Divisions of court
High Court [20A–142]—[20A–143]

Documents
Admiralty directions [6B–7]
Court of Appeal, appeals to
bundles 59/9/13
skeleton arguments 59/9/24, 59/9/28—59/9/32
discovery
without order 24/2—24/2/17
patent actions
generally 104/0/13
referred to in pleadings 104/0/20
production
objection to 24/13/3
skeleton arguments
Court of Appeal, appeals to 59/9/24, 59/9/28—59/9/32
use of
generally 24/14A/2—24/14A/3
uncertainty as to 24/14A/2

Domicile
European jurisdiction
Crown [7B–37]—[7B–38]

Duration of originating process
admiralty proceedings 75/4/3
writ of summons
extension of 6/8/6

E.C. Treaty judgment
generally 71/15/1

ECSC judgment, enforcement of 71/15/1

EFTA state judgment
Lugano Convention [7A–5]—[7A–6]

Enduring powers of attorney
fees
rules [10G–38]—[10G–39]
rules
fees [10G–38]—[10G–39]

Enduring Powers of Attorney Act 1985
rules [10G–38]—[10G–39]
supplementary provisions [10F–38]—[10F–39]

Enduring Powers of Attorney Rules 1994
fees [10G–38]—[10G–39]
schedules
fees [10G–38]—[10G–39]

Enforcement
arbitration (post-31.1.97)
appeals [21D–145]
New York Convention [21D–243]
peremptory orders [21D–93]
arbitration (pre-1.2.97)
generally [21A–248], [21A–254]
New York Convention [21B–23]
arbitration award
affidavit in support 73/31/2
generally 73/31, 73/31/3
bill of costs
generally [15A–58/54]
county court C25/5A/2
county court
interest C25/5A/2
County Court Rules
related sources C25/0/3
county court
forms [1C–6]
county court judgment, of
Q.B. Masters' direction [2A–100]
foreign judgment, of
domicile [7B–37]—[7B–38]
generally [7A–3]—[7A–4]
High Court, in
county court judgment, of [2A–100]
judgment
Q.B. Masters' direction [2A–100]
Q.B. Masters' direction
judgment [2A–100]
time limits
judgment [14–29/1]
timetable for
RSC [3D–1]
transfer of proceedings, and 78/2/2
vehicle emission penalties C48D/1—C48D/5

EURATOM inspection order
generally 71/15/1

European Convention on Human Rights
effective remedy, right to [21U–3]
introduction [21U–1]—[21U–2]
text [21T–26]—[21T–45]

European Court of Justice
judgment, enforcement of
generally 71/15/1

European Court references
QBD direction [2C–240A]
Rules of the Supreme Court
related sources 114/0/3

European jurisdiction
allocation of
E.C., within [7B–42], [7B–49], [7B–67], [7B–69]—[7B–69/1]
Brussels Convention
accession of UK [7A–2]
generally [7A–1]
implementation [7A–3]—[7A–4]
text [7B–42], [7B–49], [7B–67], [7B–69]—[7B–69/1]

European jurisdiction—*cont.*
domicile [7B–37]—[7B–38]
generally [7A–1]—[7A–6]
Lugano Convention 1988
generally [7A–5]
ratification [7A–5]
San Sebastian Convention 1989
generally [7A–4]
ratification [7A–5]

Evidence
adultery [21G–31]—[21G–31/1]
matrimonial proceedings [21G–31]—[21G–31/1]
mortgage actions
redemption figure 88/5/10
paternity [21G–31]—[21G–31/1]
patent actions
generally 104/0/21
timetable for
RSC [3D–1]

Evidence for foreign courts
principles 70/6/3

***Ex parte* applications**
Admiralty directions [6B–7]
patent actions 104/0/12

Exchange of witness statements
Admiralty directions [6B–7]

Examiner
appointment of
timetable for
RSC [3D–1]

Exchange of witness statements
timetable for
RSC [3D–1]

Execution
timetable for
RSC [3D–1]

Exempt agreement [9A–53]—[9A–54/1]

Experiments
patent actions
generally 104/0/30
undisclosed 104/0/31

Extension of time
arbitration
proceedings [21D–34]
consumer credit
generally [8F–6]

Extortionate credit bargains
interest rates [9A–159/3]
reopening
statutory basis [9A–161/1]

Family Division
chambers, proceedings in
adjournment to court 32/13/23

Fatal accidents
time limits
discretionary exclusion [14–40/4]

Fees
Court of Appeal, applications to leave to appeal 59/14/21
Court of Protection
administration [10C–81]—[10C–81/1]
commencement [10C–80]—[10C–80/1]
generally [10C–101]—[10C–104]
taxation [10C–83]—[10C–83/1]
enduring powers of attorney
rules [10G–38]—[10G–39]
House of Lords criminal appeal
appeal [19B–31]
powers of attorney
rules [10G–38]—[10G–39]
High Court
generally [4A–1]
leave to appeal to Court of Appeal 59/14/21
probate, non-contentious [4C–1]—[4C–9]

***Fieri facias*, writ of**
sheriff
duties and powers 45/1/10
stay of execution
bankruptcy 47/1/10—47/1/11
insolvency 47/1/10—47/1/11

Final orders
definition 59/1A/2

Fixed costs
person under mental disorder [10A–176]

Fixed penalties
vehicle emissions
enforcement C48D/1—C48D/5
generally C48D

Fixed-sum credit agreement
generally [9A–46/1]

Foreign courts, evidence for
principles 70/6/3

Foreign currency
judgment in
Admiralty directions [6B–14]
Court Funds Office [5C–71], [5C–73]

Foreign judgment, enforcement of
domicile [7B–37]—[7B–38]
generally [7A–3]—[7A–4]

Foreign firms
generally 81/1/21

Foreign state
default judgment against
application 13/7A/3

Forfeiture for non-payment of rent
county court
generally [8K–3], [8K–4]—[8K–4/1]
procedure [20A–814/4]

Forfeiture for non-payment of rent—*cont.*
relief against
county court [8K–3], [8K–4]—[8K–4/1]
service of summons
generally [20A–814/4]

Forms
admiralty proceedings
And see Admiralty forms
list of [6A–1A]
precedents [6A–3]—[6A–28]
county court [1C–1], [1C–3], [1C–6], [1C–10]
prescribed
list [1A–1A]
probate [11B–127]—[11B–133]

Fraud
pleading
particulars 18/12/18

Funds in court
lodgment of
Banking Act 1987, s.26, under 92/3A—92/3A/1

Funds Office
appropriation [5C–49]—[5C–50]
common investment schemes
generally [5D–2]
county court
lodgment [5C–48]—[5C–48/1]
deposit
satisfaction, money paid in [5C–58]—[5C–60/1]
foreign currency [5C–71], [5C–73]
interest bearing accounts
interest [5C–53]—[5C–54]
time of deposit [5C–55]—[5C–55/1]
investment
generally [5B–1]
satisfaction, money paid in [5C–58]—[5C–60/1]
time for [5C–66]
lodgment
court, in [5C–41]—[5C–42]
county court, in [5C–48]—[5C–48/1]
schedule, on receipt of [5C–26]—[5C–27], [5C–33]
securities, of [5C–46]]—[5C–46/1]
written request, on receipt of [5C–34], [5C–37]
management [5B–1]
payment out
without order
payee, to [5C–82], [5C–84/1]
payer, to [5C–85]—[5C–85/1]
payment schedules
certificate of Master [5C–18]—[5C–19]
rules
appropriation [5C–49]—[5C–50]
authorities [5C–18]—[5C–19]
foreign currencies [5C–71], [5C–73]
lodgment [5C–26]—[5C–27], [5C–33]—[5C–34], [5C–37], [5C–41]—[5C–42], [5C–46]—[5C–46/1], [5C–48]—[5C–48/1]
payment out [5C–92/1]

Funds Office—*cont.*
statutory basis
Administration of Justice Act 1982 [5B–1]

Garnishee proceedings
timetable for
RSC [3D–1]

Grant of representation
applications
index of [11B–113]
personal [11B–12]
service [11B–123]
solicitors, through [11B–9]
caveats
generally [11B–90]
citations
generally [11B–95]
forms [11B–127]—[11B–133]
joint administrators, to
equal priority [11B–54]
mental incapacity, persons subject to [11B–74]
minors, for
generally [11B–68]—[11B–74]
Practice Direction [11B–68]
persons of mental incapacity, to [11B–74]
records [11A–20]
renunciation
generally [11B–79]
rules
arrangement of [11B–1]
definitions [11B–4]
standing searches [11B–89]
wills
rectification [11B–109]

Gross sum costs 62/7/14

Grounds for possession
assured tenancy
notices of [8O–243], [8O–253]
protected tenancy
generally [8H–94]
reasonableness [8H–100]
secure tenancy
reasonable [8L–160]
reasonable and suitable alternative accommodation [8L–166]
suitable alternative accommodation [8L–164]—[8L–164/1]

Grounds for possession (assured tenancy)
Ground 4 [8O–243]
Ground 14 [8O–253]

Grounds for possession (protected tenancy)
Case 1 [8H–179]
Case 2 [8H–180]
discretionary [8H–179]—[8H–180]
effect [8H–94]
reasonableness [8H–100]
suitable alternative accommodation
determination [8H–173]

Grounds for possession (secure tenancy)
Ground 2 [8L–175]
Ground 5 [8L–177]
Ground 7 [8L–160]
Ground 10A [8L–164]—[8L–164/1]

Grounds for possession (secure tenancy)— *cont.*
Ground 12 [8L–166]
reasonable [8L–160], [8L–175], [8L–177]
reasonable and suitable alternative accommodation [8L–166]
suitable alternative accommodation [8L–164]—[8L–164/1]

Group actions
costs
generally 62/B/83

Guarantor of action
costs 62/10/7

Guardian *ad litem*
appointment
timetable for
RSC [3D–1]

***Habeas corpus*, writ of**
application
generally 54/1/3
generally 54/1/2
judicial review, distinction from 54/1/5

Hearings
appeals to High Court
court's powers 55/7/3
chambers, proceedings in
audience, rights of 32/6/31

Hearsay evidence
county court
generally C20/14/4
timetable for
RSC [3D–1]

High Court
allocation of business
commencement [20B–247]
enforcement
generally [20B–252]
trial [20B–249]
value of actions [20B–261]
constitution [20A–139] - [20A–140]
divisions [20A–142]—[20A–143]
interest
pleading 6/L/2

High Court and County Courts (Allocation of Arbitration proceedings) Order 1996
[21D–259]—[21D–260]

High Court and County Courts Jurisdiction Order 1991
allocation [20B–247], [20B–249]
enforcement [20B–252]
introductory note [20B–240]
savings [20B–265]
value of actions [20B–261]

High Court jurisdiction
certiorari [20A–203]—[20A–204]
Crown court appeals [20A–198]—[20A–199]
declaratory relief [20A–203]—[20A–204]
hypothetical cases [20A–191/1]
mandamus [20A–203]—[20A–204]
ouster of
generally [20A–185]
prohibition [20A–203]—[20A–204]

High Court powers
personal injury cases
general discovery [20A–219]—[20A–220]
pre-action discovery
generally [20A–215]—[20A–216]
variation of sentence [20A–259]—[20A–259/2]
vexatious litigation
procedure [20A–255]

Homelessness
asylum-seekers
eligibility for assistance [8Q–141]
deliberate act or omission
eviction after arrears [8Q–172]
generally [8Q–171]
eligibility for assistance
asylum-seekers [8Q–141]
intentionally homeless
deliberate act or omission [8Q–171], [8Q–172]
intentionally homeless
reasonable to occupy [8Q–175]—[8Q–176]
settled accommodation [8Q–178]
interim duty to accommodate
generally [8Q–155/1]—[8Q–155/2]
priority need [8Q–158], [8Q–159]
local authority duties
interim accommodation [8Q–155/1]—[8Q–155/2], [8Q–158], [8Q–159]
local authority duties
intentionally homeless [8Q–171], [8Q–172], [8Q–175]—[8Q–176], [8Q–178]
priority need and not intentionally homeless
generally [8Q–198], [8Q–200]—[8Q–200/1]
review of decisions
appeal from [8Q–246]
priority need
dependant children [8Q–158]
vulnerability [8Q–159]
reasonable to occupy
generally [8Q–175]
violence, departure after [8Q–176]
referral
generally [8Q–219]—[8Q–219/1], [8Q–222]
review of decisions
appeal from [8Q–247/1]
generally [8Q–240]—[8Q–240/1], [8Q–241]
procedure [8Q–244]

Hourly rate 62/A2/28

House of Lords
appeals
criminal cases [19B–4]
criminal cases
practice directions [19B–4]
generally [19A–1]
jurisdiction [19A–1]

House of Lords appeal
criminal cases
practice directions [19B–4]
generally [19A–1]
civil cases
practice directions [19A–7]—[19A–7/1], [19A–22]—[19A–22/1], [19A–43]—[19A–43/1], [19A–53]—[19A–53/1], [19A–57]—[19A–57/1], [19A–58]—[19A–58/1], [19A–60]—[19A–60/1], [19A–61]—[19A–61/1], [19A–63]—[19A–63/1], [19A–65]—[19A–66/1], [19A–67]—[19A–67/1], [19A–76]—[19A–76/1], [19A–99]—[19A–99/A]
standing orders [19A–107]—[19A–107/1]
criminal cases
practice directions [19B–4]—[19B–4/1], [19B–16]—[19B–16/1], [19B–20]—[19B–20/1], [19B–31], [19B–32/1], [19B–39]—[19B–40/1], [19B–43]—[19B–45/1], [19B–49]—[19B–51/1]

House of Lords civil appeal
Appeal Committee
objections [19A–22]—[19A–22/1]
preliminary steps [19A–21]
appendix
time limits [19A–53]—[19A–53/1]
application
authorities, list of [19A–65]—[19A–66/1]
bound volumes [19A–63]—[19A–63/1]
costs [19A–67]—[19A–67/1]
joint cases [19A–60]—[19A–60/1]
lodgment of cases [19A–61]—[19A–61/1]
skeleton cases [19A–57]—[19A–57/1], [19A–58]—[19A–58/1], [19A–60]—[19A–60/1], [19A–61]—[19A–61/1]
statement of facts [19A–43]—[19A–43/1]
authorities, list of [19A–65]—[19A–66/1]
bound volumes [19A–63]—[19A–63/1]
costs
application [19A–67]—[19A–67/1]
leave to appeal
admissibility [19A–7]—[19A–7/1]
legal aid
generally [19A–76]—[19A–76/1]
lodgment of cases [19A–61]—[19A–61/1]
petition for leave
form [19A–14]
procedure [19A–22]—[19A–22/1]
practice direction
appeal [19A–43]—[19A–43/1], [19A–53]—[19A–53/1], [19A–57]—[19A–57/1], [19A–58]—[19A–58/1], [19A–60]—[19A–60/1], [19A–61]—[19A–61/1], [19A–63]—[19A–63/1], [19A–65]—[19A–66/1], [19A–67]—[19A–67/1]

House of Lords civil appeal—*cont.*
appeal—*cont.*
miscellaneous [19A–76]—[19A–76/1], [19A–99]—[19A–99/A]
petition for leave [19A–7]—[19A–7/1], [19A–14], [19A–21], [19A–22]—[19A–22/1]
security for costs
standing orders [19A–107]—[19A–107/1]
settlement [19A–99]—[19A–99/A]
skeleton cases
exchange [19A–60]—[19A–60/1]
generally [19A–57]—[19A–58/1]
standing orders
judicial business [19A–107]—[19A–107/1]
statement of facts
generally [19A–43]—[19A–43/1]
time limits [19A–53]—[19A–53/1]
time limits
appendix
extension [19A–53]—[19A–53/1]
statement of facts
extension [19A–53]—[19A–53/1]

House of Lords criminal appeal
Appeal Committee
objections [19B–16]—[19B–16/1]
application
authorities, list of [19B–49]—[19B–50/1]
application
bill of costs [19B–56]
bound volumes [19B–45]—[19B–45/1]
costs [19B–51]—[19B–51/1]
fees [19B–31]
skeleton cases [19B–39]—[19B–40/1], [19B–43]—[19B–44/1]
statement of facts [19B–31]—[19B–32/1]
authorities, list of [19B–49]—[19B–50/1]
bill of costs [19B–56]
bound volumes [19B–45]—[19B–45/1]
costs
application
hearing, submissions at [19B–51]—[19B–51/1]
costs
petition for leave [19B–20]—[19B–20/1]
fees
application [19B–31]
lodgment
skeleton cases [19B–43]—[19B–43/1]
petition for leave
costs [19B–20]—[19B–20/1]
procedure [19B–16]—[19B–16/1]
petition for leave
time limits [19B–4]—[19B–4/1]
practice direction
application [19B–31], [19B–32/1], [19B–39]—[19B–40/1], [19B–43]—[19B–45/1], [19B–49]—[19B–51/1]
petition for leave [19B–4]—[19B–4/1], [19B–16]—[19B–16/1], [19B–20]—[19B–20/1]

House of Lords criminal appeal—*cont.*
skeleton cases
exchange [19B–44]—[19B–44/1]
generally [19B–39]—[19B–40/1]
lodgment [19B–43]—[19B–43/1]
statement of facts
generally [19B–31], [19B–32/1]
time limits
petition for leave [19B–4]—[19B–4/1]

Housing
anti-social behaviour
generally [8Q–66], [8Q–70], [8Q–85], [8Q–88]
assured tenancy
exempt tenancies [8O–201]—[8O–201/1], [8O–202], [8O–206], [8O–215], [8O–217/1]
generally [8O–8], [8O–19]
notice of possession [8O–243], [8O–253]
possession [8O–49]—[8O–49/1], [8O–72]—[8O–72/1]
forms [1C–10]
homelessness
assistance [8Q–141]
interim duty [8Q–155/1], [8Q–155/2], [8Q–158], [8Q–159]
local authority duties [8Q–171], [8Q–172], [8Q–175],[8Q–176], [8Q–178], [8Q–198/1], [8Q–200]—[8Q–200/1]
referral [8Q–219]—[8Q–219/1], [8Q–222]
review of decisions [8Q–240], [8Q–241], [8Q–244], [8Q–246], [8Q–247/1]
housing association tenancy [8O–176]—[8O–177]
introductory tenancy
generally [8Q–31], [8Q–47]
periodic tenancy
succession [8L–71]
protected tenancy
generally [8H–4]
protection from eviction
damages [8O–158]—[8O–168]
secure tenancy
assignment [8L–80]—[8L–81], [8L–85]
generally [8L–17]—[8L–18]
possession [8L–47]—[8L–47/1], [8L–52]
succession [8L–61], [8L–71]
statutory basis
Administration of Justice Act 1970 [8C–3]—[8C–4/1]
Consumer Credit Act 1974 [8F–6], [8F–9]—[8F–9/4]
County Courts Act 1984 [8K–3]—[8K–4/1]
Housing Act 1985 [8L–4]—[8L–7], [8L–9]—[8L–10], [8L–17]—[8L–18], [8L–47]—[8L–47/1], [8L–52], [8L–61], [8L–71], [8L–80]—[8L–81], [8L–85], [8L–106]—[8L–107], [8L–119]—[8L–120], [8L–138], [8L–149]—[8L–150], [8L–160], [8L–164]—[8L–164/1], [8L–166], [8L–172]—[8L–173, [8L–175], [8L–177]

Housing—*cont.*
Housing Act 1988 [8O–8], [8O–19]—[8O–19A], [8O–49]—[8O–49/1], [8O–60], [8O–72]—[8O–72/1], [8O–99], [8O–118, [8O–137], [8O–147], [8O–162], [8O–168], [8O–175]—[8O–177], [8O–201]—[8O–202], [8O–206], [8O–215], [8O–217/1], [8O–243], [8O–253]
Housing Act 1996 [8Q–3]—[8Q–4], [8Q–31], [8Q–47], [8Q–66], [8Q–70], [8Q–85], [8Q–88], [8Q–141]—[8Q–141/1], [8Q–155]—[8Q–155/2], [8Q–158]—[8Q–159], [8Q–171]—[8Q–172], [8Q–175]—[8Q–176], [8Q–178], [8Q–198]—[8Q–198/1], [8Q–200]—[8Q–200/1], [8Q–219]—[8Q–219/1], [8Q–222]—[8Q–222/1], [8Q–240]—[8Q–241], [8Q–244], [8Q–246], [8Q–247]—[8Q–247/1], [8Q–286]
Landlord and Tenant Act 1985 [8M–13], [8M–53], [8M–61], [8M–76/1]—[8M–77/1], [8M–81]—[8M–82], [8M–92]—[8M–93], [8M–102]—[8M–102/1]
Landlord and Tenant Act 1987 [8N–11]
Law of Property Act 1925 [8B–18]
Protection from Eviction Act 1977 [8G–13]—[8G–14]
Rent Act 1977 [8H–4], [8H–10], [8H–15], [8H–32], [8H–53]—[8H–54], [8G–58]—[8H–58/1], [8H–59]—[8H–60], [8H–94], [8H–100], [8H–121], [8H–179], [8H–179]—[8H–180]
statutory tenancy
generally [8H–10]

Housing Act 1985
definitions
generally [8L–119]—[8L–120]
landlord authority [8L–106]—[8L–107]
housing associations [8L–6]—[8L–7]
Housing Corporation [8L–9]—[8L–10]
other authorities [8L–4]—[8L–5]
periodic tenancy
succession [8L–71]
secure tenancy
assignment [8L–80]—[8L–81], [8L–85]
landlord condition [8L–17]—[8L–18]
possession [8L–47]—[8L–47/1], [8L–52]
succession [8L–61], [8L–71]

Housing Act 1988
agricultural occupancy [8O–175]
assured shorthold tenancy
county court C49/6A
assured tenancy
county court C49/6
exempt tenancies [8O–201]—[8O–201/1], [8O–202], [8O–206], [8O–215], [8O–217/1]

Housing Act 1988—*cont.*
generally [8O–8], [8O–19]
notice of possession [8O–243], [8O–253]
rent [8O–99]
security of tenure [8O–49]—[8O–49/1], [8O–60], [8O–72]—[8O–72/1]
succession [8O–118]
county court
assured shorthold tenancy C49/6A
assured tenancy C49/6
housing association tenancy [8O–176]—[8O–177]
protected tenancy [8O–175]
protection from eviction [8O–162], [8O–168]
schedules
assured tenancy [8O–201]—[8O–201/1], [8O–202], [8O–206], [8O–217/1]

Housing Act 1996
anti-social behaviour
injunctions [8Q–66], [8Q–70], [8Q–85], [8Q–88]
homelessness
assistance [8Q–141]
interim duty [8Q–155/1], [8Q–155/2], [8Q–158], [8Q–159]
local authority duties [8Q–171], [8Q–172], [8Q–175]—[8Q–176], [8Q–178], [8Q–198/1], [8Q–200]—[8Q–200/1]
referral [8Q–219]—[8Q–219/1], [8Q–222]
review of decisions [8Q–240], [8Q–241], [8Q–244], [8Q–246], [8Q–247/1]
injunctions against anti-social behaviour [8Q–66], [8Q–70], [8Q–85], [8Q–88]
introductory tenancy
generally [8Q–31]
possession [8Q–47]
registered social landlords [8Q–3]—[8Q–4]
schedule [8Q–286]

Housing association
meaning [8L–6]—[8L–7], [8O–8]
tenancy [8O–176]—[8O–177]

Housing Corporation
meaning [8L–9]—[8L–10]

Human Rights Act 1998
application [21T–24]—[21T–25]
citation [21T–24]
commencement [21T–24]
Convention rights [21T–2]—[21T–6]
definitions [21T–23]
derogations [21T–16]—[21T–19]
ECHR judges [21T–20]
generally [21T–1]—[21T–45]
legislation [21T–7]
other rights [21T–13]—[21T–15]
parliamentary procedure [21T–21]
public authorities [21T–8]—[21T–11]
recitals [21T–1]
remedial action [21T–12]

Human Rights Act 1998—*cont.*
reservations [21T–16]—[21T–19]
schedules [21T–26]—[21T–45]
supplemental provisions [21T–22]—[21T–25]

Hypothetical cases
statutory basis [20A–191/1]

Indemnity principle
costs 62/A2/27A
costs
SCTO direction 62/C/35D

Indorsement of writ
interest
pleading 6/L/2

Information for tenants
landlord's address for service [8N–11]

Inherent jurisdiction
wasted costs order
legal aid 62/11/25

Injunctions
American Cyanamid
generally 29/L/2
anti-social behaviour
generally [8Q–66], [8Q–70]
power of arrest [8Q–85], [8Q–88]
forms
adjournment of application [2C–139]
general order [2C–118]
treated as trial of action [2C–148]
undertaking [2C–128]
pre-action order [2C–107]
mandatory 29/L/1
Mareva
generally 29/L/36
pre-action
form [2C–107]
principles
generally 29/L/2
QBD direction [2C–148]
undertaking in lieu
form [2C–128]

Inquiry, order for
official referee's business
Master 36/11/2

Insolvency
fieri facias, writ of
stay of execution 47/1/10—47/1/11

Inspection of documents
timetable for
RSC [3D–1]

***Inter partes* applications**
Admiralty directions [6B–7]
Commercial Court Guide 72/A9

Interest
county court
generally C–016
judgment debt, on C25/5A/2
debts, on
pleading 6/L/2

Interest—*cont.*

High Court
pleading 6/L/2
judgment debt, on
county court C25/5A/2
pleading 6/L/2
liquidated demand, on
pleading 6/L/2
pleading
liquidated demand, on
contractual provision 6/L/2
review of taxation
costs, on 62/35/12

Interest bearing accounts
interest [5C–53]—[5C–54]
time of deposit [5C–55]—[5C–55/1]

Interim payments
affidavit
generally 29/10/6
application
affidavit 29/10/6
timetable for
RSC [3D–1]

Interim relief
service out of the jurisdiction 11/1/70A

Interlocutory applications
Admiralty directions [6B–5]
arbitration [21D–99]—[21D–101/1]

Interlocutory injunctions
patent actions 104/0/33
QBD direction [2C–148]

Interlocutory orders
definition 59/1A/2

Interpleader proceedings
assessment of costs 62/13/5

Interrogatories
Admiralty directions [6B–7]
timetable for
RSC [3D–1]

Intervention
non-parties, by
generally 15/6/8

Introductory tenancy
generally [8Q–31]
possession
generally [8Q–47]

Investment of funds
generally [5B–1]
interest bearing accounts [5C–53]—[5C–55/1]
money paid in satisfaction [5C–58]—[5C–60/1]
satisfaction, money paid in [5C–58]—[5C–60/1]
time for [5C–66]

Issue of proceedings
Q.B. Masters' direction
private room appointments [2A–27]

Joinder
causes of action
county court C5/1/1
county court
actions C5/1

Joinder of parties
alternative, in the
generally 15/4/8

Judges
rates and tax cases [20A–169] – [20A–169/1]

Judgment
county court
interest C–016
set-off [20A–745/2]
foreign, enforcement of
domicile [7B–37]—[7B–38]
generally [7A–3]—[7A–4]
interest
pleading 6/L/2
Q.B. Masters' direction
enforcement [2A–100]
signing
note [3B–1]
summary
directions 14/6/5
timetable for
RSC [3D–1]
default, in
generally 13/7A/3 , 13/9/18
foreign state, against 13/7A/3
setting aside 13/9/18

Judgment in default
foreign state, against
application 13/7A/3
procedure
proof of service 13/7/3
proof of service
affidavit of service of writ 13/7/3
setting aside
discretion 13/9/18
irregular, where
application 13/9/9

Judicial review, application for
costs
principles 62/3/6
wasted costs order 62/11/29

Judicial review
habeas corpus, writ of, distinction from 54/1/5
jurisdiction [20A–203]—[20A–204]

Judicial review, timetable (RSC) for [3D–1]

Jurisdiction
admiralty proceedings
Merchant Shipping Act 1995 [6D–209], [6D–235], [6D–252], [6D–258], [6D–262]
Supreme Court Act 1981 [6D–1], [6D–3], [6D–11], [6D–60], [6D–73]

Jurisdiction—*cont.*
allocation of
E.C., within [7B–42], [7B–49], [7B–67], [7B–69]—[7B–69/1]
Brussels Convention
exclusive jurisdiction [7B–67]
prorogation [7B–69]—[7B–69/1]
special jurisdiction [7B–49]
Court of Appeal
civil courts, appeals from [20A–172]—[20A–172/1]
Crown Court
appeals from [20A–198]—[20A–199]
sentencing [20A–263/5]—[20A–263/6]
European
Brussels Convention 1968 [7A–1]—[7A–4], [7B–42], [7B–49], [7B–67], [7B–69]—[7B–69/1]
Civil Jurisdiction and Judgments Act 1982 [7A–3]
generally [7A–1]—[7A–6]
Lugano Convention [7A–5]—[7A–6]
mortgage actions
possession 88/1/3
regulations
High and County Court Jurisdiction Order 1991 [20B–240], [20B–247], [20B–249], [20B–252], [20B–261], [20B–265]
statutes
County Courts Acts 1959 to 1984 [20A–720]—[20A–720/2], [20A–725]—[20A–725/1], [20A–726]—[20A–726/1], [20A–736]—[20A–736/2], [20A–808]—[20A–808/2], [20A–809]—[20A–809/1]
Supreme Court Act 1981 [20A–215]—[20A–216], [20A–219]—[20A–220], [20A–263/5]—[20A–263/6], [20A–465/11]—[20A–465/12]

Jury trial
county court
generally [20A–739/2]—[20A–739/3]

Knowledge
date of
generally [14–17/6], [14–17/8]
personal injury [14–17/3]

Land, recovery of
statutory basis
excepted premises [8H–15], [8H–32], [8H–53]—[8H–54], [8G–58]—[8H–58/1], [8H–59]—[8H–60]
grounds for possession [8H–94], [8H–100], [8H–121], [8H–180]
protected tenancy [8H–4]
statutory tenancy [8H–10], [8H–15]
subletting [8H–121]

Landlord
information for tenants
address for service [8N–11]

Landlord and tenant
information for tenants
landlord's address for service [8N–11]

Landlord and tenant—*cont.*
repairing obligation
generally [8M–13]
service charge
excepted cases [8M–81]—[8M–82]
information request [8M–76/1]—[8M–77/1]
limitation [8M–53], [8M–61]
statutory basis
Landlord and Tenant Act 1985 [8M–13], [8M–53], [8M–61], [8M–76/1]—[8M–77/1], [8M–81]—[8M–82], [8M–92]—[8M–93], [8M–102]—[8M–102/1]
Landlord and Tenant Act 1987 [8N–11]
transfer of proceedings [8M–102]—[8M–102/1]

Landlord and Tenant Act 1985
applications
repairing [8M–13]
definitions
qualified accountant [8M–92]—[8M–93]
generally [8M–13], [8M–76/1], [8M–92]—[8M–93], [8M–101]—[8M–102/1]
repairing obligation
generally [8M–13]
service charge
generally [8M–76/1]
timetable for
RSC [3D–1]
transfer of proceedings [8M–101]—[8M–102/1]

Landlord and Tenant Act 1987
applications
county court C43/18
county court
applications C43/18
generally [8N–11]
information for tenants [8N–11]

Landlord and tenant proceedings
applications
county court C43/18

Lands Tribunal
costs 62/B/47

Latent damage
time limits
knowledge [14–18/2]

Law of Property Act 1925
notices [8B–18]

Leave to amend
new claims 20/8/8

Leave to appeal
Court of Appeal, to
exempt categories 59/1B/5—59/1B/8
generally 59/1B – 59/1B/4
grounds 59/14/18—59/14/18A
person to grant 59/1B/9
procedure 59/14/21, 59/14/24—59/14/26C, 59/14/31, 59/14/35—59/14/35L
relevant cases 59/1/91

Leave to appeal—*cont.*
House of Lords civil case
admissibility [19A-7]—[19A-7/1]

Leave to appeal to Court of Appeal
application
bundles 59/14/24
fees 59/14/21
generally 59/14/21
bundles
application 59/14/24
inter partes referral with appeal to follow 59/14/35—59/14/35L
ex parte referral
single Lord Justice, to 59/14/25
open court, to 59/14/26 - 59/14/26C
exempt categories 59/1B/5—59/1B/8
fees 59/14/21
generally 59/1/91, 59/1B - 59/1B/4
grounds 59/14/18—59/14/18A
inter partes referral
skeleton arguments 59/14/31
with appeal to follow 59/14/35—59/14/35L
person to grant 59/1B/9
procedure
application 59/14/21, 59/14/24
referral 59/14/25—59/14/26C
referral
ex parte 59/14/25—59/14/26C
inter partes 59/14/31, 59/14/35—59/14/35L
skeleton arguments
inter partes referral 59/14/31
with appeal to follow
procedure 59/14/35—59/14/35L

Leave to defend
directions after 14/6/5
showing cause 14/4/7

Leave to serve out of the jurisdiction
discretion
forum conveniens 11/1/15

Legal aid
certificates
applications [16D-45]—[16D-46]
discharge [16D-140]—[16D-140/1]
issue [16D-91]
revocation [16D-140]—[16D-140/1]
scope [16D-91]
civil aid
remuneration regulations [16F-1]—[16F-2], [16F-4]—[16F-5]
statutory basis [16A-72], [16A-75]
effect
generally [16A-86]
selection of representatives [16A-93]
House of Lords civil appeal
generally [19A-76]—[19A-76/1]
regulations
civil aid
general [16D-169]—[16D-169/1], [16D-192], [16D-241]
remuneration [16F-1]—[16F-2], [16F-4]—[16F-5]
remuneration
civil aid [16F-1]—[16F-2], [16F-4]—[16F-5]

Legal aid—*cont.*
statutory basis
civil aid [16A-72], [16A-75]
statutory charge
generally [16D-155], [16D-164]—[16D-164/1]

Legal Aid Act 1988
definitions
generally [16A-16/1]—[16A-16/2], [16A-21]
general provisions [16A-86], [16A-93]
supplementary provisions [16A-86], [16A-93]
civil aid [16A-72], [16A-75]

Legal aid certificates
authority to incur costs
prior [16D-115]
applications
transfer of [16D-46]
patients [16D-45]
conduct of proceedings [16D-129]—[16D-129/1] , [16D-132]—[16D-132/1]
costs against assisted party
generally [16D-241], [16D-244]—[16D-244/1], [16D-246], [16D-251]
costs of assisted party
generally [16D-192], [16D-208], [16D-210]—[16D-211], [16D-221]
discharge
abuse [16D-140]—[16D-140/1]
disclosure
documents [16D-34]
information [16D-132]—[16D-132/1]
duties
progress [16D-129]—[16D-129/1]
progress, report of [16D-129]—[16D-129/1]
recovery of property
generally [16D-155], [16D-164]—[16D-164/1], [16D-169]—[16D-169/1]
revocation
abuse [16D-140]—[16D-140/1]
scope [16D-91]
statutory charge
generally [16D-155], [16D-164]—[16D-164/1], [16D-169]—[16D-169/1]

Legal Aid (General) Regulations
applications
generally [16D-45], [16D-46]
authority to incur costs [16D-115]
certificates
applications [16D-45], [16D-46]
issue [16D-91]
revocation [16D-140]—[16D-140/1]
scope [16D-91]
conduct of proceedings [16D-129]—[16D-129/1], [16D-132]—[16D-132/1]
costs against assisted party
generally [16D-241], [16D-244]—[16D-244/1], [16D-246], [16D-251]

Legal Aid (General) Regulations—*cont.*
costs of assisted party
generally [16D–192], [16D–208], [16D–210], [16D–211], [16D–221]
discharge [16D–140]—[16D–140/1]
duties [16D–129]—[16D–129/1], [16D–132]—[16D–132/1]
general provisions [16D–34]
issue [16D–91]
recovery of property
generally [16D–155], [16D–164]—[16D–164/1], [16D–169]—[16D–169/1]
revocation [16D–140]—[16D–140/1]
statutory charge
generally [16D–155], [16D–164]—[16D–164/1], [16D–169]—[16D–169/1]

Legal Aid in Civil Actions (Remuneration) Regulations 1994
citation [16F–1]
definitions [16F–2]
general provisions [16F–4]—[16F–5]

Legal aid regulations
civil aid
remuneration [16F–1]—[16F–2]
remuneration
basic allowance [16F–4]—[16F–5]

Legal professional privilege
communications in contemplation of litigation
medical advisers 24/5/22
waiver 24/5/30

Limitation Act 1980
exclusion of time limits [14–40/4]—[14–40/6]
pending actions [14–42/5]

Limitation actions
parties 75/37/2

Limitation fund
generally 75/37/5

Limitation period
amendment after
time limits [14–42/5]—[14–42/6]
date of knowledge
generally [14–17/6], [14–17/8]
personal injury [14–17/3]
discretionary exclusion of
death [14–40/4]—[14–40/6]
personal injury
actions commenced outside primary period [14–40/4]
exercise of [14–40/5]—[14–40/6]
enforcement
judgment [14–29/1]
exclusion of
death [14–40/4]—[14–40/6]
personal injury [14–40/4]—[14–40/6]
fatal accidents
discretionary exclusion [14–40/4]—[14–40/6]
date of knowledge [14–17/6], [14–17/8]

Limitation period—*cont.*
latent damage
knowledge [14–18/2]
new party [14–42/11]
ordinary
personal injury [14–17/6]
trusts [14–26]—[14–26/1]
pending actions
amendment after expiry of limitation period [14–42/5]—[14–42/6]
new party [14–42/11]
personal injury
discretionary exclusion [14–40/4]—[14–40/6]
fatal accidents [14–17/6], [14–17/8]
statutory basis
exclusion of time limits [14–40/4]—[14–40/6]
pending actions [14–42/5]
trust property [14–26]—[14–26/1]

Liquidated demand
interest
pleading 6/L/2

Liquidator
costs
generally 62/B/132

Lis pendens
service out of the jurisdiction 11/1/70

Listing
timetable for
RSC [3D–1]

Litigants in person
audience, rights of [21R–5]
costs
generally 62/18/2
Official Receiver [21R–6]

Litigants In Person (Costs and Expenses) Act 1975 [21R–4]—[21R–6]

Litigants In Person (Costs and Expenses) Act 1975
audience, rights of [21R–5]
commencement [21R–4]
Official Receiver [21R–6]

Local Government Act 1972
costs 62/B/55

Lodgment of documents
House of Lords civil appeal [19A–61]—[19A–61/1]
House of Lords criminal appeal
skeleton cases [19B-43]—[19B-43/1]

Lodgment of funds
court, in [5C–41], [5C–42]
county court, in [5C–48]—[5C–48/1]
schedule, on receipt of
generally [5C–26]—[5C–27], [5C–33]
securities, of [5C–46]—[5C–46/1]
written request, on receipt of
generally [5C–34], [5C–37]

Lugano Convention 1988
generally [7A–5]
ratification [7A–5]

Magistrates' court
case stated from, appeals by
generally 56/5/3
jurisdiction [20A–201]—[20A–202]

Maintainer of action
costs 62/10/7

Mandamus
jurisdiction [20A–203]—[20A–204]
timetable for
RSC [3D–1]

***Mareva* injunctions**
Admiralty directions [6B–7]
forms [2C–81], [2C–96]
forms
England and Wales, disposal of assets in [2C–96]
forms
worldwide, disposal of assets [2C–81]
generally 29/L/36
QBD direction
forms [2C–81] , [2C–96]
QBD directions [2C–81], [2C–96]

Masters
mode of trial 33/2/2
place of trial 33/2/2

Matrimonial proceedings
counsel's fees 62/A2/19
evidence [21G–31]—[21G–31/1]

Mental Health Act 1983
correspondence of patients [10B–34]—[10B–34/1]

Mercantile List
Bristol [2C–242]

Merchant Shipping Act 1995
assistance at sea
distress [6D–204]—[6D–205]
death
joint and several liability [6D–235]
generally [6D–209], [6D–235], [6D–252], [6D–258], [6D–262]
insurance [6D–262]
liability
joint and several [6D–235]
limitation of [6D–209]
limitation period [6D–252], [6D–258]
multiple fault
death [6D–235]
personal injury [6D–235]
personal injury
joint and several liability [6D-235]
time limits [6D–252], [6D–258]

Minors
party, as
county court [20A–720]—[20A–720/2]

Misconduct in proceedings
costs
taxation 62/28/4
unreasonableness 62/10/6

Misjoinder
intervention by non-parties 15/6/8

Misnomer
party, of 15/6/16

Mode of address
QBD direction [2C–204]—[2C–204/1]

Mode of trial
county court
arbitration, reference to [20A–737/2]
assessors [20A–736]—[20A–736/2]
generally [20A–735/1]
referee, to [20A–738/1]—[20A–738/2]
registrar, to [20A–738/1]—[20A–738/2]
Masters, before 33/2/2

Modified Brussels Convention
generally [7A–3]
special jurisdiction [7B–139]

Money in court
statutory charge against [16D–169]—[16D–169/1]

Mortgage actions
costs
heads 62/6/6
pre-emptive orders 62/B/151
pre-emptive orders
generally 62/B/151
court's powers
generally [8C–2], [8C–3]—[8C–4/1]
definitions 88/1/3
evidence
redemption figure 88/5/10
jurisdiction
possession 88/1/3
payment of secured moneys
evidence 88/5/10
procedure
evidence 88/5/10
jurisdiction 88/1/3
types 88/1/3

Motions
timetable for
RSC [3D–1]

Multi-party actions
costs
generally 62/B/83

Multiple credit agreement [9A–57/1]

Mutual discovery
relevant issues 24/2/11

Neglect in proceedings
costs
taxation 62/28/4
unreasonableness 62/10/6

New claims
amendment to raise 20/8/8

New party
time limits [14–42/11]

New trial, order for
timetable for
RSC [3D–1]

New York Convention
(post-31.1.97 arbitration) [21D–243]
(pre-1.2.97 arbitration) [21B–23]

New York Convention (post-31.1.97 arbitration)
refusal of enforcement
relevant court [21D–243]
refusal of recognition
relevant court [21D–243]

New York Convention (pre-1.2.97 arbitration)
enforcement
refusal [21B–23]
refusal of enforcement
grounds [21B–23]

Next friend
costs
solicitor and own-client basis 62/1

Non-contentious probate
fees [4C–1]—[4C–9]
rules [11B–1], [11B–4], [11B–8]—[11B–8/1], [11B–9], [11B–12], [11B–54], [11B–68], [11B–74], [11B–79], [11B–89], [11B–90], [11B–95], [11B–109], [11B–113], [11B–119A], [11B–123]

Non-Contentious Probate Rules 1987
applications [11B–9], [11B–12]
arrangement of rules [11B–1]
caveats [11B–90]
citations [11B–95]
definitions [11B–4]
generally [11B–1], [11B–4], [11B–9], [11B–12], [11B–54], [11B–68], [11B–74], [11B–79], [11B–89], [11B–90], [11B–95], [11B–109], [11B–113], [11B–119A], [11B–123]
grants [11B–68], [11B–74]
renunciation [11B–79]
schedules [11B–129], [11B–130], [11B–131]
standing searches [11B–89]

Nonjoinder
intervention by non-parties 15/6/8

Non-party
discovery against
relevant actions 24/7A/3
statutory basis [20A–219]—[20A–220]
intervention by
generally 15/6/8

Non-payment of rent, forfeiture for
county court
generally [8K–3], [8K–4]—[8K–4/1]
procedure [20A–814/4]

Non-payment of rent, forfeiture for—*cont.*
relief against
county court [8K–3], [8K–4]—[8K–4/1]
service of summons
generally [20A–814/4]

Notice
intention to defend, of
default of
generally 13/9/18
failure to give 13/9/18

Notice of motion
appeals to High Court
service 55/4/2
quash governmental decisions, etc., applications to 94/2/2

Notice to admit documents
timetable for
RSC [3D–1]

Notice to admit facts
patent actions 104/0/19
timetable for
RSC [3D–1]

Notice to produce documents
timetable for
RSC [3D–1]

Officers
county court
district judges [20A–655/1]—[20A–655/2]
registrars
county court
generally [20A–655/1]—[20A–655/2]

Official Receiver
costs
generally 62/18/2/1
litigants in person, as [21R–6]

Official referee's business
inquiry
Master 36/11/2
trial procedure
Master 36/11/2

Ombudsman
costs 62/B/132/1

Order
consent, by
Tomlin [17A–32]
county court
interest C–016
set-off [20A–745/2]
recall
generally [17A–12]
Tomlin [17A–32]

Order 14 judgment
directions 14/6/5

Originating motions
timetable for
RSC [3D–1]

Parties
addition of
application 15/6/17—15/6/18
amendment of
application 15/6/17
generally 15/6/16
terms 15/6/18
change of
death, on
generally 15/7/3
company
directors [17B–19]
county court
minors [20A–720]—[20A–720/2]
death of
generally 15/7/3
director [17B–19]
generally [17B–1]
intervention by non-parties
generally 15/6/8
introductory note [17B–1]
joinder
alternative, in the
generally 15/4/8
minors
county court [20A–720]—[20A–720/2]
misnomer 15/6/16
nonjoinder
intervention by non-parties 15/6/8
non-parties
intervention by 15/6/8
separate trials
generally 15/5/1
striking out
application 15/6/17—15/6/18
substitution of
application 15/6/17—15/6/18

Partnerships
foreign firms
generally 81/1/21
manager, service on
generally 81/3/7
service
manager, on 81/3/7

Patent actions
admissions 104/0/17
audience, rights of 104/0/26
consent orders 104/0/23
costs
assessment of 104/0/32
documents
generally 104/0/13
referred to in pleadings 104/0/20
ex parte applications 104/0/12
evidence 104/0/21
experiments
generally 104/0/30
undisclosed 104/0/31
forms
specimen minute of order 104/0/36—104/0/55
interlocutory injunctions 104/0/33
notice to admit facts 104/0/19

Patent actions—*cont.*
Practice Direction
admissions 104/0/17
amendment of patent 104/0/34
audience, rights of 104/0/26
clerk in charge of list 104/0/8
Comptroller, appeals from 104/0/11
consent orders 104/0/23
costs, assessment of 104/0/32
Court Users' Committee 104/0/28
documents 104/0/13
documents referred to in pleadings 104/0/20
draft orders 104/0/29
evidence 104/0/21
ex parte applications 104/0/12
experiments 104/0/30—104/0/31
generally 104/0/4—104/0/7
interlocutory injunctions 104/0/33
jurisdiction of Masters 104/0/22
narrowing of issues 104/0/16
notice to admit facts 104/0/19
pre-trial review 104/0/25
reading guide 104/0/15
September, sittings in 104/0/10
short applications 104/0/9
simplified trial 104/0/14
sittings outside London 104/0/27
skeleton arguments 104/0/21
specimen minute of order 104/0/35—104/0/55
technical primers 104/0/18
telephone summons 104/0/24
time estimates 104/0/15
pre-trial review 104/0/38
reading guide 104/0/15
September, sittings in 104/0/21
skeleton arguments 104/0/21
telephone summons 104/0/24
time estimates 104/0/15

Paternity proceedings
evidence of [21G–31]—[21G–31/1]

Payment into court
acceptance of
timetable for
RSC [3D–1]
Banking Act 1987, s.26, under
generally 92/3A—92/3A/1
certificate of deduction of benefits 22/1/18
costs
acceptance, on
generally 62/5/7
counterclaim
taking into account 22/2—22/2/2
county court
generally C11/1
Court Funds Rules 1987
county court, in [5C–48]—[5C–48/1]
generally [5C–41], [5C–42]
schedule, on receipt of [5C–26]—[5C–27], [5C–33]
securities, of [5C–46]—[5C–46/1]
written request, on receipt of [5C–34], [5C–37]

Payment into court, forms
notice of
generally [1A–21]

Payment into court
notice of
certificate of deduction 22/1/18
forms
generally [1A–21]
generally 22/1/16
Rules of the Supreme Court
forms 22/0/4
timetable for
RSC [3D–1]
withdrawal
generally 22/1/20

Payment of secured moneys
evidence
redemption figure 88/5/10

Payment out
Court Funds Rules 1987
without order
payee, to [5C–82], [5C—84/1]
Court Funds Rules 1987
without order
payer, to [5C–85]—[5C–85/1]
money remaining in court
generally 22/5/2
security for costs 23/3/42
without order
payee, to [5C–82], [5C–84/1]
payer, to [5C–85]—[5C–85/1]

Payment schedules
certificate of Master [5C–18]—[5C–19]

Penal notice
sequestration, writ of 45/7/7

Pending actions
time limits
amendment after expiry of limitation period [14–42/5]—[14–42/6]
new party [14–42/11]

Peremptory orders
arbitration [21D–93]

Periodic tenancy
assured tenancy
succession [8O–118]
secure tenancy
succession [8L–71]

Person under disability
compromise, approval of
Admiralty direction [6B–12]

Person under mental disorder
costs
fixed [10A–176]

Personal injury actions
county court
discovery
generally [20A–726]—[20A—726/1]
statutory basis
general discovery [20A–219]—[20A—220]

Personal injury actions—*cont.*
time limits
date of knowledge [14–17/3]
discretionary exclusion [14–40/4]—[14–40/6]
fatal accidents [14–17/6]—[14–17/8]

Personal representatives
costs
pre-emptive orders
generally 62/B/151

Petition for leave
House of Lords civil appeal
form [19A–14]
procedure [19A–22]—[19A–22/1]
House of Lords criminal appeal
costs [19B–20]—[19B–20/1]
procedure [19B–16]—[19B—16/1]
House of Lords criminal appeal
time limits [19B–4]—[19B–4/1]

Petitions
timetable for
RSC [3D–1]

Place of trial
Masters, before 33/2/2

Plaintiffs
security for costs by
limited company 23/3/21

Pleadings
Admiralty directions [6B–7]
close of
timetable for
RSC [3D–1]
fraud
particulars 18/12/18
interest
liquidated demand, on
contractual provision 6/L/2
service of
timetable for
RSC [3D–1]
timetable for
RSC [3D–1]

Point of law
Admiralty directions [6B–7]

Possession actions
land, for
generally [8H–4], [8H–10], [8H–15], [8H–32], [8H–53]—[8H–54], [8G–58]—[8H–58/1], [8H–59]—[8H–60], [8H–94], [8H–100], [8H–121]

Postal issue
Admiralty directions [6B–10]
Q.B. Masters' direction
private room appointments [2A–27]

Powers of attorney
rules [10G–38]—[10G–39]

Practice directions
admiralty proceedings [6B–1]

Practice directions—*cont.*
Court of Appeal
appeals 59/9/50
applications 59/9/40
skeleton arguments 59/9/71—59/9/75
Court of Appeal 59/9/40, 59/9/50, 59/9/71—59/9/75
House of Lords civil appeal
appeal [19A–43]—[19A–43/1], [19A–53]—[19A–53/1], [19A–57]—[19A–57/1], [19A–58]—[19A–58/1], [19A–60]—[19A–60/1], [19A–61]—[19A–61/1], [19A–63]—[19A–63/1], [19A–65]—[19A–66/1], [19A–67]—[19A–67/1]
miscellaneous [19A–76]—[19A–76/1], [19A–99]—[19A–99/A]
petition for leave [19A–7]—[19A–7/1], [19A–14], [19A–21], [19A–22]—[19A–22/1]
House of Lords criminal appeal
appeal [19B–31], [19B–32/1], [19B–39]—[19B–40/1], [19B–43]—[19B–45/1], [19B–49]—[19B–51/1]
petition for leave [19B–4]—[19B–4/1], [19B–16]—[19B–16/1], [19B–20]—[19B–20/1]
Patents Court 104/0/4—104/4/51
Q.B. Masters'
generally [2A–1]
QBD
generally [2C–1]
list [2C–11], [2C–12A]
Supreme Court Taxing Office 62/C/35D

Practice forms
county court [1C–1] , [1C–3], [1C–6], [1C–10]

Pre-action discovery
relevant actions 24/7A/3
county court
generally [20A–725]—[20A–725/1]
statutory basis
Civil Procedure Act 1997 [20A–8/2]
Supreme Court Act 1981 [20A–215]—[20A–216], [20A–219]—[20A–220]

Pre-action injunctions
form [2C–107]

Pre-emptive orders
costs
generally 62/B/151

Pre-trial checklist
Admiralty directions [6B–7]

Pre-trial review
patent actions 104/0/25

Preliminary act
timetable for
RSC [3D–1]

Preliminary issue, trial of
special case 33/3/1

Prescribed forms
list of [1A–1A]
payment into court, notice of
generally [1A–21]

Private room appointments
Q.B. Masters' direction [2A–27]

Privilege
taxing officers 62/20/2
witness statement 38/2A/12

Probate actions
fees [4C–1]—[4C–9]
forms
generally [11B–129], [11B–130], [11B–131]
grant of representation
rules [11B–1], [11B–4], [11B–8]—[11B–8/1], [11B–9], [11B–12], [11B–54], [11B–68], [11B–74], [11B–79], [11B–89], [11B–90], [11B–95], [11B–109], [11B–113], [11B–119A], [11B–123]
non-contentious
fees [4C–1]—[4C–9]
forms [11B–129], [11B–130], [11B–131]
rules [11B–1], [11B–4], [11B–8]—[11B–8/1], [11B–9], [11B–12], [11B–54], [11B–68], [11B–74], [11B–79], [11B–89], [11B–90], [11B–95], [11B–109], [11B–113], [11B–119A], [11B–123]
personal representatives
forms [11B–129], [11B–130], [11B–131]
personal representatives
rules [11B–1], [11B–4], [11B–8]—[11B–8/1], [11B–9], [11B–12], [11B–54], [11B–68], [11B–74], [11B–79], [11B–89], [11B–90], [11B–95], [11B–109], [11B–113], [11B–119A], [11B–123]
rules
grant of representation [11B–1], [11B–4], [11B–8]—[11B–8/1], [11B–9], [11B–12], [11B–54], [11B–68], [11B–74], [11B–79], [11B–89], [11B–90], [11B–95], [11B–109], [11B–113], [11B–119A], [11B–123]
statutory basis
grant of representation
generally [11A–20]

Probate forms
appearance to warning [11B–131]
caveat [11B–129]
warning to caveator [11B–130]

Production of documents
order for
necessity for 24/13/3

Prohibition
jurisdiction [20A–203]—[20A–204]

Proof of service
default judgment
affidavit of service of writ 13/7/3
generally 10/1/26

Prorogation of jurisdiction
service out of the jurisdiction 11/1/67

Protected tenancy
excepted premises
housing association, letting by [8H–59]—[8H–60]
local authority, letting by [8H–53]—[8H-54], [8H-58]—[8H-58/1]
excepted premises
rateable value, above [8H–15]
student lets [8H–32]
generally [8H–4]
grounds for possession
effect [8H–94]
reasonableness [8H–100]
post-Housing Act 1988 [8O–175]
subletting
effect on
determination of superior tenancy [8H-121]

Protection from eviction
damages
generally [8O–162]
measure [8O–168]
unlawful eviction
excluded tenancy [8G–13]—[8G–14]

Protection from Eviction Act 1977
unlawful eviction [8G–13]—[8G–14]

Protection from Harassment Act 1997
applications C45/15A

Public trustee
duties
trust accounts, audit of [12C–49]
fees
audit [12C–49]
generally [12C–40]
statutory basis
fees [12C–40]
trust accounts, audit of
statutory basis [12C–49]

Public Trustee Act 1906
fees [12C–40]
trust accounts, audit of [12C–49]

Quash governmental decisions, etc., applications to
notice of motion 94/2/2

Quasi delict
service out of the jurisdiction 11/1/55

QBD direction
Anton Piller orders
forms [2C–66]
assessment of costs [2C–259]
chambers, proceedings in
Anton Piller order [2C–66]
interlocutory injunctions [2C–148]
Mareva injunctions [2C–81], [2C–96]

QBD direction—*cont.*
costs [2C–259]
court dress [2C–207]—[2C–208/1]
European Court references [2C–240A]
generally [2C–1]
interlocutory injunctions
adjournment of application [2C–139]
general order [2C–118]
treated as trial of action [2C–148]
undertaking [2C–128]
list [2C–11], [2C–12A]
Mareva injunctions
forms [2C–81], [2C–96]
Mercantile List
Bristol [2C–242]
mode of address [2C–204]—[2C–204/1]
trial procedure
court dress [2C–207]—[2C–208/1]
mode of address [2C–204]—[2C–204/1]

Q.B. Masters
practice directions
generally [2A–1], [2C–1]
list [2C–11], [2C–12A]

Q.B. Masters' direction
enforcement
judgments [2A–100]
generally [2A–1]
judgment
enforcement [2A–100]
postal issue
private room appointments [2A–27]

Q.B. Masters' forms
security for costs
order for [1B–33]

Queen's Bench Division
chambers, proceedings in
adjournment to court 32/13/23
practice directions
generally [2A–1], [2C–1]
list [2C–11], [2C–12A]

Reading guide
patent actions 104/0/15

Receiver, court appointed
appeals 30/1/12
remuneration 30/3/2

Reciprocal enforcement of judgments
Convention states
generally [7A–1]—[7A–6]
domicile
Crown [7B–37]—[7B–38]
EC Treaty
generally 71/15/1

Recovery of land actions
statutory basis
excepted premises [8H–15], [8H–32], [8H–53]—[8H–54], [8G–58]—[8H–58/1], [8H–59]—[8H–60]
grounds for possession [8H–94], [8H–100], [8H–121]
protected tenancy [8H–4]
statutory tenancy [8H–10]
subletting [8H–121]

Recovery of property and costs
generally [16D–155], [16D–164]—[16D–164/1]

References
admiralty proceedings
disruption of business 75/42/8
costs
arbitration proceedings 62/B/12

Registered designs, actions relating to
Practice Direction 104/0/4—104/0/55

Registered social landlords
registration
generally [8Q–3]—[8Q–4]

Registrar
county court
generally [20A–655/1]—[20A–655/2]

Registrar of Civil Appeals
qualifications [20A–572/1]—[20A–572/2]

Relief against forfeiture
county court [8K–3], [8K–4]—[8K–4/1]

Remuneration
solicitors
recovery of [15A–58/54]

Rent Act 1977
discretionary grounds
Case 1
breach of obligation [8H–179]
Case 2
annoyance [8H–180]
nuisance [8H–180]
excepted premises
housing association, letting by [8H–59]—[8H–60]
local authority, letting by [8H–53]—[8H–54], [8H–58]—[8H–58/1]
rateable value, above [8H–15]
student lets [8H–32]
grounds for possession
effect [8H–94]
reasonableness [8H–100]
protected tenancy
excepted premises [8H–15], [8H–32], [8H–53]—[8H–54], [8G–58]—[8H–58/1], [8H–59]—[8H–60]
generally [8H–4]
grounds for possession [8H–94], [8H–100]
security of tenure
grounds for possession [8H–94], [8H–100]
statutory tenancy
continuing occupation [8H–10]
excepted premises [8H–15], [8H–32], [8H–53]—[8H–54], [8G–58]—[8H–58/1], [8H–59]—[8H–60]
grounds for possession [8H–94], [8H–100]

Rent Act 1977—*cont.*
subletting
effect on
determination of superior tenancy [8H–119]—[8H–121]

Reopening credit agreements
statutory basis [9A–161/1]

Repairing obligation
transfer of proceedings [8M–102]—[8M–102/1]
damages [8M–13]
generally [8M–13]
remedies
damages [8M–13]
transfer of proceedings [8M–102/1]

Reply
service
timetable for
RSC [3D–1]

Restricted-use credit agreement [9A–47/1]

Revenue proceedings
appeals
VAT Tribunals, from 91/6—91/6/1

Review of taxation
interest
costs, on 62/35/12

Rules of court
county court
application of RSC [20A–749/1]
generally [20A–748]—[20A–748/1]

Running-account credit agreement
generally [9A–46/1]

Secure tenancy
assignment
exchange, by [8L–80]—[8L–81], [8L–85]
development, approval of [8L–172]—[8L–173]
exempt tenancy
employment, occupation for [8L–138], [8L–150]
note [8L–149]
grounds for possession
reasonable, if [8L–160], [8L–175], [8L–177]
grounds for possession
reasonable and suitable accommodation, if [8L–166]
suitable alternative accommodation,if [8L–164]—[8L–164/1]
landlord condition [8L–17]—[8L–18]
possession
discretion of court [8L–52]
reasonableness [8L–47]—[8L–47/1]
discretion of court [8L–52]
succession
periodic tenancy [8L–71]
qualifying persons [8L–61]

Security for costs
Admiralty directions [6B–7]
default in giving 23/3/40

Security for costs—*cont.*
forms
order for [1B–33]
grounds
limited company 23/3/21
House of Lords civil appeal
standing orders [19A–107]—[19A–107/1]
limited company
plaintiff 23/3/21
order for
form [1B–33]
payment out 23/3/42
plaintiff, by
limited company 23/3/21
return of
payment out 23/3/42

Separate trials, order for
generally 15/5/1
special case 33/3/1

Sequestration, writ of
penal notice, indorsement of 45/7/7
requirements
penal notice 45/7/7
service of order
dispensing with 45/7/8

Service
agent of overseas principal, on
generally 10/2/2
county court
statutory basis [20A–808]—[20A–808/2]
Court of Protection Rules
generally [10C–22]—[10C–22/1]
notice of motion
appeals to High Court 55/4/2
partnerships
manager, on 81/3/7
pleadings, of
timetable for
RSC [3D–1]
proof of
default judgment
affidavit of service of writ 13/7/3
generally 10/1/26
sequestration, writ of
dispensing with 45/7/8
summons for directions
timetable for
RSC [3D–1]
timetable for
RSC [3D–1]

Service charge
definitions
qualified accountant [8M–92]—[8M–93]
excepted cases
public authority tenants [8M–81]—[8M–82]
information request
relevant costs, summary of [8M–76/1]—[8M–77/1]
limitation
consultation [8M–61]
estimates [8M–61]
reasonableness [8M–53]

Service charge—*cont.*
transfer of proceedings [8M–102]—[8M–102/1]

Service out of the jurisdiction
Admiralty directions [6B–7]
agreement of jurisdiction 11/1/67
application for leave
amendment 11/4/14
conflict of jurisdictions 11/1/70
interim relief 11/1/70A
leave required
discretion
forum conveniens 11/1/15
prorogation of jurisdiction 11/1/67
quasi delict 11/1/55
lis pendens 11/1/70
third party notice 16/1/7
third party proceedings
without leave 11/1/61
tort
without leave 11/1/55
without leave
agreement of jurisdiction 11/1/67
conflict of jurisdictions 11/1/70
exclusive jurisdiction 11/1/48
interim relief 11/1/70A
lis pendens 11/1/70
prorogation of jurisdiction 11/1/67
quasi delict 11/1/55
third party proceedings 11/1/61
tort 11/1/55

Setting aside
default judgment
irregular, where
application 13/9/8—13/9/9

Setting down
admiralty proceedings
generally 72/2/5
commercial actions 72/2/5
timetable for
RSC [3D–1]

Settlements
House of Lords civil appeal [19A–99]—[19A–99/A]

Sheriff
duties 45/1/10

Ships
assistance at sea
distress [6D–204]—[6D–205]
insurance [6D–262]
liability
insurance for [6D–262]
joint and several [6D–235]
limitation of [6D–209]
security for [6D–262]
limitation period [6D–252], [6D–258]
time limits
generally [6D–252], [6D–258]

Show cause
summary judgment
affidavit evidence 14/4/7

Single Lord Justice
application for leave to appeal to
59/14/25
application to Court of Appeal
bundles 59/14/10

Sittings
county court
place
generally [20A–652]—[20A–652/1]
time [20A–652]—[20A–652/1]
September, in
patent actions 104/0/10

Skeleton arguments
Court of Appeal, appeals to
bundles 59/9/2A
generally 59/9/24
leave to appeal
inter partes referral 59/14/31
practice directions 59/9/50,
59/14/35—59/14/35L
sequential service 59/9/32
time limits
fixtures 59/9/29
generally 59/9/28
leave to appeal 59/9/31
practice direction 59/9/50
revised arguments 59/9/28A
Short Warned List cases 59/9/30
supplemental arguments 59/9/28A
Court of Appeal direction
time limits 59/9/50
House of Lords civil appeal
exchange [19A–60]—[19A–60/1]
generally [19A–57]—[19A–58/1]
House of Lords criminal appeal
exchange [19B–44]—[19B–44/1]
generally [19B–39]—[19B–40/1]
House of Lords criminal appeal
lodgment [19B–43]—[19B–43/1]
patent actions 104/0/21

Solicitor and own-client costs
conditional fee agreements 62/15A/3
generally 62/15/2/1
next friend 62/16/4

Solicitors
accounts rules
1998 [15C–6]—[15C–15]
audience, rights of
generally [15G–107]
bill of costs
enforcement [15A–58/54]
form of [15A–58/40]
conditional fee agreements
1998 [15E–1]—[15E–4]
taxation of costs [15F–9]
conflict of interest [15G–109]
contentious business agreements
effect [15A–58/28/1]
generally [15A–58/23/1]
contentious business remuneration
bill of costs [15A–58/40]
costs
conditional fee agreements 62/15A/3
own-client
generally 62/15/2/1
next friend 62/16/4

Solicitors—*cont.*
remuneration
recovery of [15A–58/54]
statutory basis
generally [15A–24]
unqualified persons
preparing probate papers [15A–24]

Solicitors Accounts Rules 1991
generally [15C–5]

Solicitors Accounts Rules 1998
text [15C–6]—[15C–15]

Solicitors Act 1974
unqualified persons [15A–24]

Standing order
House of Lords civil appeal
judicial business [19A–107]—
[19A–107/1]

Statement of claim
amendment
timetable for
RSC [3D–1]
service
timetable for
RSC [3D–1]

Statement of facts
House of Lords civil appeal
generally [19A–43]—[19A–43/1]
time limits [19A–53]—[19A–53/1]
House of Lords criminal appeal
generally [19B–31]—[19B–32/1]

Statutory charge
generally [16D–155]
money in court [16D–169]—
[16D–169/1]
procedure [16D–164]—[16D–164/1]

Statutory tenancy
continuing occupation [8H–10]
excepted premises
housing association, letting by
[8H–59]—[8H–60]
local authority, letting by [8H–53]—
[8H–54], [8H–58]—[8H–58/1]
excepted premises
rateable value, above [8H–15]
student lets [8H–32]
grounds for possession
effect [8H–94]
reasonableness [8H–100]
subletting
effect on
determination of superior tenancy
[8H–121]

Stay of execution
fieri facias, writ of
bankruptcy 47/1/10—47/1/11
insolvency 47/1/10—47/1/11

Stay of proceedings
arbitration (post-31.1.97)
application [21D–24]
burden of proof [21D–25]
generally [21D–20], [21D–23]—
[21D–25]

Stay of proceedings—*cont.*
arbitration (pre-1.2.97)
procedure [21A–38], [21A–41]
refusal [21A–85]

Stop notice
timetable for
RSC [3D–1]

Stop orders
timetable for
RSC [3D–1]

Striking out
parties, of
application 15/6/17—15/6/18

Subletting
protected tenancy, effect on
determination of superior tenancy
[8H–121]
statutory tenancy, effect on
determination of superior tenancy
[8H–121]

Subpoena, writ of
service
timetable for
RSC [3D–1]

Substitution of parties
application 15/6/17—15/6/18

Successful unassisted party's costs
civil legal aid [16A–72], [16A–75]

Succession
assured tenancy [8O–118]
periodic tenancy [8L–71]
secure tenancy
qualifying persons [8L–61]

Summary judgment
affidavit of plaintiff in reply 14/4/7
application
relevant actions 14/1/2
costs
scale 14/7/8
directions
trial by Master 14/6/5
leave to defend
directions after 14/6/5
showing cause 14/4/7
procedure
affidavit of plaintiff in reply 14/4/7
showing cause
affidavit evidence 14/4/7
timetable for
RSC [3D–1]
trial
Master, by 14/6/5

Summary possession actions
order for possession
generally 113/8/14

Summons
county court
proof of service [20A–808]—
[20A–808/1]
sealing [20A–809—[20A–809/1

Summons—*cont.*
service of
timetable for
RSC [3D–1]

Summons for directions
Admiralty directions [6B–7]
service
timetable for
RSC [3D–1]

Supreme Court Act 1981
admiralty jurisdiction
definitions [6D–73]
generally [6D–3], [6D–11], [6D–60]
introductory note [6D–1]
applications 94/15/4
constitution
High Court [20A–139]—[20A–140]
costs
generally [20A–403]
Court of Appeal
jurisdiction [20A–172]—[20A–172/1],
[20A–177]—[20A–178]
practice [20A–406]—[20A–408],
[20A–422/2]
Crown Court
appeals [20A–198]—[20A–199]
practice [20A–465/14]—[20A–465/15]
declaratory relief [20A–203]—[20A–204]
divisions
High Court [20A–142] - [20A–145]
High Court
constitution [20A–139]—[20A–140]
divisions [20A–142]—[20A–143]
jurisdiction [20A–185], [20A–191/1],
[20A–198]—[20A–199],
[20A–201]—[20A–204]
powers [20A–255], [20A–259]—
[20A–259/2]
judges
rates and tax cases [20A–169]—
[20A–169/1]
judicial review [20A–198]—[20A–199],
[20A–201]—[20A–204]
jurisdiction
Court of Appeal [20A–172]—
[20A–172/1], [20A–177]—
[20A–178]
High Court [20A–185], [20A–191/1],
[20A–198]—[20A–199],
[20A–201]—[20A–204]
officers
qualifications
list [20A–572/1]—[20A–572/2]
practice
Court of Appeal [20A–406] -
[20A–408], [20A–422]—
[20A–422/2]
probate
grant of representation [11A–20]
schedules [20A–572/1]—[20A–572/2]
Supreme Court
judges [20A–169]—[20A–169/1]

Supreme Court Taxing Office
practice directions
generally 62/C/17, 62/C/35D

Supreme Court Taxing Office directions
indemnity principle 62/C/35D
personal injury actions 62/C/17

Taxation of costs
amount
discretionary sums 62/A2/37, 62/A2/38
Admiralty directions [6B–15]
assisted party, of
basis [16D–208]
objections [16D–221]
objections
generally [16D–221]
recovery [16D–210]—[16D–211]
audience, rights of 62/A2/38
basis
generally 62/12/1
chargeable items
hourly rate 62/A2/28
indemnity principle 62/A2/27A
taxation 62/A2/37, 62/A2/38
conditional fee agreements [15F–9]
counsel's fees
brief fee 62/A2/15/1
matrimonial proceedings 62/A2/19
personal injury actions
SCTO direction 62/C/17
three counsel 62/A2/13
vouchers 62/A2/5
discretionary sums
chargeable items 62/A2/37, 62/A2/38
fees
Court of Protection [10C–83]—[10C–83/1]
hourly rate 62/A2/28
indemnity principle
generally 62/A2/27A
SCTO direction 62/C/35D
inspection of privileged documents 62/29/8
misconduct of proceedings
generally 62/28/4
preparation
bill of costs, of 62/A2/37
hourly rate 62/A2/28
indemnity principle 62/A2/27A
procedure
commencement 62/29/6, 62/29/8
review
generally 62/35/12
Rules of the Supreme Court
related sources 62/0/3
Supreme Court Taxing Office directions 62/C/35D
taxing officers' powers
supplementary 62/20/2
timetable for
RSC [3D–1]

Taxation under Solicitors Act
client's application
expiry of 12 months [15A–58/71]
generally [15A–58/71]—[15A–58/74]

Taxing officers
powers
misconduct of proceedings 62/28/4
supplementary 62/20/2
privilege 62/20/2

Telephone summons
patent actions 104/0/24

Tenancy
assured
exempt tenancies [8O–201]—[8O–201/1], [8O–202], [8O–206], [8O–215], [8O–217/1]
generally [8O–8], [8O–19]
notices of possession [8O–243], [8O–253]
security of tenure [8O–49]—[8O–49/1], [8O–72]—[8O–72/1]
introductory
generally [8Q–31], [8Q–47]
periodic
succession [8L–71]
protected
generally [8H–4]
secure
assignment [8L–80]—[8L–81], [8L–85]
generally [8L–17]—[8L–18]
possession [8L–47]—[8L–47/1], [8L–52]
succession [8L–61], [8L–71]
statutory
generally [8H–10]

Third party notice
service
timetable for
RSC [3D–1]
service out of the jurisdiction 16/1/7

Third party proceedings
costs
indemnity 62/B/150
service out of the jurisdiction
without leave 11/1/61

Time estimates
patent actions 104/0/15

Time limits
acknowledgment of service for
generally [3D–1]
amendment
limitation period, after expiry of [14–42/5]—[14–42/6]
amendment after
time limits [14–42/6]—[14–42/6]
Court of Appeal, appeals to
skeleton arguments, lodgment of 59/9/28—59/9/32
date of knowledge
generally [14–17/6], [14–17/8]
personal injury [14–17/3]
discretionary exclusion of
death [14–40/4]—[14–40/6]
personal injury
actions commenced outside primary period [14–40/4]
exercise of [14–40/5]—[14–40/6]
generally [14–40/4]—[14–40/6]
enforcement
judgment [14–29/1]
exclusion of
death [14–40/4]—[14–40/6]
personal injury [14–40/4]—[14–40/6]

Time limits—*cont.*
fatal accidents
date of knowledge [14–17/6], [14–17/8]
discretionary exclusion [14–40/4]—[14–40/6]
House of Lords civil appeal
appendix
extension [19A–53]—[19A–53/1]
statement of facts
extension [19A–53]—[19A–53/1]
House of Lords criminal appeal
petition for leave [19B–4]—[19B–4/1]
latent damage
knowledge [14–18/2]
new party [14–42/11]
ordinary
personal injury [14–17/6]
trusts [14–26]—[14–26/1]
pending actions
amendment after expiry of [14–42/5]—[14–42/6]
new party [14–42/11]
personal injury
discretionary exclusion [14–40/4]—[14–40/6]
fatal accidents [14–17/6], [14–17/8]
skeleton arguments on appeal, lodgment of
fixtures 59/9/29
generally 59/9/28
leave to appeal 59/9/31
practice direction 59/9/50
revised arguments 59/9/28A
Short Warned List cases 59/9/30
supplemental arguments 59/9/28A
statutory basis
exclusion of time limits [14–40/4]—[14–40/6]
pending actions [14–42/5]
trust property [14–26]—[14–26/1]

Time orders
consumer credit [8F–6]

Timetables
RSC [3D–1]

***Tomlin* order**
generally [17A–32]

Tort, actions in
service out of the jurisdiction 11/1/55
service out of the jurisdiction without leave 11/1/55

Transcripts
Court of Appeal, appeals to
copy for respondent 59/9/13

Transfer of proceedings
High Court, to
enforcement, for 78/2/2
officer's duties 78/2/2
repairing obligations [8M–102]—[8M–102/1]
service charges [8M–102]—[8M–102/1]

Trial issues
assessor, assistance of 33/6—33/6/2
preliminary issue
special case 33/3/1
separate trials
special case 33/3/1

Trial procedure
Admiralty directions [6B–6]

Trial of separate issue
special case 33/3/1

Trial procedure
court dress
QBD direction [2C–207]—[2C–208/1]
mode of address
QBD direction [2C–204]—[2C–204/1]
official referee's business
Master 36/11/2
QBD direction
court dress [2C–207]—[2C–208/1]
mode of address [2C–204]—[2C–204/1]
summary judgment
Master, by 14/6/5
Master, by
generally 14/6/5

Trust accounts, audit of
statutory basis [12C–49]

Trust actions
time limits [14–26]—[14–26/1]

Trustees
costs
pre-emptive orders
generally 62/B/151

Unassisted party, costs of
civil legal aid [16A–72], [16A–75]

Undertakings
admiralty proceedings
expenses 75/23A/2
lieu of injunction, in
form [2C–128]

Unlawful eviction
excluded tenancy [8G–13]—[8G–14]

Unqualified persons
preparing probate papers [15A–24]

Unrestricted-use credit agreement [9A–47/1]

Validity of process
writ of summons
extension
principles 6/8/6

Value of action
meaning [20B–261]

Variation of sentence
statutory basis [20A–259]—[20A–259/2]

VAT Tribunal decisions
appeals from
generally 91/6—91/6/1

Vehicle emission penalties
enforcement C48D/1—C48D/5
generally C48D

Vexatious litigant
applications for leave to proceed 94/15/4

Vexatious litigation
statutory basis
procedure [20A–255]

Vouchers
counsel's fees 62/A2/5

Wages action
generally 75/1/23

Waiver
legal professional privilege 24/5/30

Warrant of arrest
admiralty proceedings
generally 75/5/10

Wasted costs order
application
procedure 62/11/14
counsel
relationship with solicitors 62/11/20
generally 62/2/9, 62/11/2, 62/11/20
grounds
improper, unreasonable or negligent conduct 62/11/5, 62/11/6
improper, unreasonable or negligent conduct
legal aid 62/11/6
pursing hopeless case 62/11/5

Wasted costs order—*cont.*
inherent jurisdiction
legal aid 62/11/25
judicial review proceedings 62/11/29
payment of fees 62/11/31
SCTO direction 62/C/6

Welsh Development Agency
compulsory purchase [8F–9/1]—[8F–9/4]

Withdrawal
payment into court
generally 22/1/20

Witness attendance
expenses 62/B/155

Witness expenses 62/B/155

Witness statement
privilege 38/2A/12
exchange of
timetable for
RSC [3D–1]

Writ of summons
admiralty proceedings
direction [6B–3]
duration 75/4/3
duration
extension of 6/8/6
interest
pleading 6/L/2
service of
timetable for
RSC [3D–1]
validity
extension
principles 6/8/6

Written offers
costs consequences
form of 62/9/9